First Workshop on Subword and Character Level Models in NLP 2017

Copenhagen, Denmark
7 September 2017

ISBN: 978-1-5108-4748-4

CURRAN ASSOCIATES INC.
proceedings
.com

EMNLP 2017

**First Workshop on Subword and Character Level
Models in NLP**

Proceedings of the Workshop

September 7, 2017
Copenhagen, Denmark

We thank our sponsor Google Inc. for a generous support.

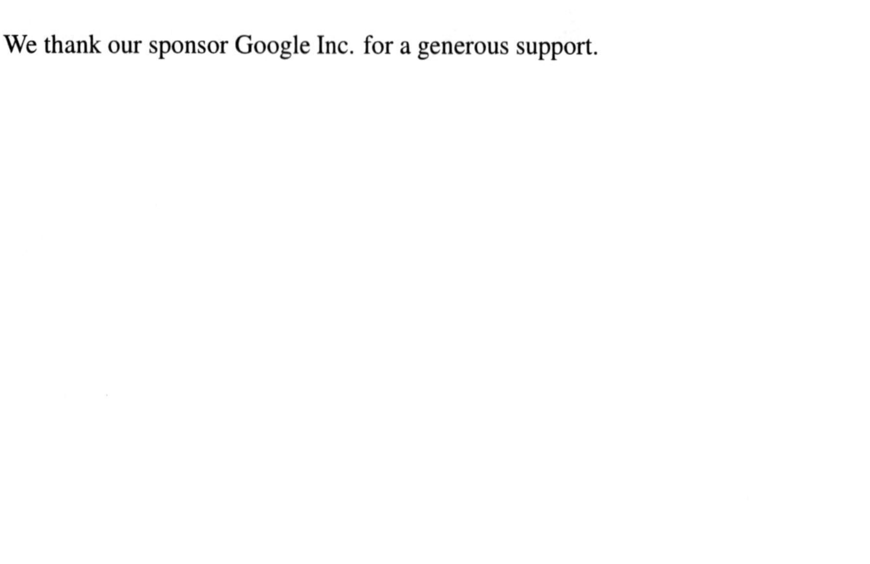

Introduction

Traditional NLP starts with a hand-engineered layer of representation, the level of tokens or words. A tokenization component first breaks up the text into units using manually designed rules. Tokens are then processed by components such as word segmentation, morphological analysis and multiword recognition. The heterogeneity of these components makes it hard to create integrated models of both structure within tokens (e.g., morphology) and structure across multiple tokens (e.g., multi-word expressions). This approach can perform poorly (i) for morphologically rich languages, (ii) for noisy text, (iii) for languages in which the recognition of words is difficult and (iv) for adaptation to new domains; and (v) it can impede the optimization of preprocessing in end-to-end learning.

The workshop provides a forum for discussing recent advances as well as future directions on sub-word and character-level natural language processing and representation learning that address these problems.

We received 37 submissions, out of which we accepted 24 as papers and 4 as extended abstracts.

Organizers:

Manaal Faruqui, Google Research, USA
Hinrich Schütze, LMU Munich, Germany
Isabel Trancoso, INESC-ID/IST, Portugal
Yadollah Yaghoobzadeh, LMU Munich, Germany

Program Committee:

Heike Adel, LMU Munich
Ehsaneddin Asgari, UC Berkeley
Miguel Ballesteros, IBM
Kris Cao, Cambridge
Grzegorz Chrupala, Tilburg
Junyoung Chung, Montreal
Trevor Cohn, Melbourne
Marta R. Costa-jussa, UPC
Ryan Cotterell, Johns Hopkins
Chris Dyer, DeepMind
Alex Fraser, LMU Munich
Kevin Gimpel, TTI Chicago
Angeliki Lazaridou, Trento
Wang Ling, DeepMind
Andrew Mass, Stanford
Chris Potts, Stanford
Marek Rei, Cambridge
Rami Al-Rfou, Google
Laura Rimcll, Cambridge
Cicero Nogueira dos Santos, IBM
Helmut Schmid, LMU Munich
Jörg Tiedemann, Helsinki
Thang Vu, IMS Stuttgart
Francois Yvon, LIMSI

Invited Speakers:

Kyunghyun Cho, NYU
Karen Livescu, TTIC
Tomas Mikolov, Facebook
Noah Smith, University of Washington

Panel Discussion:

Kyunghyun Cho, NYU
Sharon Goldwater, University of Edinburgh
Karen Livescu, TTIC
Tomas Mikolov, Facebook
Noah Smith, University of Washington

Table of Contents

Conference Program

Thursday, September 7, 2017

09:00–09:10   *Opening Remarks*
Manaal Faruqui

09:10–09:50   *Invited Talk: Subword-level Information in NLP using Neural Networks*
Tomas Mikolov

09:50–10:30   *Invited Talk: Chewing the Fat about Mincing Words*
Noah Smith

10:30–11:00   ***Coffee break***

11:00–11:40   *Invited Tutorial Talk: Neural WFSTs*
Ryan Cotterell

11:40–12:10   **Best paper presentations**

11:40–11:55   *Character and Subword-Based Word Representation for Neural Language Modeling Prediction*
Matthieu Labeau and Alexandre Allauzen

11:55–12:10   *Learning variable length units for SMT between related languages via Byte Pair Encoding*
Anoop Kunchukuttan and Pushpak Bhattacharyya

Thursday, September 7, 2017 (continued)

14:00–14:40 *Invited Talk: Fully Character Level Neural Machine Translation*
Kyunghyun Cho

14:40–15:50 Poster session and Coffee break

Character and Subword-Based word Representation for Neural Language Modeling prediction

Matthieu Labeau
LIMSI-CNRS / Orsay, France
labeau@limsi.fr

Alexandre Allauzen
LIMSI-CNRS / Orsay, France
allauzen@limsi.fr

Abstract

Most of neural language models use different kinds of embeddings for word prediction. While word embeddings can be associated to each word in the vocabulary or derived from characters as well as factored morphological decomposition, these word representations are mainly used to parametrize the input, *i.e.* the context of prediction. This work investigates the effect of using subword units (character and factored morphological decomposition) to build output representations for neural language modeling. We present a case study on Czech, a morphologically-rich language, experimenting with different input and output representations. When working with the full training vocabulary, despite unstable training, our experiments show that augmenting the output word representations with character-based embeddings can significantly improve the performance of the model. Moreover, reducing the size of the output look-up table, to let the character-based embeddings represent rare words, brings further improvement.

1 Introduction

Most of neural language models, such as n-gram models (Bengio et al., 2003) are word based and rely on the definition of a finite vocabulary $\mathcal{V}$. Therefore, a look-up table maps each word $w \in \mathcal{V}$ to a vector of real features, and is stored in a matrix. While this approach yields significant improvement for a variety of tasks and languages, see for instance (Schwenk, 2007) in speech recognition and (Le et al., 2012; Devlin et al., 2014; Bahdanau et al., 2014) in machine translation, it induces several limitations.

For morphologically-rich languages, like Czech or German, the lexical coverage is still an important issue, since there is a combinatorial explosion of word forms, most of which are hardly observed on training data. On the one hand, growing the look-up table is not a solution, since it would increase the number of parameters without having enough training examples for a proper estimation. On the other hand, rare words can be replaced by a special token. This acts as a word class merging very different words without any distinction, while using different word classes to handle out-of-vocabulary words (OOVs) (Allauzen and Gauvain, 2005) does not really solve this issue, since rare words are difficult to classify. Moreover, for most inflected or agglutinative forms, as well as for compound words, the word structure is overlooked, wasting parameters for modeling forms that could be more efficiently handled by word decomposition into subwords units.

Using subword units, whether they are built via a different supervised method with embedded language knowledge, or from the training data, has been attempted many times, especially for speech recognition. The main goal is to reduce the OOV rate. While most of them were focused on a specific language, (Creutz et al., 2007) is a representative example of such a model applied to several morphologically-rich languages.

One of the first occurrences of general language models integrating morphological features to represent words are the *factored language model* (Bilmes and Kirchhoff, 2003) and its neural version (Alexandrescu and Kirchhoff, 2006). Input words are represented by their embedding, plus several other features, some of which include morphemes. To alleviate the impact of OOVs, (Mueller and Schuetze, 2011) used morphological features for class-based predictions when input words are unknown, obtaining state-of-the-art

1

Proceedings of the First Workshop on Subword and Character Level Models in NLP, pages 1–13,
Copenhagen, Denmark, September 7, 2017. ©2017 Association for Computational Linguistics.

results on English. More recently, several types of language models represent words as function of subwords units: using a recursive structure (Luong et al., 2013), or an additive one (Botha and Blunsom, 2014). Quite a lot of work has been made on language models that extract features directly from the character sequence, whether they use character n-grams (Sperr et al., 2013), or characters composed by a convolutional layer (Santos and Zadrozny, 2014; Kim et al., 2015) or a Bi-LSTM layer (Ling et al., 2015). This avoids using an external morphological analyser. We can note that these types of models have also been applied with success to several other task, including learning word representations (Qiu et al., 2014; Cotterell et al., 2016; Bojanowski et al., 2016; Wieting et al., 2016), POS tagging (Plank et al., 2016; Ma and Hovy, 2016; Heigold et al., 2017), Named entity recognition (Gillick et al., 2016), Parsing (Ballesteros et al., 2015) and Machine translation (Costa-jussà and Fonollosa, 2016). Recently, an exhaustive summary of previous work on word representation by composing subword units was presented in (Vania and Lopez, 2017). This work also compares the types of subword unit, how they are composed, and their impact on various morphological typologies.

While recurrent neural networks have shown excellent performances for character-level language modeling (Sutskever et al., 2011; Hermans and Schrauwen, 2013), the results of such models are usually worse than those that use word-level prediction, since they have to consider a far longer history of tokens to be able to predict the next one correctly. However, more recent work (Hwang and Sung, 2017) seems to obtain very satisfactory results with a supplementary word-level layer that allows a better processing of the longer history.

Our work focuses on replacing output word embeddings by representations built from subwords. To the best of our knowledge, such a model has only been proposed in (Józefowicz et al., 2016), which evaluates the use of convolutional and LSTM layers to build word representations for outputs words. They allow the model to trade size against perplexity, since their model performs worse than the classic softmax approach, but with far less parameters. We first propose to study the training of a language model which augments or completely replaces output words representations with character-based representations. We compare the effect of different architectures, as well as the effect of different input representations. Our results show that:

- When evaluating perplexity on the full training vocabulary, using an augmented output representation improves the model performance.

- Not using the look-up table for rare words also improves the model performance.

Finally, we describe a short experiment with factoring the output predictions using a morphological analysis, which we believe could lead to a facilitated word generation when combined with re-inflexion models.

Our paper is organized as follows: Section 2 describes the general architecture of the language model, and of the representations used, as well as its training, Section 3 presents the experiments and Section 4 gives our results and discussion.

2 Language model

We use a recurrent neural language model (Mikolov et al., 2010). The input of the network is a sequence of words $S = (w_1, \ldots, w_{|S|})$. Given a fixed sized vocabulary $\mathcal{V}$, the language model outputs a multinomial distribution $P(w_i = j | w_1^{i-1}), \forall j \in \mathcal{V}$ for each position i in the sequence, and with the prediction contexte $w_1^{i-1} = w_1, \ldots, w_{i-1}$. This allows us to compute the following probability :

$$P(w_1, \ldots, w_{|S|}) = \prod_{i=1}^{|S|} P(w_i | w_1^{i-1})$$

Our model uses the LSTM variant (Hochreiter and Schmidhuber, 1997). The hidden state $\mathbf{h}_i$ will be computed using the previous hidden state and a computed representation $\mathbf{r}_{w_i}$ of the word in position i in the sequence:

$$\mathbf{h}_i = LSTM(\mathbf{r}_{w_i}, \mathbf{h}_{i-1})$$

The conditional probability distribution of the next word is computed with a softmax function:

$$P(w_i = j | w_1^{i-1}) = \frac{\exp\left(\mathbf{h}_i \mathbf{r}_j^{out} + b_j\right)}{\sum_{k \in \mathcal{V}} \exp\left(\mathbf{h}_i \mathbf{r}_k^{out} + b_k\right)} \quad (1)$$

We propose to improve output word embeddings by using representations built from sub-words, as it is often done for input words.

Usually, input and output word embeddings are parameters, stored in look-up matrices $\mathbf{W}$ and $\mathbf{W}_{out}$. The word embedding $\mathbf{r}_w^{word}$ of a word w is simply the column of $\mathbf{W}$ corresponding to its index in the vocabulary $\mathcal{V}$:

$$\mathbf{r}_w^{word} = [\mathbf{W}]_w$$

2.1 Representing words

We consider two other types of representations: decomposition of the words into characters (or n-grams of characters), and decomposing them into a Lemma and positional tags using a morphological analysis. An example of these different decompositions is shown in table 1.

Representation	Decomposition
Word	počátku
Characters	p+o+č+á+t+k+u
Character 3-grams	poč+očá+čát+átk+tku
Lemma + Tags	počátek+N+MascIn+Sg+Loc+Act

Table 1: Example of subword decompositions used for Czech word

2.1.1 Character-based representations

A word w is a character sequence $\{c_1, .., c_{|w|}\}$ represented by their embeddings $\{\mathbf{r}_{c_1}^{char}, .., \mathbf{r}_{c_{|w|}}^{char}\}$, where $\mathbf{r}_{c_i}^{char} = [\mathbf{C}]_{c_i}$ denotes the vector associated to the character c_i. To infer a word embedding from its character embeddings, we use two different architectures:

First, a *convolution layer* (Waibel et al., 1990; Collobert et al., 2011), similar to layers used in (Santos and Zadrozny, 2014; Kim et al., 2015), applies a convolution filter $\mathbf{W}_{n_c}^{CNN}$ over a sliding window of n_c characters, producing local features:

$$x_{n_c}^n = \mathbf{W}_{n_c}^{CNN}(\mathbf{r}_{c_{n-n_c+1}}^{char} : ... : \mathbf{r}_{c_n}^{char})^T + \mathbf{b}_{n_c}^{CNN}$$

where $x_{n_c}^n$ is a vector obtained for each position n in the word. The embeddings of w is then obtained by applying a max-pooling and the activation function ϕ:

$$[\mathbf{r}_w^{n_c}]_i = \phi\left(\max_{n=1}^{|w|-n_c+1}[\mathbf{x}_{n_c}^n]_i\right) \qquad (2)$$

We can use multiple filters of n_{c_f} different sizes and concatenate their results:

$$\mathbf{r}_w^{CharCNN} = (\mathbf{r}_w^{n_{c_1}} : ... : \mathbf{r}_w^{n_{c_f}}) \qquad (3)$$

Our second method uses a *bi-LSTM* (Hochreiter and Schmidhuber, 1997; Graves et al., 2005), on characters, similarly to (Ling et al., 2015). It combines the final states $\overrightarrow{\mathbf{h}_{|w|}}$ and $\overleftarrow{\mathbf{h}_1}$ of two LSTMs, respectively over the character sequence and the reverse character sequence, which are computed as such:

$$\overrightarrow{\mathbf{h}_i} = LSTM(\mathbf{r}_{c_i}^{char}, \overrightarrow{\mathbf{h}_{i-1}})$$

$$\overleftarrow{\mathbf{h}_j} = LSTM(\mathbf{r}_{c_j}^{char}, \overleftarrow{\mathbf{h}_{j+1}})$$

$$\mathbf{r}_w^{CharBiLSTM} = \overrightarrow{\mathbf{h}_{|w|}} : \overleftarrow{\mathbf{h}_1} \qquad (4)$$

2.1.2 Lemma+Tags decomposition

For morphologically-rich languages, the different morphological properties of a word (gender, case, ...) are usually encoded using mutliple tags as shown in table 1. Therefore a word w is decomposed into a lemma l along with a set of associated sub-tags $T = \{t_1, .., t_{|T|}\}$ of fixed size $|T|$. For a given word, a single tag can be simply created by the concatenation of the subtags. However, this implies a large tagset and mitigates the generalization power since some sub-tags combinations can remain unobserved on training data. In this work we prefer a factored representation where each sub-tags is considered independently.

Lemmas, similarly to surface forms, are represented by $|\mathcal{V}_L|$ vectors stored in a look-up matrix $\mathbf{L}$, and $\mathbf{r}_l^{lemma} = [\mathbf{L}]_l$. For every words, each sub-tag has its own vocabulary and its own look-up matrix. However, the additional cost is negligible given their small size (see table 3). To infer a word embedding from a sub-tags set, we also use two methods. First, we simply concatenate their embeddings:

$$\mathbf{r}_T^{TagConcat} = \mathbf{r}_{t_1}^{tag_1} : ... : \mathbf{r}_{t_i}^{tag_i} : ... : \mathbf{r}_{t_{|T|}}^{tag_{|T|}} \qquad (5)$$

The second method uses a bidirectionnal LSTM on the sequence of tags T, using exactly the same structure as in section 2.1.1:

$$\mathbf{r}_T^{TagBiLSTM} = \overrightarrow{\mathbf{h}_{|T|}} : \overleftarrow{\mathbf{h}_1} \qquad (6)$$

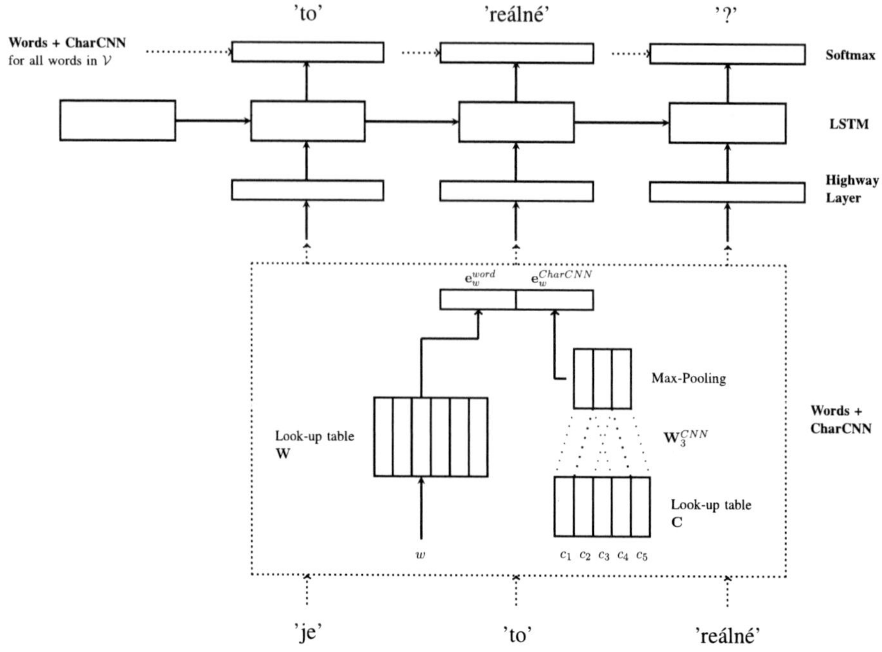

Figure 1: Example architecture of our language model, when using word embeddings and a character CNN to build both input and output word representations.

2.2 Training

Our final model, as illustrated in figure 1, uses concatenation of word, character-based or lemma and tags embeddings, to obtain input and output word representations. Following (Kim et al., 2015), we used a Highway layer (Srivastava et al., 2015) to model interactions between concatenated embeddings of various sources.

Usually, such a model is trained by maximizing the log-likelihood. For a given word w_i given its preceding sequence $w_1, \ldots, w_{i-1}$, the model parameters θ are estimated in order to maximize the following function for all the sequences observed in the training data:

$$LL(\theta) = \sum_{i=1}^{|S|} \log P_\theta(w_i|w_1^{i-1}) \qquad (7)$$

This objective function implies a very costly summation imposed by the softmax activation of the output layer: large output vocabularies cause a computational bottleneck due to the output normalization.

Different solutions have been proposed, as *shortlists* (Schwenk, 2007), *hierarchical softmax* (Morin and Bengio, 2005; Mnih and Hinton, 2009; Le et al., 2011), or self-normalisation techniques (Devlin et al., 2014; Andreas et al., 2015; Chen et al., 2016). Sampling-based techniques explore a different solution, where a limited number of negative examples are sampled to reduce the normalization cost. Working with a large vocabulary, and with output representations potentially more costly to compute, we choose to use the following sampling-based training algorithms:

- Target sampling, which is based on importance sampling (Bengio and Sénécal, 2008; Jean et al., 2015), directly approximates the normalization over $\mathcal{V}$ by normalizing over a sampled subset.

Indeed, the gradient of the objective described in equation 7 is written as:

$$\frac{\partial}{\partial\theta} \log P_\theta(w_i|w_1^{i-1}) = \frac{\partial}{\partial\theta}(\mathbf{h}_i \mathbf{r}_{w_i}^{out} + b_{w_i})$$
$$- \mathbb{E}_{w \sim P_\theta(.|w_1^{i-1})} \left[\frac{\partial}{\partial\theta}(\mathbf{h}_i \mathbf{r}_{w_i}^{out} + b_{w_i}) \right] \qquad (8)$$

The idea is to approximate the expectation of the second term by importance sampling a subset of $\mathcal{V}$ from a proposal distribution $\mathcal{Q}$. Target sampling implies associating with a part

$\mathcal{D}_i$ of the training data a subset $\mathcal{V}_i$ of $\mathcal{V}$ that corresponds to the target words of $\mathcal{D}_i$ plus a small subset of the remaining words. The resulting objective is equivalent to approximating the probability computed in equation 1 by normalizing it only over $\mathcal{V}_i$.

- Noise contrastive estimation (NCE), introduced in (Gutmann and Hyvärinen, 2012; Mnih and Teh, 2012), aims to discriminate between one example sampled from the real data $\mathcal{D}$ and k from a noise distribution P_n, and results in the model being theoretically unnormalized. The idea is to sample examples according to a mixture:

$$P(w|w_1^{i-1}) = \frac{1}{k+1} P_{\mathcal{D}}(w|w_1^{i-1}) \\ + \frac{k}{k+1} P_n(w|w_1^{i-1}) \tag{9}$$

and train the model to recover whether the sample came from the data or the noise distribution. This is done by minimizing the binary cross-entropy of recognizing the current sample's origin, using the posterior probabilities:

$$P(w \sim P_{\mathcal{D}}|w, w_1^{i-1}) = \\ \frac{P_\theta(w|w_1^{i-1})}{P_\theta(w|w_1^{i-1}) + kP_n(w|w_1^{i-1})} \tag{10}$$

$$P(w \sim P_n|w, w_1^{i-1}) = 1 \\ - P(w \sim P_{\mathcal{D}}|w, w_1^{i-1}) \tag{11}$$

Besides, the probabilities intervening in equation 10 can be replaced by unnormalized scores at training time, since we can consider normalizing quantities as parameters to be learned.

- BlackOut (Ji et al., 2015), also approximating the normalization computation, with a weighted sampling scheme and a discriminative objective.It can be considered as a variant from NCE where we sample a set of k examples S_k from a proposal distribution $\mathcal{Q}$. We then proceed to apply NCE with a re-weighted noise distribution

$$P_n(w|w_1^{i-1}) = \frac{1}{k} \sum_{w_j \in S_k} \frac{\mathcal{Q}(w_j)}{\mathcal{Q}(w)} P_\theta(w_w|w_1^{i-1}) \tag{12}$$

which empirically behaves far better than NCE, providing an improved stability. BlackOut can also be linked to Importance sampling.

Ultimately, these three algorithms approximate the negative log-likelihood computed on a number k of negative samples from $\mathcal{V}$, using an easy to sample distribution.

3 Experiments

Experiments are carried out on Czech, a morphologically rich language using the different criteria described in section 2.2.

3.1 Data

We used data from the parallel corpus *News-commentary* 2015, from the WMT News MT Task. The data consists in 210K word sequences, amounting in about 4,7M tokens. We divided the data into a training, development and testing sets, these last two amounting to 150K tokens each. In our experiments, we use different vocabulary sizes by varying the frequency threshold: words are selected when their frequency in the training data are stricly higher than the threshold. Table 2 shows the correspondences between vocabulary sizes and these thresholds.

f_{Th}	$|\mathcal{V}_{Th}|$
0 (All words)	159142
1	66743
5	37010
10	25295

Table 2: Vocabulary sizes for different frequency thresholds

The lemma and tags decomposition presented in section 2.1.2 were obtained with Morphodita (Straková et al., 2014). There is 12 tag categories for Czech. Vocabulary sizes for characters, lemma and tags are detailed in table 3.

$|\mathcal{V}_C|$	$|\mathcal{V}_L|$	$|\mathcal{V}_{tag_i}|_{i=1..|T|}$
155	61364	[12, 65, 11, 6, 9, 6, 3, 5, 5, 4, 3, 3]

Table 3: Vocabulary sizes for subword units

3.2 Setup

The different versions of our model used in experiments are shown in table 4. We used a Highway layer when there is a concatenation of embeddings of different sources, which is for almost all architectures. We tried applying a Highway layer to the output representation, but it seemed almost always counter-productive, rendering training more unstable. In all experiments presented here, weights are not tied between input and output representations, since our preliminary experiments with tied weights always gave worst results. Besides, we didn't mix structures for character-level representations (for example, using an input Char-CNN and output CharLSTM) since our first experiments gave systematically worse results than using the same structures). When using different types of representations, we kept consistency between vocabularies: if both lemmas and words are used in a model, any lemma considered unknown will have its corresponding word unknown, and inversely. The same (or corresponding) vocabularies are used for inputs, outputs, and evaluation. The only exception is presented in section 4.4. When using a character-based output representation, during evaluation, the *unknown* token is built from a specific character token, a specific lemma token, and 12 specific tag tokens that are parameters of the model.

Input representation	$\mathbf{r}_w$	Eq
Words	$\mathbf{r}_w^{word}$	
CharCNN	$Hw(\mathbf{r}_w^{CharCNN})$	3
CharBiLSTM	$Hw(\mathbf{r}_w^{CharBiLSTM})$	4
Words + CharCNN	$Hw(\mathbf{r}_w^{word} : \mathbf{r}_w^{CharCNN})$	
Words + CharBiLSTM	$Hw(\mathbf{r}_w^{word} : \mathbf{r}_w^{CharBiLSTM})$	
Lemma + Tags Concat.	$Hw(\mathbf{r}_l^{lemma} : \mathbf{r}_T^{TagConcat})$	5
Lemma + TagsBiLSTM	$Hw(\mathbf{r}_l^{lemma} : \mathbf{r}_T^{TagBiLSTM})$	6
Output representation	$\mathbf{r}_w^{out}$	
Words	$\mathbf{r}_w^{word}$	
Words + CharCNN	$\mathbf{r}_w^{word} : \mathbf{r}_w^{CharCNN}$	
Words + CharBiLSTM	$\mathbf{r}_w^{word} : \mathbf{r}_w^{CharBiLSTM}$	
Lemmas	$\mathbf{r}_l^{lemma}$	
Lemmas + CharCNN	$\mathbf{r}_l^{lemma} : \mathbf{r}_l^{CharCNN}$	
Lemmas + CharLSTM	$\mathbf{r}_l^{lemma} : \mathbf{r}_l^{BiLSTM}$	

Table 4: Detail of input and output representations used in our experiments. Hw designate the use of a Highway layer

Our experiments aim at comparing potential use of subword-based word representation, and thus are not directed towards performance. For this reason, we used the same implementation for all experiments and did not specifically try to optimize the general model structure or the dimensional hyperparameters, neither compared our results with benchmarks on Czech corpora.

3.3 Training and evaluation

Language models are evaluated with perplexity:

$$PPL = \exp\left(\sum_{i=1}^{|S|} \frac{-\log P_\theta(w_i|w_1^{i-1})}{|S|}\right)$$

over all sequences in the testing data. Perplexity is computed for a fixed output vocabulary $\mathcal{V}$, which allows to compare models using the same output vocabulary. However, we can't evaluate model performance on out-of-vocabulary words, since those are to be classified as the unknown token in $\mathcal{V}$.

Our models are implemented with Tensor flow (Abadi et al., 2015). We use the Adam algorithm (Kingma and Ba, 2014) with an initial learning rate of $5 * 10^{-4}$ for training, over a maximum of 10 epochs, with a batch size of 128 sequences. However, since the training is often unstable, the model backtracks to the last checkpoint if it does not improve its performance on validation data after $1/10$ of an epoch, and stop training after 10 unsuccessful loadings in a row. To avoid overfitting, we use dropout with probability 0.5 on recurrent layers, and $L2$ regularization on feedforward layers.

We use two hidden layers, and choose our embeddings dimensions in order to obtain, for each type of representation, an embedding dimension of 150. In the case of the CNN, we used filters of 3, 5 and 7 characters, of dimension 30, 50, and 70. Whether we use NCE, blackOut, or importance sampling, we draw $k = 500$ noise samples by batch. For all experiments, we report the perplexity on test data at the end of training. Results presented in tables 5, 6, 7 are the average of the results obtained on 5 models, and the standard deviation.

4 Results

4.1 Influence of the vocabulary size

We first train our model with different vocabulary sizes. As shown in figure 2, our model fails to improve upon the conventional word model when the output vocabulary size is relatively small (shown on the two leftmost graphs). More precisely, models that use word and character-based representations at the output seem unable to learn after a couple of iterations. We first link this behaviour to the difficulty met by the authors in (Józefowicz et al., 2016): since most logits are tied when we use an output character-based representation - as

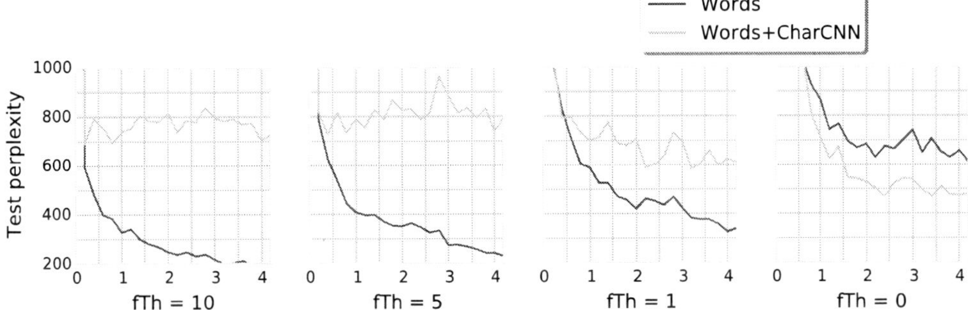

Figure 2: Test perplexities obtained when training models using Words as input representation and Words+CharCNN as output representations, for various vocabulary sizes. Corresponding vocabulary sizes are given in table 2. The models are trained with target sampling.

opposed to independently learned word embeddings, the function mapping from word to word representation is smoother and training becomes more difficult. They used a smaller learning rate and a low dimensional correction factor, learned for each word, as a work-around.

However, increasing the vocabulary size reduces this effect . This is especially clear with the whole training vocabulary (on the rightmost graph of figure 2): in this setup, using a character-based representation improves the performance of the model. We can assume that, for rare words, learning independent embeddings fails since scarce updates of these embeddings are insufficient. For the rare words, combining word and character-based embeddings allows the model to better counteract the sparsity issue.

4.2 Choice of the training criterion

Given the previous results, we use the full training vocabulary to assess the impact of the training criterion. However, using this full training vocabulary renders training very unstable, especially with sampling-based algorithms. Stability issues, especially for the Noise-contrastive estimation, have previously been discussed (Chen et al., 2016; Józefowicz et al., 2016). We shortly experimented to choose the most practical criterion to use. Figure 3 shows the shape of the training curves. While target sampling and blackOut both seem to work properly, NCE needs far more noise samples to converge. We believe this is related to the tensorflow implementation, which re-use the same noise samples for every example in the batch, which leads to a lack of diversity in negative

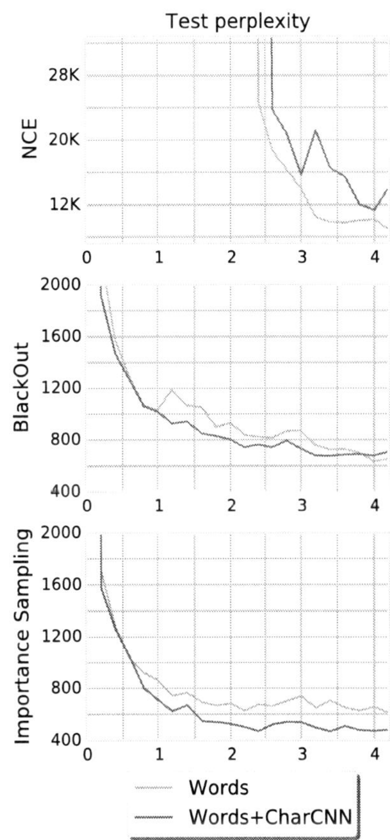

Figure 3: Test perplexities obtained when training models using Words as input representation and Words+CharCNN as output representations, for various training methods: Noise contrastive estimation, blackOut and Target sampling.

examples. Augmenting the number of samples or reducing the size of the batch are possible solutions, but they increase the training time. BlackOut obtains better results because, while very similar to NCE, the scores used as coming from the noise distribution are context-dependent, which brings diversity to negative examples.

Overall, across several experiments, target sampling performs better than blackOut, and we choose to use it for the rest of our experiments. Since training is still quite unstable, depending on the architecture, we report results across 5 trainings for the next sections.

Output Representation Input Representation		Words	Words + Char	
			CNN	BiLSTM
Words		563 ± 53	432 ± 18	480 ± 31
Char	CNN	698 ± 41	543 ± 16	-
	BiLSTM	971 ± 24	-	938 ± 48
Words + Char	CNN	$\mathbf{495 \pm 34}$	$\mathbf{411 \pm 40}$	-
	BiLSTM	537 ± 24	-	$\mathbf{480 \pm 21}$
Lemmas + Tags	Concat.	521 ± 47	424 ± 22	502 ± 54
	BiLSTM	541 ± 8	445 ± 24	496 ± 39

Table 5: Average test perplexities obtained when training 5 models with target sampling, for various input/output representations. Results in bold are the best models for a given output representation.

4.3 Effects of the representation choice

Table 5 gathers the main experimental results to assess which combination of input and output representations gives the best performance. For any input representation, augmenting the output representation with a character-based embedding improves the performance of the model. It is especially true for convolutional layers. We also can notice that the improvement is better for models that performed badly with basic output word embeddings.

Overall, biLSTMs perform worse than their convolution/concatenation counterparts. Finally, the best average perplexity of 495 for word only output representations is improved to an average of 411 for augmented output representations.

Other output representations: First, our experiments with only character-based embeddings as output representations give results far worse than those reported in 5, with our best model obtaining an average perplexity of ≈ 2500. Training is also far more unstable. We believe these results are linked to the difficulties mentioned in (Józefowicz et al., 2016) and in section 4.1.

We also tried to use the lemma+tags decomposition presented in section 2.1.2, but without success. When tags were ambiguous across several occurrences of the same words, we tried using specific tokens, or choosing the most frequent tags, but in both cases the model severely overfits.

Finally, we tried to use word embeddings pretrained with word2vec (Mikolov et al., 2013) as output representations. We obtained results very similar to those of classical word cmbcddings, with a small but noticeable improvement when the input representation used LSTM. However, these improvements are still well under those obtained by augmenting the output representation with a character-based embedding.

4.4 Influence of the size of the word embeddings vocabulary

Input Representation	f_{Th}^W	Words + CharCNN		
		All words	Frequent words	Rare words
Words	0	432 ± 18	286 ± 13	$\mathbf{5170 \pm 1310}$
	1	415 ± 26	258 ± 13	6510 ± 780
	5	$\mathbf{390 \pm 20}$	$\mathbf{250 \pm 14}$	7210 ± 1290
	10	416 ± 20	265 ± 11	8100 ± 580
CharCNN	0	543 ± 16	348 ± 10	6400 ± 1480
	1	523 ± 17	328 ± 22	$\mathbf{5070 \pm 1080}$
	5	$\mathbf{478 \pm 16}$	$\mathbf{316 \pm 27}$	7000 ± 1800
	10	488 ± 31	338 ± 25	8210 ± 2160
Words + CharCNN	0	411 ± 40	271 ± 30	$\mathbf{4470 \pm 190}$
	1	374 ± 10	$\mathbf{242 \pm 7}$	5020 ± 870
	5	$\mathbf{367 \pm 14}$	$\mathbf{241 \pm 8}$	5560 ± 1220
	10	393 ± 19	254 ± 13	6600 ± 1910
Lemma + TagsConcat.	All	449 ± 26	293 ± 16	5830 ± 760
	1	439 ± 34	287 ± 11	6220 ± 1080
	5	$\mathbf{408 \pm 32}$	$\mathbf{269 \pm 20}$	$\mathbf{4600 \pm 1280}$
	10	430 ± 32	$\mathbf{269 \pm 20}$	8410 ± 1140
Lemma + TagsBiLSTM	All	445 ± 24	288 ± 13	7150 ± 1560
	1	424 ± 34	281 ± 21	5380 ± 1000
	5	$\mathbf{387 \pm 9}$	$\mathbf{258 \pm 5}$	$\mathbf{4300 \pm 1390}$
	10	442 ± 17	287 ± 13	7390 ± 1690

Table 6: Test perplexity averaged on 5 models trained with target sampling, for various input representations and output word look-up table sizes. Corresponding vocabulary sizes are given in table 2. Test perplexities are given for all words, frequent words (frequency > 10) and rare words (frequency < 10). In bold are the best models for a given input representation.

Following our observations in section 4.1, we then assess the effect of reducing the word vocabulary size for Words+CharCNN output representation. We don't change the size of the event space: when constructing output representations for words under a chosen frequency, we simply don't use the word representation. For example, using a threshold of $f_{Th}^{W} = 10$ means that words that appear less thant ten times won't have their own word embedding, and will be represented by the unknown word token combined with their character-based representation. Results are shown in table 6. We can see that for all input representations, using a specific unknown token in place of a specific word embedding for words appearing less than 5 times in training data gives the best performance. Reducing the look-up table to words only appearing more than 10 times gives worse results, while they are still better than if we keep the full table. However, there is no clear trend when looking at the rare words perplexities, which are very hard to interpret, given their very high standard deviation. With a smaller output word look-up table, our best average perplexity of 411 is reduced to 376, which is a very sizeable overall improvement.

Input Representation	Output Representation	Lemmas	Lemmas + Char	
			CNN	BiLSTM
Words		240 ± 12	220 ± 9	222 ± 12
Char	CNNN	308 ± 15	270 ± 11	-
	BiLSTM	477 ± 17	-	429 ± 9
Words + Char	CNN	234 ± 9	$\mathbf{203 \pm 7}$	-
	BiLSTM	238 ± 6	-	225 ± 11
Lemmas + Tags	Concat.	239 ± 3	211 ± 5	217 ± 9
	BiLSTM	$\mathbf{232 \pm 5}$	$\mathbf{203 \pm 6}$	$\mathbf{212 \pm 6}$

Table 7: Test perplexities averaged on 5 models on lemmas with a multiple objectives cost function. Results are given for various input/output representations. In bold are the best models for a given output representation.

4.5 Predicting root and tags jointly

While using the lemma+tags decomposition to build output representation was not, in our experiments, successful, we investigated a factorised prediction of lemma and tags. We used different costs for predicting lemmas and each tag, which are summed into a final objective function. As recently seen in (Martinez et al., 2016; Burlot and Yvon, 2017), these objectives are individually easier when working with morphologically-rich languages, and fully inflected words can be obtained by using morphological inflection models, which have been shown to be quite successful (Faruqui et al., 2016; Kann et al., 2017).

Table 7 shows the test perplexities on lemmas for various input and output representations. We can observe that in all cases training is far more stable, with generally lower standard deviations. In this case, using a lemma+tags with a BiLSTM or a Words+CharCNN input representation both give the best results, while augmenting the output representation of the lemma with a character-build embedding also improves results. This makes the joint learning of a factored prediction and reinflection language model a very interesting direction for future work.

5 Conclusion

We described a neural language model allowing the use of subword units for both input and output word representations. While in our experiments training with a full vocabulary is unstable, we can identify important trends: augmenting output representations with character-based embeddings improves the model performance, and in this setup, replacing independent word embeddings by the unknown token for rare words yields further improvement. It is worth noticing that this also opens the vocabulary, since our model can be used to rescore unknown words. Additional experiments suggest that factoring the output of the model with a lemma+tags decomposition, then re-inflecting these into words, could make generation easier: this is a direction we plan to investigate.

Acknowledgements

We wish to thank the anonymous reviewers for their helpful comments. This work has been funded by the European Union's Horizon 2020 research and innovation programme under grant agreement No. 645452 (QT21).

References

Martín Abadi, Ashish Agarwal, Paul Barham, Eugene Brevdo, Zhifeng Chen, Craig Citro, Greg S. Corrado, Andy Davis, Jeffrey Dean, Matthieu Devin, Sanjay Ghemawat, Ian Goodfellow, Andrew Harp, Geoffrey Irving, Michael Isard, Yangqing Jia, Rafal Jozefowicz, Lukasz Kaiser, Manjunath Kudlur, Josh

Levenberg, Dan Mané, Rajat Monga, Sherry Moore, Derek Murray, Chris Olah, Mike Schuster, Jonathon Shlens, Benoit Steiner, Ilya Sutskever, Kunal Talwar, Paul Tucker, Vincent Vanhoucke, Vijay Vasudevan, Fernanda Viégas, Oriol Vinyals, Pete Warden, Martin Wattenberg, Martin Wicke, Yuan Yu, and Xiaoqiang Zheng. 2015. TensorFlow: Large-scale machine learning on heterogeneous systems. Software available from tensorflow.org. http://tensorflow.org/.

Andrei Alexandrescu and Katrin Kirchhoff. 2006. Factored neural language models. In *Proceedings of the Human Language Technology Conference of the NAACL, Companion Volume: Short Papers*. Association for Computational Linguistics, New York City, USA, pages 1–4. http://www.aclweb.org/anthology/N/N06/N06-2001.

A. Allauzen and J.L Gauvain. 2005. Open vocabulary asr for audiovisual document indexation. In *IEEE International Conference on Acoustics, Speech and Signal Processing (ICASSP)*.

Jacob Andreas, Maxim Rabinovich, Michael I. Jordan, and Dan Klein. 2015. On the accuracy of self-normalized log-linear models. In *Advances in Neural Information Processing Systems 28: Annual Conference on Neural Information Processing Systems 2015, December 7-12, 2015, Montreal, Quebec, Canada.* pages 1783–1791. http://papers.nips.cc/paper/5806-on-the-accuracy-of-self-normalized-log-linear-models.

Dzmitry Bahdanau, Kyunghyun Cho, and Yoshua Bengio. 2014. Neural machine translation by jointly learning to align and translate. *CoRR* abs/1409.0473.

Miguel Ballesteros, Chris Dyer, and Noah A. Smith. 2015. Improved transition-based parsing by modeling characters instead of words with lstms. In *Proceedings of the 2015 Conference on Empirical Methods in Natural Language Processing*. Association for Computational Linguistics, Lisbon, Portugal, pages 349–359. http://aclweb.org/anthology/D15-1041.

Yoshua Bengio, Réjean Ducharme, Pascal Vincent, and Christian Janvin. 2003. A neural probabilistic language model. *Journal of Machine Learning Research* 3:1137–1155.

Yoshua Bengio and Jean-Sébastien Sénécal. 2008. Adaptive importance sampling to accelerate training of a neural probabilistic language model. *IEEE Trans. Neural Networks* 19(4):713–722.

Jeff A. Bilmes and Katrin Kirchhoff. 2003. Factored language models and generalized parallel backoff. In *Proceedings of the 2003 Conference of the North American Chapter of the Association for Computational Linguistics on Human Language Technology: Companion Volume of the Proceedings of HLT-NAACL 2003–short Papers - Volume 2*. Association for Computational Linguistics, Stroudsburg, PA, USA, NAACL-Short '03, pages 4–6. https://doi.org/10.3115/1073483.1073485.

Piotr Bojanowski, Edouard Grave, Armand Joulin, and Tomas Mikolov. 2016. Enriching word vectors with subword information. *CoRR* abs/1607.04606. http://arxiv.org/abs/1607.04606.

Jan A. Botha and Phil Blunsom. 2014. Compositional Morphology for Word Representations and Language Modelling. In *Proceedings of the International Conference of Machine Learning (ICML)*. Beijing, China.

Franck Burlot and François Yvon. 2017. Learning morphological normalization for translation from and into morphologically rich language. *The Prague Bulletin of Mathematical Linguistics (Proc. EAMT)* (108):49–60.

Wenlin Chen, David Grangier, and Michael Auli. 2016. Strategies for training large vocabulary neural language models. In *Proceedings of the 54th Annual Meeting of the Association for Computational Linguistics (Volume 1: Long Papers)*. Association for Computational Linguistics, Berlin, Germany, pages 1975–1985. http://www.aclweb.org/anthology/P16-1186.

Ronan Collobert, Jason Weston, Léon Bottou, Michael Karlen, Koray Kavukcuoglu, and Pavel Kuksa. 2011. Natural language processing (almost) from scratch. *J. Mach. Learn. Res.* 12:2493–2537. http://dl.acm.org/citation.cfm?id=1953048.2078186.

Marta R. Costa-jussà and José A. R. Fonollosa. 2016. Character-based neural machine translation. In *Proceedings of the 54th Annual Meeting of the Association for Computational Linguistics (Volume 2: Short Papers)*. Association for Computational Linguistics, Berlin, Germany, pages 357–361. http://anthology.aclweb.org/P16-2058.

Ryan Cotterell, Hinrich Schütze, and Jason Eisner. 2016. Morphological smoothing and extrapolation of word embeddings. In *Proceedings of the 54th Annual Meeting of the Association for Computational Linguistics (Volume 1: Long Papers)*. Association for Computational Linguistics, Berlin, Germany, pages 1651–1660. http://www.aclweb.org/anthology/P16-1156.

Mathias Creutz, Teemu Hirsimäki, Mikko Kurimo, Antti Puurula, Janne Pylkkönen, Vesa Siivola, Matti Varjokallio, Ebru Arisoy, Murat Saraçlar, and Andreas Stolcke. 2007. Morph-based speech recognition and modeling of out-of-vocabulary words across languages. *ACM Trans. Speech Lang. Process.* 5(1):3:1–3:29.

Jacob Devlin, Rabih Zbib, Zhongqiang Huang, Thomas Lamar, Richard Schwartz, and John Makhoul.

2014. Fast and robust neural network joint models for statistical machine translation. In *Proceedings of the 52nd Annual Meeting of the Association for Computational Linguistics (Volume 1: Long Papers)*. Association for Computational Linguistics, Baltimore, Maryland, pages 1370–1380. http://www.aclweb.org/anthology/P14-1129.

Manaal Faruqui, Yulia Tsvetkov, Graham Neubig, and Chris Dyer. 2016. Morphological inflection generation using character sequence to sequence learning. In *Proceedings of the 2016 Conference of the North American Chapter of the Association for Computational Linguistics: Human Language Technologies*. Association for Computational Linguistics, San Diego, California, pages 634–643. http://www.aclweb.org/anthology/N16-1077.

Dan Gillick, Cliff Brunk, Oriol Vinyals, and Amarnag Subramanya. 2016. Multilingual language processing from bytes. In *Proceedings of the 2016 Conference of the North American Chapter of the Association for Computational Linguistics: Human Language Technologies*. Association for Computational Linguistics, San Diego, California, pages 1296–1306. http://www.aclweb.org/anthology/N16-1155.

Alex Graves, Santiago Fernández, and Jürgen Schmidhuber. 2005. Bidirectional LSTM networks for improved phoneme classification and recognition. In *Artificial Neural Networks: Formal Models and Their Applications - ICANN 2005, 15th International Conference, Warsaw, Poland, September 11-15, 2005, Proceedings, Part II*. pages 799–804.

Michael U. Gutmann and Aapo Hyvärinen. 2012. Noise-contrastive estimation of unnormalized statistical models, with applications to natural image statistics. *J. Mach. Learn. Res.* 13(1):307–361.

Georg Heigold, Guenter Neumann, and Josef van Genabith. 2017. An extensive empirical evaluation of character-based morphological tagging for 14 languages. In *Proceedings of the 15th Conference of the European Chapter of the Association for Computational Linguistics: Volume 1, Long Papers*. Association for Computational Linguistics, Valencia, Spain, pages 505–513. http://www.aclweb.org/anthology/E17-1048.

Michiel Hermans and Benjamin Schrauwen. 2013. Training and analysing deep recurrent neural networks. In C. J. C. Burges, L. Bottou, M. Welling, Z. Ghahramani, and K. Q. Weinberger, editors, *Advances in Neural Information Processing Systems 26*, Curran Associates, Inc., pages 190–198. http://papers.nips.cc/paper/5166-training-and-analysing-deep-recurrent-neural-networks.pdf.

Sepp Hochreiter and Jürgen Schmidhuber. 1997. Long short-term memory. *Neural Comput.* 9(8):1735–1780. https://doi.org/10.1162/neco.1997.9.8.1735.

Kyuyeon Hwang and Wonyong Sung. 2017. Character-level language modeling with hierarchical recurrent neural networks. In *2017 IEEE International Conference on Acoustics, Speech and Signal Processing, ICASSP 2017, New Orleans, LA, USA, March 5-9, 2017*. pages 5720–5724. https://doi.org/10.1109/ICASSP.2017.7953252.

Sébastien Jean, Kyunghyun Cho, Roland Memisevic, and Yoshua Bengio. 2015. On using very large target vocabulary for neural machine translation. In *Proceedings of the 53rd Annual Meeting of the Association for Computational Linguistics and the 7th International Joint Conference on Natural Language Processing (Volume 1: Long Papers)*. Association for Computational Linguistics, Beijing, China, pages 1–10. http://www.aclweb.org/anthology/P15-1001.

Shihao Ji, S. V. N. Vishwanathan, Nadathur Satish, Michael J. Anderson, and Pradeep Dubey. 2015. Blackout: Speeding up recurrent neural network language models with very large vocabularies. *CoRR* abs/1511.06909. http://arxiv.org/abs/1511.06909.

Rafal Józefowicz, Oriol Vinyals, Mike Schuster, Noam Shazeer, and Yonghui Wu. 2016. Exploring the limits of language modeling. *CoRR* abs/1602.02410. http://arxiv.org/abs/1602.02410.

Katharina Kann, Ryan Cotterell, and Hinrich Schütze. 2017. Neural multi-source morphological reinflection. In *Proceedings of the 15th Conference of the European Chapter of the Association for Computational Linguistics: Volume 1, Long Papers*. Association for Computational Linguistics, Valencia, Spain, pages 514–524. http://www.aclweb.org/anthology/E17-1049.

Yoon Kim, Yacine Jernite, David Sontag, and Alexander M Rush. 2015. Character-aware neural language models. *arXiv preprint arXiv:1508.06615* .

Diederik P. Kingma and Jimmy Ba. 2014. Adam: A method for stochastic optimization. *CoRR* abs/1412.6980. http://arxiv.org/abs/1412.6980.

Hai-Son Le, Alexandre Allauzen, and François Yvon. 2012. Continuous space translation models with neural networks. In *Proceedings of the 2012 Conference of the North American Chapter of the Association for Computational Linguistics: Human Language Technologies*. Association for Computational Linguistics, Montréal, Canada, pages 39–48. http://www.aclweb.org/anthology/N12-1005.

Hai-Son Le, Ilya Oparin, Alexandre Allauzen, Jean-Luc Gauvain, and Francois Yvon. 2011. Structured output layer neural network language model. In *IEEE International Conference on Acoustics, Speech and Signal Processing (ICASSP)*. Prague, Czech Republic, pages 5524–5527.

Wang Ling, Chris Dyer, Alan W Black, Isabel Trancoso, Ramon Fermandez, Silvio Amir, Luis Marujo, and Tiago Luis. 2015. Finding function in form: Compositional character models for open vocabulary word representation. In *Proceedings of the*

2015 Conference on Empirical Methods in Natural Language Processing. Association for Computational Linguistics, Lisbon, Portugal, pages 1520–1530. http://aclweb.org/anthology/D15-1176.

Thang Luong, Richard Socher, and Christopher Manning. 2013. Better word representations with recursive neural networks for morphology. In *Proceedings of the Seventeenth Conference on Computational Natural Language Learning*. Association for Computational Linguistics, Sofia, Bulgaria, pages 104–113. http://www.aclweb.org/anthology/W13-3512.

Xuezhe Ma and Eduard Hovy. 2016. End-to-end sequence labeling via bi-directional lstm-cnns-crf. In *Proceedings of the 54th Annual Meeting of the Association for Computational Linguistics (Volume 1: Long Papers)*. Association for Computational Linguistics, Berlin, Germany, pages 1064–1074. http://www.aclweb.org/anthology/P16-1101.

Mercedes Garcia Martinez, Loc Barrault, and Fethi Bougares. 2016. Factored neural machine translation architectures. In *International Workshop on Spoken Language Translation (IWSLT'16)*. Seattle (USA).

Tomas Mikolov, Martin Karafiát, Lukás Burget, Jan Cernocký, and Sanjeev Khudanpur. 2010. Recurrent neural network based language model. In *INTERSPEECH 2010, 11th Annual Conference of the International Speech Communication Association, Makuhari, Chiba, Japan, September 26-30, 2010*. pages 1045–1048.

Tomas Mikolov, Ilya Sutskever, Kai Chen, Greg S Corrado, and Jeff Dean. 2013. Distributed representations of words and phrases and their compositionality. In C. J. C. Burges, L. Bottou, M. Welling, Z. Ghahramani, and K. Q. Weinberger, editors, *Advances in Neural Information Processing Systems 26*. Curran Associates, Inc., pages 3111–3119. http://papers.nips.cc/paper/5021-distributed-representations-of-words-and-phrases-and-their-compositionality.pdf.

Andriy Mnih and Geoffrey E Hinton. 2009. A scalable hierarchical distributed language model. In D. Koller, D. Schuurmans, Y. Bengio, and L. Bottou, editors, *Advances in Neural Information Processing Systems 21*, Curran Associates, Inc., pages 1081–1088. http://papers.nips.cc/paper/3583-a-scalable-hierarchical-distributed-language-model.pdf.

Andriy Mnih and Yee Whye Teh. 2012. A fast and simple algorithm for training neural probabilistic language models. In *ICML*. icml.cc / Omnipress.

Frederic Morin and Yoshua Bengio. 2005. Hierarchical probabilistic neural network language model. In Robert G. Cowell and Zoubin Ghahramani, editors, *Proceedings of the Tenth International Workshop on Artificial Intelligence and Statistics*. Society for Artificial Intelligence and Statistics, pages 246–252.

http://www.iro.umontreal.ca/ lisa/pointeurs/hierarchical-nnlm-aistats05.pdf.

Thomas Mueller and Hinrich Schuetze. 2011. Improved modeling of out-of-vocabulary words using morphological classes. In *Proceedings of the 49th Annual Meeting of the Association for Computational Linguistics: Human Language Technologies*. Association for Computational Linguistics, Portland, Oregon, USA, pages 524–528. http://www.aclweb.org/anthology/P11-2092.

Barbara Plank, Anders Søgaard, and Yoav Goldberg. 2016. Multilingual part-of-speech tagging with bidirectional long short-term memory models and auxiliary loss. In *Proceedings of the 54th Annual Meeting of the Association for Computational Linguistics (Volume 2: Short Papers)*. Association for Computational Linguistics, Berlin, Germany, pages 412–418. http://anthology.aclweb.org/P16-2067.

Siyu Qiu, Qing Cui, Jiang Bian, Bin Gao, and Tie-Yan Liu. 2014. Co-learning of word representations and morpheme representations. In *Proceedings of COLING 2014, the 25th International Conference on Computational Linguistics: Technical Papers*. Dublin City University and Association for Computational Linguistics, Dublin, Ireland, pages 141–150. http://www.aclweb.org/anthology/C14-1015.

Cicero D. Santos and Bianca Zadrozny. 2014. Learning character-level representations for part-of-speech tagging. In Tony Jebara and Eric P. Xing, editors, *Proceedings of the 31st International Conference on Machine Learning (ICML-14)*. JMLR Workshop and Conference Proceedings, pages 1818–1826. http://jmlr.org/proceedings/papers/v32/santos14.pdf.

Holger Schwenk. 2007. Continuous space language models. *Comput. Speech Lang.* 21(3):492–518.

Henning Sperr, Jan Niehues, and Alex Waibel. 2013. Letter n-gram-based input encoding for continuous space language models. In *Proceedings of the Workshop on Continuous Vector Space Models and their Compositionality*. Association for Computational Linguistics, Sofia, Bulgaria, pages 30–39. http://www.aclweb.org/anthology/W13-3204.

Rupesh Kumar Srivastava, Klaus Greff, and Jürgen Schmidhuber. 2015. Training very deep networks. *CoRR* abs/1507.06228. http://arxiv.org/abs/1507.06228.

Jana Straková, Milan Straka, and Jan Hajič. 2014. Open-source tools for morphology, lemmatization, pos tagging and named entity recognition. In *Proceedings of 52nd Annual Meeting of the Association for Computational Linguistics: System Demonstrations*. Association for Computational Linguistics, Baltimore, Maryland, pages 13–18. http://www.aclweb.org/anthology/P14-5003.

Ilya Sutskever, James Martens, and Geoffrey Hinton. 2011. Generating text with recurrent neural networks. In Lise Getoor and Tobias Scheffer, editors, *Proceedings of the 28th International Conference on Machine Learning (ICML-11)*. ACM, New York, NY, USA, ICML '11, pages 1017–1024.

Clara Vania and Adam Lopez. 2017. From characters to words to in between: Do we capture morphology? *CoRR* abs/1704.08352. http://arxiv.org/abs/1704.08352.

Alexander Waibel, Toshiyuki Hanazawa, Geofrey Hinton, Kiyohiro Shikano, and Kevin J. Lang. 1990. *Readings in Speech Recognition*, Morgan Kaufmann Publishers Inc., San Francisco, CA, USA, chapter Phoneme Recognition Using Time-delay Neural Networks, pages 393–404.

John Wieting, Mohit Bansal, Kevin Gimpel, and Karen Livescu. 2016. Charagram: Embedding words and sentences via character n-grams. In *Proceedings of the 2016 Conference on Empirical Methods in Natural Language Processing*. Association for Computational Linguistics, Austin, Texas, pages 1504–1515. https://aclweb.org/anthology/D16-1157.

Learning variable length units for SMT between related languages via Byte Pair Encoding

Anoop Kunchukuttan, Pushpak Bhattacharyya
Center For Indian Language Technology
Department of Computer Science & Engineering
Indian Institute of Technology Bombay
{anoopk,pb}@cse.iitb.ac.in

Abstract

We explore the use of segments learnt using Byte Pair Encoding (referred to as *BPE units*) as basic units for statistical machine translation between *related* languages and compare it with *orthographic syllables*, which are currently the best performing basic units for this translation task. BPE identifies the most frequent character sequences as basic units, while orthographic syllables are linguistically motivated pseudo-syllables. We show that BPE units modestly outperform orthographic syllables as units of translation, showing up to 11% increase in BLEU score. While orthographic syllables can be used only for languages whose writing systems use vowel representations, BPE is writing system independent and we show that BPE outperforms other units for non-vowel writing systems too. Our results are supported by extensive experimentation spanning multiple language families and writing systems.

1 Introduction

The term, *related languages*, refers to languages that exhibit lexical and structural similarities on account of sharing a **common ancestry** or being in **contact for a long period of time** (Bhattacharyya et al., 2016). Examples of languages related by common ancestry are Slavic and Indo-Aryan languages. Prolonged contact leads to convergence of linguistic properties even if the languages are not related by ancestry and could lead to the formation of *linguistic areas* (Thomason, 2000). Examples of such linguistic areas are the Indian subcontinent (Emeneau, 1956), Balkan (Trubetzkoy, 1928) and Standard Average European (Haspelmath, 2001)

linguistic areas. Genetic as well as contact relationship lead to related languages sharing vocabulary and structural features.

There is substantial government, commercial and cultural communication among people speaking related languages (Europe, India and South-East Asia being prominent examples and linguistic regions in Africa possibly in the future). As these regions integrate more closely and move to a digital society, translation between *related* languages is becoming an important requirement. In addition, translation to/from related languages to a *lingua franca* like English is also very important. However, despite significant communication between people speaking related languages, most of these languages have few parallel corpora resources. It is therefore important to leverage the relatedness of these languages to build good-quality statistical machine translation (SMT) systems given the lack of parallel corpora.

Modelling lexical similarity among related languages is the key to building good-quality SMT systems with limited parallel corpora. **Lexical similarity** implies related languages share many words with similar form (spelling/pronunciation) and meaning *e.g.* blindness is andhapana in Hindi, aandhaLepaNaa in Marathi. These words could be cognates, lateral borrowings or loan words from other languages.

Subword level transformations are an effective way for translation of such shared words. In this work, we propose use of Byte Pair Encoding (BPE) (Gage, 1994; Sennrich et al., 2016), a encoding method inspired from text compression literature, to learn basic translation units for translation between related languages. In previous work, the basic units of translation are either linguistically motivated (word, morpheme, syllable, etc.) or ad-hoc choices (character n-gram). In contrast, BPE is motivated by **statistical properties of text**.

Proceedings of the First Workshop on Subword and Character Level Models in NLP, pages 14–24,
Copenhagen, Denmark, September 7, 2017. ©2017 Association for Computational Linguistics.

The major contributions of our work are:

- We show that BPE units **modestly outperform orthographic syllable units** (Kunchukuttan and Bhattacharyya, 2016b), the best performing basic unit for translation between related languages, resulting in up to 11% improvement in BLEU score.
- Unlike orthographic syllables, BPE units are **writing system independent**. Orthographic syllables can only be applied to alphabetic and abugida writing systems. We show BPE units improve translation over word and morpheme level models for languages using *abjad* and *logographic* writing systems. Average BLEU score improvements of 18% and 6% over a baseline word-level model for language pairs involving abjad and logographic writing systems respectively were observed.
- Like orthographic syllables, BPE units outperform character, morph and word units when the language pairs show relatively less lexical similarity or belong to different language families (but have sufficient contact relation).
- While orthographic syllables approximate true syllables, we observe that BPE units learnt from the corpus **span various linguistic entities** (syllables, suffixes, morphemes, words, *etc.*). This may enable BPE level models to learn translation mappings at various levels simultaneously.
- We have reported results over a large number of languages (16 language pairs and 17 languages) which span 4 major language families and 10 writing systems of various types. To the best of our knowledge, this is the largest experiment for translation over related languages and the **broad coverage strongly supports our results**.
- We also show BPE units outperform other translation units in a **cross-domain translation** task.

The paper is organized as follows. Section 2 discusses related work. Section 3 discusses why BPE is a promising method for learning subword units and describes how we train BPE unit level translation models. Section 4 describes our experimental set-up. Section 5 reports the results of our experiments and analyses the results. Based on experimental results, we analyse why BPE units outperform other units in Section 6. Section 7 concludes the paper by summarizing our work and discussing further research directions.

2   Related Work

There are two broad set of approaches that have been explored in the literature for translation between related languages that leverage lexical similarity between source and target languages.

The first approach involves **transliteration of source words** into the target languages. This can done by transliterating the untranslated words in a post-processing step (Nakov and Tiedemann, 2012; Kunchukuttan et al., 2014), a technique generally used for handling named entities in SMT. However, transliteration candidates cannot be scored and tuned along with other features used in the SMT system. This limitation can be overcome by integrating the transliteration module into the decoder (Durrani et al., 2010), so both translation and transliteration candidates can be evaluated and scored simultaneously. This also allows transliteration *vs.* translation choices to be made.

Since a high degree of similarity exists at the subword level between related languages, the second approach looks at **translation with subword level basic units**. Character-level SMT has been explored for very closely related languages like *Bulgarian-Macedonian, Indonesian-Malay, Spanish-Catalan* with modest success (Vilar et al., 2007; Tiedemann, 2009a; Tiedemann and Nakov, 2013). Unigram-level learning provides very little context for learning translation models (Tiedemann, 2012). The use of character n-gram units to address this limitation leads to data sparsity for higher order n-grams and provides little benefit (Tiedemann and Nakov, 2013). These results were demonstrated primarily for very close European languages. Kunchukuttan and Bhattacharyya (2016b) proposed *orthographic syllables*, a linguistically-motivated variable-length unit, which approximates a syllable. This unit has outperformed character n-gram, word and morpheme level models as well as transliteration post-editing approaches mentioned earlier. They also showed orthographic syllables can outperform other units even when: (i) the lexical distance between related languages is reasonably large, (ii) the languages do not have a genetic relation, but only a contact relation.

Recently, subword level models have also generated interest for neural machine translation (NMT) systems. The motivation is the need to limit the **vocabulary of neural MT systems** in encoder-decoder architectures (Sutskever et al., 2014). It is in this context that Byte Pair Encoding, a data compression method (Gage, 1994), was adapted to learn subword units for NMT (Sennrich et al., 2016). Other subword units for NMT have also been proposed: character (Chung et al., 2016), Huffman encoding based units (Chitnis and DeNero, 2015), wordpieces (Schuster and Nakajima, 2012; Wu et al., 2016). Our hypothesis is that such subword units learnt from corpora are particularly suited for translation between related languages. In this paper, we test this hypothesis by using BPE to learn subword units.

3   BPE for related languages

We discuss why BPE is a promising method for learning subword units (subsections 3.1 and 3.2) and describe how we trained our BPE unit level translation models (subsections 3.3 and 3.4).

3.1   Motivation

Byte Pair Encoding is a data compression algorithm which was first adapted for Neural Machine Translation by Sennrich et al. (2016). For a given language, it is used to build a **vocabulary** relevant to translation by *discovering the most frequent character sequences* in the language.

For NMT, BPE enables efficient, high quality, open vocabulary translation by (i) limiting core vocabulary size, (ii) representing the most frequent words as atomic BPE units and rare words as compositions of the atomic BPE units. These benefits of BPE are not particular to NMT, and apply to SMT between related languages too. Given the lexical similarity between related languages, we would like to *identify a small, core vocabulary of subwords* from which words in the language can be composed. These subwords represent stable, frequent patterns (possibly linguistic units like syllables, morphemes, affixes) for which mappings exist in other related languages. This alleviates the need for word level translation.

3.2   Comparison with orthographic syllables

We primarily compare BPE units with orthographic syllables (OS) (Kunchukuttan and Bhattacharyya, 2016b), which are good translation units for related languages. The *orthographic syllable* is a sequence of one or more consonants followed by a vowel, *i.e.* a C^+V unit, which approximates a linguistic syllable (*e.g. spacious* would be segmented as *spa ciou s*). Orthographic syllabification is rule based and applies to writing systems which represent vowels (alphabets and abugidas).

Both OS and BPE units are variable length units which provide longer and more relevant context for translation compared to character n-grams. In contrast to orthographic syllables, the BPE units are highly frequent character sequences reflecting the underlying statistical properties of the text. Some of the character sequences discovered by the BPE algorithm may be different linguistic units like syllables, morphemes and affixes. Moreover, BPE can be applied to text in any writing system.

3.3   The BPE Algorithm

We briefly summarize the BPE algorithm (described at length in Sennrich et al. (2016)). The input is a monolingual corpus for a language (one side of the parallel training data, in our case). We start with an *initial vocabulary viz.* the characters in the text corpus. The vocabulary is updated using an iterative greedy algorithm. In every iteration, the most frequent bigram (based on current vocabulary) in the corpus is added to the vocabulary (the *merge* operation). The corpus is again encoded using the updated vocabulary and this process is repeated for a pre-determined number of merge operations. The number of merge operations is the only hyperparameter to the system which needs to be tuned. A new word can be segmented by looking up the learnt vocabulary. For instance, a new word `scion` may be segmented as `sc ion` after looking up the learnt vocabulary, assuming `sc` and `ion` as BPE units learnt during training.

3.4   Training subword level translation model

We train subword level phrase-based SMT models between related languages. Along with BPE level, we also train PBSMT models at morpheme and OS levels for comparison.

For BPE, we learn the vocabulary separately for the source and target languages using the respective part of the training corpus. We segment the data into subwords during pre-processing and indicate word boundaries by a boundary marker (_) as shown in the example below. The boundary marker helps keep track of word boundaries, so the word level representation can be reconstructed after decoding.

ben	Bengali	kok	Konkani	pan	Punjabi
bul	Bulgarian	kor	Korean	swe	Swedish
dan	Danish	mac	Macedonian	urd	Urdu
hin	Hindi	mar	Marathi	tam	Tamil
ind	Indonesian	mal	Malayalam	tel	Telugu
jpn	Japanese	may	Malay		

(a) List of languages used in experiments along with ISO 639-3 codes. These codes are used in the paper.

Language Family		Type of writing system	
Dravidian	mal,tam,tel	Alphabet	dan[1],swe[1],may[1] ind[1],buc[2],mac[2]
Indo-Aryan	hin,urd,ben kok,mar,pan	Abugida	mal,tam,tel,hin ben,kok,mar,pan
Slavic	bul,mac		
Germanic	dan,swe	Syllabic	kor
Polynesian	may,ind	Logographic	jpn
Altaic	jpn,kor	Abjad	urd

(b) Classification of the languages and writing systems. (i) Indo-Aryan, Slavic and Germanic belong to the larger Indo-European language family. (ii) Alphabetic writing systems used by selected languages: Latin[1] and Cyrillic[2].

Table 1: Languages under experiments: details

word: `Childhood means simplicity .`

subword: `Chi ldhoo d _ mea ns _ si mpli ci ty _ .`

While building phrase-based SMT models at the subword level, we use (a) monotonic decoding since related languages have similar word order, (b) higher order languages models (10-gram) since data sparsity is a lesser concern owing to small vocabulary size (Vilar et al., 2007), and (c) word level tuning (by post-processing the decoder output during tuning) to optimize the correct translation metric (Nakov and Tiedemann, 2012). Following decoding, we used a simple method to regenerate words from subwords (desegmentation): concatenate subwords between consecutive occurrences of boundary marker characters.

4 Experimental Setup

We trained translation systems over the following basic units: character, morpheme, word, orthographic syllable and BPE unit. In this section, we summarize the languages and writing systems chosen for our experiments, the datasets used and the experimental configuration of our translation systems, and the evaluation methodology.

4.1 Languages and writing systems

Our experiments spanned a diverse set of languages: 16 language pairs, 17 languages and 10 writing systems. Table 1 summarizes the key aspects of the languages involved in the experiments.

The chosen languages span 4 major language families (6 major sub-groups: Indo-Aryan, Slavic and Germanic belong to the larger Indo-European language family). The languages exhibit diversity in word order and morphological complexity. Of course, between related languages, word order and morphological properties are similar. The classification of Japanese and Korean into the Altaic family is debated, but various lexical and grammatical similarities are indisputable, either due to genetic or cognate relationship (Robbeets, 2005; Vovin, 2010). However, the source of lexical similarity is immaterial to the current work. For want of a better classification, we use the name *Altaic* to indicate relatedness between Japanese and Korean.

The chosen language pairs also exhibit varying levels of lexical similarity. Table 3 shows an indication of the lexical similarity between them in terms of the Longest Common Subsequence Ratio (LCSR) (Melamed, 1995). The LCSR has been computed over the parallel training sentences at character level (shown only for language pairs where the writing systems are the same or can be easily mapped in order to do the LCSR computation). At one end of the spectrum, Malayalam-India, Urdu-Hindi, Macedonian-Bulgarian are dialects/registers of the same language and exhibit high lexical similarity. At the other end, pairs like Hindi-Malayalam belong to different language families, but show many lexical and grammatical similarities due to contact for a long time (Subbarao, 2012).

The chosen languages cover 5 types of writing systems. Of these, alphabetic and abugida writing systems represent vowels, logographic writing systems do not have vowels. The use of vowels is optional in abjad writing systems and depends on various factors and conventions. For instance, Urdu word segmentation can be very inconsistent (Durrani and Hussain, 2010) and generally short vowels are not denoted. The Korean *Hangul* writing system is syllabic, so the vowels are implicitly represented in the characters.

4.2 Datasets

Table 2a shows train, test and tune splits of the parallel corpora used. The Indo-Aryan and Dravidian language parallel corpora are obtained from the multilingual Indian Language Corpora Initiative (ILCI) corpus (Jha, 2012). Parallel corpora

Language Pair	train	tune	test
ben-hin,pan-hin, kok-mar, mal-tam,tel-mal, hin-mal,mal-hin	44,777	1000	2000
urd-hin,ben-urd urd-mal,mal-urd	38,162	843	1707
bul-mac	150k	1000	2000
dan-swe	150k	1000	2000
may-ind	137k	1000	2000
kor-jpn,jpn-kor	69,809	1000	2000

(a) Parallel Corpora Size (no. of sentences)

Language	Size	Language	Size
hin (Bojar et al., 2014)	10M	urd (Jawaid et al., 2014)	5M
tam (Ramasamy et al., 2012)	1M	mar (news websites)	1.8M
mal (Quasthoff et al., 2006)	200K	swe (OpenSubtitles2016)	2.4M
mac (Tiedemann, 2009b)	680K	ind (Tiedemann, 2009b)	640K

(b) Details of additional monolingual corpora for training word-level language models (source and size in number of sentences)

Table 2: Training Corpus Statistics

for other pairs were obtained from the *OpenSubtitles2016* section of the OPUS corpus collection (Tiedemann, 2009b). Language models for word-level systems were trained on the target side of training corpora plus additional monolingual corpora from various sources (See Table 2b for details). We used just the target language side of the parallel corpora for character, morpheme, OS and BPE-unit level LMs.

4.3 System details

We trained phrase-based SMT systems using the *Moses* system (Koehn et al., 2007), with the *grow-diag-final-and* heuristic for extracting phrases, and Batch MIRA (Cherry and Foster, 2012) for tuning (default parameters). We trained 5-gram LMs with Kneser-Ney smoothing for word and morpheme level models and 10-gram LMs for character, OS and BPE-unit level models. Subword level representation of sentences is long, hence we speed up decoding by using cube pruning with a smaller beam size (pop-limit=1000). This setting has been shown to have minimal impact on translation quality (Kunchukuttan and Bhattacharyya, 2016a).

We used unsupervised morphological-segmenters for generating morpheme representations (trained using *Morfessor* (Smit et al., 2014)). For Indian languages, we used the models distributed as part of the *Indic NLP Library*[1] (Kunchukuttan et al., 2014). We used orthographic syllabification rules from the *Indic NLP Library* for Indian languages, and custom rules for Latin and Slavic scripts. For training BPE models, we used the *subword-nmt*[2] library. We used *Juman*[3] and *Mecab*[4] for Japanese and Korean tokenization respectively.

For mapping characters across Indic scripts, we used the method described by Kunchukuttan et al. (2015) and implemented in the *Indic NLP Library*.

4.4 Evaluation

The primary evaluation metric is *word-level* BLEU (Papineni et al., 2002). We also report LeBLEU (Virpioja and Grönroos, 2015) scores as an alternative evaluation metric. LeBLEU is a variant of BLEU that does an edit-distance based, soft-matching of words and has been shown to be better for morphologically rich languages. We used bootstrap resampling for testing statistical significance (Koehn, 2004).

5 Results and Analysis

This section describes the results of various experiments and analyses them. A comparison of BPE with other units across languages and writing systems, choice of number of merge operations and effect of domain change and training data size are studied. We also report initial results with a joint bilingual BPE model.

5.1 Comparison of BPE with other units

Table 3 shows translation accuracies of all the language pairs under experimentation for different translation units, in terms of BLEU as well as LeBLEU scores. The number of BPE merge operations was chosen such that the resultant vocabulary size would be equivalent to the vocabulary size of the orthographic syllable encoded corpus. Since we could not do orthographic syllabification for Urdu, Korean and Japanese, we selected the merge operations as follows: For Urdu, number of merge operations were selected based on Hindi OS vocabulary since Hindi and Urdu are registers of the same language. For Korean and Japanese, the number of BPE merge operations was set to 3000, discovered by tuning on a separate validation set.

---

[1] http://anoopkunchukuttan.github.io/indic_nlp_library
[2] https://github.com/rsennrich/subword-nmt
[3] http://nlp.ist.i.kyoto-u.ac.jp/EN/index.php?JUMAN
[4] https://bitbucket.org/eunjeon/mecab-ko

Language Pair		BLEU					LeBLEU				
Src-Tgt	LCSR	C	W	M	O	$\mathbf{B}_{match}$	C	W	M	O	$\mathbf{B}_{match}$
ben-hin	52.30	27.95	32.47	32.17	**33.54**	33.22	0.672	0.682	0.708	0.715	**0.716**
pan-hin	67.99	71.26	70.07	71.29	**72.41**	72.22	0.905	0.871	0.899	0.906	**0.907**
kok-mar	54.51	19.83	21.30	22.81	23.43	**23.63**	0.632	0.636	0.659	**0.671**	0.665
mal-tam	39.04	4.50	6.38	7.61	7.84	**8.67†**	0.311	0.314	0.409	0.447	**0.465**
tel-mal	39.18	6.00	6.78	7.86	8.50	**8.79**	0.346	0.314	0.383	0.439	**0.443**
hin-mal	33.24	6.28	8.55	9.23	10.46	**10.73**	0.324	0.393	0.436	**0.477**	0.468
mal-hin	33.24	12.33	15.18	17.08	18.44	**20.54**	0.444	0.460	0.528	0.551	**0.565**
urd-hin	-	52.57	55.12	52.87	NA	**55.55**	0.804	0.795	0.792	NA	**0.823**
ben-urd	-	18.16	27.06	27.31	NA	**28.06**	0.607	0.660	0.671	NA	**0.692**
urd-mal	-	3.13	6.49	7.05	NA	**8.44**	0.247	0.350	0.379	NA	**0.416**
mal-urd	-	8.90	13.22	15.30	NA	**18.48**	0.444	0.454	0.522	NA	**0.568**
bul-mac	62.85	20.61	21.20	-	**21.95**	21.73	0.603	0.606	-	**0.613**	0.599
dan-swe	63.39	35.36	35.13	-	35.46	**35.77**	0.692	**0.694**	-	0.682	0.682
may-ind	73.54	60.50	**61.33**	-	60.79	59.54†	0.827	**0.832**	-	0.828	0.825
kor-jpn	-	8.51	9.90	-	NA	**10.23**	0.396	0.372	-	NA	**0.408**
jpn-kor	-	8.17	8.44	-	NA	**9.02**	0.372	0.350	-	NA	**0.374**

Table 3: Translation accuracies for various translation units (BLEU and LeBLEU scores reported). The reported scores are:- **W**: word-level, **M**: morpheme, **O**: orthographic syllable, $\mathbf{B}_{match}$: BPE units with number of merge operations selected to match vocabulary size of OS encoding. See discussion related to exceptions for pairs involving Urdu, Korean and Japanese. (a) The values marked in **bold** indicate best score for a language pair (b) **LCSR** indicates lexical similarity (c) *NA: Not Applicable.* (d) † indicates that difference in BLEU scoresbetween $\mathbf{B}_{match}$ and **O** are statistically significant ($p < 0.05$)

Our major observations are described below (based on BLEU scores):

• BPE units are clearly better than the traditional word and morpheme representations. The average BLEU score improvement is 15% over word-based results and 11% over morpheme-based results. The only exception is Malay-Indonesian, which are registers of the same language.

• BPE units also show modest improvement over the recently proposed orthographic syllables over most language pairs (average improvement of 2.6% and maximum improvement of up to 11%). The improvements are not statistically significant for most language pairs. The only exceptions are Bengali-Hindi, Punjabi-Hindi and Malay-Indonesian - all these languages pairs have relatively less morphological affixing (*Bengali-Hindi, Punjabi-Hindi*) or are registers of the same language (Malay-Indonesian). For Bengali-Hindi and Punjabi-Hindi, the BPE unit translation accuracies are quite close to OS level accuracies. Since OS level models have been shown to be better than character level models (Kunchukuttan and Bhattacharyya, 2016b), BPE units are better than character level models by transitivity.

• BPE units also outperform other units for translation between language pairs belonging to different language pairs, but having a long contact relationship *viz.* Malayalam-Hindi and Hindi-Malayalam.

• It is worth mentioning that BPE units provide a substantial benefit over OS units when translation involves a morphologically rich language. In translations involving Malayalam, Tamil and Telugu, average accuracy improvement of 6.25% were observed.

The LeBLEU scores also show the same trends as the BLEU scores.

5.2 Applicability to different writing systems

The utility of orthographic syllables as translation units is limited to languages that use writing systems which represent vowels. Alphabetic and abugida writing systems fall into this category. On the other hand, logographic writing systems (Japanese Kanji, Chinese) and abjad writing systems (Arabic, Hebrew, Syriac, etc.) do not represent vowels. To be more precise, abjad writing systems may represent some/all vowels depending on language, pragmatics and conventions. Syllabic writing systems like Korean Hangul do not explicitly represent vowels, since the basic unit (the syllable) implicitly represents the vowels. The major advantage of Byte Pair Encoding is its **writing system independence** and our results show

	O	B_{match}	B_{1k}	B_{2k}	B_{3k}	B_{4k}
ben-hin	**33.54**	33.22	33.16	33.25	<u>33.30</u>	32.99
pan-hin	**72.41**	72.22	<u>72.28</u>	72.19	72.08	71.94
kok-mar	23.43	23.63	**23.84**	23.73	23.79	23.30
mal-tam	7.84	8.67	8.66	8.71	8.63	**8.74**
tel-mal	8.50	8.79	8.99	8.83	**9.12**	8.76
hin-mal	10.46	10.73	**10.96**	10.89	10.61	10.55
mal-hin	18.44	20.54	**21.23**	20.53	20.64	20.19
urd-hin	NA	55.55	**55.69**	55.49	55.57	55.47
ben-urd	NA	28.06	28.12	**28.19**	28.03	27.93
urd-mal	NA	8.44	8.22	8.04	8.02	**8.57**
mal-urd	NA	18.48	18.72	18.47	**18.79**	18.18
bul-mac	21.95	21.73	21.74	**22.27**	21.95	21.94
dan-swe	35.46	35.77	36.38	36.18	**36.61**	36.2
may-ind	**60.79**	59.54	<u>60.63</u>	60.24	60.35	60.15
kor-jpn	NA	NA	10.13	9.8	**10.23**	9.92
jpn-kor	NA	NA	**9.29**	9.23	9.02	8.96

Table 4: Translation accuracies for BPE models trained with different number of merge operations (BLEU). Underlined scores indicate the best BPE configuration when OS is the best-performing for a language pair.

that BPE encoded units are useful for translation involving abjad (Urdu uses an extended Arabic writing system), logographic (Japanese Kanji) and syllabic (Korean Hangul) writing systems. For language pairs involving Urdu, there is an 18% average improvement over word-level and 12% average improvement over morpheme-level translation accuracy. For Japanese-Korean language pairs, an average improvement of 6% in translation accuracy over a word-level baseline is observed.

5.3 Choosing number of BPE merges

The above mentioned results for BPE units do not explore optimal values of the number of merge operations. This is the only hyper-parameter that has to be selected for BPE. We experimented with number of merge operations ranging from 1000 to 4000 and the translation results for these are shown in Table 4. Selecting the optimal value of merge operations lead to a modest, average increase of 1.6% and maximum increase of 3.5% in the translation accuracy over B_{match} across different language pairs .

We also experimented with higher number of merge operations for some language pairs, but there seemed to be no benefit with a higher number of merge operations. Compared to the number of merge operations reported by Sennrich et al. (2016) in a more general setting for NMT (60k), the number of merge operations is far less for

Pair	C	W	M	O	B_{match}
pan-hin	58.07	58.95	**59.71**	57.95	59.66[†]
kok-mar	17.97	18.83	18.53	**19.12**	18.42[†]
mal-tam	4.12	5.49	5.84	5.93	**6.75**[†]
tel-mal	3.11	3.26	**4.06**	3.83	3.75
hin-mal	3.85	5.18	5.99	6.24	**6.37**
mal-hin	8.42	9.92	11.12	13.36	**14.45**[†]

(a) BLEU scores

Pair	C	W	M	O	B_{match}
pan-hin	0.869	0.825	0.868	0.863	**0.876**
kok-mar	0.647	0.641	0.643	**0.665**	0.653
mal-tal	0.301	0.261	0.378	0.452	**0.475**
tel-mal	0.246	0.198	0.238	0.297	**0.300**
hin-mal	0.281	0.336	0.354	**0.404**	0.384
mal-hin	0.439	0.371	0.466	0.548	**0.565**

(b) LeBLEU scores

Table 5: Translation accuracies for Agriculture Domain [†] indicates statistically significant difference in BLEU score between **O** and B_{match}. BLEU score differences between B_{match} and **W** are also statistically significant (except Konkani-Marathi) ($p < 0.05$)

translation between related languages with limited parallel corpora. We must bear in mind that their goal was different: available parallel corpus was not an issue, but they wanted to handle as large a vocabulary as possible for open-vocabulary NMT. Yet, the low number of merge operations suggest that BPE encoding captures the core vocabulary required for translation between related tasks.

5.4 Robustness to Domain Change

Since we are concerned with low resource scenarios, a desirable property of subword units is robustness of the translation models to change of translation domain. Kunchukuttan and Bhattacharyya (2016b) have shown that OS level models are robust to domain change. Since BPE units are learnt from a specific corpus, it is not guaranteed that they would also be robust to domain changes. To study the behaviour of BPE unit trained models, we also tested the translation models trained on tourism & health domains on an agriculture domain test set of 1000 sentences (see Table 5 for results). *In this cross-domain translation scenario, the BPE level model outperforms the OS-level and word-level models*

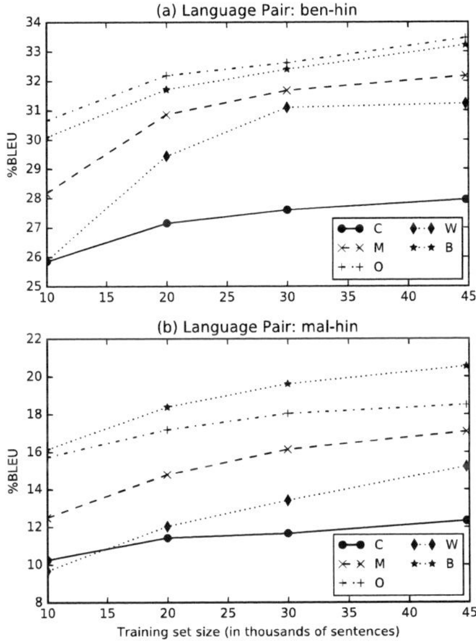

Figure 1: Effect of training data size on translation accuracy for different basic units

	$\textbf{Best}_{prev}$	$\textbf{JB}_{1k}$	$\textbf{JB}_{2k}$	$\textbf{JB}_{3k}$	$\textbf{JB}_{4k}$
ben-hin	O (33.46)	**33.54**	33.23	33.54	33.35
pan-hin	O (**72.51**)	<u>72.41</u>	72.35	72.13	72.04
kok-mar	B_{1k} (23.84)	**24.01**	23.76	23.8	23.86
mal-tam	B_{4k} (8.74)	8.6	**8.82**	8.74	8.72
tel-mal	B_{3k} (**9.12**)	8.47	8.84	8.89	<u>8.92</u>
hin-mal	B_{1k} (10.96)	**11.19**	11.09	11.1	10.96
mal-hin	B_{1k} (**21.23**)	20.79	<u>21.22</u>	21.12	21.06
bul-mac	B_{2k} (**22.27**)	22.11	22.17	21.58	<u>22.24</u>
dan-swe	B_{3k} (36.61)	36.15	**36.86**	36.51	36.71
may-ind	O (61.24)	**61.26**	60.98	61.11	60.66

Table 6: Translation accuracies for Joint BPE models trained with different number of merge operations (BLEU). The $\textbf{Best}_{prev}$ indicates the best performing units and their accuracy scores from Tables 3 and 4 shown for comparison.

for most language pairs. The Konkani-Marathi pair alone shows a degradation using the OS level model. The BPE model is almost on par with the OS level model for Telugu-Malayalam and Hindi-Malayalam.

5.5 Effect of training data size

For different training set sizes, we trained SMT systems with various representation units (Figure 1 shows the learning curves for two language pairs). BPE level models are better than OS, morpheme and word level across a range of dataset sizes. Especially when the training data is very small, the OS and BPE level models perform significantly better than the word and morpheme level models. For Malayalam-Hindi, the BPE level model is better than the OS level model at utilizing more training data.

5.6 Joint bilingual learning of BPE units

In the experiments discussed so far, we learnt the BPE vocabulary separately for the source and target languages. In this section, we describe our experiments with jointly learning BPE vocabulary over source and target language corpora as suggested by Sennrich et al. (2016). The idea is to learn an encoding that is consistent across source and target languages and therefore helps alignment. We expect a significant number of common BPE units between related languages. If source and target languages use the same writing system, then a joint model is created by learning BPE over concatenated source and target language corpus. If the writing systems are different, then we transliterate one corpus to another by one-one character mappings. This is possible between Indic scripts. But this scheme cannot be applied between Urdu and Indic scripts as well as between Korean Hangul and Japanese Kanji scripts.

Table 6 shows the results of the joint BPE model for language pairs where such a model is built. We do not see any major improvement over the mono lingual BPE model due to the joint BPE model.

6 Why are BPE units better than others?

The improved performance of BPE units compared to word-level and morpheme-level representations is easy to explain: with a limited vocabulary they **address the problem of data sparsity**. But character level models also have a limited vocabulary, yet they do not improve translation performance except for very close languages. Character level models learn character mappings effectively, which is sufficient for translating related languages which are very close to each other (translation is akin to transliteration in these cases). But they are not sufficient for translating related languages that are more divergent. In this case, translating cognates, morphological affixes, non-cognates *etc.* require a larger context. So, BPE and OS units — which **provide more**

Src-Tgt	Word	Morph	BPE	OS	Char
ben-hin	0.40	0.58	0.60	0.62	0.71
pan-hin	0.50	0.64	0.69	0.70	0.72
kok-mar	0.66	0.63	0.64	0.67	0.74
mal-tam	0.46	0.56	0.70	0.71	0.77
tel-mal	0.45	0.52	0.62	0.64	0.78
hin-mal	0.39	0.46	0.52	0.58	0.79
mal-hin	0.37	0.45	0.54	0.60	0.71

Table 7: Pearson's correlation coefficient between lexical similarity and translation accuracy (both in terms of LCSR at character level). *This was computed over the test set between: (i) sentence level lexical similarity between source and target sentences and (ii) sentence level translation accuracy between hypothesis and reference.*

	hin	mar	mal
OS	tI, stha	mA, nA	kka, nI
Suffix	ke, me.m	ChyA, madhIla	unnu, .e~Nkill.m
Word	paryaTaka, athavA	prAchIna, aneka	bhakShaN.m, yAtra

Table 8: Examples of BPE units for Indian languages. (ITRANS transliteration shown)

context — outperform character units.

A study of the correlation between lexical similarity and translation quality makes this evident (See Table 7). We see that character models work best when the source and target sentences are lexically very similar. The additional context decouples OS and BPE units from lexical similarity. Words and morphemes show the least correlation since they do not depend on lexical similarity.

Why does BPE performs better than OS which also provides a larger contextual window for translation? While orthographic syllables represent just approximate syllables, we observe that BPE units also **represent higher level semantic units like frequent morphemes, suffixes and entire words**. Table 8 shows a few examples for some Indian languages. So, BPE level models can learn semantically similar translation mappings in addition to lexically similar mappings. In this way, BPE units enable the translation models to **balance the use of lexical similarity with semantic similarity**. This further decouples the translation quality from lexical similarity as seen from the table. BPE units also have an **additional degree of freedom** (choice of vocabulary size), which allows tuning for best translation performance. This could be important when larger parallel corpora

are available, allowing larger vocabulary sizes.

7 Conclusion & Future Work

We show that translation units learnt using BPE can outperform all previously proposed translation units, including the best-performing orthographic syllables, for SMT between related languages when limited parallel corpus is available. Moreover, BPE encoding is writing system independent, hence it can be applied to any language. Experimentation on a large number of language pairs spanning diverse language families and writing systems lend strong support to our results. We also show that BPE units are more robust to change in translation domain. They perform better for morphologically rich languages and extremely data scarce scenarios.

BPE seems to be beneficial because it enables discovery of translation mappings at various levels simultaneously (syllables, suffixes, morphemes, words, *etc.*). We would like to further pursue this line of work and investigate better translation units. This is also a question relevant to translation with subwords in NMT. NMT between related languages using BPE and similar encodings is also an obvious direction to explore.

Given the improved performance of the BPE-unit, tasks involving related languages *viz.* pivot based MT, domain adaptation (Tiedemann, 2012) and translation between a *lingua franca* and related languages (Wang et al., 2012) can be revisited with BPE units.

Acknowledgments

We thank the Technology Development for Indian Languages (TDIL) Programme and the Department of Electronics & Information Technology, Govt. of India for their support. We also thank the reviewers for their feedback.

References

Pushpak Bhattacharyya, Mitesh Khapra, and Anoop Kunchukuttan. 2016. Statistical machine translation between related languages. In *Annual Conference of the North American Chapter of the Association for Computational Linguistics: Tutorials*.

Ondřej Bojar, Vojtěch Diatka, Pavel Rychlý, Pavel Straňák, Vít Suchomel, Aleš Tamchyna, and Daniel Zeman. 2014. HindEnCorp – Hindi-English and Hindi-only Corpus for Machine Translation. In *Proceedings of the 9th International Conference on Language Resources and Evaluation*.

Colin Cherry and George Foster. 2012. Batch tuning strategies for statistical machine translation. In *Proceedings of the Conference of the North American Chapter of the Association for Computational Linguistics: Human Language Technologies*.

Rohan Chitnis and John DeNero. 2015. Variable-length word encodings for neural translation models. In *Proceedings of the 2015 Conference on Empirical Methods in Natural Language Processing*.

Junyoung Chung, Kyunghyun Cho, and Yoshua Bengio. 2016. A character-level decoder without explicit segmentation for neural machine translation. In *Proceedings of the Meeting of the Association for Computational Linguistics*.

Nadir Durrani and Sarmad Hussain. 2010. Urdu word segmentation. In *Proceedings of Human Language Technologies: The 2010 Annual Conference of the North American Chapter of the Association for Computational Linguistics*.

Nadir Durrani, Hassan Sajjad, Alexander Fraser, and Helmut Schmid. 2010. Hindi-to-Urdu machine translation through transliteration. In *Proceedings of the 48th Annual Meeting of the Association for Computational Linguistics*.

Murray B Emeneau. 1956. India as a lingustic area. *Language* .

Philip Gage. 1994. A new algorithm for data compression .

Martin Haspelmath. 2001. The european linguistic area: Standard average european. In Martin Haspelmath, editor, *Language typology and language universals: An international handbook*, Walter de Gruyter.

Bushra Jawaid, Amir Kamran, and Ondřej Bojar. 2014. Urdu monolingual corpus. LINDAT/CLARIN digital library at the Institute of Formal and Applied Linguistics, Charles University in Prague. http://hdl.handle.net/11858/00-097C-0000-0023-65A9-5.

Girish Nath Jha. 2012. The TDIL program and the Indian Language Corpora Initiative. In *Proceedings of the Language Resources and Evaluation Conference*.

Philipp Koehn. 2004. Statistical significance tests for machine translation evaluation. In *Proceedings of the Conference on Empirical Methods in Natural Language Processing*.

Philipp Koehn, Hieu Hoang, Alexandra Birch, Chris Callison-Burch, Marcello Federico, Nicola Bertoldi, Brooke Cowan, Wade Shen, Christine Moran, Richard Zens, et al. 2007. Moses: Open source toolkit for Statistical Machine Translation. In *Proceedings of the 45th Annual Meeting of the ACL on Interactive Poster and Demonstration Sessions*.

Anoop Kunchukuttan and Pushpak Bhattacharyya. 2016a. Faster decoding for subword level phrase-based smt between related languages. In *Third Workshop on NLP for Similar Languages, Varieties and Dialects*.

Anoop Kunchukuttan and Pushpak Bhattacharyya. 2016b. Orthographic syllable as basic unit for smt between related languages. In *Proceedings of the Conference on Empirical Methods in Natural Language Processing*.

Anoop Kunchukuttan, Ratish Puduppully, and Pushpak Bhattacharyya. 2015. Brahmi-Net: A transliteration and script conversion system for languages of the Indian subcontinent. In *Proceedings of Conference of the North American Chapter of the Association for Computational Linguistics - Human Language Technologies: System Demonstrations*.

Anoop Kunchukuttan, Ratish Pudupully, Rajen Chatterjee, Abhijit Mishra, and Pushpak Bhattacharyya. 2014. The IIT Bombay SMT System for ICON 2014 Tools contest. In *Proceedings on the NLP Tools Contest at International Conference on Natural Language Processing*.

I Dan Melamed. 1995. Automatic evaluation and uniform filter cascades for inducing n-best translation lexicons. In *Proceedings of Third Workshop on Very Large Corpora*.

Preslav Nakov and Jörg Tiedemann. 2012. Combining word-level and character-level models for machine translation between closely-related languages. In *Proceedings of the 50th Annual Meeting of the Association for Computational Linguistics: Short Papers-Volume 2*.

Kishore Papineni, Salim Roukos, Todd Ward, and Wei-Jing Zhu. 2002. BLEU: a method for automatic evaluation of machine translation. In *Proceedings of the Meeting of the Association for Computational Linguistics*.

Uwe Quasthoff, Matthias Richter, and Christian Biemann. 2006. Corpus portal for search in monolingual corpora. In *Proceedings of the fifth international conference on language resources and evaluation*.

Loganathan Ramasamy, Ondřej Bojar, and Zdeněk Žabokrtský. 2012. Morphological Processing for English-Tamil Statistical Machine Translation. In *Proceedings of the Workshop on Machine Translation and Parsing in Indian Languages*.

Martine Irma Robbeets. 2005. *Is Japanese Related to Korean, Tungusic, Mongolic and Turkic?*. Otto Harrassowitz Verlag.

Mike Schuster and Kaisuke Nakajima. 2012. Japanese and korean voice search. In *2012 IEEE International Conference on Acoustics, Speech and Signal Processing (ICASSP)*.

Rico Sennrich, Barry Haddow, and Alexandra Birch. 2016. Neural machine translation of rare words with subword units. In *Proceedings of the Meeting of the Association for Computational Linguistics*.

Peter Smit, Sami Virpioja, Stig-Arne Grönroos, and Mikko Kurimo. 2014. Morfessor 2.0: Toolkit for statistical morphological segmentation .

Karumuri Subbarao. 2012. *South Asian Languages: A Syntactic Typology*. Cambridge University Press.

Ilya Sutskever, Oriol Vinyals, and Quoc V Le. 2014. Sequence to sequence learning with neural networks. In *Proceedings of Advances in Neural Information Processing Systems*.

Sarah Thomason. 2000. Linguistic areas and language history. In John Nerbonne and Jos Schaeken, editors, *Languages in Contact*, Editions Rodopi B.V., Brill.

Jörg Tiedemann. 2009a. Character-based PBSMT for closely related languages. In *Proceedings of the 13th Conference of the European Association for Machine Translation*.

Jörg Tiedemann. 2009b. News from opus-a collection of multilingual parallel corpora with tools and interfaces. In *Proceedings of the Conference on Recent Advances in Natural Language Processing*.

Jörg Tiedemann. 2012. Character-based pivot translation for under-resourced languages and domains. In *EACL*.

Jörg Tiedemann and Preslav Nakov. 2013. Analyzing the use of character-level translation with sparse and noisy datasets. In *Proceedings of the Conference on Recent Advances in Natural Language Processing*.

Nikolai Trubetzkoy. 1928. Proposition 16. In *Actes du premier congres international des linguistes La Haye*.

David Vilar, Jan-T Peter, and Hermann Ney. 2007. Can we translate letters? In *Proceedings of the Second Workshop on Statistical Machine Translation*.

Sami Virpioja and Stig-Arne Grönroos. 2015. Lebleu: N-gram-based translation evaluation score for morphologically complex languages. In *Proceedings of the Workshop on Machine Translation*.

Alexander Vovin. 2010. *Korea-Japonica: A Re-Evaluation of a Common Genetic Origin*. University of Hawaii Press.

Pidong Wang, Preslav Nakov, and Hwee Tou Ng. 2012. Source language adaptation for resource-poor machine translation. In *Proceedings of the 2012 Joint Conference on Empirical Methods in Natural Language Processing and Computational Natural Language Learning*.

Y. Wu, M. Schuster, Z. Chen, Q. V. Le, and M. Norouzi. 2016. Google's neural machine translation system: Bridging the gap between human and machine translation. *ArXiv e-prints: abs/1609.08144* .

Character Based Pattern Mining for Neology Detection

Gaël Lejeune and **Emmanuel Cartier**
LIPN, Paris XIII University
99 avenue Jean-Baptiste Clément
93430 Villetaneuse FRANCE
`firstname.lastname@lipn.univ-paris13.fr`

Abstract

Detecting neologisms is essential in real-time natural language processing applications. Not only can it enable to follow the lexical evolution of languages, but it is also essential for updating linguistic resources and parsers. In this paper, neology detection is considered as a classification task where a system has to assess whether a given lexical item is an actual neologism or not. We propose a combination of an unsupervised data mining technique and a supervised machine learning approach. It is inspired by current researches in stylometry and on token-level and character-level patterns. We train and evaluate our system on a manually designed reference dataset in French and Russian. We show that this approach is able to outperform state-of-the-art neology detection systems. Furthermore, character-level patterns exhibit good properties for multilingual extensions of the system.

1 Introduction

This paper deals with automatic detection of formal neologisms in French and Russian, with a language-agnostic objective. Formal neologisms are composed of a new form linked to a new meaning, in opposition to semantic neologisms, composed of a new meaning with an existing form. Whereas formal neologisms represent a tiny part of lexical items in corpora, and thus are not yet attracting a lot of research, they are part of the living lexicon of a given language and notably the gate to understand the evolution of languages.

The remainder of the paper is organized as follows. Section 2 details related works on computational approaches to neology. Section 3 describes key aspects of our method and experiments for neology detection. Section 4 presents evaluation results for French and Russian. Finally, Section 5 summarizes the experiments and evokes future developments.

2 Previous work

The study of neology has not been a high level priority within computational linguistics for two reasons. First, large diachronic electronic corpora were scarcely available for different languages until recently. Second, novel lexical units represent less than 5 percent of lexical units in corpora, according to several studies (Renouf, 1993, e.g.). But, from a bird-eyes view, linguistic change is the complementary aspect of the synchronic structure, and every unit in every language is time-related and has a life-cycle.

As shown by (Lardilleux et al., 2011), new words and hapaxes are continuously appearing in textual data. Every lexical unit is subjected to time, form and meaning can change, due to socio-linguistic (*diastraty*) and geographical (*diatopy*) variations. The increasing availability of electronic (long or short-term) diachronic corpora, advances on word-formation theory and in machine learning techniques motivated the recent emergence of neology tracking systems (Cabré and De Yzaguirre, 1995; Kerremans et al., 2012; Gérard et al., 2014; Cartier, 2016). These tools have a two-fold objective: gaining a better overview on language lifecyle(s), and allow lexicographers and computational linguists to update lexicographic resources, language processing tools and re-

Proceedings of the First Workshop on Subword and Character Level Models in NLP, pages 25–30,
Copenhagen, Denmark, September 7, 2017. ©2017 Association for Computational Linguistics.

sources.

From a NLP point of view, the main questions are : how can we automatically track neologisms, categorize them and follow their evolution, from their first appearance to their integration or disappearance? is it possible to induce neology-formation procedures from expert-curated examples and therefore predict new words formation?

The standard, and rather unique, approach to formal neology tracking consists in extracting novel forms from monitor corpora using lexicographic resources as a reference dictionary to induce unknown words. This is often call the "exclusion dictionary architecture" (EDA). The first system designed for English is due to Renouf (Renouf, 1993) : a monitor corpora and a reference dictionary from which unknown words can be derived. Further filters are then applied to eliminate spellings errors and proper nouns.

Four main difficulties arise from this approach. First, the design of a reference exclusion dictionary requires large machine-readable dictionaries: this entails specific procedures to apply this architecture to under-resourced languages, and an up-to-date dictionary for other languages. Second, the EDA architecture is not sufficient by itself : most of the unknown words are proper nouns, spelling errors or other cases derived from boilerplate removal: this entails a post-processing phase. Third, these systems do not take into account the sociological and diatopic aspects of neologism, as they limit their corpora to specific domains: an ideal system should be able to extend its monitoring to new corpora and maintain diastratic meta-data to characterize novel forms. Fourth, post-filtering has to be processed carefully. For instance, excluding all proper nouns makes it impossible to detect antonomasia (i.e. the fact that a proper noun is used as a common noun, for example "Is he a new kind of Kennedy?").

In many cases, the EDA technique is complemented by a human validation phase, in which experts have to assign each detected "neologism candidate" (NC) a label, either "excluded" or "neologism". This phase enables to complement the exclusion dictionary and to filter candidates to achieve a 100% precision for subsequent analysis. Usually, the guidelines for assessing the class of NCs are as follows : a formal neologism is defined as a word not yet pertaining to usage in the given language at assessment time[1]. A non-neologism is a word pertaining to one of the following categories : a spelling mistake, a boilerplate outcome, a word already in usage... With this procedure, Cartier (Cartier, 2016) evaluated on a one-year subset, that 59.87% of French NC were actual neologisms. In Russian, nevertheless, they evaluated that only 30% of NC were actual neologisms, mainly due to the fact that the EDA technique was in its early phases and that the POS-tagger and spell-checker were not accurate enough. Thus, this approach is not suitable for real time detection or multilingual extension.

In this paper, we advocate a new method to overcome the drawbacks of this method. It combines an unsupervised text mining component to retrieve salient features of positive and negative examples, and a supervised method using these features to automatically detect new neologisms from on-going texts.

3   Dataset and Methods

To the best of our knowledge, there are no existing NLP techniques that take advantage of text mining techniques for detecting neologisms. Intuitively and practically, formal neologisms, as new form-meaning pairs, appear in specific contexts, such as quotation marks(*c'est une véritable "trumperie"*[2]) or metalinguistic markers (*ce que nous pouvons appeler des catholibans*[3].The word-formation rules at stake (Schmid, 2015) involve affixation, composition and borrowings, each implying specific character-based features. From these intuition and analysis, we propose a novel method combining an unsupervised technique to retrieve the salient features of neologisms (internal structure and context), and a supervised machine learning approach to de-

---

[1] This definition is complemented by other clues like Google Ngrams Viewer statistics or reference dictionaries

[2] *It is a pure deception*, built from Trump + -erie suffix, phonetically near the French word for deception, tromperie.

[3] What we can call catholibans

	French	Russian
#Documents	15559	1750
#Candidates (occ.)	4321 (21511)	807(3563)
#Positives (occ.)	1903 (6339)	245 (715)
Positive ratio (Precision)	44.04%	30.3%

Table 1: Composition of the dataset for French and Russian

tect formal neologisms in on-going texts. In the following, we will first present our corpora and reference data and detail the algorithms used.

3.1 Corpora and Reference Data

As reference data, we use the evaluation data proposed by (Cartier, 2016). It contains a list of NCs and a label : excluded or neologism. In order to see the candidates in context we queried their website[4] to retrieve texts containing one or more NC occurrences. The dataset used here is then limited to NCs having at least one context available. Table 1 exhibits the statistics about this dataset[5]. One can see that the lack of experts for Russian has led to a much smaller dataset. Furthermore, the ratio of positive candidates is smaller in Russian due to a lower quality of the components.

3.2 Contextual character-level features for classification

The data mining component presented here aims to model the context of the candidates in order to classify them. It is an important tool to detect salient contextual and internal features of formal neologisms. Many Data Mining techniques have been used to deal with textual data (Borgelt, 2012), among them we chose an algorithm suitable for the particular type of patterns we wanted to compute (character-level patterns). Character-level analysis has received a growing attention from the scientific in recent years. This approach has proved its efficiency in various tasks (in particular in multilingual settings), among which Authorship Attribution (Brixtel, 2015), Information Extraction (Lejeune et al., 2015), Hashtags Prediction (Dhingra et al., 2016) or Terminology Extraction (Korenchuk, 2017). In this ex-

periment, we mine closed frequent token and character sequences from the candidates contexts using the maximal repeated strings algorithm from Ukkonen (Ukkonen, 2009). These character level patterns (CLP) are computed in linear time thanks to augmented suffix arrays (Kärkkäinen et al., 2006). The CLP computed in this paper have two properties :

- they have a minimal frequency of 2 (in other words they are repeated);

- they are closed: CLP cannot be expanded to the left nor to the right without lowering the frequency.

Patterns are extracted by comparing the contexts of each occurrence of the candidates belonging to the training set. Two kinds of patterns are computed. First, we computed token-level patterns (TLP) which are words and punctuation marks. In some extent, the TLP method can be viewed as a variant of the Lesk algorithm (Lesk, 1986) where in addition to words unigrams there are n-grams mixing graphical words and punctuation. Second, character-level patterns (CLP) pattern which are sequences of characters without any filtering. With CLP, the objective is to represent different levels of linguistic description in the same time: morphology (prefixes, suffixes), lexicon (words or group of words) and style (punctuation and combinations between words and punctuation).

3.2.1 Patterns and contexts

For each attested neologisms found in our corpus, the start and end offsets of their occurrences in the corpus are computed. We model the context as a vector of CLP and TLP frequencies, afterwards we are able to compare the contexts of neologisms and compare them to the context of non-neologisms. Four types of contexts have been identified:

- Internal (resp. bilateral): n characters before the start offset of the NC and n characters after the end offset of the NC, including (resp. excluding) the NC itself

- Left (resp. right): n characters before (resp. after) the start offset (resp. end offset) of the NC plus the NC itself

---

[4] http://www.neoveille.org

[5] The precision is even worse than on the original data, due to the lack of contexts in the retrieval phase.

Various context sizes have been experimented, from 10 to 400 characters, in order to assess the influence of the window size on the classification results. The context size is always computed in characters in order to have the same data for computing CLP and TLP.

3.2.2 Learning Framework and Evaluation Metrics

Once the CLP are computed in all the training set, they are used as features to train classifiers. For each candidate, the value of each feature will be the frequency of the CLP in the given context (bilateral, internal, left or right). The training of the classifiers has been performed with Scikit-learn (Pedregosa et al., 2011). Various classifiers (decision trees, support vector machines, bayesian networks). 10-fold cross validation has been performed so that the figures presented here after are the mean of the results for each fold. In order to avoid learning biases, all the occurrences of a given candidate will be grouped in only one set per fold : the train set or the test set. Therefore, with TLP internal and bilateral contexts yield the same results : the NC itself can not be used by this method.

4 Results

Table 1 shows the results obtained with TLP for the French dataset with a SVM classifier (linear kernel) and C-parameter set at 1. We will only focus on SVM since this classifier outperformed Decision trees, random forests and bayesian networks . The results for the internal end bilateral context are the same because of the design of the train and test sets (see Section 3.2.2). Two results have to be highlighted here. First, the left context gave by far the best results, suggesting that there are clues announcing neologisms. Second, if we forget about left contexts, the results can be improved by expanding the windows size to 50 characters[6]. Our hypothesis is that expanding the context only improves the bad results and that expanding the left context mostly yields noise. With 72% F-measure in the best case, the TLP method was promising but it was quickly outperformed by the CLP method.

---

[6]More precisely, the best results for bilateral context are obtained with a window-size of 47.

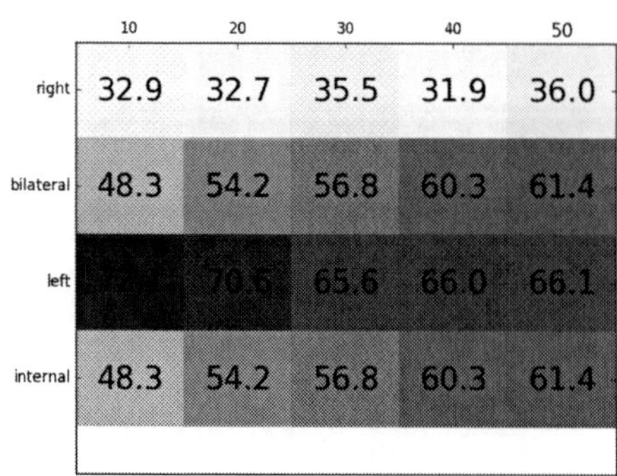

	10	20	30	40	50
right	32.9	32.7	35.5	31.9	36.0
bilateral	48.3	54.2	56.8	60.3	61.4
left	[illegible]	70.6	65.6	66.0	66.1
internal	48.3	54.2	56.8	60.3	61.4

Table 1: French Data : F-measure for TLP according to the context length (10 to 50) and context types.

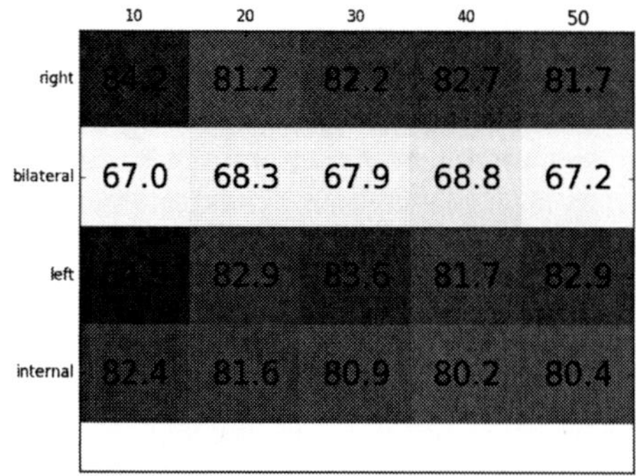

	10	20	30	40	50
right	84.2	81.2	82.2	82.7	81.7
bilateral	67.0	68.3	67.9	68.8	67.2
left	[illegible]	82.9	83.6	81.7	82.9
internal	82.4	81.6	80.9	80.2	80.4

Table 2: French Data : F-measure for CLP according to the context length (10 to 50) and context types.

On a first approach, we managed to tune the minimal ($minlen$) and maximal length ($maxlen$) of the CLP in order to reduce the search space because even in small windows there are a huge amount of CLP.

We first observed that the optimal F_1-measure scores were obtained with $minlen = 3$ and $maxlen = 7$. This result seemed to be consistent with what has been observed with comparable methodology used for the Authorship Attribution task (see for instance (Brixtel, 2015)). However, subsequent experiments with the same cross-validation method showed that removing these length constraints lead to similar results. Filtering patterns according to their support (relative frequency) has been tested as well but it gave instable results.

Finally, taking all the CLP appeared to

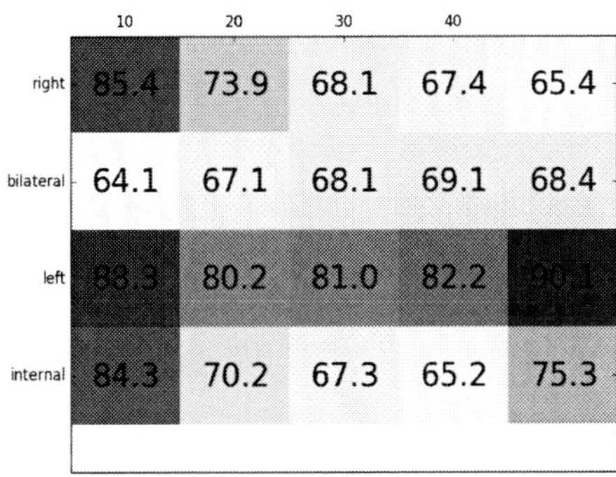

Table 3: Russian Data : F-measure for CLP according to the context length (10 to 50) and context types.

be the best configuration. These results are showed (Table 2). The CLP method takes advantage of internal properties of the candidates (prefixes and suffixes) and it allows us to get more clues in the immediate context of the NC. With a 84.9% F-measure, this method performs better than the 75%[7] presented in (Cartier, 2016). The bilateral context is the least efficient configuration. It shows that CLP including the candidate itself are very good features. Furthermore, it reduces the differences between the left and right contexts. The best results are still found in the immediate contexts but we do not find with CLP the same shift in the results when the context-size is modified.

In Russian we observed the same phenomena with TLP. Therefore, we only present here the results for the CLP method (Table 3). Here, the results are even better than the results for the French dataset with more than 90% F-measure with a left context of length 50. The main difference is that there is more instability when the size and the types of contexts changes. This instability may come from the size of the dataset and the subsequent lower number of features.

There may be room for improvement for the bilateral and internal configurations by taking into account the relative position of the pattern (e.g. if the pattern has been found on the left side, right side or both sides of the candidate) and not only its number of occurences.

Finally, among the classifiers we tested, SVM with linear kernels offers the best results. This is a result we expected since it is consistent with state-of-the-art results in stylometry (Sun et al., 2012). Decision trees perform a bit worse and, interestingly, random forests offer very little added-value. We plan to experiment Conditional Random Fields in order to take advantage of the sequential aspect of our input data.

According to the data we collected, the EDA approach shows a precision around 44 % (61% F-measure) for French and 30 % (46% F-measure). Even if it is difficult to precisely assess recall, we can only say that the method presented here shows a real improvement : 82% for French (84.9% F-Measure) and 87% for Russian (90.1% F-measure) in terms of precision.

5 Discussion and Perspectives

The preliminary study we have conducted demonstrates that a combination of unsupervised data mining and supervised Machine learning techniques can largely outperform the EDA approach used to detect formal neologisms. Moreover, this technique does not need any NLP pre-processing (tokenization, lemmatization, POS tagging...) of the textual data, which is a great advantage for poorly endowed languages. It reduces the marginal cost for processing new languages.

We plan additional experiments to back the legitimacy of the approach :

- experiment on other languages : we are currently collecting data Chinese, Czech and Portuguese;

- compare with other machine learning techniques, especially CRF, which have proved good accuracy in sequence labelling;

Additionally, we want to experiment the model to detect not only neologisms as a unique category, but categories of neologisms, as affixation, composition and borrowing are likely to retain specific and discriminative features that could be exploited in the detection process.

---

[7]60% precision and probably a recall close to 100%

References

Christian Borgelt. 2012. Frequent item set mining. In *Wiley Interdisciplinary Reviews: Data Mining and Knowledge Discovery 2(6)*. pages 437–456.

Romain Brixtel. 2015. Maximal repeats enhance substring-based authorship attribution. In *Recent Advances in Natural Language Processing, RANLP 2015, 7-9 September, 2015, Hissar, Bulgaria*. pages 63–71.

M. Teresa Cabré and Luis De Yzaguirre. 1995. Stratégie pour la détection semi-automatique des néologismes de presse. *TTR : traduction, terminologie, rédaction, 8 (2), p. 89-100.* .

Emmanuel Cartier. 2016. Néoveille, système de repérage et de suivi des néologismes en sept langues. *Neologica, 10, Revue internationale de néologie, p.101-131* .

Bhuwan Dhingra, Zhong Zhou, Dylan Fitzpatrick, Michael Muehl, and William Cohen. 2016. Tweet2vec: Character-based distributed representations for social media. In *Proceedings of the 54th Annual Meeting of the Association for Computational Linguistics (Volume 2: Short Papers)*. Association for Computational Linguistics, Berlin, Germany, pages 269–274. http://anthology.aclweb.org/P16-2044.

Christophe Gérard, Ingrid Falk, and Delphine Bernhard. 2014. Traitement automatisé de la néologie : pourquoi et comment intégrer l'analyse thématique ? *Actes du 4e Congrès mondial de linguistique française (CMLF 2014), Berlin, p. 2627-2646.* .

Juha Kärkkäinen, Peter Sanders, and Stefan Burkhardt. 2006. Linear work suffix array construction. *Journal of the ACM* 53(6):918–936.

Daphné Kerremans, Susanne Stegmayr, and Hans-Jörg Schmid. 2012. The NeoCrawler: identifying and retrieving neologisms from the internet and monitoring on-going change. *Kathryn Allan and Justyna A. Robinson, eds., Current methods in historical semantics, Berlin etc.: de Gruyter Mouton, 59-96.* .

Yuliya Korenchuk. 2017. *Méthode d'enrichissement et d'élargissement d'une ontologie à partir de corpus de spécialité multilingues.* Ph.D. thesis, Université de Strasbourg.

Adrien Lardilleux, Yves Lepage, and François Yvon. 2011. The Contribution of Low Frequencies to Multilingual Sub-sentential Alignment: a Differential Associative Approach. *International Journal of Advanced Intelligence* 3(2):189–217.

Gaël Lejeune, Romain Brixtel, Antoine Doucet, and Nadine Lucas. 2015. Multilingual event extraction for epidemic detection. *Artificial Intelligence in Medicine* Doi: 10.1016/j.artmed.2015.06.005.

Michael Lesk. 1986. Automatic sense disambiguation using machine readable dictionaries: How to tell a pine cone from an ice cream cone. In *Proceedings of the 5th Annual International Conference on Systems Documentation*. ACM, New York, NY, USA, SIGDOC '86, pages 24–26. https://doi.org/10.1145/318723.318728.

F. Pedregosa, G. Varoquaux, A. Gramfort, V. Michel, B. Thirion, O. Grisel, M. Blondel, P. Prettenhofer, R. Weiss, V. Dubourg, J. Vanderplas, A. Passos, D. Cournapeau, M. Brucher, M. Perrot, and E. Duchesnay. 2011. Scikit-learn: Machine learning in Python. *Journal of Machine Learning Research* 12:2825–2830.

Antoinette Renouf. 1993. Sticking to the Text : a corpus linguist's view of language. *ASLIB Proceedings, 45 (5), p. 131-136* .

Hans-Jörg Schmid. 2015. The scope of word-formation research. *Peter O. Müller, Ingeborg Ohnheiser, Susan Olsen and Franz Rainer, eds., Word-Formation. An International Handbook of the Languages of Europe. Vol. I.* .

Jianwen Sun, Zongkai Yang, Sanya Liu, and Pei Wang. 2012. Applying stylometric analysis techniques to counter anonymity in cyberspace. *JNW* 7(2):259–266. https://doi.org/10.4304/jnw.7.2.259-266.

Esko Ukkonen. 2009. Maximal and minimal representations of gapped and non-gapped motifs of a string. *Theoretical Computer Science* 410(43):4341–4349.

Automated Word Stress Detection in Russian

Maria Ponomareva and **Kirill Milintsevich** and **Ekaterina Chernyak** and **Anatoly Starostin**
National Research University Higher School of Economics, Russian Federation
maponomareva_2@edu.hse.ru, knmilintsevich@edu.hse.ru
echernyak@hse.ru, anatoli.starostin@gmail.com

Abstract

In this study we address the problem of automated word stress detection in Russian using character level models and no part-speech-taggers. We use a simple bidirectional RNN with LSTM nodes and achieve the accuracy of 90% or higher. We experiment with two training datasets and show that using the data from an annotated corpus is much more efficient than using a dictionary, since it allows us to take into account word frequencies and the morphological context of the word.

1 Introduction

Character level models and character embeddings have received a lot of attention recently. The character embeddings were used for several NLP tasks, such as word similarity (Wieting et al., 2016), sentence similarity (Wieting et al., 2016), part-of-speech tagging (Wieting et al., 2016), NER (Klein et al., 2003), speech recognition (Mikolov et al., 2012), question answering (Lukovnikov et al., 2017), language identification (Jaech et al., 2016), etc.

In this study we concentrate on a lesser known problem, which to our knowledge has not been completely solved yet, namely the automatic detection of word stress. For some languages, e.g. Russian, this problem might be crucial for speech processing and generation.

Only a few authors touch upon the problem of automated word stress detection in Russian. Among them, one research project in particular is worth mentioning (Hall and Sproat, 2013). The authors restricted the task of stress detection to finding the correct order within an array of stress assumptions where valid stress patterns were closer to the top of the list than the invalid

ones. Then, the first stress assumption in the rearranged list was considered to be correct. The authors used the Maximum Entropy Ranking method to address this problem (Collins and Koo, 2005) and took character bi- and trigrams, suffixes and prefixes of ranked words as features as well as suffixes and prefixes represented in an "abstract" form where most of the vowels and consonants were replaced with their phonetic class labels. The study features the results obtained using the corpus of Russian wordforms generated on the basis of Zaliznyaks Dictionary (approx. 2m wordforms). Testing the model on randomly split train and test samples showed the accuracy of 0.987. According to the authors, they observed such a high accuracy because splitting the sample randomly during testing helped the algorithm benefit from the lexical information i.e. different wordforms of the same lexical item often share the same stress position. The authors then tried to solve a more complicated problem and tested their solution on a small number of wordforms for which the paradigms were not included the training sample. As a result, the accuracy of 0.839 was achieved. The evaluation technique that the authors proposed is quite far from real-life application which is the main disadvantage of their study. Usually the solutions in the field of automated stress detection are applied to real texts where the frequency distribution of wordforms differs drastically from the one in a bag of words obtained from "unfolding" of all the items in a dictionary.

In addition, another study (Reynolds and Tyers, 2015) describes the rule-based method of automated stress detection without the help of machine learning. The authors proposed a system of finite-state automata imitating the rules of Russian stress accentuation and formal grammar that partially solved stress ambiguity by applying syntactical restrictions. Thus, using all the above-

31

Proceedings of the First Workshop on Subword and Character Level Models in NLP, pages 31–35,
Copenhagen, Denmark, September 7, 2017. ©2017 Association for Computational Linguistics.

mentioned solutions together with wordform frequency information, the authors achieved the accuracy of 0.962 on a relatively small hand-tagged Russian corpus (7689 tokens) that was not found to be generally available. We can treat the proposed method as a baseline for the automated word stress detection problem in Russian.

In many languages, such as French, Czech, Finnish and German the rules for automated word stress detection can be formalized quite easily. Nevertheless there are languages where phonological characteristics do not predict stress position, for instance such word prosodic systems can be found in North-West Caucasian (Abkhaz) and Balto-Slavic languages (Lithuanian, Serbo-Croatian, Russian) (van der Hulst, 1999).

In Russian every word has one and only one stressed syllable. Lexical stress is free in its positioning (any syllable can be stressed as shown in (1)) and is movable (for many lexemes lexical stress depends on the word form, as shown in (2)).

1. *éta* [This-Sg.F.Nom] *neyrosét'* [network-Gg.Nom] *búdet* [be-3Sg.Fut] *rasstavl'át'* [put-Inf] *udaréniya* [stress-Pl.Acc] [in] *slováh* [word-Pl.Loc] *rússkogo* [russian-Sg.M.Gen] *yaziká* [language-Sg.Gen]

2. *dérevo* [tree-Sg.Nom] *derévya* [tree-Pl.Nom]

   Lexical stress can be crucial in disambiguating between homographs, both between two wordforms ((3)) as well as between two lexemes ((4)):

3. *rukí* [hand-Sg.Gen] *rúki* [hand-Pl.Nom]

4. *béregu* [river.bank-Sg.Dat] *beregú* [protect-1Sg.Pres]

The position of lexical stress in Russian depends on many factors including the morphological content of the word, but also the type of word formation, its frequency and its meaning. A complex system of markers which are defined for all morphemes has been developed in fundamental research (Zaliznyak, 1985). There are rules that define the hierarchy and interaction of markers but some of them are not strict and can be considered more of a tendency.

For practical purposes the dictionary approach to text accentuation can be appropriate. It is possible to imagine a system that finds an accented form for each token using some predefined list.

However such a system would have several disadvantages, the most important of which would be its inability to predict stress for unknown words.

In this paper we propose a formal approach to the problem of automatic accentuation of Russian text by trying to exploit neural character models for these purposes. Furthermore, we try to avoid using any additional or third-party tools for part of speech tagging and try to develop a simplistic approach that is based only on using the training data.

2 Datasets

We considered two datasets:

1. Zaliznyak's Russian Grammar Dictionary, which lists over 100,000 lexemes (Zaliznyak, 1985). Each lexeme and its wordforms are stressed. The dictionary was split into a train and test datasets in a 2:1 ratio, so that all forms of one lexeme belong either to the train or to the test dataset and no lexeme belongs to both. We've assigned the name Dictionary Model (DictM) to the RNN trained on this dataset.

2. Transcriptions from the speech subcorpus[1] of Russian National Corpus (RNC) (Grishina, 2003). The spoken corpus was collected by recording people talking in different situations after which it was transcribed and annotated with word stress, also the transcripts of the Russian movies were included. The main difference between these transcriptions and Zaliznyak's Dictionary is that the transcription usually doesnt contain all forms of a word and, more importantly contains word contexts, i.e. previous words. By taking context into account we can attempt to differentiate between cases such as *"óblaka"* [cloud-Sg.Gen] and *"oblaká"* [clouds-Pl.Nom], since the previous word in most instances will reveal whether the word is singular or plural. This dataset was split into train and test datasets using the same 2:1 ratio. We trained two models on the corpus. Let us call the first RNN a Context Dependant Model (CDM). In order

---

[1]Word stress in spoken texts database in Russian National Corpus[Baza dannykh aktsentologicheskoy razmetki ustnykh tekstov v sostave Natsional'nogo korpusa russkogo yazyka], `http://www.ruscorpora.ru/en/search-spoken.html`

to take the previous word into account we used the following algorithm: if the previous word has less than three letters, we remove its word stress and concatenate it with the current word (for example, *"te‿oblaká"* [that-Pl.Nom cloud-Pl.Nom]). If the previous word has 3 or more letters, we use the last three, since Russian endings are typically 2-3 letters long and derivational morphemes are usually located on the right periphery of the word. As such we get, for example *"ogo‿óblaka"* [Sg.N.Gen cloud-Sg.Gen] from *"belogo‿óblaka"* [white-Sg.N.Gen cloud-Sg.Gen]. The second model (Context Free Model, CFM) has the same architecture but it doesn't take context into account.

3 Architecture

We adopted a character level architecture from standard tutorials on Keras framework[2]. Our neural network is a bidirectional recurrent neural network with 64 LSTM nodes and dropout regularization. Every input word is represented by a 40 by 33 matrix, where 40 stands for the maximum observed word length in characters. Shorter words are padded with a padding symbol. 33 is the number of letters in the Russian alphabet and every letter in a word is encoded with one-hot encodings.

Stress can be considered a characteristic of a vowel that has two possible values. A syllable in Russian has a (C)V(C) structure, so the number of vowels equals the number of syllables and in every word only one vowel will be stressed. The word stress is encoded by one-hot encoding too and shows which of the 40 letters is annotated with the word stress. The output layer of the RNN again has 40 nodes and is activated by `softmax`. In order to evaluate the quality of word stress detection we used accuracy.

4 Results and discussion

While testing[3] the presented approach on Zaliznyakś Dictionary we had 1,767,041 instances in the train dataset and 878,306 instances in the test dataset. We trained DictM for 10 epochs and received the best results on the fourth epoch with 88.7% accuracy for the test set from the dictionary. The score can be compared with the results of the

---

[2] https://keras.io
[3] Our implementation of the method can be found here: `https://github.com/MashaPo/accent_lstm`.

# of sylla-bles	Correct detections, %	Correct detections
2	0.690	182,285 of 263,952
3	0.721	127,012 of 176,144
4	0.846	85,675 of 101,229
5	0.918	42,124 of 45,879
6	0.952	15,241 of 16,009
7	0.958	3,813 of 3,979
8	0.96	744 of 775
9	0.928	156 of 168
Micro-average	0.751	

Table 1: Word length in syllables and the number of correct detections for Dictionary Model

second experiment in (Hall and Sproat, 2013) and proves that RNN is as efficient as Maximum Entropy Ranking for this problem.

The second dataset was slightly bigger and comprised 2,306,776 unique train instances and 1,154,067 unique test instances. We used this dataset to train CDM and CFM for 10 epochs. CDM achieved the best results during the fifth epoch with 97.7% accuracy on all words. CFM showed the highest accuracy of 97.9% during the sixth epoch.

The significant difference between those values shows that taking the previous context into account increases the accuracy, although by using corpus we could have ignored some complex cases that are not widely used in actual speech but are present in Zaliznyak's dictionary and increase the weight of most frequent words that do not necessarily have a common type of stress placement. Here we are referring to numerals and frequent adverbs that have their own special type of stress placement. Due to their frequency such cases negatively influenced the accuracy of DictM.

We implemented the following method to compare the RNN's. We used those three models to detect word stress in the test set of the corpus. We then computed the number of correct predictions for words of different length and calculated the micro-average of accuracy for every model. It is worth mentioning that the accuracy value for the DictM dropped in comparison to the score obtained from the dictionary test set (88.7% for the dictionary test set and 75.1% for the corpus test set). The results for DictM, CFM, CDM are presented in tables 1, 2 and 3 respectively.

The comparison of the results proves that training the model using the corpus gives us a visible increase in accuracy even when the left context is

# of sylla-bles	Correct detec-tions, %	Correct detections
2	0.981	259,179 of 263,952
3	0.974	171,645 of 176,144
4	0.975	98,707 of 101,229
5	0.975	44,774 of 45,879
6	0.972	15,567 of 16,009
7	0.950	3,782 of 3,979
8	0.940	729 of 775
9	0.934	157 of 168
Micro-average		0.977

Table 2: Word length in syllables and the number of correct detections for Context Free Model

# of sylla-bles	Correct detec-tions, %	Correct detections
2	0.983	259,656 of 263,952
3	0.977	172,164 of 176,144
4	0.976	98,887 of 101,229
5	0.977	44,837 of 45,879
6	0.973	15,591 of 16,009
7	0.955	3,802 of 3,979
8	0.923	716 of 775
9	0.952	160 of 168
Micro-average		0.979

Table 3: Word length in syllables and the number of correct detections for Context Dependant Model

# of sylla-bles	Correct detec-tions, %	Correct detections
2	0.756	17,852 of 23,606
3	0.829	5,402 of 6,510
4	0.823	1,011 of 1,227
Micro-average		0.77

Table 4: **CFM** score on 50 homograph pairs

# of sylla-bles	Correct detec-tions, %	Correct detections
2	0.810	19,143 of 23,606
3	0.844	5,498 of 6,510
4	0.847	1,040 of 1,227
Micro-average		0.819

Table 5: **CDM** score on 50 homograph pairs

Stressed wordform	#	CDM accuracy		CFM accuracy	
slová [word-Pl.Nom]	984	0.871	0.80	1.0	0.54
slóva [word-Sg.Gen]	812	0.714		0.0	
delá [affair-Pl.Nom]	976	0.929	0.86	1.0	0.62
déla [affair-Sg.Gen]	588	0.753		0.0	
nógi [leg-Pl.Nom]	542	0.797	0.74	1.0	0.85
nogí [leg-Sg.Gen]	92	0.44		0.0	
vólny [wave-Pl.Nom]	88	0.72	0.77	1.0	0.60
volný [wave-Sg.Gen]	57	0.85		0.0	

Table 6: **CDM** and **CFM** detailed results for some of the homograph pairs

not considered. For DictM there is a clear positive correlation between the number of words and the accuracy of predictions, DictM gets better results then CDM on 8- and 9-syllable words, which are rare in the corpus and can be new for CFM and CDM, while DictM could have learned the whole paradigm. CFM and DFM show negative correlation between the accuracy and the number of syllables which is expected due to lower frequency of longer words.

Next, the results from CDM clearly present the advantages of training the RNN while taking the previous word into account, since it increases the number of correctly detected word stresses including homograph cases. The similar way of model testing makes our results comparable with those obtained in (Reynolds and Tyers, 2015), our Context Free Model and Context Dependant Model showed higher micro-average of accuracy than the baseline.

In order to show CDM to be more accurate than CFM due to the homograph disambiguation we conducted additional tests to learn how both models treat the homographs. More precisely, we extracted the tuples of words from the dictionary that only differed in stress position (*"dorogóy"* [expensive-M.Sg.Nom] *"dorógoy"* [road-Sg.Instr]). Next, we selected such homograph pairs that for both words the number of occurrences in the corpus was above the predetermined threshold. Tables 4 and 5 show the scores after testing CFM and CDM on 50 most frequent pairs. More detailed results for four homograph pairs are displayed in Table 6. The data clearly indicates that CFM simply chooses the most frequent word in a homograph pair. Even though CDM makes mistakes when analysing more frequent words in the pair, it significantly increases the accuracy for less frequent words. The overall accuracy for cases where the frequency of the homographs is comparable (rows 1,2 and 4 of the table) is notably higher for CDM than CFM.

We have also conducted error analysis. First of all, a huge source of errors are proper names both first names and surnames. Several typical Russian surnames are derived from nouns or adjectives and differ from other wordforms only in stress position. We may address this issue by exploiting NER algorithms and introducing special rules for proper names. Another kind of error is related to words with ambiguous word stress. For example, in words like *"musoroprovod"* [garbage.chute-Sg.Nom] two word stress positions are possible in modern Russian: *musoropróvod* or *musoroprovód*. Last but not the least, in Russian the letter *ë* is always stressed, but if this letter is written as a regular *e*, the RNN may erroneously ignore it.

5 Future work

There are a few directions for future work:

1. improving the way we take word context into account. We may use more sophisticated techniques to define the ending and morphological features of the previous word. We may also explore how considering the next word improves the performance.

2. introducing rules for named entities in general and proper names in particular;

3. experimenting with reducing the number of instances in a train dataset to both lower the training time and to find specific important examples for training;

4. experimenting with RNNs carefully in order to gain more linguistic intuition on how word stress is chosen.

6 Conclusions

In this study we conducted a few experiments on training RNNs to detect word stress in Russian words. Our results show that, first of all, the character level RNNs are quite suitable for the task, since on average we achieve the accuracy around 90% or higher. Secondly, we explored two different sources of training data (namely, a dictionary and an annotated corpus) and we can definitively state that using the corpus suits the task better, since it allows us to take frequent cases and morphological context into account and use this information for further disambiguation.

Acknowledgements

The research was prepared within the framework of the Basic Research Program at the National Research University Higher School of Economics (HSE) and supported within the framework of a subsidy by the Russian Academic Excellence Project "5-100".

References

Michael Collins and Terry Koo. 2005. Discriminative reranking for natural language parsing. *Computational Linguistics* 31:25–70.

Elena B. Grishina. 2003. Spoken russian in russian national corpus. *Russian National Corpus* 2005:94–110.

Keith Hall and Richard Sproat. 2013. Russian stress prediction using maximum entropy ranking. In *Proceedings of the 2013 Conference on Empirical Methods in Natural Language Processing*. Association for Computational Linguistics, Seattle, Washington, USA, pages 879–883. http://www.aclweb.org/anthology/D13-1088.

Aaron Jaech, George Mulcaire, Shobhit Hathi, Mari Ostendorf, and Noah A Smith. 2016. Hierarchical character-word models for language identification. *arXiv preprint arXiv:1608.03030* .

Dan Klein, Joseph Smarr, Huy Nguyen, and Christopher D Manning. 2003. Named entity recognition with character-level models. In *Proceedings of the seventh conference on Natural language learning at HLT-NAACL 2003-Volume 4*. Association for Computational Linguistics, pages 180–183.

Denis Lukovnikov, Asja Fischer, Jens Lehmann, and Sören Auer. 2017. Neural network-based question answering over knowledge graphs on word and character level. In *Proceedings of the 26th International Conference on World Wide Web*. International World Wide Web Conferences Steering Committee, pages 1211–1220.

Tomáš Mikolov, Ilya Sutskever, Anoop Deoras, Hai-Son Le, Stefan Kombrink, and Jan Cernocky. 2012. Subword language modeling with neural networks. *preprint (http://www. fit. vutbr. cz/imikolov/rnnlm/char. pdf)* .

Robert Reynolds and Francis Tyers. 2015. Automatic word stress annotation of russian unrestricted text. In *Proceedings of the 20th Nordic Conference of Computational Linguistics (NODALIDA 2015)*. Linköping University Electronic Press, Sweden, Vilnius, Lithuania, pages 173–180. http://www.aclweb.org/anthology/W15-1822.

Harry van der Hulst. 1999. *Word prosodic systems in the languages of Europe*, volume 20. Walter de Gruyter.

John Wieting, Mohit Bansal, Kevin Gimpel, and Karen Livescu. 2016. Charagram: Embedding words and sentences via character n-grams. *arXiv preprint arXiv:1607.02789* .

Andrey A. Zaliznyak. 1985. From proto-slavic word-stress to russian [ot praslavyanskoy aktsentuatsii k russkoy].

A Syllable-based Technique for Word Embeddings of Korean Words

Sanghyuk Choi[*] and **Taeuk Kim** and **Jinseok Seol** and **Sang-goo Lee**
Department of Computer Science and Engineering
Seoul National University
{sanghyuk, taeuk, jamie, sglee}@europa.snu.ac.kr

Abstract

Word embedding has become a fundamental component to many NLP tasks such as named entity recognition and machine translation. However, popular models that learn such embeddings are unaware of the morphology of words, so it is not directly applicable to highly agglutinative languages such as Korean. We propose a syllable-based learning model for Korean using a convolutional neural network, in which word representation is composed of trained syllable vectors. Our model successfully produces morphologically meaningful representation of Korean words compared to the original Skip-gram embeddings. The results also show that it is quite robust to the Out-of-Vocabulary problem.

1 Introduction

Continuous word representation has been a fundamental ingredient to many NLP tasks with the advent of simple and successful approaches such as Word2Vec (Mikolov et al., 2013a) and GloVe (Pennington et al., 2014). Although it has been verified that they are effective in formulating semantic and syntactic relationship between words, there are some limitations. First, they are only available to words in pre-defined vocabulary thus prone to the Out-of-Vocabulary(OOV) problem. Second, they cannot utilize subword information at all because they regard word as a basic unit. Those problems become more magnified when applying word-based methods to agglutinative languages such as Korean, Japanese, Turkish, and Finnish. In this work, we propose a new model

that utilizes syllables as basic components of word representation to alleviate the problems, especially for Korean. In our experiment, we confirm that our model constructs representation of words which contains a semantic and syntactic relationship between words. We also show that our model can handle OOV problem and capture morphological information without dedicated analysis.

2 Related Work

Recent works that utilize subword information to construct word representation could be largely divided into two families: The models that use morphemes as a component and the others taking advantage of characters.

Morpheme-based representation models

A morpheme is the smallest unit of meaning in linguistics. Therefore, there are many researches that consider morphemes when building word representations (Luong et al., 2013; Botha and Blunsom, 2014; Cotterell and Schütze, 2015).

Luong et al. (2013) applies a recursive neural network over morpheme embeddings to obtain word embeddings. Although morpheme-based models are good at capturing semantics, one major drawback is that most of them require manually annotated data or an explicit morphological analyzer which could introduce unintended errors. Our model doesn't need such a preprocessing.

Character-based representation models

Recently, utilizing information from characters has become one of the active NLP research topics. One way to extract knowledge from a sequence of characters is using character n-grams (Wieting et al., 2016; Bojanowski et al., 2016).

Bojanowski et al. (2016) suggests an approach based on the Skip-gram model (Mikolov et al., 2013a), where the model sums character n-gram vectors to represent a word. On the other hand,

---

36

* Portions of this research were done while the author was a student at Seoul National University.

Proceedings of the First Workshop on Subword and Character Level Models in NLP, pages 36–40,
Copenhagen, Denmark, September 7, 2017. ©2017 Association for Computational Linguistics.

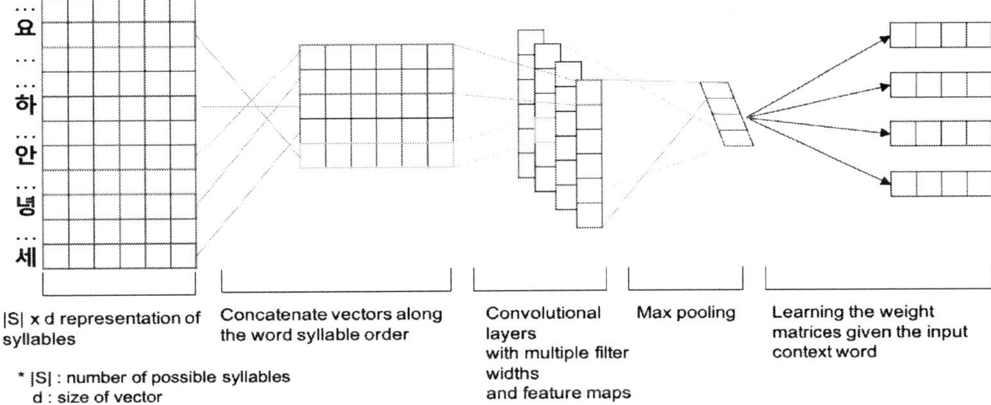

Figure 1: Overall architecture of our model. Each syllable is a d-dimensional vector. For a given word '안녕하세요' (hello, *annyeonghaseyo*), we concatenate vectors according to syllable order in word. After passing through the convolutional layer and max pooling layer, word representation is produced. All parameters are jointly trained by Skip-gram scheme.

there are some approaches (Dos Santos and Gatti, 2014; Ling et al., 2015; Santos and Guimaraes, 2015; Zhang et al., 2015; Kim et al., 2016; Jozefowicz et al., 2016; Chung et al., 2016) in which word representations are composed of character embeddings via deep neural networks such as convolutional neural networks (CNN) or recurrent neural networks (RNN).

Kim et al. (2016) introduces a language model that aggregates subword information through a character-level CNN. Models based on characters have shown competitive results on many tasks. A problem of character-based models is that characters themselves have no semantic meanings so that models often concentrate on only local syntactic features of words. To avoid the problem, we select syllables which have fine-granularity like a character but has its own meaning in Korean as a basic component of the representation of words.

3 Proposed Model

Characteristics of Korean Words

Morphologically, unlike many other languages, a Korean word (*Eojeol*) is not just a concatenation of characters. It is constructed by the following hierarchy: a sequence of syllables (*Eumjeol*) forms a word, and the composition of 2 or 3 characters (*Jaso*) forms a syllable (Kang and Kim, 1994).

In linguistics, Korean language is categorized as an agglutinative language, where each word is made of a set of morphemes. To complete the Korean word (*Eumjeol*), a root morpheme must be combined with a bound morpheme (*Josa*), or a postposition (*Eomi*). This derivation produces about 60 different forms of the similar meaning, which causes the explosion of vocabulary. For the same reason, the number of occurrences of each word is relatively small even with a large corpus, which prevents the model from an efficient learning. Thus, most of the Korean word representation models use morphemes as an embedding unit, though it requires an additional preprocessing. The problem is that errors coming from an immature morpheme analyzer might be propagated to the word representation model. Moreover, a single Korean syllable possess a semantic meaning. For example, the word '대학'(college, *daehag*) is a composition of '대'(big, or great, *dae*) and '학'(learn, or a study, *hag*). Therefore, our model regards syllables as embedding units rather than words or morphemes. For instance, the representations of '나는'(I am, *naneun*), '나의'(my, *naui*), or '나에게'(to me, *na-ege*) are constructed by leveraging the same syllable vector '나'(I, *na*).

Syllable-based Representation

Similar to (Kim et al., 2016), let $\mathcal{S}$ be a set of all Korean syllables. We embed each syllables into d-dimensional vector space, so that $Q \in \mathbb{R}^{d \times |\mathcal{S}|}$ becomes a syllable embedding matrix. Let $(s_1, s_2, ..., s_l)$ denote a word $t \in V$ which consists of l syllables, t is represented by concatenating syllable vectors as a column vector: $(Qs_1, Qs_2, ..., Qs_l) \in \mathbb{R}^{d \times l}$. Then we apply a convolution filter $H \in \mathbb{R}^{d \times w}$ having a width w, we get a feature map $f^t \in \mathbb{R}^{l-w+1}$. For filters whose widths are more than 1, they need a zero padding when processing words coming from only a single syllable.

In detail, for the given filter H, the feature map can be calculated as follows:

$$f_i^t = \tanh(\langle (Qs_i, ..., Qs_{i+w-1}), H \rangle + b) \quad (1)$$

where $\langle A, B \rangle = \mathrm{tr}(AB^\mathsf{T})$ denoting Frobenius inner product. We then apply a max pooling $y^t = \max_i f_i^t$ to extract the most important feature. By using multiple filters, namely $H_1, H_2, ..., H_h$, we get a final representation $y^t = (y_1^t, ..., y_h^t)$ for the word t.

For training, we adopt Skip-gram (Mikolov et al., 2013b) method with negative sampling so that for a given center word y^t, we maximize the log-probability of predicting context word y^c. We jointly train syllable embedding matrix and convolution filters all together. Figure 1 shows overall architecture of our model.

4 Experiments and Results

Datasets and Baselines

The Experiments are performed on a randomly sampled subset of Korean News corpus collected from 2012 to 2014, containing approximately 2.7M tokens, 11k vocabulary, and 1k syllables. We compare our model to the original *skip-gram model with negative sampling* (Mikolov et al., 2013b) as a baseline.

Implementation details

For all experiments, we use the following common parameters for both our model and baseline. We use vector representations of dimension 320, the size of window is 4 and the negative-sampling parameter is 7. We train over twelve epochs. In our model, the dimension of syllable embedding is 320. Empirically, using filters with size 1~4 was enough since most of Korean words are composed of 2~4 syllables[1].

---

[1] About 95% of words in a training set had a length less than 5.

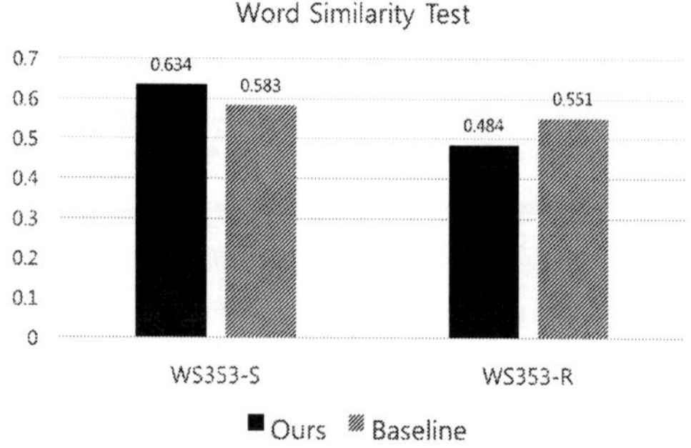

Figure 2: Test result on translated WordSim353 dataset. It contains similarity and relatedness test and measured by Pearson correlation. Our model outperformed the baseline in similarity task.

4.1 Quantitative Evaluation

We use the WordSim353 dataset (Finkelstein et al., 2001; Agirre et al., 2009) for the word similarity and relatedness task. As WordSim353 dataset is an English data, we translated it into Korean. The quality of the word vector representation is evaluated by computing Pearson correlation coefficient between human judgment scores and the cosine similarity between word vectors.

The graph in Figure 2 shows that our model outperforms the baseline on WS353-Similarity dataset. We estimated it since a lot of similar words share the same syllable(s) in Korean. On the other hand, on WS353-Relatedness, the performance is not as good in comparison with the similarity task. We presume that leveraging syllables on computing representations can be a noise among related words without common syllables.

4.2 Qualitative Evaluation

Out-Of-Vocabulary Test

Since our model uses syllable vectors when computing word representation, it is possible to achieve representation of OOV words by combining syllables. To evaluate the representations of OOV words, we manually chose 4 newly coined words not appear in training data (Table 1). These words were derived from original words. For example, '구글신'(God Google, *gugeulsin*) is derived from '구글'(Google, *gugeul*) and '갤노트'(Gal'Note, *gaelnoteu*) is a abbreviation form of '갤럭시노트'(Galaxy Note, *gaelleogsinoteu*). Morphologically, two of them concatenate additional syllables to the original word, and the other

Original word	Newly coined word
구글	구글신
(Google, *gugeul*)	(God google, *gugeulsin*)
이득	개이득
(Profit, *ideug*)	(Real profit, *gaeideug*)
퇴근	퇴근각
(Leave work,	(Time to leave work,
toegeun)	*toegeungag*)
갤럭시노트	갤노트
(Galaxy Note,	(Gal'Note,
gaelleogsinoteu)	*gaelnoteu*)

Table 1: 4 newly coined words in Korean which did not appear in training data. Proposed model successfully recognized stem from the original word, and predicted it as the most similar word.

two remove some syllables.

We examined the nearest neighbor of the representations of OOV words, and confirmed that each original word vector is placed in the nearest distance. It is no wonder since almost every newly coined word keeps the syllables of original word with their positions fixed.

Morphological Representation Test

We now evaluate our model on language morphology by observing how word representation leverages morphological characteristics. As mentioned above, the process of forming a sentence of Korean is totally different from many other languages. In case of Korean, a word can function in the sentence only if it is combined with the bound morpheme. For example, '서울을'(of Seoul, *seoul-eul*) is a combination of full morpheme '서울'(Seoul, *seoul*) + bound morpheme '을'(of, *eul*).

To compare how models learn the morphological characteristics, we randomly sampled hundred words and the same words combined with certain postposition('을', *eul*) from the training data. The graph in Figure 3 shows this result more clearly. We can observe that words forming the discriminative parallel clusters against postposition-combined-words while the baseline doesn't.

5 Conclusion

We present a syllable-based word representation model experimented with Korean, which is one of morphologically rich languages. Our model keeps

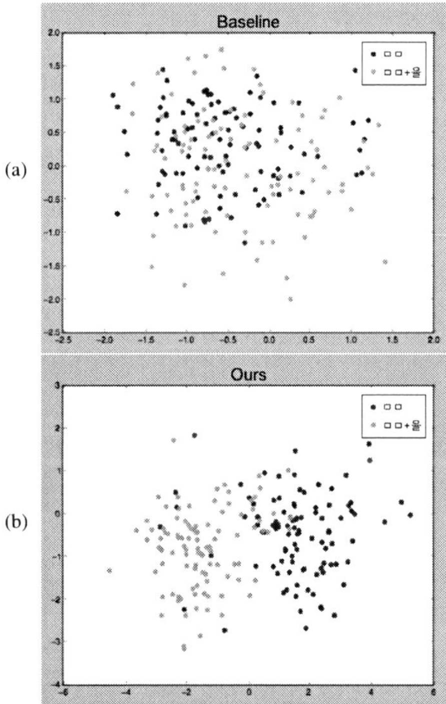

Figure 3: PCA projections of vector representation of 100 randomly sampled pairs of word. Each pair is composed of a word and the same word with postposition. In (b), our model shows that words forming the discriminative parallel clusters against postposition-combined-words.

the characteristics of Skip-gram models, in which word representation learns from context words. It also takes into account the morphological characteristics by sharing parameters between the words that contain common syllables. We demonstrate that our model is competitive on quantitative evaluations. Furthermore, we show that the model can handle OOV words, and capture morphological relationships. As a future work, we have a plan to expand our model so that it can utilize overall information extracted from words, morphemes and characters.

Acknowledgments

This work was supported by the National Research Foundation of Korea(NRF) funded by the Ministry of Science, ICT and Future Planning (NRF-2016M3C4A7952587, PF Class Heterogeneous High Performance Computer Development).

References

Eneko Agirre, Enrique Alfonseca, Keith Hall, Jana Kravalova, Marius Paşca, and Aitor Soroa. 2009. A study on similarity and relatedness using distributional and wordnet-based approaches. In *Proceedings of Human Language Technologies: The 2009 Annual Conference of the North American Chapter of the Association for Computational Linguistics*. Association for Computational Linguistics, pages 19–27.

Piotr Bojanowski, Edouard Grave, Armand Joulin, and Tomas Mikolov. 2016. Enriching word vectors with subword information. *arXiv preprint arXiv:1607.04606* .

Jan Botha and Phil Blunsom. 2014. Compositional morphology for word representations and language modelling. In *International Conference on Machine Learning*. pages 1899–1907.

Junyoung Chung, Kyunghyun Cho, and Yoshua Bengio. 2016. A character-level decoder without explicit segmentation for neural machine translation. *arXiv preprint arXiv:1603.06147* .

Ryan Cotterell and Hinrich Schütze. 2015. Morphological word-embeddings. In *HLT-NAACL*. pages 1287–1292.

Cícero Nogueira Dos Santos and Maira Gatti. 2014. Deep convolutional neural networks for sentiment analysis of short texts. In *COLING*. pages 69–78.

Lev Finkelstein, Evgeniy Gabrilovich, Yossi Matias, Ehud Rivlin, Zach Solan, Gadi Wolfman, and Eytan Ruppin. 2001. Placing search in context: The concept revisited. In *Proceedings of the 10th international conference on World Wide Web*. ACM, pages 406–414.

Rafal Jozefowicz, Oriol Vinyals, Mike Schuster, Noam Shazeer, and Yonghui Wu. 2016. Exploring the limits of language modeling. *arXiv preprint arXiv:1602.02410* .

Seung-Shik Kang and Yung Taek Kim. 1994. Syllable-based model for the korean morphology. In *Proceedings of the 15th conference on Computational linguistics-Volume 1*. Association for Computational Linguistics, pages 221–226.

Yoon Kim, Yacine Jernite, David Sontag, and Alexander M Rush. 2016. Character-aware neural language models. In *Thirtieth AAAI Conference on Artificial Intelligence*.

Wang Ling, Tiago Luís, Luís Marujo, Ramón Fernandez Astudillo, Silvio Amir, Chris Dyer, Alan W Black, and Isabel Trancoso. 2015. Finding function in form: Compositional character models for open vocabulary word representation. *arXiv preprint arXiv:1508.02096* .

Thang Luong, Richard Socher, and Christopher D Manning. 2013. Better word representations with recursive neural networks for morphology. In *CoNLL*. pages 104–113.

Tomas Mikolov, Kai Chen, Greg Corrado, and Jeffrey Dean. 2013a. Efficient estimation of word representations in vector space. *arXiv preprint arXiv:1301.3781* .

Tomas Mikolov, Ilya Sutskever, Kai Chen, Greg S Corrado, and Jeff Dean. 2013b. Distributed representations of words and phrases and their compositionality. In *Advances in neural information processing systems*. pages 3111–3119.

Jeffrey Pennington, Richard Socher, and Christopher D Manning. 2014. Glove: Global vectors for word representation. In *EMNLP*. volume 14, pages 1532–1543.

Cicero Nogueira dos Santos and Victor Guimaraes. 2015. Boosting named entity recognition with neural character embeddings. *arXiv preprint arXiv:1505.05008* .

John Wieting, Mohit Bansal, Kevin Gimpel, and Karen Livescu. 2016. Charagram: Embedding words and sentences via character n-grams. *arXiv preprint arXiv:1607.02789* .

Xiang Zhang, Junbo Zhao, and Yann LeCun. 2015. Character-level convolutional networks for text classification. In *Advances in neural information processing systems*. pages 649–657.

Supersense Tagging with a Combination of Character, Subword, and Word-level Representations

Youhyun Shin and **Sang-goo Lee**
Department of Computer Science and Engineering
Seoul National University
`shinu89,sglee@europa.snu.ac.kr`

Abstract

Recently, there has been increased interest in utilizing characters or subwords for natural language processing (NLP) tasks. However, the effect of utilizing character, subword, and word-level information simultaneously has not been examined so far. In this paper, we propose a model to leverage various levels of input features to improve on the performance of an supersense tagging task. Detailed analysis of experimental results show that different levels of input representation offer distinct characteristics that explain performance discrepancy among different tasks.

1 Introduction

Recently, there has been increased interest in using characters or subwords, instead of words, as the basic unit of language feature in natural language processing tasks. Utilizing subword information has been shown to be very effective for named entity alignment of parallel corpus (Sennrich and Haddow, 2016) and named entity recognition (Lample et al., 2016; Santos and Guimaraes, 2015). Some recent advancements were achieved using character or subword features in neural machine translation and language modeling (Sennrich et al., 2015; Chung et al., 2016; Lee et al., 2016; Kim et al., 2016).

The main benefit of utilizing features below word-level is the ability to overcome out-of-vocabulary (OOV) and the rare word problems. When faced with very infrequent or OOV words in the test data, word-level models must resort to replacing them with "unknown word" tokens; and in many cases, this discarded information could be vital for understanding certain semantics of the text, hence word-level models could per-

form poorly when said types of words appear frequently.

Traditionally, words are segmented into subwords using carefully engineered morpheme analyzers (Smit et al., 2014). Recently, we see a rise in popularity of data-driven methods such as employing an efficient encoding scheme of character sequences (e.g. byte-pair encoding (Sennrich et al., 2016)). Words could also be split into individual characters to capture even finer syntactic details. Subword schemes of varying linguistic granularity offer a trade-off between capturing semantic and syntactic features.

Despite of the success of character or subword-level approaches, there has been lack of studies on ways to combine different levels of features, namely character, subword, and word-level features. To the best of our knowledge, utilization of subword units have not even been applied to supersense tagging yet. In this paper, we present a novel neural network architecture that incorporates all three types of word-feature units (Section 3). We conduct experiments on SemCor dataset using our model (Section 4.2). Then we analyze the optimal combination of the word features for each classs of the 41 supersenses in detail (Section 4.3).

2 Background

2.1 Supersense Tagset

The supersense tagset consists of a total of 41 supersenses which are top-level semantic classes used in WordNet (Fellbaum, 1998) as shown in Table 1. This set is generally used for evaluating the approaches to coarse-grained word sense disambiguation and information extraction such as extended NER (Ciaramita and Johnson, 2003; Ciaramita and Altun, 2006). In this paper, we use the SemCor dataset (Table 2) for evaluation.

Proceedings of the First Workshop on Subword and Character Level Models in NLP, pages 41–45,
Copenhagen, Denmark, September 7, 2017. ©2017 Association for Computational Linguistics.

Nouns							
Supersense	Freq.	Supersense	Freq.	Supersense	Freq.	Supersense	Freq.
person	17%	attribute	5%	object	2%	process	1%
artifact	10%	time	5%	possession	2%	plant	1%
act	9%	state	4%	phenomenon	1%	shape	<1%
cognition	8%	body	3%	animal	1%	motive	<1%
group	7%	substance	2%	relation	1%	Tops	<1%
communication	8%	quantity	2%	feeling	1%		
location	5%	event	2%	food	1%		
Verbs							
stative	26%	social	7%	perception	5%	body	2%
communication	13%	motion	8%	creation	4%	competition	<1%
change	9%	possession	6%	emotion	2%	weather	<1%
cognition	9%	contact	6%	consumption	2%		

Table 1: The 41 WordNet supersenses (26 nouns and 15 verbs) and their frequency percentages. Note the sum of the percentages of the nouns is 100%, and that of the verbs is 100%.

	Train	Test	Total
Documents	150	36	186
Sentences	15,462	4,676	20,138
Subwords	436,101	104,264	540,365
Words	348,987	85,787	434,774
Supersenses	109,183	25,952	135,135
Nouns	71,919	15,506	87,425
Verbs	37,264	10,446	47,710

Table 2: The statistics of the SemCor dataset.

2.2 Subword Segmentation

We use Byte Pair Encoding (BPE) (Sennrich et al., 2016) to segment words into subwords. First, BPE produces the most efficient character encoding scheme given a corpus. The encoding scheme consists of a fixed-size dictionary containing the most frequent character sequences. If a word is not frequent enough to be listed in the dictionary, it is broken down into subwords that exist in the dictionary and the meaning of the word is inferred from the meanings of the subwords. For example, an infrequent word "transition" could be split into frequent character sequences "transi@@" and "tion".

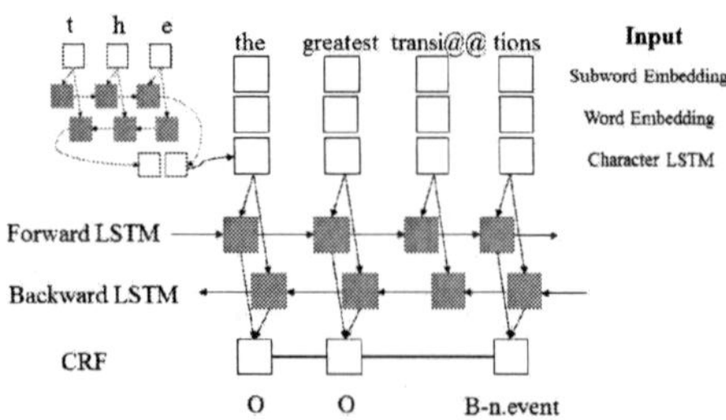

Figure 1: Model architecture

3 Model Description

We define *supersense tagging* as a sequence labeling problem: given an input word sequence $W = (w_1, w_2, \ldots, w_n)$, it is segmented into subword sequences using some encoding scheme (e.g. BPE) $X = (x_1, x_2, \ldots, x_m)$, and then a sequence of supersense labels $Y = (y_1, y_2, \ldots, y_n)$ is predicted, where $y \in \{1, \ldots, k\}$.

We present a novel neural network model that incorporates all of varying levels of word features: character, subword, and word (Figure 1). This model is similar to (Lample et al., 2016), but differs from it in that (i) our model uses subword-level features as the basic unit of the main LSTM architecture (Section 3.2), (ii) uses delayed prediction to synchronize subword-level sequences with word-level predictions (Section 3.2), and (iii) takes subword-level input representations along with characters and words (Section 3.1).

3.1 Input Representation

For each x, our model produces three types of embeddings: (i) character-level embedding $\mathbf{z}^{(c)}$, (ii) subword embedding $\mathbf{z}^{(s)}$, and (iii) word-level embedding $\mathbf{z}^{(w)}$. In order to produce character-level representation, a bidirectional long short-term memory cell (LSTM) $\mathrm{BiLSTM_c}$ is utilized. The hidden states of either directions of the cells are concatenated into a single character-level representation: $\mathbf{c} = \left[\mathbf{h}^{(f)}; \mathbf{h}^{(b)}\right]$. Producing subword embeddings is trivial, as each x is assigned a trainable vector $\mathbf{z}^{(s)}$. Lastly, a word embedding $\mathbf{z}^{(w)}$ is produced by taking the embedding of the word in which x belongs. Note for some experiments, we use Glove to initialize word embeddings [1]. These representations are concatenated to produce a single vector $\mathbf{z} \in \mathbb{R}^r$ for each x, where r is the subword embedding dimension:

$$\mathbf{z} = \left[\mathbf{z}^{(c)}; \mathbf{z}^{(s)}; \mathbf{z}^{(w)} \right] \quad (1)$$

3.2 BiLSTM-CRF Architecture

We employ BiLSTM-CRF as the base architecture. Unlike previous work, subword-level embeddings instead of word-level embeddings are fed in at each time step. Given a subword-level embedding sequence $\mathbf{Z} = (\mathbf{z}_1, \mathbf{z}_2, \ldots, \mathbf{z}_m)$, the main bidirectional LSTM, BiLSTM_s, along with a synchronization layer L_s, and a linear layer L_o, produce prediction scores $\mathbf{O} = (\mathbf{o}_1, \mathbf{o}_2, \ldots, \mathbf{o}_n)$.

$$\mathbf{H}^{(s)} = \text{BiLSTM}_s\left(\mathbf{Z}\right) \quad (2)$$

$$\mathbf{H}^{(w)} = L_s\left(\mathbf{H}^{(s)}\right) \quad (3)$$

$$\mathbf{O} = L_o\left(\mathbf{H}^{(w)}\right) \quad (4)$$

Note that due to the difference between input and output lengths m and n, synchronization between the two adjacent layer is required. The synchronization layer delays the supersense prediction until a word is fully formed by its subwords. Untrainable layer L_s is implemented by selectively allowing hidden outputs, where the subword aligns with the ending of the word it belongs to, pass through the layer:

$$\mathbf{H}^{(w)} = \mathbf{W}^{(s)} \cdot \mathbf{H}^{(s)} \quad (5)$$

Where $\mathbf{W}^{(s)} \in \mathbb{R}^{n \times m}$ and each element is defined as $\mathbf{W}^{(s)}_{i,j} = \mathbb{1}\left(\text{end}\left(x_j, w_i\right)\right)$. Then the output layer L_o applies linear transformation on $\mathbf{H}^{(w)}$ to produce label scores $\mathbf{O} \in \mathbb{R}^{n \times k}$.

As the final layer, the conditional random field (CRF) takes time-independent label scores $\mathbf{O}$ and produces a joint score of the entire sequence by considering interdependency among labels:

$$s\left(W, Y\right) = \sum_{i=0}^{n} \mathbf{A}_{y_i, y_{i+1}} + \sum_{i=1}^{n} \mathbf{O}_{i, y_i} \quad (6)$$

Where $\mathbf{A}$ is the transition matrix among labels. For all Y, we maximize

$$\log p\left(Y|W\right) = s\left(W, Y\right) - \log \sum_{\bar{Y}} e^{s\left(W, \bar{Y}\right)} \quad (7)$$

Where $\bar{Y}$ is all possible combinations. Maximizing the objective encurges the valid sequence of labels to be produced.

4 Experiments

4.1 Experimental Setup

Dropout rate was 0.5, stochastic gradient descent (SGD) was used as learning method, and learning rate was 0.005. The gradient clipping is 5.0.

4.2 SemCor Evaluations[2]

without pre-trained vectors			
	Precision	Recall	F-score
char	51.4	48.7	50.02
sub	63.5	63.6	63.54
word	64.9	63.6	64.30
s+w	64.1	62.0	63.04
c+s	65.1	65.9	65.46
c+w	66.8	66.3	66.51
c+s+w	64.0	65.0	64.47
with pre-trained word vector			
word	66.9	67.5	67.20
s+w	68.0	68.4	68.20
c+w	68.6	69.5	69.04
c+s+w	68.1	69.5	68.82
with pre-trained subword & word vectors			
c+s+w	68.9	69.7	69.32

Table 3: Comparison of character, subword, and word-level models with/without pre-trained vectors.

The classification results of SemCor dataset using different combinations of input representations are shown in Table 3. We note that in uni-representation settings the word-level model performs better than the character or subword-level model. This is presumably because supersense tagging predicts labels for each word. We also note that when word embeddings are pre-trained, the performance is always improved by the addition of character or subword-level embeddings. Overall, the best result is obtained when the subword and word embeddings are pre-trained and all embeddings are utilized.

4.3 Detailed Analysis

To investigate the effect of using character or subword-level embeddings, we select 15 supersenses and examine each of them individually (Table 4). With pre-trained vectors, *c+s+w* performs much better than other combinations, outperforming others in many classes. However, without the

[1]https://nlp.stanford.edu/projects/glove/

[2]We use shorthands *c*, *s* and *w* to denote *character*, *subword* and *word*, respectively.

	without pre-trained vectors							with pre-trained vectors				
	c	s	w	c+s	c+w	s+w	c+s+w	w	c+w	s+w	c+s+w	c+s+w
Named Entity Recognition supersenses												
person	77.8	75.6	72.7	**84.7**	84.6	70.2	82.2	86.4	90.6	86.1	89.3	**90.7**
group	50.8	58.7	60.4	**64.4**	63.7	61.0	63.6	62.5	65.1	62.0	64.2	**65.6**
location	46.1	56.3	57.6	60.3	**60.9**	51.4	59.9	61.0	69.5	63.7	67.7	**70.2**
3 most frequent noun and verb supersenses												
artifact	50.2	65.8	67.5	67.0	67.6	67.5	**67.9**	70.8	**74.8**	74.4	73.8	73.6
act	40.4	55.8	58.4	58.8	**60.3**	56.6	57.9	58.9	62.6	60.7	**63.3**	62.5
cognition	41.7	59.2	59.2	**60.6**	58.1	56.2	60.1	59.8	59.8	60.8	61.2	**61.6**
stative	72.0	76.3	75.9	77.0	**77.7**	75.2	75.6	76.1	77.4	77.3	**78.6**	78.2
communication	55.1	73.7	**76.4**	75.4	72.7	76.3	73.5	75.9	76.6	76.4	**78.8**	78.3
change	32.9	54.4	52.9	54.7	**55.9**	54.4	54.5	56.2	**59.9**	56.5	58.6	59.5
3 rarest noun and verb supersenses												
shape	0.0	16.7	28.6	17.9	28.2	**30.2**	26.5	23.3	31.4	26.8	22.2	**32.9**
motive	57.6	75.0	73.9	68.8	76.3	**84.2**	75.9	**76.9**	69.1	75.0	71.8	76.6
Tops	71.4	80.0	**85.7**	**85.7**	66.7	**85.7**	75.0	**85.7**	71.4	76.9	80.0	75.0
body	8.5	43.3	**49.7**	40.4	45.7	43.8	44.1	50.0	49.9	49.4	47.9	**51.1**
competition	0.0	34.7	32.9	35.5	**37.0**	32.6	34.6	34.6	36.3	34.3	36.7	**39.0**
weather	0.0	0.0	**27.3**	10.5	19.1	0.0	17.4	0.0	0.0	9.5	**22.2**	19.1

Table 4: F-score comparison for NER, the most frequent and rarest supersense classification. Bold values are best cases in with/without pre-trained vectors, respectively. Underlined values represent the cases that use pre-trained embeddings.

	char	sub	word	c+s	c+w	s+w	c+s+w
Mr.	Griston	Thomas	Bob	Dr.	Pope	William	Mrs.
	Ledford	Bob	Dr.	Mrs.	Vice	Bob	Dr.
	Jasper	Sam	Alexander	Sen.	Mollie	Dr.	Bob
States	Swedes	states	states	State	Paris	states	Angeles
	Pisces	cities	State	Moscow	State	places	heaven
	Seldes	S.	state	Lewis	Spots	Manchester	outside
with	wither	With	With	from	With	With	With
	With	by	o'clock	With	from	on	possible
	within	By	breakin	behind	without	On	On

Table 5: Nearest neighbors analysis based on different representation vectors.

pre-trained vectors, it fails to maintain the dominance.

Also, 5 out of the 7 combinations perform better than others in at least one class. This shows that character, subword, and word-level embeddings offer features of different characteristics that could be either advantageous or disadvantageous depending on the class.

We further conduct nearest neighbor analysis on various embedding combinations (Table 5). We find that, in most cases, words of the same supersenses are mapped closely to each other in the word embedding space. Similar to our findings in previous analysis, we also find that each model exhibits distinct characteristics. For example, in $c+s$ model, the nearest neighbors of *Mr.* are *Dr.* and *Mrs.*. However, in *sub* model, male names such as *Thomas* and *Bob* are identified as the nearest neighbors.

5 Conclusion

In this paper, we examine the effect of various combinations of input representations on the performance of supersense tagging task. Furthermore, a modified BiLSTM-CRF model which is able take subword sequences and predict word labels is proposed. Our experiments on supersense tagging show that utilizing all token units (character, subword, and word-level) along with pre-trained word vectors perform the best. Based on detailed analysis of selective supersense classes, we conjecture that each granlarity level of input representations offers different semantic and syntactic features that could have varying effects depending on the task. As future work, we intend to investigate the feasibility of a model that self-learns the optimal continuous combination of different levels of subword information depending on the task and data characteristics.

References

Junyoung Chung, Kyunghyun Cho, and Yoshua Bengio. 2016. A character-level decoder without explicit segmentation for neural machine translation. In *Proceedings of the 54th Annual Meeting of the Association for Computational Linguistics*.

Massimiliano Ciaramita and Yasemin Altun. 2006. Broad-coverage sense disambiguation and information extraction with a supersense sequence tagger. In *Proceedings of the 2006 Conference on Empirical Methods in Natural Language Processing*. Association for Computational Linguistics, pages 594–602.

Massimiliano Ciaramita and Mark Johnson. 2003. Supersense tagging of unknown nouns in wordnet. In *Proceedings of the 2003 conference on Empirical methods in natural language processing*. Association for Computational Linguistics, pages 168–175.

Christiane Fellbaum. 1998. Wordnet: An electronic lexical database.

Yoon Kim, Yacine Jernite, David Sontag, and Alexander M Rush. 2016. Character-aware neural language models. In *Thirtieth AAAI Conference on Artificial Intelligence*.

Guillaume Lample, Miguel Ballesteros, Sandeep Subramanian, Kazuya Kawakami, and Chris Dyer. 2016. Neural architectures for named entity recognition. In *Proceedings of NAACL-HLT*. pages 260–270.

Jason Lee, Kyunghyun Cho, and Thomas Hofmann. 2016. Fully character-level neural machine translation without explicit segmentation. *arXiv preprint arXiv:1610.03017* .

Cicero Nogueira dos Santos and Victor Guimaraes. 2015. Boosting named entity recognition with neural character embeddings. *arXiv preprint arXiv:1505.05008* .

Rico Sennrich and Barry Haddow. 2016. Linguistic input features improve neural machine translation. In *Proceedings of the First Conference on Machine Translation*.

Rico Sennrich, Barry Haddow, and Alexandra Birch. 2015. Neural machine translation of rare words with subword units. *arXiv preprint arXiv:1508.07909* .

Rico Sennrich, Barry Haddow, and Alexandra Birch. 2016. Neural machine translation of rare words with subword units. In *Proceedings of the 54th Annual Meeting of the Association for Computational Linguistics*.

Peter Smit, Sami Virpioja, Stig-Arne Grönroos, Mikko Kurimo, et al. 2014. Morfessor 2.0: Toolkit for statistical morphological segmentation. In *The 14th Conference of the European Chapter of the Association for Computational Linguistics (EACL), Gothenburg, Sweden, April 26-30, 2014*. Aalto University.

Weakly supervised learning of allomorphy

Miikka Silfverberg and **Mans Hulden**
Department of Linguistics
University of Colorado
`first.last@colorado.edu`

Abstract

Most NLP resources that offer annotations at the word segment level provide morphological annotation that includes features indicating tense, aspect, modality, gender, case, and other inflectional information. Such information is rarely aligned to the relevant parts of the words—i.e. the allomorphs, as such annotation would be very costly. These unaligned weak labelings are commonly provided by annotated NLP corpora such as treebanks in various languages. Although they lack alignment information, the presence/absence of labels at the word level is also consistent with the amount of supervision assumed to be provided to L1 and L2 learners. In this paper, we explore several methods to learn this latent alignment between parts of word forms and the grammatical information provided. All the methods under investigation favor hypotheses regarding allomorphs of morphemes that re-use a small inventory, i.e. implicitly minimize the number of allomorphs that a morpheme can be realized as. We show that the provided information offers a significant advantage for both word segmentation and the learning of allomorphy.

1 Introduction

Many NLP resources provide weakly labeled morphological resources in data sets that are primarily annotated for higher-level constructs besides morphology. Most treebanks, for example, include some morphological annotation on the word level of varying granularity. The Penn treebank (Marcus et al., 1993) uses a limited label set of 45, while the Universal Dependencies (UD) (Nivre et al., 2017) project annotates word forms with a much larger set of morphological feature-value pairs. Noteworthy is that such annotation is not in any way aligned with the substrings in the word forms themselves: if the Finnish word **kaatuisi** 'would fall down' is annotated as `kaatua,V,Cond,Pres,3,Sg`, there is no indication that **kaatu** corresponds to the stem, **isi** to `Cond`, and that `V`, `3` and `Sg` are realized as zero allomorphs.

In essence, such labeled resources provide an inference problem in the realm of inflectional morphology in that one can exploit statistical regularities in the data to perform a morpheme segmentation and labeling of the data. A linguistically informed observation based on a simple assumption of systematic regularity between form and meaning is that it is very unlikely that a single morpheme such as the Finnish conditional be realized in more than a handful of different allomorphs. Conversely, it is unlikely that a part of a word, such as the affix **isi** carry many disparate meanings, i.e. be associated with a large array of different labels. Still, morphemes are often realized by more than one allomorph although the number of allomorphs is typically small. Consider for example English plural number which is realized by different allomorphs in the forms **dogs**, **chur<u>ch</u>es**, **ox<u>en</u>** and **child<u>ren</u>**. From a data-driven perspective, the inference problem thus becomes to find a globally good allomorph segmentation and labeling of all word forms given in a large resource of inflected word forms.

Besides NLP applications, this type of input and the related inference problem is consistent with the assumptions of relevant inputs witnessed in L1 acquisition—a combination of stems and other affixes where the learner knows from the environment some semantic signal from the immediate discourse, e.g. plurality, tense, etc. Children tend

Proceedings of the First Workshop on Subword and Character Level Models in NLP, pages 46–56,
Copenhagen, Denmark, September 7, 2017. ©2017 Association for Computational Linguistics.

to show the ability to analyze affixes before they can use them productively. For example, three-year-olds have been shown to be able to associate agentive meaning to an **-er** morpheme in English, but can only produce the suffix later (Clark and Hecht, 1982; Clark and Berman, 1984).

In this paper we explore and evaluate several methods for automatically segmenting and labeling each allomorph present in resources that are labeled with morphosyntactic features at the word level. This means that our training data consists of plain unsegmented word forms (for example **kaatuisi**) and morphological feature sets (for example {V, Cond, Pres, 3, Sg}). The result is a morphologically segmented corpus where each morphological segment is associated with at least one morphological feature as shown in Figure 1. In order to account for fusional morphology, we allow one segment to be associated with multiple morphological features.

We treat the problem of joint segmentation and feature assignment as a search problem in the space of all possible segmentations and labelings of each word form in a (weakly) annotated corpus. The crucial constraint provided by the weak labeling is that not all labels can be present in a word form—the set of labels present for each inflected word must be restricted to those given by the resource. To our knowledge, this weakly supervised task has not previously been explored although joint segmentation and labeling has been explored in a fully supervised setting by Cotterell et al. (2015).

To solve the problem, we explore global metrics that indirectly favor re-use of allomorphs according to the intuition given above. We formalize a generic objective function that scores the goodness of segmentations and labeling globally in a corpus. The scoring portion of this objective function is tested with several metrics: symmetric conditional probability, which favors that allomorphs be good predictors of labels and vice versa, a perceptron learner that weights allomorph-label association, a Rescorla-Wagner model based on classical conditioning that also learns such association weights, and a model of Kullback-Leibler divergence that favors that labels and allomorphs have similar distributions throughout a data set.[1] We also compare the performance of the various meth-

ods to a baseline unsupervised model, Morfessor[2], augmented with the capacity to also provide labels of allomorphs in addition to segmenting.

2   Related Work

In the realm of natural language processing, morphological segmentation is a well-researched and established problem (Goldsmith (2001), Creutz and Lagus (2005), Poon et al. (2009), Dreyer and Eisner (2011), Ruokolainen et al. (2016)). While most approaches to pure segmentation are unsupervised, semi-supervised work usually assumes the availability of a limited number of gold segmentations (Dasgupta and Ng, 2007; Kohonen et al., 2010; Grönroos et al., 2014; Sirts and Goldwater, 2013). Using vector space representations of words to produce a weak labeling that identifies related forms has also been investigated (Schone and Jurafsky, 2000; Soricut and Och, 2015). Kann et al. (2016) perform unsupervised *canonicalization* of allomorphs, transforming words such as **having** to **have ing**, a task which is somewhat related to the problem addressed in this paper. Many methods that tackle specific morphology-related NLP tasks implicitly learn some model of allomorphy. This includes semi-supervised vocabulary expansion (Faruqui et al., 2016), and morphological inflection from examples (Cotterell et al., 2016a).

To our knowledge, the weakly supervised learning problem addressed in this paper has not been considered in the literature. Cotterell et al. (2015) present a closely related task. They investigate *labeled morphological segmentation*, that is, simultaneous segmentation and labeling of segments with morphological features. The crucial difference between our work and the work by Cotterell et al. (2015) is that our models are learned in a weakly supervised manner from plain word forms and sets of morphological features. In contrast, Cotterell et al. (2015) learn segmentation models in a fully supervised manner from data where each word is morphologically segmented and the segments are annotated with morphological features.

In the cognitive literature on L1 and L2 learning, statistical learning -based approaches that attempt to explain language learning through observations about statistical regularities have explored the extent to which relatively simple generalizations based on co-occurrence observations and

---

[1]Our code is freely available at https://github.com/mpsilfve/learn-allomorphs

[2]http://www.cis.hut.fi/projects/morpho/morfessor2.shtml

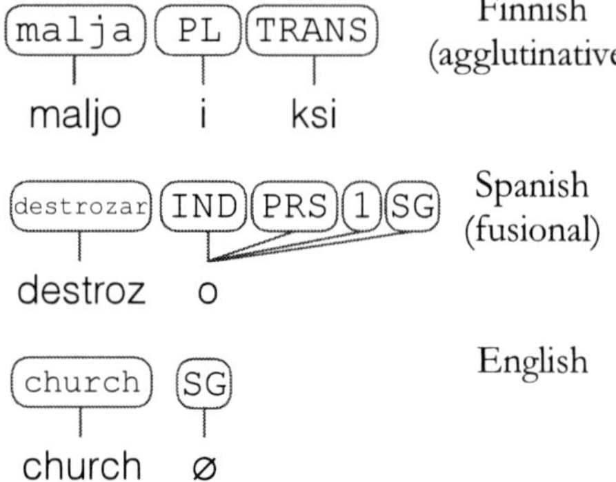

Figure 1: Morphological feature alignments in agglutinative and fusional languages; in the Finnish word (**malja** 'cup') each allomorph has a single feature while in the Spanish word (**destrozar** 'destroy') several features are associated with a single allomorph. In the English example, a zero allomorph is declared to which the feature SG is aligned.

statistical generalizations can be used to model learning of various levels of structure in natural language, including discovery of words (Saffran et al., 1996), grammatical categories (Reeder et al., 2013), and syntactic structure (Newport, 2016).

3 Methods

Given a corpus of word forms and associated morphological features, we want to find the correct segmentation for a word such as **barked** into *segments* which correspond to morphemes **bark**, **ed**, ∅, and the correct assignment of *morphological features* in a feature set {bark, V, Past} onto the segments. In this case: **bark**/bark, **ed**/Past and ∅/V. Note that we treat the lemma as a morphological feature.

Zero morphs (∅) are required because several languages have morphological features which are not visible in the word form, for example singular number of English nouns. In our gold standard segmented test data, we align word class markers such as N and V with a zero morph because they do not correspond to any substring of the word form. This decision is somewhat arbitrary. Other options include aligning them with the word stem and simply removing them from the corpus. In some cases, as in the case of English adverbs with suffix **-ly**, one could also consider aligning

the word class marker with an affix.

We propose to accomplish segmentation and feature assignment by learning a real-valued scoring function $\Theta : \Sigma^* \times Y \to \mathbb{R}$, where Σ^* is the set possible segments and Y is the finite set of morphological features.[3] The scoring function Θ expresses the strength of association between a segment such as **ed** and a morphological feature such as Past. It is learned from a set of unsegmented word forms and their morphological label sets. We present several alternative formulations for Θ.

Using the scoring function Θ, we find the optimal segmentation $x_{max} = x_1...x_n$ of the input word form and optimal feature assignment $y_{max} = y_1 \cup ... \cup y_n$ which together maximize the value of Θ as given by Equation 1. We perform the maximization using an exact search algorithm over the set of segmentations and feature assignments. Therefore, we are guaranteed to find the optimal segmentation and feature assignment.

$$(x_{max}, y_{max}) = \arg\max_{\substack{x_1...x_n=\mathbf{x} \\ y_1\cup...\cup y_n=\mathbf{y}}} \sum_{x_i} \sum_{y \in y_i} \Theta(x_i, y) \tag{1}$$

We perform the maximization in Equation 1 in the following way. Let $\mathbf{x}$ be an input string and let $\mathbf{y} = \{f_1, ..., f_k\}$ be a set of morphological features. We first form an exhaustive set of segmentations of $\mathbf{x}$ (in order to allow for tractable inference, we only consider segmentations into maximally 5 segments). We then consider each segmentation $x_1...x_n = \mathbf{x}$ in turn and find the feature assignment $y_1 \cup ... \cup y_n = \mathbf{y}$ which maximizes the score Θ using a recursive algorithm presented below.

Given a partition $y_1, ..., y_n$ of a possibly empty prefix of $\mathbf{y} = \{f_1, ..., f_k\}$ (that is a collection of pointwise disjoint sets $y_1, ..., y_n$ where $y_1 \cup ... \cup y_n = \{f_1, ..., f_j\}$ and $j \leq k$), we can find the optimal score M for assigning the remaining morphological features $\mathbf{y}_{rest} = \mathbf{y} - \{f_1, ..., f_j\}$ into sets in $y_1, ..., y_n$ using the following recursive algorithm.[4] Set $M := -\infty$ and iterate over i in $\{1, ..., n\}$.

- If $\mathbf{y}_{rest}$ is empty, then $y_1 \cup ... \cup y_n = \mathbf{y}$. If each $y_l \neq \emptyset$, assign $M := \max(M, \Theta((x_1, ..., x_n), (y_1, ..., y_n)))$.

---

[3] Y is finite because the inventory of morphological features is derived from a finite corpus.

[4] A natural extension of this algorithm will recover the optimal feature assignment.

- If $\mathbf{y}_{rest}$ is not empty, assign $y_i := y_i \cup \{f_{j+1}\}$ and find the optimal score M' for $\mathbf{y}'_{rest} = \{f_{j+1}, ..., f_k\} - \{f_{j+1}\}$. Set $M := \max(M, M')$.

Finally, return M.

By initially setting $y_1 = ... = y_n = \emptyset$, we can find the optimal feature assignment for the entire segmentation $x_1, ..., x_n$.

We limit the set of segmentations of a word to those which have maximally one empty substring and explore assignments where each segment is aligned with at least one morphological feature. One segment may, however, be aligned with several features. This is required when a morpheme encodes for several morphological features.

These assumptions are in line with typological considerations—agglutinative languages such as Finnish and Turkish largely associate allomorphs with a single morphological feature, while fusional languages, such as Swedish and Spanish, may associate many features with a substring (see figure 1). Allomorph overlap, where a substring **xyz** in a word has **xy** associated with one feature and **yz** with another, is generally not attested cross-linguistically which narrows down the set of hypotheses we need to consider. However, a typologically interesting case not modeled in our approach is templatic, or root-and-pattern morphology, where a discontinuous subsequence may be associated with a feature, such as in the classic Arabic example **kataba** 'to write', where root radicals associate with a stem (**ktb** = related to writing) and intervening vowels with inflectional and derivational patterns. The objective functions we develop may be adapted to this case, however, at the cost of enlarging the search space since all subsequences would need to be considered when associating parts of word forms and morphological features. Moreover, even languages with templatic morphology can be handled using the current system, provided that templatic phenomena are not annotated in the corpus. For example, a model of Arabic may represent vowel changes in the stem by declaring different stem allomorphs instead of treating the discontinuous root radical consonants as the stem, e.g. **kataba** ('to write' perfect indicative 2p masculine) vs. **taktubu** ('to write' imperfective indicative 2p masculine).

Below, we present several alternative formulations for the scoring function Θ. Two of the functions *symmetric conditional probability* and *KL-*

divergence are statistics which can be computed in a straightforward manner given a training data set. The two remaining functions, the *perceptron* and *Rescorla-Wagner*, are derived by learning multi-class classifiers which predict the morphological labels of a word based on its sub-strings. The parameters of these classifiers express associations between morphological labels and substrings. We use these associations as the scoring function Θ.

3.1 Symmetric conditional probability

Intuitively, a substring x is a good candidate allomorph for a morphological feature y if x and y frequently co-occur. Symmetric conditional probability (SCP), introduced by da Silva et al. (1999) for mining of lexical multi-word units, is a mathematical realization of this principle.

The SCP of a segment x and a feature y is given by equation 2. The probability $p(x)$ is the frequency of words having substring x, $p(y)$ the frequency of words having morphological label y and $p(x, y)$ the frequency of words having both substring x and label y.

$$\mathrm{SCP}(x, y) = p(x|y)p(y|x) = \frac{p(x, y)^2}{p(x)p(y)} \quad (2)$$

By setting $\Theta(x, y) = \mathrm{SCP}(x, y)$, we can use the symmetric conditional probability as a scoring function.

3.2 Perceptron

We explore a simple extension of the classical perceptron learning algorithm (Rosenblatt, 1958) for multi-label classification (Tsoumakas and Katakis, 2007). Instead of predicting a single label for each input instance, we predict a set of outputs corresponding to the morphological features related to a word.

We start with a standard perceptron classifier defined by a feature extraction function $f : \Sigma^* \to \{0, 1\}^k$, which maps word forms x into a vector, and one parameter vector $\phi_y \in \mathbb{R}^k$ for each morphological feature $y \in Y$. Here, k is the total number of distinct substrings that occur in the data set $\mathcal{D}$.[5] Intuitively, f extracts substrings of x. More formally, it maps a word form x into a vector in a space where each dimension corresponds to a string in Σ^* and $f(x)[i] = 1$, iff x has a substring corresponding to the ith dimension. Inference in

---

[5] k is between 144,000 and 423,000 for all of the data sets considered in this paper.

the model is defined by Equation 3 and parameter updates are defined by Equation 4, where y_{gold} is the gold standard label.

$$y_{max} = \arg\max_{y \in Y} \phi_y^\top f(x) \qquad (3)$$

$$\phi_{y_{max}} := \phi_{y_{max}} - f(x) \text{ and } \phi_{y_{gold}} := \phi_{y_{gold}} + f(x) \qquad (4)$$

We modify standard perceptron updates in the following way: For a word x with a set of morphological labels Y, where $|Y| = n$, we examine the set N consisting of the top-n labels returned by the perceptron classifier using the current parameter estimates. We then perform a negative update for parameters corresponding to labels which were not associated with the word form x in the gold standard, that is labels in the set $N - Y$. Conversely, we perform a positive update for parameters which were associated with word form x, that is morphological features in the set $Y - N$.

Clearly, we perform no updates for a particular word form x, iff the top-n candidates returned by the classifier exactly correspond to the set of morphological features of x.

We first train a system using the aforementioned variant of the perceptron algorithm. As feature templates, we us the substrings of words in $\mathcal{D}$. We then use the parameter values corresponding to associations of substrings x and features y, learned by the perceptron algorithm, as scores $\Theta(x, y)$.

3.3 Rescorla-Wagner learning

The Rescorla-Wagner (R-W) rule (Rescorla and Wagner, 1972) is a model of classical conditioning that provides an account of the association strength between a conditioned stimulus (CS) and an unconditioned stimulus (US); or, alternatively, the strength between a *stimulus* and the expectation of *reward*. This type of a learning model has been applied to acquisition of plurals (Ramscar and Yarlett, 2007; Ramscar, 2013), number names (Ramscar et al., 2011) word recognition (Baayen et al., 2011), and typology of number encoding in inflectional morphology (Ackerman et al., 2016).

In the single stimulus case, we have an expected reward v which is calculated as a linear combination of a binary stimulus u and a learned weight w:

$$v = wu \qquad (5)$$

As stimuli arrive possibly paired with a reward, the weight w is updated depending on whether the reward was present as $w = w + \varepsilon\delta u$, where δ is set in proportion to r, the 'actual' reward, usually set to 1 or 100 if the association is valid, else 0. The quantity $\delta = r - v$ is hence the prediction error which drives association updates toward 0 or toward the maximum association score and ε is a learning rate (set to 0.01 here). In our model, the *reward* is a morphological label, and the *stimuli* are the substrings present in the word forms witnessed. We extend the common single-stimulus/single-reward R-W model to one which learns association strengths of multiple stimuli and multiple rewards in a standard way (Dayan and Abbott, 2001). Each possible morphological label is associated with a weight vector $\mathbf{w}$ where each dimension corresponds to a string in Σ^*, as in the perceptron case. As stimuli arrive, weight updates are performed per label as:

$$\mathbf{w} = \mathbf{w} + \varepsilon\delta\mathbf{u} \text{ where } \delta = r - v \qquad (6)$$

Here, as before, r is 0 if the label is absent and 100 if it is present.

Learning is very similar to perceptron learning—the conditions under which R-W learning and perceptron training is identical is explored in detail in Dawson (2008). The main difference between our R-W and perceptron implementations is that perceptron updates are only performed if the n labels present in a word form do not appear in the n-best scoring list, while R-W updates are always done if the expectation produced by summing the individual expectations caused by the substrings in a word fails to match the maximum label 'reward'.

3.4 Kullback-Leibler divergence

Given a set of labeled words $U \subset \mathcal{D}$ in our data set, we can examine the distribution of morphological features in U defined by $p(f|U) \propto |\{(x, y) \in U | f \in y\}|$ for all $f \in Y$. We can examine different subsets of $\mathcal{D}$ defined by criteria concerning (1) morphological features, or (2) existence of a given substring in word forms. Intuitively, a substring s is a good candidate morpheme for a morphological feature f, if $U_s = \{(x, y) \in \mathcal{D} | s$ is a substring of $x\}$ and $U_f = \{(x, y) \in \mathcal{D} | f \in y\}$ define similar distributions of morphological features.

Kullback-Leibler (KL) divergence is a widely

	# train wf	# test wf	# lemmas	feat. types
Eng	10,000	300	8591	7
Fin	12,693	300	10049	39
Swe	10,000	300	6589	23
Tur	7,645	300	2523	36

Table 1: Data set sizes for English, Finnish, Swedish and Turkish.

used measure for the distance of two discrete probability distributions defined on the same sample space defined by Equation 7.

$$\mathrm{KL}(p||q) = \sum_x p(x) \log \frac{p(x)}{q(x)} \qquad (7)$$

We use the negative KL divergence of the distributions over morphological features defined by a substring x and a morphological feature f, respectively, as score $\Theta(x, f)$.

3.5 Baseline

As our baseline, we use the unsupervised morphological segmentation given by the Morfessor Baseline method (Creutz and Lagus, 2005). We use its default settings for all parameters.

We assign labels to segments based on maximum likelihood as defined by co-occurrence of segments and labels in the segmented data set. When there are fewer segments than morphological features, we assign at least one feature per segment. Otherwise, we assign at most one feature per segment while maximizing the joint probability of segments and morphological features.

This baseline was chosen because it is easily accessible to most researchers and very easy and fast to apply.

4 Data

We use data from the 2016 SIGMORPHON shared task on morphological re-inflection (Cotterell et al., 2016b) (Finnish and Turkish) and the 2017 CoNLL shared task on morphological re-inflection[6] (English and Swedish). Figure 2 shows an example of the data format and Table 1 shows details for each data set.

We use the training and test sets from subtask 1 from the SIGMORPHON shared task (Cotterell et al., 2016a) and the task 1 high training set together with the task 1 development set from the

---

[6]`https://sites.google.com/view/conll-sigmorphon2017/`

CoNLL shared task 2017 (Cotterell et al., 2017). Figure 3 shows an example of the annotated test data.

5 Experiments

We first train each of the scoring functions presented in Section 3 on the combined training data and *unsegmented* test data. After that, we find the optimal segmentation and label alignment for each word in the test data using each scoring function. We explore all segmentations consisting of maximally 5 segments and all assignments of morphological features to the segments using a dynamic algorithm in order to speed up inference.

For perceptron and R-W learning, we run the training algorithm for three epochs over the train and test data. The learning rate ε for R-W learning is fixed to 0.01 and the maximum possible association response r is fixed to 100.

We evaluate each scoring function with regard to three different criteria: (1) identification of morpheme boundaries, (2) identification of unlabeled morphemes, and (3) identification of labeled morphemes. For each criterion, we give recall, precision and F_1-score. Evaluation criteria (1) and (2) are very similar, but we include both for easier comparison with earlier work in the field of unsupervised morphological segmentation.

To illustrate our evaluation scheme, consider the following gold standard segmentation and alignment for English

`ping/ping ing/V.PTCP,PRS NULL/V`

The aligned form contains three morpheme boundaries: at index 1 (start of word), at index 4 (between the stem and participle suffix) and at index 7 (end of word). It contains two unlabeled morphemes: **ping** and **ing**, and four labeled morphemes: **ping/ping**, **ing/V.PTCP**, **ing/PRS** and **NULL/V**. Counts for these units are used to compute recall, precision and F_1-score for each evaluation criterion.

6 Results

Table 2 shows the results of all experiments for each language.

In general, each of the scoring functions performs substantially better than the baseline Morfessor system. However, SCP delivers lower unlabeled morpheme F-scores for Turkish and KL-divergence gives lower performance on morpheme boundary detection for Finnish.

51

psychoanalyse	V,V.PTCP,PRS	psychoanalysing
aalloittaisuus	pos=N,case=ON+ESS,num=PLN	aalloittaisuuksilla
centralbank	N,DEF,GEN,SG	centralbankens
haberleşmek	V,IND,3,SG,PST,PROG,POS,DECL	haberleşiyordu

Figure 2: Example lines from the English, Finnish, Swedish and Turkish training data set of. The first field contains the lemma, the second field contains additional morphological features and the last field contains the word form.

```
autofocuss/autofocus ed/PST NULL/V
paali/paali n/case=ACC NULL/num=SGN,pos=N
kammarrätt/kammarrätt s/GEN NULL/N,INDF,SG
âmâ/âmâ lar/PL dan/ABL NULL/N
```

Figure 3: Example entries from the annotated English, Finnish, Swedish and Turkish test sets. We align the stem with the lemma and the part-of-speech with the zero allomorph.

R-W seems to deliver consistently competitive performance when compared to the other systems on morpheme boundary recovery and morpheme identification. The performance of the perceptron algorithm is quite similar to the R-W but, in general, lower. The perceptron algorithm, however, delivers the best performance for Turkish.

KL divergence seems to perform the worst of all of the scoring functions. It delivers markedly worse performance on the Swedish data set than the other systems.

SCP delivers superior performance when compared to R-W for Finnish on morpheme boundary recovery and morpheme identification. However, its performance on English and and Turkish is substantially worse than both R-W and the perceptron algorithm.

In the case of labeled morphemes, SCP seems to deliver consistently good performance. It outperforms R-W even in the case of Turkish and English, where it delivers substantially worse performance on unlabeled morpheme identification.

7 Discussion

The results show clear improvement over the baseline approach of first applying unsupervised morphological segmentation and then assigning labels based on co-occurrence counts of segments and labels. That is, including information about morphological features in the segmentation process is clearly beneficial.

The perceptron and R-W learning algorithms have very similar performance, which can be explained by the fact that the algorithms themselves are quite similar. However, the R-W algorithm seems to deliver somewhat superior performance. One possible reason for this is that the R-W will prefer solutions where one substring in the word explains one morphological feature, whereas the perceptron algorithm does not have such a bias. This can be attributed to the 'blocking' effect of R-W learning: when one feature (substring) has already been weighted early during training enough to yield a maximum response (label), no updates are made for other features which may also co-occur with the same label.

The fact that both R-W and the perceptron algorithm seem to perform poorly for labeled morpheme identification can be explained by the fact that both algorithms are trained to predict each of the morphological labels of the word from all substrings occurring in the word. This can lead to confusion of features for morphemes occurring in the same word. For example, the R-W performs comparatively poorly on labeled morpheme identification for the Finnish, Swedish and English data sets. This happens because it assigns the part-of-speech feature to the stem in many words but the gold standard analysis is that the part-of-speech is aligned with the zero morpheme. Conversely, it also assigns the lemma to the zero morpheme in many words, whereas the gold standard instead assigns lemmas to stems. Note that the decision to align part-of-speech with the zero morpheme instead of the word stem is fairly arbitrary. Therefore, a different gold standard segmentation could give substantially higher labeled morpheme performance for R-W.

The arbitrariness of the gold standard annotation as regards certain features may be avoided by a different evaluation scheme where no gold standard is used. One can, for example, leave a held-out data set and first segment and label the data on a training section, and then investigate

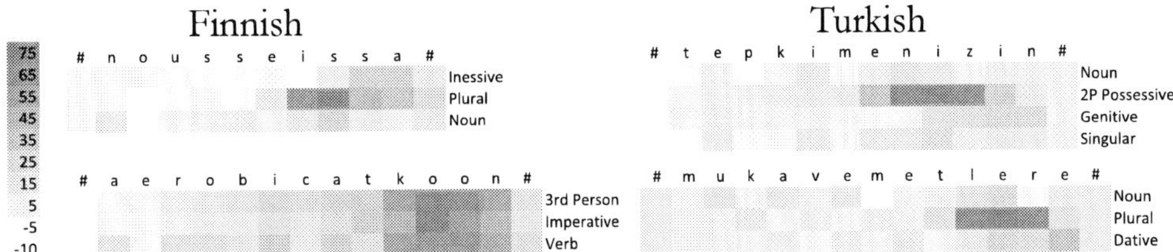

Figure 4: Example activations for two inflected Finnish words (**noussut** 'risen', **aerobicata** 'to do aerobics') and two Turkish words (**tepkime** 'reaction', **mukavemet** 'durability') with Rescorla-Wagner learning. The activation score at each character is calculated as a sum of the activations associated with the substrings that the character participates in. Standard linguistic analyses have the Finnish inessive as **-ssa**, the plural as **-i-**, and both the imperative and 3rd person fused as **-koon**. For Turkish, the 2P Possessive is **-niz-**, the genitive is **-in**, the plural is **-ler-**, and the dative is **-e**.

	(a) Eng	Fin	Swe	Tur		(b) Eng	Fin	Swe	Tur		(c) Eng	Fin	Swe	Tur
Kullback-Leibler Divergence					Kullback-Leibler Divergence					Kullback-Leibler Divergence				
R	93.91	82.74	73.81	81.25	R	69.52	45.66	15.71	44.28	R	74.18	39.70	8.88	31.36
P	87.15	80.36	65.89	76.60	P	62.02	43.82	13.35	40.97	P	74.11	37.07	7.64	27.09
F_1	90.41	81.54	69.63	78.86	F_1	65.56	44.72	14.43	42.56	F_1	74.15	38.34	8.22	29.07
Perceptron					Perceptron					Perceptron				
R	98.81	80.67	86.15	86.68	R	90.15	47.62	44.55	61.32	R	90.06	34.77	30.30	59.91
P	95.06	88.05	76.54	90.54	P	84.94	54.05	37.57	65.13	P	90.06	33.59	27.30	54.70
F_1	96.90	84.20	81.06	**88.57**	F_1	87.47	50.63	40.76	**63.16**	F_1	**90.06**	34.17	28.72	**57.19**
Rescorla-Wagner					Rescorla-Wagner					Rescorla-Wagner				
R	98.93	83.74	82.58	82.88	R	94.98	50.84	43.91	56.84	R	43.96	29.98	24.31	43.14
P	97.87	86.81	82.22	91.96	P	93.42	53.53	43.63	65.76	P	43.96	29.98	24.96	43.58
F_1	**98.40**	85.23	82.40	87.18	F_1	**94.19**	52.16	**43.77**	60.97	F_1	43.96	29.98	24.63	43.36
Symmetric Conditional Probability					Symmetric Conditional Probability					Symmetric Conditional Probability				
R	89.02	81.56	77.38	70.65	R	64.31	50.14	37.82	27.99	R	66.37	56.45	62.88	52.81
P	95.15	91.58	94.33	90.28	P	71.49	59.37	51.53	39.89	P	66.37	53.90	64.07	53.35
F_1	91.99	**86.28**	**85.02**	79.27	F_1	67.71	**54.37**	43.62	32.89	F_1	66.37	**55.15**	**63.47**	53.08
Morfessor baseline					Morfessor baseline					Morfessor baseline				
R	80.79	67.36	76.19	77.26	R	21.19	9.94	21.79	39.93	R	1.77	9.66	20.11	8.74
P	61.10	65.67	72.35	93.22	P	14.14	9.59	20.27	52.20	P	1.76	10.97	25.09	11.21
F_1	69.58	66.50	74.22	84.50	F_1	16.96	9.77	21.00	45.24	F_1	1.77	10.27	22.32	9.82

Table 2: Results for (a) morpheme boundaries; (b) unlabeled morphemes; (c) labeled morphemes. For each language and each task, the scoring function delivering the best performance is shown in boldface.

how many new allomorphs are implicitly detected when the held-out data is also segmented and labeled. The expectation is that very few new allomorphs should be found in a held-out set if a model assigns labels to substrings in a consistent manner. Whether a good score on such an evaluation would correspond to linguistically motivated allomorph sets is a question we intent to investigate in the future. If so, a robust evaluation could potentially be made without any gold segmentation and labeling at all.

In addition to the scoring functions presented in Section 3, we investigated a number of other scoring functions, for example pointwise mutual information (PMI)[7] of segments and morphological features, but these did not yield competitive performance according to preliminary experiments. We also experimented with IBM models (Brown et al., 1993) for alignment of characters to morphosyntactic labels, which also performed poorly.

SCP performs poorly on the English and Turkish data sets. For English, a major problem is that SCP does not find the present participle suffix **ing**. This suffix is problematic because it is associated with a combination of morphological features, namely present tense and the participle feature. Both of these co-occur more frequently with other suffixes (**ed** in the case of participle and **NULL** in the case of present tense), however, when they co-occur, they always occur with the **ing** suffix. This seems to be a problem for SCP which encodes a strong preference that there be a one-to-one mapping between morphemes and features.

A possible explanation for the poor performance of SCP on the Turkish data set is that this is the smallest of all data sets, while still having a very large number of morphological features.

In this investigation, we have not exhausted the set of reasonable scoring functions. One objective function that is particularly interesting is to simply try to minimize the total number of different allomorphs discovered in the data. This objective function is difficult to integrate in our current approach since the function is discontinuous. In essence, this objective function calls for an algorithm that discovers a segmentation and labeling of the data such that the sum total of different allomorph types is minimized. The problem appears to be computationally intractable in principle, since it bears strong similarities to other intractable problems such as set covering. But good heuristic solvers for NP-complete problems such as Moskewicz et al. (2001) may perhaps be harnessed to find good solutions under this formulation. A thorough analysis and evaluation of this type of model remains future work.

8 Conclusion

We have presented a new learning problem for natural language processing, namely weakly supervised learning of allomorphy. The problem is important from a practical point of view because there are many morphologically annotated corpora where the annotation is not extended to the morpheme level. It is also relevant from a theoretical point of view because it is related to L1 morphology learning.

We explored four different learning methods: KL divergence, perceptron learning, R-W learning and SCP. We compared these to a baseline consisting of unsupervised morphological segmentation augmented by a straightforward labeling mechanism. Our results show that weak supervision delivers sizable improvements when evaluated with regard to F_1-score on labeled and unlabeled segmentation. According to our experiments, R-W learning, while not only efficient, also delivers the best results on this task.

Acknowledgements

We wish to thank Jordan Boyd-Graber, Koen Claessen, Gerlof Bouma, and Hubie Chen for very helpful discussion and comments. This work has been supported in part by the Defense Advanced Research Projects Agency (DARPA) in the program Low Resource Languages for Emergent Incidents (LORELEI).

---

[7] The reason for the poor performance of PMI is that it will often align features with rare substrings and, therefore, it can assign a great number of distinct allomorphs to the same morphological feature. To illustrate this, let $\mathrm{pmi}(x, y) = \log p(x, y)/(p(x)p(y))$ be the PMI of segment x and feature y. This quantity can never exceed $\log 1/p(y)$ because $p(x, y) \leq p(x)$. Assume that x only occurs once in the training corpus and the sole occurrence is in a word with feature y. Thus $p(x, y) = p(x)$ and $\mathrm{pmi}(x, y) = \log 1/p(y)$, i.e. the maximal PMI for any segment x given feature y.

References

Farrell Ackerman, Robert Malouf, and James P. Blevins. 2016. Patterns and discriminability in language analysis. *Word Structure* 9(2):132–155.

R. Harald Baayen, Petar Milin, Dusica Filipović Đurđević, Peter Hendrix, and Marco Marelli. 2011. An amorphous model for morphological processing in visual comprehension based on naive discriminative learning. *Psychological review* 118(3):438–481.

Peter F. Brown, Stephen A. Della Pietra, Vincent J. Della Pietra, and Robert L. Mercer. 1993. The mathematics of statistical machine translation: Parameter estimation. *Computational Linguistics* 19(2):263–313.

Eve V. Clark and Ruth A. Berman. 1984. Structure and use in the acquisition of word formation. *Language* pages 542–590.

Eve V. Clark and Barbara Frant Hecht. 1982. Learning to coin agent and instrument nouns. *Cognition* 12(1):1–24.

Ryan Cotterell, Christo Kirov, John Sylak-Glassman, Géraldine Walther, Ekaterina Vylomova, Patrick Xia, Manaal Faruqui, Sandra Kübler, David Yarowsky, Jason Eisner, and Mans Hulden. 2017. The CoNLL-SIGMORPHON 2017 shared task: Universal morphological reinflection in 52 languages. In *Proceedings of the CoNLL-SIGMORPHON 2017 Shared Task: Universal Morphological Reinflection*. Association for Computational Linguistics, Vancouver, Canada.

Ryan Cotterell, Christo Kirov, John Sylak-Glassman, David Yarowsky, Jason Eisner, and Mans Hulden. 2016a. The SIGMORPHON 2016 shared task—morphological reinflection. In *Proceedings of the 14th SIGMORPHON Workshop on Computational Research in Phonetics, Phonology, and Morphology*. Association for Computational Linguistics, Berlin, Germany, pages 10–22.

Ryan Cotterell, Thomas Müller, Alexander M. Fraser, and Hinrich Schütze. 2015. Labeled morphological segmentation with semi-Markov models. In *CoNLL*. pages 164–174.

Ryan Cotterell, Tim Vieira, and Hinrich Schütze. 2016b. A joint model of orthography and morphological segmentation. In *Proceedings of the 2016 Conference of the North American Chapter of the Association for Computational Linguistics: Human Language Technologies*. Association for Computational Linguistics, San Diego, California, pages 664–669.

Mathias Creutz and Krista Lagus. 2005. Unsupervised morpheme segmentation and morphology induction from text corpora using Morfessor 1.0. Technical Report A81, Helsinki University of Technology.

Joaquim Ferreira da Silva, Gaël Dias, Sylvie Guilloré, and José Gabriel Pereira Lopes. 1999. Using Local-Maxs algorithm for the extraction of contiguous and non-contiguous multiword lexical units. In *Progress in Artificial Intelligence: 9th Portuguese Conference on Artificial Intelligence, EPIA '99 Évora, Portugal, September 21–24, 1999 Proceedings*, Springer Berlin Heidelberg, Berlin, Heidelberg, pages 113–132.

Sajib Dasgupta and Vincent Ng. 2007. High-performance, language-independent morphological segmentation. In *Human Language Technologies 2007: The Conference of the North American Chapter of the Association for Computational Linguistics; Proceedings of the Main Conference*. Association for Computational Linguistics, Rochester, New York, pages 155–163.

Michael R. W. Dawson. 2008. Connectionism and classical conditioning. *Comparative Cognition and Behavior Reviews* 3:1–115.

P. Dayan and L. F. Abbott. 2001. Classical conditioning and reinforcement learning. *Theoretical Neuroscience* .

Markus Dreyer and Jason Eisner. 2011. Discovering morphological paradigms from plain text using a Dirichlet process mixture model. In *Proceedings of EMNLP 2011*. Association for Computational Linguistics, Edinburgh, pages 616–627.

Manaal Faruqui, Ryan McDonald, and Radu Soricut. 2016. Morpho-syntactic lexicon generation using graph-based semi-supervised learning. *Transactions of the Association for Computational Linguistics* 4:1–16.

John Goldsmith. 2001. Unsupervised learning of the morphology of a natural language. *Computational linguistics* 27(2):153–198.

Stig-Arne Grönroos, Sami Virpioja, Peter Smit, and Mikko Kurimo. 2014. Morfessor FlatCat: An HMM-based method for unsupervised and semi-supervised learning of morphology. In *Proceedings of COLING 2014, the 25th International Conference on Computational Linguistics*. Dublin City University and Association for Computational Linguistics, Dublin, Ireland, pages 1177–1185.

Katharina Kann, Ryan Cotterell, and Hinrich Schütze. 2016. Neural morphological analysis: Encoding-decoding canonical segments. In *Proceedings of the 2016 Conference on Empirical Methods in Natural Language Processing*. Association for Computational Linguistics, Austin, Texas, pages 961–967.

Oskar Kohonen, Sami Virpioja, and Krista Lagus. 2010. Semi-supervised learning of concatenative morphology. In *Proceedings of the 11th Meeting of the ACL Special Interest Group on Computational Morphology and Phonology (SIGMORPHON)*. Association for Computational Linguistics, pages 78–86.

Mitchell P. Marcus, Mary Ann Marcinkiewicz, and Beatrice Santorini. 1993. Building a large annotated corpus of english: The penn treebank. *Computational linguistics* 19(2):313–330.

Matthew W. Moskewicz, Conor F. Madigan, Ying Zhao, Lintao Zhang, and Sharad Malik. 2001. Chaff: Engineering an efficient SAT solver. In *Proceedings of the 38th annual Design Automation Conference*. ACM, pages 530–535.

Elissa L. Newport. 2016. Statistical language learning: Computational, maturational, and linguistic constraints. *Language and Cognition* 8(03):447–461.

Joakim Nivre, Željko Agić, Lars Ahrenberg, Maria Jesus Aranzabe, Masayuki Asahara, Aitziber Atutxa, et al. 2017. Universal dependencies 2.0. LINDAT/CLARIN digital library at the Institute of Formal and Applied Linguistics, Charles University in Prague.

Hoifung Poon, Colin Cherry, and Kristina Toutanova. 2009. Unsupervised morphological segmentation with log-linear models. In *Proceedings of Human Language Technologies: The 2009 Annual Conference of the North American Chapter of the Association for Computational Linguistics*. Association for Computational Linguistics, pages 209–217.

Michael Ramscar. 2013. Suffixing, prefixing, and the functional order of regularities in meaningful strings. *Psihologija* 46(4):377–396.

Michael Ramscar, Melody Dye, Hanna Muenke Popick, and Fiona O'Donnell-McCarthy. 2011. The enigma of number: Why children find the meanings of even small number words hard to learn and how we can help them do better. *PloS one* 6(7).

Michael Ramscar and Daniel Yarlett. 2007. Linguistic self-correction in the absence of feedback: A new approach to the logical problem of language acquisition. *Cognitive Science* 31(6):927–960.

Patricia A. Reeder, Elissa L. Newport, and Richard N. Aslin. 2013. From shared contexts to syntactic categories: The role of distributional information in learning linguistic form-classes. *Cognitive psychology* 66(1):30–54.

Robert A. Rescorla and Allan R. Wagner. 1972. A theory of Pavlovian conditioning: Variations in the effectiveness of reinforcement and nonreinforcement. *Classical conditioning II: Current research and theory* 2:64–99.

Frank Rosenblatt. 1958. The perceptron: A probabilistic model for information storage and organization in the brain. *Psychological Review* 65(6):386–408.

Teemu Ruokolainen, Oskar Kohonen, Kairit Sirts, Stig-Arne Grönroos, Mikko Kurimo, and Sami Virpioja. 2016. A comparative study of minimally supervised morphological segmentation. *Computational Linguistics* 42(1):91–120.

Jenny R. Saffran, Richard N. Aslin, and Elissa L. Newport. 1996. Statistical learning by 8-month-old infants. *Science* 274(5294):1926–1928.

Patrick Schone and Daniel Jurafsky. 2000. Knowledge-free induction of morphology using latent semantic analysis. In *Proceedings of the 2nd workshop on Learning language in logic and the 4th conference on Computational natural language learning*. Association for Computational Linguistics, pages 67–72.

Kairit Sirts and Sharon Goldwater. 2013. Minimally-supervised morphological segmentation using adaptor grammars. *Transactions of the Association for Computational Linguistics* 1:255–266.

Radu Soricut and Franz Och. 2015. Unsupervised morphology induction using word embeddings. In *Proceedings of the 2015 Conference of the North American Chapter of the Association for Computational Linguistics: Human Language Technologies*. Association for Computational Linguistics, Denver, Colorado, pages 1627–1637.

Grigorios Tsoumakas and Ioannis Katakis. 2007. Multi-label classification: An overview. *IJDWM* 3(3):1–13.

Character-based recurrent neural networks
for morphological relational reasoning

Olof Mogren
Chalmers University of Technology
Sweden
mogren@chalmers.se

Richard Johansson
University of Gothenburg
Sweden
richard.johansson@gu.se

Abstract

We present a model for predicting word forms based on *morphological relational reasoning* with analogies. While previous work has explored tasks such as morphological inflection and reinflection, these models rely on an explicit enumeration of morphological features, which may not be available in all cases. To address the task of predicting a word form given a *demo relation* (a pair of word forms) and a *query word*, we devise a character-based recurrent neural network architecture using three separate encoders and a decoder. We also investigate a multiclass learning setup, where the prediction of the relation type label is used as an auxiliary task.

Our results show that the exact form can be predicted for English with an accuracy of 94.7%. For Swedish, which has a more complex morphology with more inflectional patterns for nouns and verbs, the accuracy is 89.3%. We also show that using the auxiliary task of learning the relation type speeds up convergence and improves the prediction accuracy for the word generation task.

1 Introduction

Recently, a number of papers have been published that use character-level neural models as a way to address the inherent drawbacks of traditional models that represent words as atomic symbols. This offers a number of advantages: the vocabulary in a character-based model can be much smaller, as it only needs to represent a finite and fairly small alphabet, and as long as the characters are in the alphabet, no words will be out-of-vocabulary (OOV). Character-level models can capture distributional properties, not only of frequent words but also of words that occur rarely (Luong and Manning, 2016). This type of model needs no tokenization, freeing the system from one source of errors. Character-level neural models have been applied in several NLP tasks, ranging from relatively basic tasks such as text categorization (Zhang et al., 2015) and language modeling (Kim et al., 2016) to complex prediction tasks such as translation (Luong and Manning, 2016; Sennrich et al., 2016).

In particular, character-based neural models are attractive because they can take sub-word units, such as the *morphology*, into account. Morphological analysis and prediction models using character-based recurrent neural networks have recently become popular, as evidenced by their complete dominance at the SIGMORPHON shared task on morphological reinflection (Cotterell et al., 2016). However, in these models, including the top-performing system in the shared task (Kann and Schütze, 2016), an explicit feature representation of the morphological inflection needs to be provided as an input. These features represent number, gender, case, tense, aspect, etc.

In this paper, we take a new approach to predicting word forms that bypasses the need for an explicit representation of morphological features. We present a model that learns morphological *analogy relations* between words: given a *demo relation* $R_{demo} = (w_1, w_2)$, represented as a pair of words w_1 and w_2, and a *query word* q, can we apply the same relation as represented by R_{demo} to the query word, and arrive at the correct target t? The task may be illustrated with a simple example: *see* is to *sees* as *eat* is to what?

The relation in the example above is trivial on a superficial level, as the model just needs to add an *s* to the query word. However, the analogy task is more challenging in the general case. The

57

Proceedings of the First Workshop on Subword and Character Level Models in NLP, pages 57–63,
Copenhagen, Denmark, September 7, 2017. ©2017 Association for Computational Linguistics.

model needs to take into account that words belong to groups whose inflectional patterns are different – morphological *paradigms*. For instance, if we consider the past tense instead of the present in the example above, the relation is more complex: *see* is to *saw* as *eat* is to what? The model also needs to pick up general patterns that cut across paradigms, including phonological processes such as umlaut and vowel harmony, as well as orthographic quirks such as the rule in English that turns *y* into *ie* in certain contexts.

The fact that our model does not rely on explicit features makes it applicable in scenarios where features are unavailable, such as when working with under-resourced languages. However, since the model is trained using a weaker signal than in the traditional feature-based scenario, it needs to learn a latent representation from the analogies that plays the same role as the morphological features otherwise would. This makes the task more challenging to learn, and we compare the training time of a purely feature-free model to one where features are available during training as an auxiliary prediction task in a multi-task learning setup.

2 Recurrent neural networks

A recurrent neural network (RNN) is an artificial neural network that can model a sequence of arbitrary length. The basic layout is simply a feedforward neural network with weight sharing at each position in the sequence, making it a recursive function on the hidden state h_t. The network has an input layer at each position t in the sequence, and the input x_t is combined with the the previous internal state h_{t-1}. In a language setting, it is common to model sequences of words, in which case each input x_t is the vector representation of a word. In the basic variant ("vanilla" RNN), the transition function is a linear transformation of the hidden state and the input, followed by a pointwise nonlinearity.

$$h_t = \tanh(W x_t + U h_{t-1} + b),$$

where W and U are weight matrices, and b is a bias term.

Basic "vanilla" RNNs have some shortcomings. One of them is that these models are unable to capture longer dependencies in the input. Another one is the vanishing gradient problem that affects many neural models when many layers get stacked after each other, making these models difficult to train (Hochreiter, 1998; Bengio et al., 1994).

Some variants have been proposed to solve these shortcomings. The Long Short Term Memory (LSTM) (Schmidhuber and Hochreiter, 1997) is an RNN where the layer at each timestep is a cell that contains three gates controlling what parts of the internal memory will be kept (the forget gate f_t), what parts of the input that will be stored in the internal memory (the input gate i_t), as well as what will be included in the output (the output gate o_t).

The Gated Recurrent Unit (GRU) (Cho et al., 2014a) is a simplification of this approach, having only two gates by replacing the input and forget gates with an update gate u_t that simply erases memory whenever it is updating the state with new input. The GRU is thus a network that has fewer parameters, and has obtained similar experimental results as the original LSTM.

Gated recurrent networks have been used successfully for language modelling, sentiment analysis (Tang et al., 2015), textual entailment (Rocktäschel et al., 2016), and machine translation (Sutskever et al., 2014; Cho et al., 2014b).

3 Character RNN for morphological word relation transfer

In this work, we present a neural approach for the transfer of word relations. We use a deep recurrent neural network with GRU cells that take the raw character-sequences as input. In the proposed model, the demo relation $R_{demo} = (w_1, w_2)$ is encoded using one separate encoder RNN for each of the two words w_1 and w_2. The outputs of the demo encoders are fed into a fully connected layer, *"FC relation"*. The query word q is encoded separately using a third encoder RNN. The final output from the query encoder is concatenated with the output from *"FC relation"*, and fed via a second fully connected layer *"FC merge"* into the RNN decoder which generates the output sequence. The decoder employs a standard attention mechanism (Bahdanau et al., 2014) allowing access to the outputs at all locations of the query encoder. The whole model is similar to a sequence-to-sequence model used for translation, with the extra modules that encodes the demo relation. Figure 1 shows the architecture of the model.

The implementation of the model will be avail-

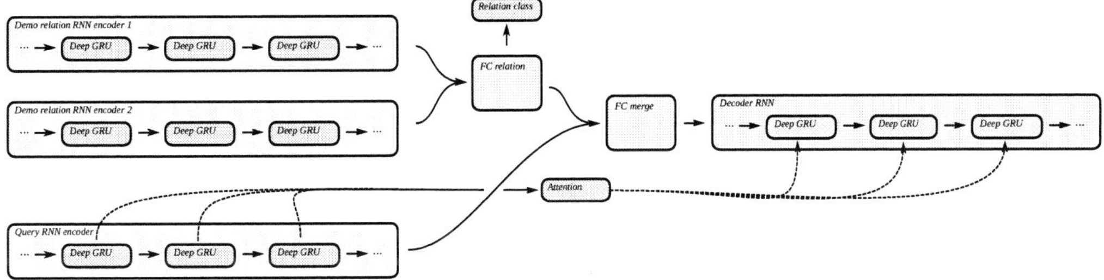

Figure 1: The layout of the proposed model. The demo relation is encoded using one separate encoder RNN for each of the two words. A fully connected layer follows the demo relation pair, with a softmax classification output layer, to guide the training. This speeds up the training drastically. The query word is encoded separately. the output from the fully connected relation layer is concatenated with the hidden state from the query encoder, and fed into the RNN decoder which generates the output while using an attention pointer to the query encoder.

able online, along with instructions on how to download the datasets.

3.1 Learning the relation type as an auxiliary training task

Since we are interested in how hard it is for the model to learn morphological relations without a signal representing the relation explicitly, we investigated a multitask learning setup where the prediction of the type of the relation is an auxiliary task. The purpose of this approach is that the auxiliary task could help the model learn a useful intermediate representation that facilitates the generation of the output string. We implemented this as a softmax classification output layer that was attached to the *"FC relation"*, and trained it to predict a label for the type of relation. We stress that this information is not available to the model during evaluation.

4 Experimental setup

This section explains the setup of the empirical study of our model. How it is designed, trained, and evaluated.

4.1 Hyperparameters

The hyperparameters relevant to the proposed model are presented in Table 1. The hidden size parameter decides the dimensionality of all RNN parts of the model, as well as the character embedding size. The final configuration amounted to hidden size: 100, depth: 2, initial learning rate: 1×10^{-3}, L2 weight decay parameter 5×10^{-5}, and drop probability 0.0. In the dropout experi-

ments, dropout were applied to encoder RNN outputs, and to the fully connected layers.

Hyperparameter	Explored	Selected
Hidden size	50-350	100
Depth	1-2	2
Learning rate		1×10^{-3}
L2 weight decay		5×10^{-5}
Drop probability	0.5, 0.0	0.0

Table 1: Hyperparameters in the model.

4.2 Datasets

The model was trained and evaluated on words in English and Swedish. In both languages, a total of seven relations, and their corresponding inverse relations, were considered:

- singular–plural for nouns, e.g. *dog–dogs*
- base form–comparative for adjectives, e.g. *high–higher*
- base form–superlative for adjectives, e.g. *high–highest*
- comparative–superlative for adjectives, e.g. *higher–highest*
- infinitive–past for verbs, e.g. *sit–sat*
- infinitive–present for verbs, e.g. *sit–sits*
- infinitive–progressive for verbs (English), e.g. *sit–sitting*
- active infinitive–passive infinitive for verbs (Swedish), e.g. *äta–ätas* 'eat–be eaten'

For English, the word list with inflected froms from the SCOWL project was downloaded[1]. In the

---

[1] See http://wordlist.aspell.net/.

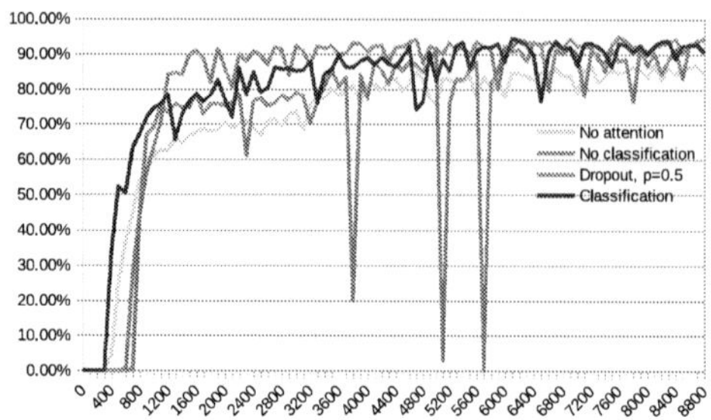

Figure 2: Prediction accuracy on the English validation set during training when using the auxiliary classification loss signal and when not using it.

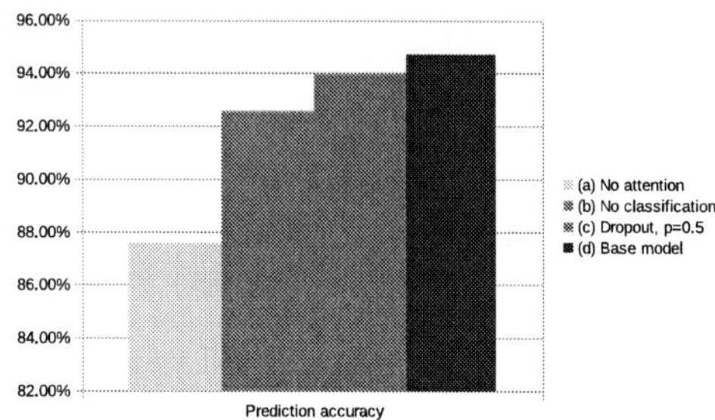

Figure 3: Prediction accuracy on English test set: (a) without attention mechanism, (b) when not using the auxiliary classification loss signal, (c) using dropout, and (d) using all standard values, (see Section 4.1).

English data, 25,052 nouns, 1,433 adjectives, and 7,806 verbs were used for training. For each class, 200 words were used for validation, and 200 for testing. For Swedish, words were extracted from SALDO (Borin et al., 2013). In the Swedish data, 64,460 nouns, 12,507 adjectives, and 7,764 verbs were used for training. The same size of validation and test sets were used.

4.3 Training

Training was done with backpropagation through time (BPTT) and minibatch learning with the Adam optimizer (Kingma and Ba, 2015). Training duration was decided using early stopping (Wang et al., 1994).

4.4 Evaluation

To evaluate the performance of the model, the datasets were split into training, validation, and test sets. Where nothing else is specified, reported numbers are prediction accuracy. This is the frac-

Size	English	Swedish	English & Swedish
350	90.3%	81.6%	82.3%
150	93.3%	84.1%	87.4%
100	**94.7%**	**88.3%**	**89.9%**
50	90.9%	83.1%	88.0%

Table 2: Prediction accuracy of the proposed model using different hidden sizes. Column labels denote training set: the *English & Swedish* model were simultaneously trained on both languages, and has no explicit signal about the language it is seeing, the other columns show results for models trained on only one language.

Size	English	Swedish	English & Swedish
350	85.3%	79.3%	82.3%
150	88.0%	86.9%	87.4%
100	**90.6%**	**89.3%**	**89.9%**
50	87.9%	88.1%	88.0%

Table 3: Prediction accuracy of the proposed model trained using both English and Swedish simultaneously. Column labels here denotes test dataset: English, Swedish, and combined.

tion of predictions that were exactly matching the target words.

5 Results

This section presents the results of the experimental evaluation of the system. Table 2 shows prediction accuracy on the test set for different hidden sizes, and for different training sets: *English*, *Swedish*, and *English & Swedish* (trained simultaneously in the same model). These are evaluated on the test set in the same language as the training set. Table 3 shows prediction accuracy on the different test sets (*English*, *Swedish*, and *English & Swedish*), for the same model, trained simultaneously on *English & Swedish*. The model trained on the combined training data (both English and Swedish) performs slightly better on the Swedish test-data (89.3% prediction accuracy compared to 88.3%).

Figure 2 shows the prediction accuracy on validation during the normal training procedure with auxiliary training *(Classification)*, without the auxiliary training *(No classification)*, and using dropout with drop probability 0.5 *(Dropout)*. The auxiliary output drastically speeds up training, to the point where we haven't obtained the same

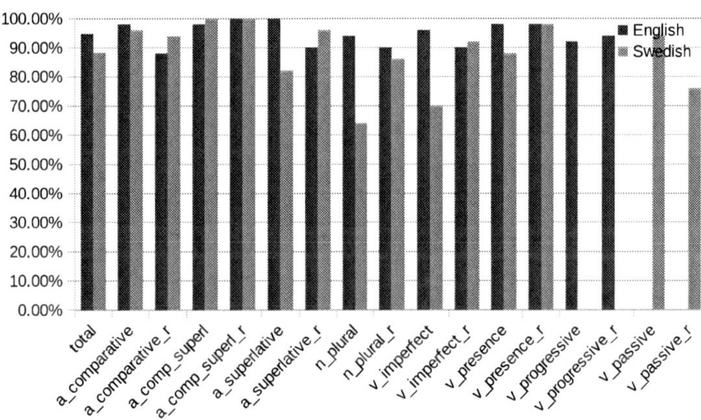

Figure 4: Results for all relations (total), and for each specific relation. One can see the difference between English and Swedish for plural forms of nouns, where Swedish can be more complex, and harder to learn.

performance without it. While the dropout seems to stabilize the performance of the model somewhat during training, we obtained the best validation performance without it. The final prediction accuracy results for the test set can be seen in Figure 3, illustrating once again, that the performance is best using the auxiliary training task, reaching an accuracy of 94.7% for English.

Figure 3 also includes a comparison between the different training architectures evaluated on the English test set. Whereas it is surprising that dropout does not help, both the attention mechanism and the auxiliary training objective are clearly helping the model learn and perform well. However, it is a positive result that the model that does not use the auxiliary task is still able to reach a high accuracy, as that type of supervision might not be available in low-resource situations.

Figure 4 separates the performance for each relation type, showing that our model obtains 100% test set accuracy for several classes, such as the transform from comparative to superlative for both English and Swedish, while dropping as low as to 64% for the singular-to-plural relation in Swedish, a relation that shows more complex patterns: while English nouns almost exclusively form the plural with -s, Swedish nouns are divided into two genders, each of which has several declension patterns (e.g. *-er*, *-ar*, *-or*, *-n*), and are also affected by processes such as umlaut (e.g. *fot–fötter*) and syncope (e.g. *nyckel–nycklar*).

6 Related work

The benefits of character based RNNs have been demonstrated in a number of works. (Graves, 2013) demonstrated how a character-based LSTM network could generate Wikipedia content with the markup. (Kim et al., 2016) presented a character-aware language model working with characters, but computing a distribution over words. Some work has tried to leverage the strengts of character-based RNNs, while combatting its main weakness; that character sequences tend to get much longer than the corresponding word sequences. (Luong and Manning, 2016) presented a neural machine translation (NMT) system using character RNNs only for OOV words, dropping the RNN output into a conventional word-based NMT system. They demonstrated that the resulting character-based word embeddings showed the same properties as the embeddings trained on word-level, having semantically similar words close in the embedding space. (Sennrich et al., 2016) proposed an NMT system that used the Byte-Pair Encoding (BPE), initially an algorithm to compress strings and represent frequent substrings with compacter symbols, to create a sub-word-level vocabulary. The authors mention that this can be seen as a compressed character-based model. (Kann and Schütze, 2016) proposed a character-based neural model for morphological inflection and reinflection. Both source word and tags were encoded using a special alphabet using one encoder RNN. The paper was the winner in the

SIGMORPHON 2016 shared task (Cotterell et al., 2016). This task has a similar goal to ours, but the input is a query word along with the source and target tags for the morphological forms. This is a simpler task, as their system does not need to find out the forms from examples.

7 Discussion and conclusions

In this paper, we have presented a neural model that can learn to do *morphological relational reasoning* on a given query word q, given a demo relation consisting of a word in the two different forms (source form and desired target form). Our approach uses one character based encoder RNN for each of the three input words, and generates the output word as a character sequence. The model is able to generalize to unseen words as demonstrated by good prediction accuracy on the held-out test sets in both English and Swedish. We note that the model learns faster, and reaches a higher prediction accuracy using an auxiliary training task requiring the model to output a classification of the relation observed in the demo relation encoder RNN (see Figure 2 and Figure 3). When training the model on the combined training data (both English and Swedish) we obtain slightly better prediction accuracy on the Swedish test-data (89.3% compared to 88.3%). This may need more investigation, but it indicates that training the model in a multi-lingual setting is beneficial at least for some languages. A similar observation was made in (Firat et al., 2017): a neural machine translation system that obtains better results on low-resource languages when trained in a multi-lingual setting.

7.1 Future work

Our motivation for carrying out this work is that it would be applicable in situations where linguistic resources (e.g. morphological tables) might not be available, for instance in under-resourced and under-described languages. The current work has been limited to English and Swedish, two languages where morphological resources are abundant, but in future work we would like to evaluate our system with languages that are less well provided in terms of resources.

Furthermore, while our model has been able to successfully predict the correct form in the majority of cases in our experiments, our evaluation setup is still fairly close to a traditional reinflec-

tion scenario that relies on morphological features. A more challenging and interesting task would be a zero-shot scenario where the test data contains unseen relations and possibly even unseen morphemes. Such a setup could not possibly be handled by a feature-based model without providing external knowledge, but it would be interesting to investigate how successful an analogy-based approach would be in that case.

Acknowledgments

RJ was supported by the Swedish Research Council under grant 2013–4944. OM was supported by Swedish Foundation for Strategic Research (SSF) under grant IIS11-0089.

References

Dzmitry Bahdanau, Kyunghyun Cho, and Yoshua Bengio. 2014. Neural machine translation by jointly learning to align and translate. *arXiv preprint arXiv:1409.0473* .

Yoshua Bengio, Patrice Simard, and Paolo Frasconi. 1994. Learning long-term dependencies with gradient descent is difficult. *Neural Networks, IEEE Transactions on* 5(2):157–166.

Lars Borin, Markus Forsberg, and Lennart Lönngren. 2013. SALDO: a touch of yin to WordNet's yang. *Language Resources and Evaluation* 47(4):1191–1211.

Kyunghyun Cho, Bart van Merrienboer, Dzmitry Bahdanau, and Yoshua Bengio. 2014a. On the properties of neural machine translation: Encoder–decoder approaches. In *Proceedings of SSST-8, Eighth Workshop on Syntax, Semantics and Structure in Statistical Translation*. Association for Computational Linguistics, Doha, Qatar, pages 103–111. http://www.aclweb.org/anthology/W14-4012.

Kyunghyun Cho, Bart van Merrienboer, aglar Glehre, Dzmitry Bahdanau, Fethi Bougares, Holger Schwenk, and Yoshua Bengio. 2014b. Learning phrase representations using rnn encoder-decoder for statistical machine translation. In Alessandro Moschitti, Bo Pang, and Walter Daelemans, editors, *EMNLP*. ACL, pages 1724–1734. http://dblp.uni-trier.de/db/conf/emnlp/emnlp2014.html#ChoMGBBSB14.

Ryan Cotterell, Christo Kirov, John Sylak-Glassman, David Yarowsky, Jason Eisner, and Mans Hulden. 2016. The SIGMORPHON 2016 shared task – morphological reinflection. In *Proceedings of the 14th Annual SIGMORPHON Workshop on Computational Research in Phonetics, Phonology, and Morphology*. pages 10–22.

Orhan Firat, Kyunghyun Cho, Baskaran Sankaran, Fatos T Yarman Vural, and Yoshua Bengio. 2017. Multi-way, multilingual neural machine translation. *Computer Speech & Language* 45:236–252.

Alex Graves. 2013. Generating sequences with recurrent neural networks. *arXiv preprint arXiv:1308.0850* .

Sepp Hochreiter. 1998. The vanishing gradient problem during learning recurrent neural nets and problem solutions. *International Journal of Uncertainty, Fuzziness and Knowledge-Based Systems* 6(02):107–116.

Katharina Kann and Hinrich Schütze. 2016. MED: The LMU system for the SIGMORPHON 2016 shared task on morphological reinflection. In *Proceedings of the 14th Annual SIGMORPHON Workshop on Computational Research in Phonetics, Phonology, and Morphology*. pages 62–70.

Yoon Kim, Yacine Jernite, David Sontag, and Alexander M Rush. 2016. Character-aware neural language models. In *Thirtieth AAAI Conference on Artificial Intelligence*.

Diederik Kingma and Jimmy Ba. 2015. Adam: A method for stochastic optimization. *International Conference on Learning Representations* .

Minh-Thang Luong and Christopher D. Manning. 2016. Achieving open vocabulary neural machine translation with hybrid word-character models. In *Proceedings of the 54th Annual Meeting of the Association for Computational Linguistics (Volume 1: Long Papers)*. Association for Computational Linguistics, Berlin, Germany, pages 1054–1063. http://www.aclweb.org/anthology/P16-1100.

Tim Rocktäschel, Edward Grefenstette, Karl Moritz Hermann, Tomáš Kočiský, and Phil Blunsom. 2016. Reasoning about entailment with neural attention. In *International Conference on Learning Representations*.

Jürgen Schmidhuber and Sepp Hochreiter. 1997. Long short-term memory. *Neural computation* 7(8):1735–1780.

Rico Sennrich, Barry Haddow, and Alexandra Birch. 2016. Neural machine translation of rare words with subword units. In *Proceedings of the 54th Annual Meeting of the Association for Computational Linguistics (Volume 1: Long Papers)*. Association for Computational Linguistics, Berlin, Germany, pages 1715–1725. http://www.aclweb.org/anthology/P16-1162.

Ilya Sutskever, Oriol Vinyals, and Quoc V Le. 2014. Sequence to sequence learning with neural networks. In *Advances in neural information processing systems*. pages 3104–3112.

Duyu Tang, Bing Qin, and Ting Liu. 2015. Document modeling with gated recurrent neural network for sentiment classification. In *Proceedings of the 2015 Conference on Empirical Methods in Natural Language Processing*. pages 1422–1432.

C. Wang, S. S. Venkatesh, and J. S. Judd. 1994. Optimal stopping and effective machine complexity in learning. In *Advances in Neural Information Processing Systems 6*. Morgan Kaufmann.

Xiang Zhang, Junbo Zhao, and Yann LeCun. 2015. Character-level convolutional networks for text classification. In *Advances in Neural Information Processing Systems*. pages 649–657.

Glyph-aware Embedding of Chinese Characters

Falcon Z. Dai[*] and **Zheng Cai**[*]
Toyota Technological Institute at Chicago
dai@ttic.edu, jontsai@ttic.edu

Abstract

Given the advantage and recent success of English character-level and subword-unit models in several NLP tasks, we consider the equivalent modeling problem for Chinese. Chinese script is logographic and many Chinese logograms are composed of common substructures that provide semantic, phonetic and syntactic hints. In this work, we propose to explicitly incorporate the visual appearance of a character's glyph in its representation, resulting in a novel glyph-aware embedding of Chinese characters. Being inspired by the success of convolutional neural networks in computer vision, we use them to incorporate the spatio-structural patterns of Chinese glyphs as rendered in raw pixels. In the context of two basic Chinese NLP tasks of language modeling and word segmentation, the model learns to represent each character's task-relevant semantic and syntactic information in the character-level embedding.

1 Introduction

Recently, in combination with deep learning, character-level and subword-unit-level models has achieved the state-of-the-art performance in various natural language processing (NLP) tasks involving Western languages (Wu et al., 2016), we consider the equivalent modeling problem for solving NLP tasks in Chinese. Unlike English script which is *alphabetic* with a small alphabet, Chinese script is *logographic* with a large set of characters which are meaningful individually. According to *Table of General Standard Characters* (通用规范汉字表) compiled by the Chinese government in 2013, there are 3,500 level-1 (being the most common) characters and more than 8,105 characters in total (Wikipedia, 2017). At the same time, it is not correct to treat Chinese characters as equivalent to English words because the distribution of Chinese characters deviate markedly from Zipf's law (Zipf, 1935; Shtrikman, 1994). Furthermore, there is evidence suggesting that segmented Chinese words, - some of them are unigrams -, distribute according to Zipf's law (Xiao, 2008). Arguably, the closest equivalent linguistic unit in English corresponding to a Chinese character is a subword unit, i.e., word fragments.

Furthermore, there is a strong case for modeling at character-level for task involving Chinese corpora, since Chinese text is usually written without word boundaries to indicate the *segmentation* of characters into words. As a consequence, word-segmented corpora is rare. Traditionally, systems are designed to process words as input, so often, a separately trained or hand crafted routine would first segment the contiguous sequence of characters into words as part of the preprocessing. However, this pipeline design might unnecessarily accumulate error due to segmentation ambiguity that can be resolved in a later stage. The trend of *end-to-end* training of differentiable, neural network-based models also enables training character-level models jointly with the rest of the system under the task objective. It is well-known that many Chinese characters' written form, their *glyphs*, share common sub-structures and some of these sub-structure are informative of the semantics, syntactic role and phonetics of the characters. For example, for semantics, 雨 (rain) 雪 (snow) 雹 (hail) 雷 (thunder) all have a sub-structure 雨, which commonly denote meteorological phenomena.[1] For

───────────
[*] These authors contributed equally and their names are randomly ordered

───────────
[1] A sub-structure such as 雨 in 雪 is called a *radical*.

Proceedings of the First Workshop on Subword and Character Level Models in NLP, pages 64–69,
Copenhagen, Denmark, September 7, 2017. ©2017 Association for Computational Linguistics.

syntactic roles, 打 (hit) 提 (lift) 抓 (grab) all contain 扌 which is indicative of a verb. For phonetics, 乙 (yǐ) 亿 (yì) 忆 (yì) all share 乙. However, as far as we are aware of, at the time of our work[2], there is no study that explicitly exploits the *spatio-structural* information of a Chinese character's glyph for NLP tasks.[3] In this work, we explore the effect of incorporating glyphs as additional features in the context of two common Chinese NLP tasks, segmentation and language modeling, resulting in a novel *glyph-aware embedding* of Chinese characters. This work's major contributions are

- a novel character embedding model that explicitly incorporates visual appearance of Chinese characters.

- new state-of-the-art results on a segmentation benchmark task.

2 Hypotheses

We hypothesize that the semantic and syntactic information of sub-glyph structures can help improve the character embeddings and thus improve performance in Chinese NLP tasks.

Intuitively, representing each character only by their ID's implies that any pair of characters are as distinct as any other pair. This ignores any common sub-glyph structures shared by characters. Therefore incorporating the glyph's visual information we should be able to generalize knowledge learned about a character to another via their shared sub-glyph structures.

However, this hypothesis is not trivial because there are many Chinese characters that share strikingly similar visual appearances yet not their meanings. For example, 土 (soil) ↔ 士 (roughly means -er as fighter translates to 斗 (fight) 士), and 人 (person) ↔ 入 (enter). By identifying a character with only its visual appearance, we are vulnerable to this new source of ambiguity which can harm performance. Due to this concern, we also include a mixed embedding in our experiments which combine both ID and glyph representation.

3 Method

In keeping with the common neural network model architectures, we decided to feed the glyph as an input to a feed-forward neural network (FNN) model, an *embedder*, that outputs an *embedding vector* which, in both the segmentation task and the language modeling task, is then consumed by a recurrent neural network to make predictions. In order to compare the proposed glyph-aware embeddings with the glyph-unaware embeddings, we shall keep the recurrent neural network (RNN) architecture fixed and only change the embedder in our experiments.

Considering that there are many different layouts for sub-glyph structures[4], and the same radical can appear at different positions[5], we think the most promising representation that preserves both the *identities* and the *spatial arrangement* of sub-structures is to use the raw pixels of a glyph.

Being inspired by the success of *convolutional neural networks* (CNN) (LeCun et al., 1995) in learning feature representation in computer vision (Krizhevsky et al., 2012), we used CNN to implement the embedder (see Figure 1). We believe that the spatial translational invariance induced by CNN's filter structure is particularly suited for modeling radicals that can appear at different locations of a glyph. After the CNN, a fully connected layer outputs an embedding vector of some dimension k. To apply our method, we first render the glyph for a character using a font file[6] and then feed the glyph as a gray-scale image into the CNN embedder.

We implemented our models and experiments efficiently with Tensorflow (Abadi et al., 2016). In particular, we cached rendered glyphs to reduce repeated render calls of the same character by 1,000 times. We open-source our implementation[7] for replicability

4 Results

Chinese language modeling

Following the common approach in language modeling (LM), we model the likelihood of a sentence

---

[2]Since then, we discovered two independent, concurrent studies with approaches similar to ours by Liu et al. (2017) and Costa-jussà et al. (2017).

[3]A character's visual appearance is essential in solving hand-writing recognition tasks which are challenges in computer vision.

[4]昌 has a vertical layout, 明, horizontal, and 晶, compound.

[5]the radical 口 (mouth) can appear on the left 喊, top 员, bottom 含, inner 向.

[6]We used Google's free Noto font (Google Inc.) throughout this work including the Chinese characters rendered in this paper.

[7]http://github.com/falcondai/chinese-char-lm

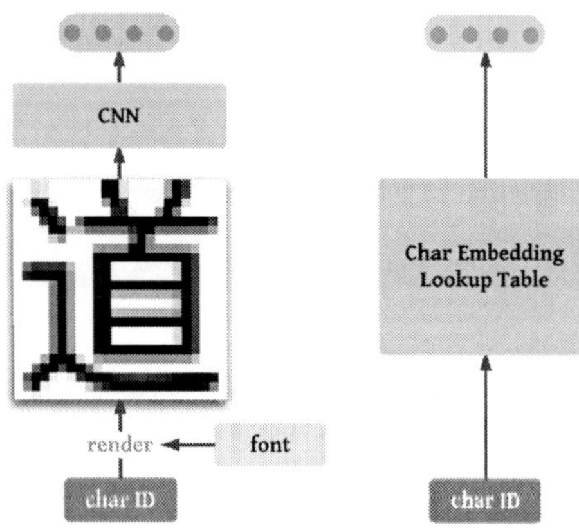

Figure 1: Left: our proposed glyph-aware CNN embedder. Right: the commonly used embedding model (we refer to this as ID embedder). The trainable parameters are labeled in orange.

as

$$p(c_1, \cdots, c_n) = p(c_1) \prod_{i=2}^{n} p(c_i | c_1, \cdots, c_{i-1})$$

where c_i is the i-th character in a sentence of n characters. The conditional distribution of $p(c_i | c_1, \cdots, c_{i-1})$ is modeled as a gated recurrent unit (GRU) (Chung et al., 2014) together with an embedder. In all the experiments, we used a GRU with a 128-dimensional hidden state, and 300-dimensional embedding vectors for all embedders. For the CNN embedder, we use a two layer CNN: 32 (7, 7) filters with (2, 2) stride in the first layer, 16 (5, 5) filters (2, 2) stride in the second layer, and a fully-connected layer at the end. For all the layers, we use ReLU non-linearity throughout (Nair and Hinton, 2010). For the linear embedder, we used only one fully-connected layer. For the last row "ID + CNN embedder" in Table. 1, we combine the embedding vectors output by ID and CNN embedders via vector addition. In all the runs, we limited the vocabulary size to 4000 with one unknown class.

We experimented with language modeling on the Microsoft Research dataset (MSR) from the Second International Chinese Word Segmentation Bakeoff (Emerson, 2005). First, we should note that the CNN embedder outperformed the linear embedder by a large margin (see the second and the third row in Table. 1. This is expected as the CNN is more suitable for modeling image data. Second,

embedders	test perplexity
ID embedder	**47.53**
linear embedder	71.51
CNN embedder	55.51
ID + CNN embedder	**47.75**

Table 1: LM performance of different embedders on the test split of MSR.

the ID embedder (see the first row in Table. 1) remains a very strong baseline and the mixed embedder is only as good as the ID embedder by itself (see the fourth row in Table. 1). It seems that CNN embedder did *not* provide extra information useful for the task.

Chinese word segmentation

We use Peking University dataset (PKU) and Microsoft Research dataset (MSR) from the Second International Chinese Word Segmentation Bakeoff (Emerson, 2005) to compare the proposed CNN embedder with the ID embedder. We formulated the segmentation task as a structured prediction problem of predicting whether to insert word boundary behind a character for each character given the whole input sentence. An example would be:

这 是 一句 话 。
1 1 0 1 1 1

We experimented with both single-directional GRU and bidirectional long short-term memory (LSTM) recurrent networks (Graves and Schmidhuber, 2005; Hochreiter and Schmidhuber, 1997; Schuster and Paliwal, 1997) as the sequence prediction models in our experiments (RNN segmentor). (see Table. 2 and Table. 3). RNN segmentor takes sequence of embeddings from embedder. For the CNN embedder, we used a single layer ReLU-gated CNN: 16 (5,5) filters with (2,2) stride and a fully-connected layer to output a 100-dimensional embedding vector at the end. For the RNN segmentor, the hidden unit is set to be 100 dimensional with a fully-connected layer mapping the output hidden state to a binary prediction at each character. Overall, on both PKU and MSR, the proposed mixed embedder and bidirectional LSTM achieved the best performance outperforming the previous state-of-the-art on by a significant margin. Similar to the LM experiments, we use a vocabulary of 4000 and one unknown class.

RNN segmentors	embedder	precision	recall	F1
GRU	ID	87.41	84.14	85.75
	CNN	90.03	**89.54**	**89.78**
	ID + CNN	**90.46**	88.80	89.62
Bidirectional LSTM	ID	96.06	94.66	95.36
	CNN	94.73	94.88	94.81
	ID + CNN	**96.91**	**95.41**	**96.15**
NWS (Cai and Zhao, 2016)		95.5	94.9	95.16

Table 2: segmentation results on PKU dataset

RNN segmentors	embedder	precision	recall	F1
GRU	ID	86.97	85.25	86.10
	CNN	**89.93**	86.79	**88.33**
	ID + CNN	88.81	**87.19**	88.00
Bidirectional LSTM	ID	97.34	**97.25**	97.29
	CNN	97.07	96.98	97.03
	ID + CNN	**97.82**	97.04	**97.43**
NWS (Cai and Zhao, 2016)		96.1	96.7	96.4

Table 3: segmentation results on MSR dataset

We use Adam (Kingma and Ba, 2014) optimizer throughout all our experiments.

5 Analysis

Due to the lack of improvement of the proposed mixed embedder over the ID embedder in the language modeling task, we suspect that the CNN embedder is under-trained. Unlike a digit class in MNIST (LeCun et al., 2010) which has 6,000 training examples, given one font, a character only has one glyph and every sub-glyph structure appears on average in only about 40 characters. Thus we suspect that the variability in input to the CNN is too limited. Modeling after common image augmentation technique (Krizhevsky et al., 2012), we applied random jitters, i.e., 2D translation with $\Delta x, \Delta y \in \{-2, -1, 0, +1, +2\}$, to the input glyphs at training time. This increases the input variations by 25-fold but the perplexity degrades slightly to 49.66.

Since we mix the ID embedding and CNN embedding by summation in the proposed mixed embedder, the norm of each component embedding determines the relative importance of that representation in the resulting embedding. In Figure. 2, we observe that the CNN embeddings distribute differently in the trained segmentation model and the trained language modeling model. In the case of language modeling, the norm of CNN embeddings is squashed suggesting that CNN embedding is largely ignored.

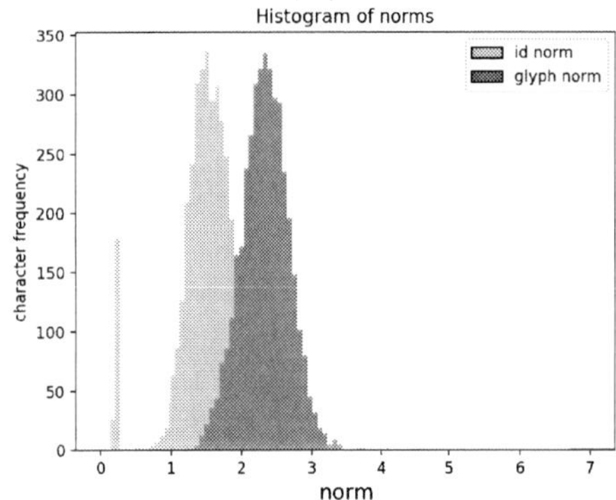

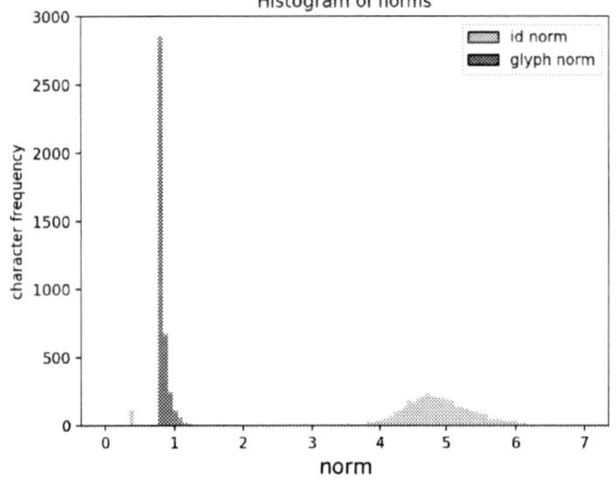

Figure 2: The distribution of the Frobenius norm of ID embeddings (id norm) and CNN embeddings (glyph norm) from the mixed embedder. Top: the segmentation task. Bottom: the language modeling task.

6 Discussion

It should be noted that the number of parameters of the proposed CNN embedder is different than that of the ID embedder. Suppose the dimensionality of the embedding vectors is K, and the vocabulary size is N, the CNN embedder has $O(N + K)$ many parameters: $O(K)$ many *trainable* parameters and $O(N)$ glyphs rendered from a font file. In contrast, the ID embedder has $O(N K)$ many parameters, all of which are *trainable*. This means that the CNN embedder is a more compact representation with competitive performance as the ID embedder.

Related work

Shi et al. (2015) represented a character by its radicals based on Wubi input method but this ignores the scales and spatial arrangement of each radical which are present in our rendered glyphs.

It came to our late attention that independently, Liu et al. (2017) considered the same character-level modeling problem and experimented with vanilla CNN models almost identical to ours. They evaluated their method on a new document classification task instead of the commonly considered tasks or benchmarks we considered in this work. Consistent with their findings, we also observed similar effects of CNN embedder, ID embedder and mixed embedder in our tasks. Our mixed embedded corresponds roughly to their early fusion model. Costa-jussà et al. (2017) also considered incorporating Chinese glyphs as additional features in their Chinese-Spanish machine translation system and their modeling approach corresponds roughly to our linear embedder.

Future work

We hope to delve deeper into the cause of the CNN embedder's low performance in the LM task. In particular, we want to experiment with using bag-of-stroke prediction in a multi-task loss to provide CNN with extra supervision during training. Furthermore, we have only explored two NLP tasks that emphasize semantic and syntactic information in this work. In the future, we hope to explore tasks that requires more phonetic information to do well, such as phoneme prediction.

7 Conclusion

Our experiments show that glyph-aware embedding can improve performance in some Chinese NLP tasks, in particular, the word segmentation task. Further studies are needed to understand the usefulness of glyph features in a more comprehensive way. However, given the visual ambiguity inherent in Chinese characters and the difficulty to interpret neural network models, any further research that uses glyph features and deep learning methods should exercise caution when measuring and verifying the contribution of the glyph features.

References

Martín Abadi, Ashish Agarwal, Paul Barham, Eugene Brevdo, Zhifeng Chen, Craig Citro, Greg S. Corrado, Andy Davis, Jeffrey Dean, Matthieu Devin, and others. 2016. Tensorflow: Large-scale machine learning on heterogeneous distributed systems. *CoRR*.

Deng Cai and Hai Zhao. 2016. Neural word segmentation learning for chinese. *CoRR*.

Junyoung Chung, Caglar Gulcehre, KyungHyun Cho, and Yoshua Bengio. 2014. Empirical evaluation of gated recurrent neural networks on sequence modeling. *CoRR*.

Marta R Costa-jussà, David Aldón, and José AR Fonollosa. 2017. Chinese–spanish neural machine translation enhanced with character and word bitmap fonts. *Machine Translation*, pages 1–13.

Tom Emerson. 2005. Second international chinese word segmentation bakeoff. http://sighan.cs.uchicago.edu/bakeoff2005/. Accessed: 2017-04-15.

Google Inc. Google noto fonts. https://www.google.com/get/noto/help/cjk/. Accessed: 2017-07-21.

Alex Graves and Jürgen Schmidhuber. 2005. Framewise phoneme classification with bidirectional lstm and other neural network architectures. *Neural Networks*, 18(5):602–610.

Sepp Hochreiter and Jürgen Schmidhuber. 1997. Long short-term memory. *Neural computation*, 9(8):1735–1780.

Diederik Kingma and Jimmy Ba. 2014. Adam: A method for stochastic optimization. *CoRR*.

Alex Krizhevsky, Ilya Sutskever, and Geoffrey E Hinton. 2012. ImageNet Classification with Deep Convolutional Neural Networks. In F. Pereira, C. J. C. Burges, L. Bottou, and K. Q. Weinberger, editors, *Advances in Neural Information Processing Systems 25*, pages 1097–1105. Curran Associates, Inc.

Yann LeCun, Yoshua Bengio, et al. 1995. Convolutional networks for images, speech, and time series. *The handbook of brain theory and neural networks*, 3361(10):1995.

Yann LeCun, Corinna Cortes, and Christopher JC Burges. 2010. Mnist handwritten digit database. *AT&T Labs [Online]. Available: http://yann.lecun.com/exdb/mnist*, 2.

Frederick Liu, Han Lu, Chieh Lo, and Graham Neubig. 2017. Learning Character-level Compositionality with Visual Features. *CoRR*. ArXiv: 1704.04859.

Vinod Nair and Geoffrey E Hinton. 2010. Rectified linear units improve restricted boltzmann machines. In *Proceedings of the 27th international conference on machine learning (ICML-10)*, pages 807–814.

Mike Schuster and Kuldip K Paliwal. 1997. Bidirectional recurrent neural networks. *IEEE Transactions on Signal Processing*, 45(11):2673–2681.

Xinlei Shi, Junjie Zhai, Xudong Yang, Zehua Xie, and Chao Liu. 2015. Radical embedding: Delving deeper to chinese radicals. In *Proceedings of the 53rd Annual Meeting of the Association for Computational Linguistics and the 7th International Joint Conference on Natural Language Processing (Volume 2: Short Papers)*, pages 594–598, Beijing, China. Association for Computational Linguistics.

S. Shtrikman. 1994. Some comments on Zipf's law for the Chinese language. *Journal of Information Science*, 20(2):142–143.

Wikipedia. 2017. Table of general standard chinese characters — wikipedia, the free encyclopedia. [Online; accessed 21-July-2017].

Yonghui Wu, Mike Schuster, Zhifeng Chen, Quoc V. Le, Mohammad Norouzi, Wolfgang Macherey, Maxim Krikun, Yuan Cao, Qin Gao, Klaus Macherey, Jeff Klingner, Apurva Shah, Melvin Johnson, Xiaobing Liu, Łukasz Kaiser, Stephan Gouws, Yoshikiyo Kato, Taku Kudo, Hideto Kazawa, Keith Stevens, George Kurian, Nishant Patil, Wei Wang, Cliff Young, Jason Smith, Jason Riesa, Alex Rudnick, Oriol Vinyals, Greg Corrado, Macduff Hughes, and Jeffrey Dean. 2016. Google's neural machine translation system: Bridging the gap between human and machine translation. *CoRR*, abs/1609.08144.

Hang Xiao. 2008. On the Applicability of Zipf's Law in Chinese Word Frequency Distribution. *Journal of Chinese Language and Computing*, 18(1):33–46.

George K Zipf. 1935. The psychology of language. *NY Houghton-Mifflin*.

Exploring Cross-Lingual Transfer of Morphological Knowledge In Sequence-to-Sequence Models

Huiming Jin
Beihang University, China
huiming.jin.buaa@gmail.com

Katharina Kann
CIS
LMU Munich, Germany
kann@cis.lmu.de

Abstract

Multi-task training is an effective method to mitigate the data sparsity problem. It has recently been applied for cross-lingual transfer learning for paradigm completion—the task of producing inflected forms of lemmata—with sequence-to-sequence networks. However, it is still vague how the model transfers knowledge across languages, as well as if and which information is shared. To investigate this, we propose a set of data-dependent experiments using an existing encoder-decoder recurrent neural network for the task. Our results show that indeed the performance gains surpass a pure regularization effect and that knowledge about language and morphology can be transferred.

1 Introduction

Neural sequence-to-sequence models define the state of the art for paradigm completion (Cotterell et al., 2016, 2017; Kann and Schütze, 2016), the task of generating inflected forms of a lemma's paradigm, e.g., filling the empty fields in Table 1 using one of the non-empty fields.

However, those models are in general very data-hungry, and do not reach good performances in low-resource settings. Therefore, Kann et al. (2017) propose to leverage morphological knowledge from a high-resource language (*source language*) to improve paradigm completion in a closely related language with insufficient resources (*target language*). This is achieved by a form of multi-task learning – they train an encoder-decoder model simultaneously on training examples for both languages. While closer related languages seem to help more than distant ones, the mechanisms *how* this transfer works still

	Present		Past	
	Singular	Plural	Singular	Plural
1	*sueño*	*soñamos*	*soñé*	*soñamos*
2	*sueñas*	*???*	*soñaste*	*soñasteis*
3	*sueña*	*sueñan*	*soñó*	*???*

Table 1: Partial inflection table for indicative forms of the Spanish verb *soñar*.

remain largely obscure. Several possibilities exist: (i) learning of target tag specific word transformations from the high-resource language (**trans**); (ii) training of the character language model of the decoder (**LM**); (iii) learning a bias to copy a large part of the input (**copy**), since members of the same paradigm mostly share the same stem; (iv) a general regularization effect obtained by multi-task training (**reg**).

In this work, we intend to shed light on the way cross-lingual transfer learning for paradigm completion with an encoder-decoder model works, and will especially focus on the role of the character and tag embeddings. In particular we aim at answering the following questions: (i) What does the neural model learn from the tags of a high-resource language for the tags of a low-resource language? (ii) Is sharing an alphabet important for the transfer? (iii) How much of the transfer learning can be reduced to a regularization effect achieved by multi-task learning?

For our analysis, we present a set of detailed experiments for the target language Spanish [ES]. Source languages are either members of the Romance language family (Catalan [CA], French [FR], Italian [IT], Portuguese [PT]) of different levels of similarity to Spanish, cf. Table 2, or an unrelated language (Arabic [AR]). We show which parts of the information are learned from the characters or tags and discuss where sequences of letters or tags from a second language contribute to or restrain performance on the paradigm comple-

Proceedings of the First Workshop on Subword and Character Level Models in NLP, pages 70–75,
Copenhagen, Denmark, September 7, 2017. ©2017 Association for Computational Linguistics.

	PT	CA	IT	FR
similarity to ES	89%	85%	82%	75%

Table 2: Lexical similarities of Spanish and the Romance languages used for our experiments (Lewis, 2009).

tion task in the low-resource language.

2 Transfer Learning for Paradigm Completion

In this section, we describe cross-lingual transfer learning for morphology and the model used for it.

Cross-lingual transfer. Transfer learning for paradigm completion is much more language-specific than most semantic natural language processing tasks, like entity typing or machine translation. An extreme example is the infeasible task of transferring morphological knowledge from Chinese to Portuguese as Chinese does not make use of inflection at all. Even between two morphologically rich languages transfer is difficult if they are unrelated, since inflections often mark dissimilar subcategories and word forms do not share similarities.

However, Kann et al. (2017) show that transferring morphological knowledge from Spanish to Portuguese, two languages with similar morphology and 89% lexical similarity, works well and, more surprisingly, even supposedly very different languages like Arabic and Spanish can benefit from each other. They make this possible by training an encoder-decoder model and appending a special tag (i.e., embedding) for each language to the input of the system, similar to (Johnson et al., 2016). It is currently unclear, though, what the nature of this transfer is, motivating our work which explores this in more detail.

Model description. The model Kann et al. (2017) use and we explore in more detail here is an encoder-decoder recurrent neural network (RNN) with attention (Bahdanau et al., 2015). It is trained on maximizing the following log-likelihood:

$$\mathcal{L}(\boldsymbol{\theta}) = \sum_{(k, w_{\ell_t}) \in \mathcal{D}_t} \log p_{\boldsymbol{\theta}} \left(f_k[w_{\ell_t}] \mid \ell_t, w_{\ell_t}, t_k \right)$$
$$+ \sum_{(k, w_{\ell_s}) \in \mathcal{D}_s} \log p_{\boldsymbol{\theta}} \left(f_k[w_{\ell_s}] \mid \ell_s, w_{\ell_s}, t_k \right) \quad (1)$$

We denote the source training examples as $\mathcal{D}_s$ and the target training examples as $\mathcal{D}_s$. w_{ℓ_s} represents

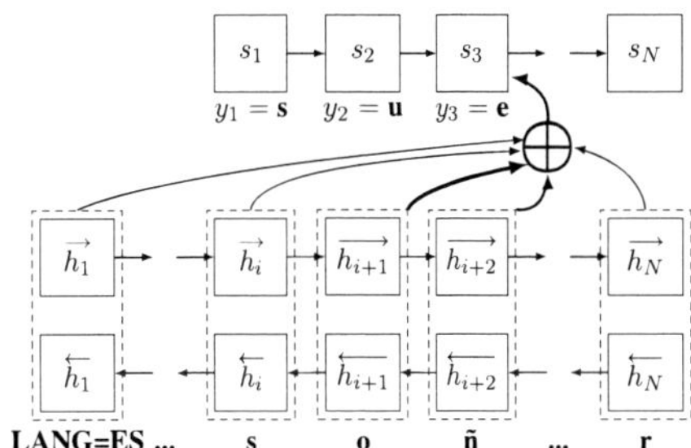

Figure 1: Overview of an encoder-decoder RNN, mapping the Spanish lemma *soñar* to the target form *sueña*. The thickness of the arrows towards the circled plus symbol corresponds to each *attention weight*. All tags in the input are omitted.

a lemma in a high-resource source language ℓ_s and w_{ℓ_t} represents a lemma in a low-resource target language ℓ_t. k represents a given slot in the paradigm and $f_k[w_\ell]$ is the inflected form of w_ℓ corresponding to the morphological tag t_k. The parameters θ of the model are tied for both the high-resource language and the low-resource language to enable transfer learning.

In detail, a bidirectional gated RNN is used to *encode* the input sequence, which consists of a language tag, morphological tags and characters of the input language. The decoder generates the output sequence from the characters of the same language, and consists of a unidirectional RNN with an attention mechanism over the encoder hidden states. Notably, the elements of the input and the output are represented by embeddings living in separate spaces.

Hyperparameters. Encoder and decoder RNNs have 100 hidden units and we use 300-dimensional embeddings. We train using ADADELTA (Zeiler, 2012) with minibatch size 20. All models for all experiments are trained for a maximum of 150 epochs. The best model is applied at test time.

3 Exploration of Transfer Learning

In order to answer the questions raised in the introduction, we conduct the following experiments.

3.1 Data

We use the Romance and Arabic language data from Kann et al. (2017). In particular, each training file contains $12,000$ high-resource examples mixed with 50 or 200 fixed Spanish instances. We

	trans	LM	copy	reg
l-ciph	X	X		
t-ciph	X			
l-emb	X	X	X	
t-emb	X			

Table 3: Expected effect of different modifications of the high-resource training data. Learning of the marked fields is likely to be influenced, descriptions in the text, cf. §1.

use the same development and test files for all experiments. Arabic is transcribed into Latin characters.

3.2 Experiments

Letter cipher (l-ciph). Let $\mathcal{C} = \mathcal{C}_{low} \cup \mathcal{C}_{high}$ be the union of the sets of all characters in the alphabets of the low-resource language and the high-resource language, respectively.[1] We define a bijective cipher function $f_{ciph} : \mathcal{C} \mapsto \mathcal{C}$, mapping each character to a different character, chosen at random. Then, we apply this function to the elements of the input and output words in the high-resource language and train the model on this modified data. The low-resource samples in train, dev and test remain unchanged.

We expect this to have the following effects: (i) languages do not share affixes anymore; (ii) as we use the same embeddings for the changed and unchanged characters, the model might learn *wrong* affixes for tags; (iii) an incorrect character language model could be learned; and (iv) a general bias to copy should remain unchanged.

Tag cipher (t-ciph). We further consider the union of the sets of all morphological tags existing in the low- and high-resource languages: $\mathcal{T} = \mathcal{T}_{low} \cup \mathcal{T}_{high}$. We define a bijective cipher function $f_{ciph} : \mathcal{T} \mapsto \mathcal{T}$. We then apply this function to all tags in the high-resource language input and train a new model. The low-resource examples in train, dev and test are not changed.

We expect this to: (i) disturb the learning of correspondences between target tags and output characters; (ii) not influence anything else.

Language-dependent letter embeddings (l-emb). We now use different embeddings for the characters of the two languages. This corresponds to a setting where the source and target languages do not share the same vocabulary.

This should result in: (i) making it impossible for the model to learn which affixes have to be produced for which tag, maybe resulting in benefits for more distant and worse performance for extremely close languages; and (ii) transfer of the decoder's character language model getting impossible.

Language-dependent tag embedding (t-emb). Additionally, we also experiment with different embeddings for the morphological tags in different languages.

We expect the following to happen: (i) the model can learn a character language model in the output, which might be good for related and bad for more distant languages; (ii) it should not be possible for the model to learn a correspondence between tags and characters in the output sequence; and (iii) the model cannot get information about tags in the low-resource language from the high-resource language's examples.

We additionally perform two last experiments:
Language-dependent letter embeddings with separation symbol (l-emb-sep). This is the same as l-emb, but we introduce a new separation symbol SEP between the tags and the characters, solving the problem that it is not clear where the tag ends and the word starts. We expect equal or better performance than for l-emb.
Language-dependent tag embedding with separation symbol (t-emb-sep). This is equivalent to t-emb, but we again insert a new separation symbol SEP between the tags and the input word's characters. We expect equal or better performance than for t-emb.

3.3 Intuition

In Table 3 we display an overview of which of the working mechanisms of cross-lingual transfer learning we expect to be effected by which changes to the high-resource training data. Depending on the relationship between the source and the target language, e.g., whether they use the same affixes to express the same morphosyntactic properties, we anticipate stronger or weaker effects. The regularization effect should not be influenced by our changes to the data.

3.4 Results and Analysis

For the low-resource training set of size 50, the models with the original setup and without transfer perform best and worst, respectively. However,

---

[1] Note that for the languages considered in our experiments we have $\mathcal{C}_{low} \approx \mathcal{C}_{high}$.

	50						200					
	ES (+0)	AR	FR	IT	CA	PT	ES (+0)	AR	FR	IT	CA	PT
original	**.0075(.00)**	.1496(.01)	.4277(.02)	**.5161(.01)**	**.6216(.02)**	**.4755(.01)**	.5012(.03)	.6596(.01)	.7080(.01)	.7713(.01)	.8142(.01)	.6885(.01)
l-ciph	-	.1209(.01)	.1837(.03)	.3207(.02)	.2937(.02)	.1005(.06)	-	.6626(.01)	.6491(.02)	.7032(.02)	.7151(.00)	.6155(.03)
t-ciph	-	.1208(.02)	.3491(.01)	.4823(.01)	.4963(.02)	.3623(.02)	-	.6405(.01)	.7058(.01)	.7768(.01)	.8040(.01)	.6317(.01)
l-emb	-	.1353(.06)	.2905(.01)	.2842(.09)	.4327(.03)	.2723(.06)	-	**.7109(.02)**	.7048(.01)	.7412(.01)	.7655(.02)	**.7323(.01)**
t-emb	-	.1363(.03)	.3941(.02)	.5012(.02)	.5610(.02)	.4300(.02)	-	.6464(.00)	.7364(.01)	.7760(.01)	.8142(.01)	.6690(.01)
l-emb-sep	-	.1312(.03)	.3240(.03)	.3554(.04)	.4282(.03)	.2883(.06)	-	.6464(.00)	.7180(.02)	.7522(.01)	.7757(.01)	.7250(.02)
t-emb-sep	-	**.1672(.02)**	**.4516(.01)**	.5138(.01)	.5944(.02)	.4608(.02)	-	.6668(.01)	**.7434(.00)**	**.7946(.01)**	**.8305(.01)**	.6824(.01)

Table 4: Results for all experiments and all high-resource source languages. ES denotes experiments without transfer. 50 and 200 are the numbers of low-resource training examples. All results are averaged over 5 training runs, standard deviation in parenthesis.

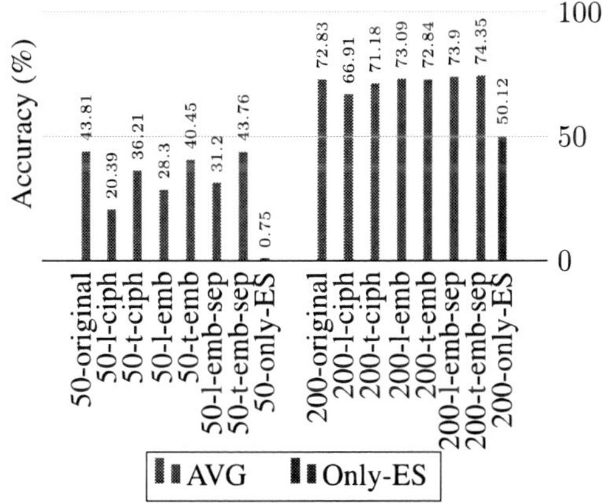

Figure 2: Results for all experiments, averaged over all languages. *only*-ES denotes a model trained exclusively on 50 or 200 Spanish examples.

for low-resource training size 200, t-emb-sep performs best in most case, and without transfer still performs worst. The order of the accuracies averaged over all languages can be seen in Figure 2: original > t-emb-sep > t-emb > t-ciph > l-emb-sep > l-emb > l-ciph for 50 and t-emb-sep > l-emb-sep > l-emb > t-emb > original > t-ciph > l-ciph for 200 low-resource examples. The detailed results of each language can be found in Table 4.

First, this shows clearly that the character embeddings are more important for the task than the tag embeddings. Second, l-emb (resp. t-emb) and l-ciph (resp. t-ciph) correspond to a setting with *no* additional information vs. a setting with *potentially wrong* information. Generally higher accuracies for separate embedding spaces indicate that the model can learn incorrect information via transfer. Thus, the choice of the source language seems to be very important. The differences in performance between original and l-emb represent the influence of shared vs. separate embedding

spaces, i.e., vocabularies in the case of the letters. Sharing a vocabulary seems to influence the final accuracy a lot, and more positively for 50 low-resource examples. We can explain this with the model learning to copy – it has no intrinsic way of knowing which input character equals which output character in the vocabulary unless it has seen it at least once. However, for 200 Spanish examples, we can expect all characters to appear in the Spanish training data, such that the character language model and tag-output correspondence get more important. This explains the unexpected result that l-emb performs best for Arabic (200) and Portuguese (200): both source languages potentially confuse the language model; in Portuguese we contribute this to a big overlap of lemmata in the two languages with Portuguese often inflecting in a different way (Kann et al., 2017). Further, the differences in performance between original and t-emb show that the model indeed learns information from the tags, supposedly which output sequence is more likely to appear with which tag.

The l-emb-sep and t-emb-sep results show that a separation symbol clearly improves the model's performance.

4 Related Work

Transfer learning with encoder-decoder networks. Encoder-decoder RNNs were introduced by Cho et al. (2014) and Sutskever et al. (2014) and extended by an attention mechanism by Bahdanau et al. (2015). Lately, much work was done on *multi-task learning* and *transfer learning* with encoder-decoder RNNs. Luong et al. (2015) investigated multi-task setups for sequence-to-sequence learning, combining multiple encoders and decoders. In contrast, in our experiments, we use only one encoder and one decoder. There exists much work on multi-task learning with encoder-decoder RNNs for machine translation (Johnson et al., 2016; Dong et al., 2015; Firat et al., 2016;

Ha et al., 2016). Alonso and Plank (2016) explored multi-task learning empirically, analyzing *when* it improves performance. Here, we focus on *how* transfer via multi-task learning works.

Paradigm completion. SIGMORPHON hosted two shared tasks on paradigm completion (Cotterell et al., 2016, 2017), in order to encourage the development of systems for the task. One approach is to treat it as a string transduction problem by applying an alignment model with a semi-Markov model (Durrett and DeNero, 2013; Nicolai et al., 2015). Recently, neural sequence-to-sequence models are also widely used (Faruqui et al., 2016; Kann and Schütze, 2016; Aharoni and Goldberg, 2017; Zhou and Neubig, 2017). All the above mentioned work were designed for one single language.

5 Conclusion

We conducted a set of experiments to explore the mechanisms behind cross-lingual transfer learning for morphological reinflection. Our findings indicate that knowledge about a language's typical character sequences and outputs for certain morphological tags can be transferred. In particular, this means that the effect cannot be reduced to sole regularization.

Acknowledgments

We would like to thank Hinrich Schütze and the anonymous reviewers for their helpful comments.

References

Roee Aharoni and Yoav Goldberg. 2017. Sequence to sequence transduction with hard monotonic attention. In *ACL*.

Héctor Martínez Alonso and Barbara Plank. 2016. Multitask learning for semantic sequence prediction under varying data conditions. *arXiv preprint arXiv:1612.02251* .

Dzmitry Bahdanau, Kyunghyun Cho, and Yoshua Bengio. 2015. Neural machine translation by jointly learning to align and translate. In *ICLR*.

Kyunghyun Cho, Bart Van Merriënboer, Dzmitry Bahdanau, and Yoshua Bengio. 2014. On the properties of neural machine translation: Encoder-decoder approaches. In *SSST*.

Ryan Cotterell, Christo Kirov, John Sylak-Glassman, Géraldine Walther, Ekaterina Vylomova, Patrick Xia, Manaal Faruqui, Sandra Kübler, David Yarowsky, Jason Eisner, and Mans Hulden. 2017.

The CoNLL-SIGMORPHON 2017 shared task: Universal morphological reinflection in 52 languages. In *CoNLL-SIGMORPHON*.

Ryan Cotterell, Christo Kirov, John Sylak-Glassman, David Yarowsky, Jason Eisner, and Mans Hulden. 2016. The SIGMORPHON 2016 shared task—morphological reinflection. In *SIGMORPHON*.

Daxiang Dong, Hua Wu, Wei He, Dianhai Yu, and Haifeng Wang. 2015. Multi-task learning for multiple language translation. In *ACL*.

Greg Durrett and John DeNero. 2013. Supervised learning of complete morphological paradigms. In *HLT-NAACL*.

Manaal Faruqui, Yulia Tsvetkov, Graham Neubig, and Chris Dyer. 2016. Morphological inflection generation using character sequence to sequence learning. In *NAACL-HLT*.

Orhan Firat, Kyunghyun Cho, and Yoshua Bengio. 2016. Multi-way, multilingual neural machine translation with a shared attention mechanism. *arXiv preprint arXiv:1601.01073* .

Thanh-Le Ha, Jan Niehues, and Alexander Waibel. 2016. Toward multilingual neural machine translation with universal encoder and decoder. *arXiv preprint arXiv:1611.04798* .

Melvin Johnson, Mike Schuster, Quoc V. Le, Maxim Krikun, Yonghui Wu, Zhifeng Chen, Nikhil Thorat, Fernanda Vigas, Martin Wattenberg, Greg Corrado, Macduff Hughes, and Jeffrey Dean. 2016. Google's multilingual neural machine translation system: Enabling zero-shot translation. *arXiv preprint arXiv:1611.04558* .

Katharina Kann, Ryan Cotterell, and Hinrich Schütze. 2017. One-shot neural cross-lingual transfer for paradigm completion. In *ACL*.

Katharina Kann and Hinrich Schütze. 2016. Single-model encoder-decoder with explicit morphological representation for reinflection. In *ACL*.

M Paul Lewis, editor. 2009. *Ethnologue: Languages of the World*. SIL International, Dallas, Texas, 16 edition.

Minh-Thang Luong, Quoc V Le, Ilya Sutskever, Oriol Vinyals, and Lukasz Kaiser. 2015. Multi-task sequence to sequence learning. *arXiv preprint arXiv:1511.06114* .

Garrett Nicolai, Colin Cherry, and Grzegorz Kondrak. 2015. Inflection generation as discriminative string transduction. In *HLT-NAACL*.

Ilya Sutskever, Oriol Vinyals, and Quoc V Le. 2014. Sequence to sequence learning with neural networks. In *NIPS*.

Matthew D Zeiler. 2012. ADADELTA: an adaptive learning rate method. *CoRR* abs/1212.5701.

Chunting Zhou and Graham Neubig. 2017. Multi-space variational encoder-decoders for semi-supervised labeled sequence transduction. In *ACL*.

Unlabeled Data for Morphological Generation With Character-Based Sequence-to-Sequence Models

Katharina Kann and **Hinrich Schütze**
LMU Munich, Germany
kann@cis.lmu.de

Abstract

We present a semi-supervised way of training a character-based encoder-decoder recurrent neural network for morphological reinflection, the task of generating one inflected word form from another. This is achieved by using unlabeled tokens or random strings as training data for an autoencoding task, adapting a network for morphological reinflection, and performing multi-task training. We thus use limited labeled data more effectively, obtaining up to 9.9% improvement over state-of-the-art baselines for 8 different languages.

1 Introduction

Morphologically rich languages use inflection—the adaptation of a surface form to its syntactic context—to mark the properties of a word, e.g., *gender* or *number* of nouns or *tense* of verbs. This drastically increases the type-token ratio, and thus negatively effects natural language processing (NLP), making morphological analysis and generation an important field of research.

In this work, we focus on morphological reinflection (MRI), the task of mapping one inflected form of a lemma to another, given the morphological properties of the target, e.g., (*smiling*, *Past-Part*) → *smiled*. The lemma does not have to be known. Recently, there have been some advances on the topic, motivated by the SIGMOR-PHON 2016 shared task on morphological reinflection (Cotterell et al., 2016) and the CoNLL-SIGMORPHON 2017 shared task on universal morphological reinflection (Cotterell et al., 2017). In 2016, neural sequence-to-sequence models, specifically attention-based encoder-decoder models, outperformed all other approaches by a wide

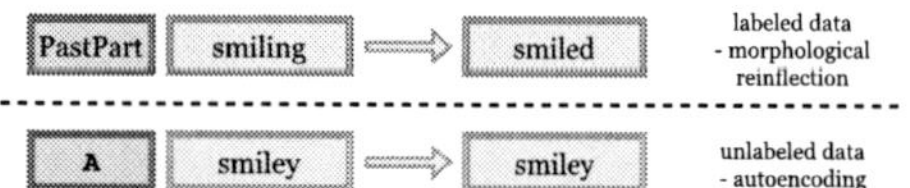

Figure 1: Examples for labeled and unlabeled input. The content of the red boxes (very left in both rows) signalizes if the sample belongs to the MRI task or the autoencoding task.

margin (Faruqui et al., 2016; Kann and Schütze, 2016). However, those models require a lot of training data, while in contrast many morphologically rich languages are low-resource, and little work has been done so far on neural models for morphology in settings with limited training data. This makes sequence-to-sequence models not applicable to morphological generation in most languages.

An abundance of *unlabeled* data, in contrast, can be assumed available for each language in the focus of NLP. Thus, we propose a semi-supervised training method for a state-of-the-art encoder-decoder network for MRI using both labeled and unlabeled data, mitigating the need for time-expensive annotations. We achieve this by treating unlabeled words as training examples for an *autoencoding* (Vincent et al., 2010) task and multi-task training (cf. Figure 1). We intuit the following reasons why this should be beneficial: (i) The decoder's character language model can be trained using unlabeled data. (ii) Training on a second task reduces the problem of overfitting. (iii) By forcing the model to additionally learn autoencoding, we give it a strong prior to copy the input string. This might be advantageous as often many forms of a paradigm share the same stem, e.g., *smiling* and *smiled*. In order to investigate the importance of the latter, we further experiment with autoencoding of *random strings* and find that for our experimental settings and non-templatic languages the performance gain is comparable to using corpus words.

Proceedings of the First Workshop on Subword and Character Level Models in NLP, pages 76–81,
Copenhagen, Denmark, September 7, 2017. ©2017 Association for Computational Linguistics.

2 Model Description

The log-likelihood for joint training on the tasks of MRI and autoencoding is:

$$\mathcal{L}(\boldsymbol{\theta}) = \sum_{(f_s, f_t, t) \in \mathcal{T}} \log p_{\boldsymbol{\theta}}\left(f_t \mid e(f_s, t)\right) \quad (1)$$
$$+ \sum_{w \in \mathcal{W}} \log p_{\boldsymbol{\theta}}(w \mid e(w)),$$

$\mathcal{T}$ is the MRI training data, with each example consisting of a source form f_s, a target form f_t and a target tag t. $\mathcal{W}$ denotes a set of words in the language of the system. The encoding function e depends on $\boldsymbol{\theta}$. The parameters $\boldsymbol{\theta}$ are shared across the two tasks, resulting in a share of information. We obtain this by giving our model data from both sets at the same time, and marking each example with a task-specific input symbol, cf. Figure 1. Following (Kann and Schütze, 2016), we employ a neural encoder-decoder model.

Encoder. For the input of the encoder, we adapt the format by Kann and Schütze (2016), but modify it to be able to handle unlabeled data: Given the set of morphological subtags M each target tag is composed of (e.g., the tag *1SgPresInd* contains the subtags *1*, *Sg*, *Pres* and *Ind*), and the alphabet Σ of the language of application, our input is of the form B[**A**/M*]Σ*E, i.e., it consists of *either* a sequence of subtags *or* the symbol **A** signaling that the input is not annotated and should be autoencoded, and (in both cases) the character sequence of the input word. B and E are start and end symbols. Each part of the input is represented by an embedding.

We then encode the input $x = x_1, x_2, \ldots, x_{T_x}$ using a bidirectional gated recurrent neural network (GRU) (Cho et al., 2014b), i.e., $\overrightarrow{h}_i = f\left(\overrightarrow{h}_{i-1}, x_i\right)$ and $\overleftarrow{h}_i = f\left(\overleftarrow{h}_{i+1}, x_i\right)$, with f being the update function of the hidden layer. Forward and backward hidden states are concatenated to obtain the input h_i for the decoder.

Decoder. The decoder is an attention-based GRU, defining a probability distribution over strings in Σ^*:

$$p(y \mid x) = \prod_{t=1}^{T_y} p(y_t \mid y_1, \ldots, y_{t-1}, s_t, c_t),$$

with s_t being the decoder hidden state for time t and c_t being a context vector, calculated using the encoder hidden states together with attention weights. A detailed description of the model can be found in Bahdanau et al. (2015).

3 Experiments

Dataset. We experiment on the task 3 dataset of the SIGMORPHON 2016 shared task on MRI (Cotterell et al., 2016) and all standard languages provided: Arabic, Finnish, Georgian, German, Navajo, Russian, Spanish and Turkish. German, Spanish and Russian are suffixing and exhibit stem changes. Russian differs from the other two in that those stem changes are consonantal and not vocalic. Finnish and Turkish are agglutinating, almost exclusively suffixing and have vowel harmony systems. Georgian uses both prefixiation and suffixiation. In contrast, Navajo mainly makes use of prefixes with consonant harmony among its sibilants. Finally, Arabic is a templatic, non-concatenative language.

For each language, we further add randomly sampled words from the respective Wikipedia dumps. We exclude tokens that are not exclusively composed from characters of the language's alphabet, e.g., digits, or do not appear at least 2 times in the corpus. The exact amount of unlabeled data added is treated as a hyperparameter depending on the number of available annotated examples and optimized on the development set, cf. Section 4.1. Evaluation is done on the official shared task test set.

Training, hyperparameters and evaluation. We mainly adopt the hyperparameters of (Kann and Schütze, 2016). Embeddings are 300-dimensional, the size of all hidden layers is 100 and for training we use ADADELTA (Zeiler, 2012) with a batch size of 20. We train all models which use $\frac{1}{8}$ or more of the labeled data for 200 epochs, and models that see $\frac{1}{16}$ and $\frac{1}{32}$ of the original data for 400 and 800 epochs, respectively. In all cases, we apply the last model for testing.

We evaluate using two metrics: accuracy and edit distance. Accuracy reports the percentage of completely correct solutions, while the edit distance between the system's guess and the gold solution gives credit to systems that produce forms that are close to the right form.

Baselines. We compare our system to three baselines: The first one is **MED**[1], the winning sys-

---

[1]http://cistern.cis.lmu.de/med/

Table 1:

		ar				fi				ka				de				nv				ru				sp				tu			
		SIG16	SIG17	MED	Our	SIG16	SIG17	MED	Our	SIG16	SIG17	MED	Our	SIG16	SIG17	MED	Our	SIG16	SIG17	MED	Our	SIG16	SIG17	MED	Our	SIG16	SIG17	MED	Our	SIG16	SIG17	MED	Our
$\frac{1}{4}$	acc	.188	.094	.716	**.722**	.293	.325	.809	**.854**	.814	.831	.910	**.912**	.721	.687	.882	**.888**	.317	.403	.706	**.711**	.641	.638	**.825**	.824	.558	.539	.939	**.942**	.181	.129	.904	**.910**
	ED	2.26	3.06	0.94	**0.92**	1.90	1.47	0.47	**0.35**	0.42	0.38	**0.28**	0.30	0.47	0.54	0.33	**0.31**	2.04	1.95	1.01	**0.97**	0.69	0.65	**0.43**	**0.43**	0.96	0.97	**0.15**	**0.15**	2.92	3.33	0.27	**0.23**
$\frac{1}{8}$	acc	.104	.063	.600	**.640**	.207	.227	.687	**.732**	.798	.791	.883	**.894**	.618	.593	.851	**.873**	.247	.350	.516	**.619**	.516	.523	.766	**.772**	.441	.409	.896	**.916**	.120	.080	**.846**	.832
	ED	2.76	3.32	1.37	**1.20**	2.32	1.91	0.85	**0.77**	0.47	0.44	0.45	**0.42**	0.67	0.73	0.42	**0.35**	2.40	2.23	1.75	**1.40**	0.95	0.92	**0.60**	**0.60**	1.36	1.35	0.26	**0.22**	3.42	3.80	**0.47**	0.54
$\frac{1}{16}$	acc	.052	.043	.470	**.533**	.126	.149	.543	**.620**	.709	.751	.860	**.875**	.504	.495	.791	**.839**	.204	.329	.350	**.473**	.384	.422	.645	**.695**	.317	.308	.807	**.862**	.070	.049	.717	**.739**
	ED	3.36	3.53	1.80	**1.59**	2.84	2.34	1.33	**1.16**	0.62	**0.50**	0.58	0.52	0.90	0.94	0.60	**0.45**	2.71	2.41	2.63	**2.05**	1.23	1.17	0.94	**0.82**	1.80	1.70	0.47	**0.36**	3.81	4.09	0.99	**0.94**
$\frac{1}{32}$	acc	.028	.027	.263	**.381**	.073	.088	.314	**.402**	.595	.648	.818	**.852**	.384	.386	.661	**.722**	.174	.303	.174	**.369**	.249	.293	.406	**.502**	.196	.245	.657	**.756**	.044	.028	.524	**.571**
	ED	3.73	3.73	2.79	**2.22**	3.18	2.76	2.48	**2.00**	0.87	0.70	0.76	**0.65**	1.15	1.18	1.01	**0.90**	2.94	**2.65**	3.85	2.73	1.61	1.45	1.71	**1.38**	2.22	2.06	0.97	**0.62**	4.19	4.27	1.98	**1.80**

Table 1: Accuracy (the higher the better) and edit distance (the lower the better) for our system and the three baselines on the official test set of task 3 of the SIGMORPHON 2016 shared task. Only the indicated amount (row labels) of the original training data is used, emulating a low-resource setting. Best results for each language in bold.

tem of the 2016 shared task. The network architecture is the same as in our system, but it is trained exclusively on labeled data. Thus, we expect it to suffer stronger from a lack of resources.

The second baseline is the official SIGMORPHON 2016 shared task baseline (**SIG16**) (Cotterell et al., 2016), which is similar in spirit to the system described by Nicolai et al. (2015). The system treats the prediction of edit operations to be performed on the input string as a sequential decision-making problem, greedily choosing each edit action given the previously chosen actions. The selection of operations is made by an averaged perceptron, using the binary features described in (Cotterell et al., 2016).[2]

Third, we compare to the baseline system of the CoNLL-SIGMORPHON 2017 shared task on universal morphological reinflection (**SIG17**) (Cotterell et al., 2017), which is extremely suitable for low-resource settings. It splits all source and target forms in the training set into prefix, middle part and suffix, and uses those to find prefix or suffix substitution rules. Every evaluation example is searched for the longest contained prefix or suffix and the rule belonging to the affix and given target tag is applied to obtain the output.

Results and discussion. As shown in Table 1, additionally training on unlabeled examples improves the performance of the encoder-decoder network for nearly all settings and languages, especially for the very low-resource scenarios with $\frac{1}{16}$ and $\frac{1}{32}$ of the training data. The biggest increase in accuracy can be seen for Russian and Spanish, both in the $\frac{1}{32}$ setting, with 0.0963 $(0.5023 - 0.4060)$ and 0.0992 $(0.7564 - 0.6572)$, respectively. For the settings with bigger amounts

of training data available, the unlabeled data does not change performance a lot. This was expected, as the model already gets enough information from the annotated data. However, semi-supervised training never *hurts* performance, and can thus always be employed. Overall, our semi-supervised training method shows to be a useful extension of the original system.

Furthermore, there are only two cases— Georgian, $\frac{1}{16}$, and Navajo, $\frac{1}{32}$—where any of the SIGMORPHON baselines outperforms the neural methods. This clearly shows the superiority of neural networks for the task and emphasizes the need to reduce the amount of labeled training data required for their training.

4 Analyses

4.1 Amount of Unlabeled Data

We now consider the amount of unlabeled examples as a function of the number of annotated examples. Data and training regime are the same as in Section 3. This analysis is performed on the development set and we report the highest accuracy obtained during training.

The resulting accuracies for Arabic and German can be seen in Figure 2. The other languages behave similarly to German. The loss of performance for reducing the training data varies a lot between languages, depending on how regular and thus "easy to learn" those are. Concerning the amount of unlabeled examples, it seems that even though in single cases other ratios are slightly better, using 4 times more unlabeled examples mostly obtains highest accuracy. Thus, a general rule could be that the more additional examples are used the better. The only exception is Arabic in the $\frac{1}{32}$ setting, where using half as many unlabeled as labeled examples obtains much better results. We explain this with the Semitic language being templatic. Since words in Arabic paradigms do

---

[2]Note that our use of the system differs from the official baseline in that we perform a direct form-to-form mapping. The shared task system predicts first form-to-lemma and then lemma-to-form. However, we assume no lemmata to be given, and thus are unable to train such a system.

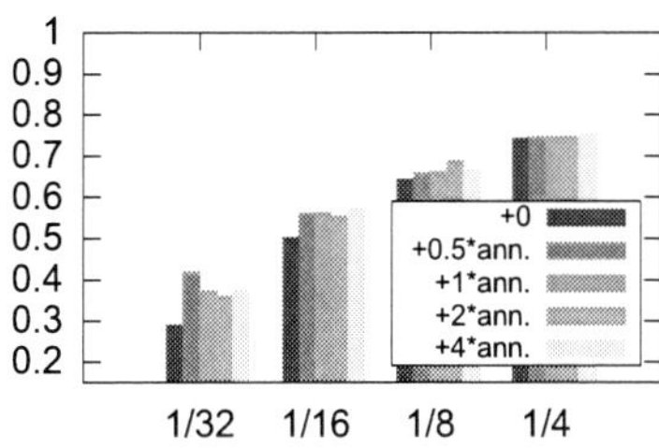

Arabic

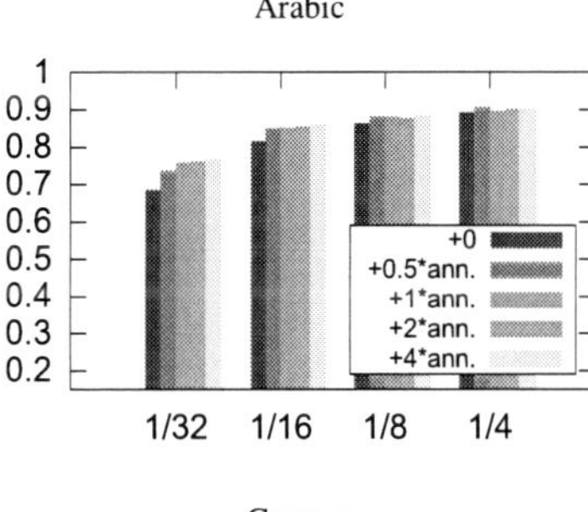

German

Figure 2: Comparison of different amounts of unlabeled data, sorted by the amount of labeled training examples in portions of the original data. Evaluated on the development set.

	ar	fi	ka	de	nv	ru	es	tu
MED	.2628	.3144	.8184	.6608	.1738	.4060	.6572	.5238
MED+*corpus*	**.3811**	**.4015**	.8523	.7221	**.3688**	**.5023**	.7564	**.5713**
MED+*random*	.3064	.3793	**.8531**	**.7313**	.3250	.4958	**.7676**	.5706

Table 2: Accuracies for MED (Kann and Schütze (2016)), MED+*corpus* and MED+*random*. Descriptions in the text.

not share a connected stem, we expect that giving the model too much bias to copy might be harming performance in low-resource settings. However, even for low-resource Arabic, using a ratio of 1:4 of labeled to unlabeled examples still yields a better performance than not using unlabeled examples at all. Thus, we can conclude that if aiming for a language-independent setup, this is a good ratio.

4.2 Autoencoding of Random Strings

We expect the network to benefit from a bias to copy strings. This suggests that *any* random combination of characters from the language's alphabet could be autoencoded in order to improve the performance in low-resource settings. To verify this, we train models on new datasets with $\frac{1}{32}$ of the labeled examples from task 3 of the SIGMOR-PHON 2016 shared task and the optimal number of unlabeled examples for each language, cf. §4.1. However, the unlabeled examples are now random strings of a length between 3 and 20. All models are trained as before. Accuracies on the official test sets are shown in Table 2, and compared to (i) training without unlabeled examples and (ii) the data being enhanced by corpus words. Several aspects of the results are eye-catching. First, for Arabic, the gap to the performance with cor-

pus words is the biggest, showing that indeed the tendency of languages to copy the stem when inflecting is playing an important role. Second, for some languages the performance gains for corpus words and random words are comparable. Third, the performance of random strings is closer to the performance of corpus words the higher the overall accuracy is. The additional unlabeled examples might be acting as regularizers in this case.

Overall, this experiment shows clearly that giving the model a bias to copy strings helps for inflection in non-templatic languages, and that random strings can improve a network for MRI.

5 Related Work

For the SIGMORPHON 2016 and the CoNLL-SIGMORPHON 2017 shared tasks (Cotterell et al., 2016, 2017), multiple MRI systems were developed, e.g., (Nicolai et al., 2016; Taji et al., 2016; Kann and Schütze, 2016; Aharoni et al., 2016; Östling, 2016; Makarov et al., 2017). Encoder-decoder neural networks (Cho et al., 2014a; Sutskever et al., 2014; Bahdanau et al., 2015) performed best, such that we extend them in this work. Earlier work on paradigm completion included (Faruqui et al., 2016; Nicolai et al., 2015; Durrett and DeNero, 2013). Work directly tackling MRI was more rare, e.g., (Dreyer and Eisner, 2009). Our work relates to the line of research on minimally supervised and unsupervised methods for morphology, e.g., Creutz and Lagus (2007) and Goldsmith (2001) presenting the unsupervised morphological segmentation systems Morfessor and Linguistica, or (Dreyer and Eisner, 2011; Poon et al., 2009; Snyder and Barzilay, 2008). However, none of those focused directly on MRI or on training neural networks for morphology. The only case we know of where this *was* done was work by Kann et al. (2017). They leveraged morphologically annotated data in a closely related high-resource language to reduce the need for labeled data in the target language. This works well for similar languages, but has the shortcoming to require annotations in such a language to be at hand. A similar approach was presented by Ha et al. (2016) for machine translation (MT). Unlabeled corpora were used for semi-supervised training of models for MT, e.g., by Cheng et al. (2016); Vincent et al. (2010); Socher et al. (2011); Ramachandran et al. (2016). Those approaches differ from ours, due to a fundamental difference between the two tasks: For MRI, the source vocabulary and the target vocabulary are mostly the same. This makes it intuitive for MRI to train the final model jointly on MRI and autoencoding.

6 Conclusion

We presented a way of semi-supervised training of a state-of-the-art model for low-resource MRI, using words from an unlabeled corpus. We found that the best ratio of labeled to unlabeled data depends of the morphological typology of the language. Finally, we showed that autoencoding random strings also increases performance, for some languages as much as using corpus words.

Acknowledgments

We would like to thank the anonymous reviewers for their insightful comments. This work was supported by DFG (SCHU2246/10).

References

Roee Aharoni, Yoav Goldberg, and Yonatan Belinkov. 2016. Improving sequence to sequence learning for morphological inflection generation: The BIU-MIT systems for the SIGMORPHON 2016 shared task for morphological reinflection. In *SIGMORPHON*.

Dzmitry Bahdanau, Kyunghyun Cho, and Yoshua Bengio. 2015. Neural machine translation by jointly learning to align and translate. In *ICLR*.

Yong Cheng, Wei Xu, Zhongjun He, Wei He, Hua Wu, Maosong Sun, and Yang Liu. 2016. Semi-supervised learning for neural machine translation. *arXiv preprint arXiv:1606.04596* .

Kyunghyun Cho, Bart van Merrienboer, Dzmitry Bahdanau, and Yoshua Bengio. 2014a. On the properties of neural machine translation: Encoder–decoder approaches. In *SSST*.

Kyunghyun Cho, Bart Van Merriënboer, Çalar Gülçehre, Dzmitry Bahdanau, Fethi Bougares, Holger Schwenk, and Yoshua Bengio. 2014b. Learning phrase representations using RNN encoder–decoder for statistical machine translation. In *EMNLP*.

Ryan Cotterell, Christo Kirov, John Sylak-Glassman, Géraldine Walther, Ekaterina Vylomova, Patrick Xia, Manaal Faruqui, Sandra Kübler, David Yarowsky, Jason Eisner, and Mans Hulden. 2017. The CoNLL-SIGMORPHON 2017 shared task: Universal morphological reinflection in 52 languages. In *CoNLL-SIGMORPHON*.

Ryan Cotterell, Christo Kirov, John Sylak-Glassman, David Yarowsky, Jason Eisner, and Mans Hulden. 2016. The SIGMORPHON 2016 shared task—morphological reinflection. In *SIGMORPHON*.

Mathias Creutz and Krista Lagus. 2007. Unsupervised models for morpheme segmentation and morphology learning. *TSLP* 4(1):3.

Markus Dreyer and Jason Eisner. 2009. Graphical models over multiple strings. In *EMNLP*.

Markus Dreyer and Jason Eisner. 2011. Discovering morphological paradigms from plain text using a Dirichlet process mixture model. In *EMNLP*.

Greg Durrett and John DeNero. 2013. Supervised learning of complete morphological paradigms. In *NAACL*.

Manaal Faruqui, Yulia Tsvetkov, Graham Neubig, and Chris Dyer. 2016. Morphological inflection generation using character sequence to sequence learning. In *NAACL*.

John Goldsmith. 2001. Unsupervised learning of the morphology of a natural language. *Computational linguistics* 27(2):153–198.

Thanh-Le Ha, Jan Niehues, and Alexander Waibel. 2016. Toward multilingual neural machine translation with universal encoder and decoder. *arXiv preprint arXiv:1611.04798* .

Katharina Kann, Ryan Cotterell, and Hinrich Schütze. 2017. One-shot neural cross-lingual transfer for paradig completion. In *ACL*.

Katharina Kann and Hinrich Schütze. 2016. MED: The LMU system for the SIGMORPHON 2016 shared task on morphological reinflection. In *ACL*.

Peter Makarov, Tatiana Ruzsics, and Simon Clematide. 2017. Align and copy: UZH at SIGMORPHON 2017 shared task for morphological reinflection. In *CoNLL-SIGMORPHON*.

Garrett Nicolai, Colin Cherry, and Grzegorz Kondrak. 2015. Inflection generation as discriminative string transduction. In *NAACL*.

Garrett Nicolai, Bradley Hauer, Adam St Arnaud, and Grzegorz Kondrak. 2016. Morphological reinflection via discriminative string transduction. In *SIGMORPHON*.

Robert Östling. 2016. Morphological reinflection with convolutional neural networks. In *SIGMORPHON*.

Hoifung Poon, Colin Cherry, and Kristina Toutanova. 2009. Unsupervised morphological segmentation with log-linear models. In *NAACL*.

Prajit Ramachandran, Peter J Liu, and Quoc V Le. 2016. Unsupervised pretraining for sequence to sequence learning. *arXiv preprint arXiv:1611.02683* .

Benjamin Snyder and Regina Barzilay. 2008. Unsupervised multilingual learning for morphological segmentation. In *ACL*.

Richard Socher, Jeffrey Pennington, Eric H Huang, Andrew Y Ng, and Christopher D Manning. 2011. Semi-supervised recursive autoencoders for predicting sentiment distributions. In *EMNLP*.

Ilya Sutskever, Oriol Vinyals, and Quoc V Le. 2014. Sequence to sequence learning with neural networks. In *NIPS*.

Dima Taji, Ramy Eskander, Nizar Habash, and Owen Rambow. 2016. The Columbia University - New York University Abu Dhabi SIGMORPHON 2016 morphological reinflection shared task submission. In *SIGMORPHON*.

Pascal Vincent, Hugo Larochelle, Isabelle Lajoie, Yoshua Bengio, and Pierre-Antoine Manzagol. 2010. Stacked denoising autoencoders: Learning useful representations in a deep network with a local denoising criterion. *Journal of Machine Learning Research* 11(Dec):3371–3408.

Matthew D Zeiler. 2012. ADADELTA: An adaptive learning rate method. *arXiv preprint arXiv:1212.5701* .

Vowel and Consonant Classification through Spectral Decomposition

Patricia Thaine and **Gerald Penn**
Department of Computer Science
University of Toronto
{pthaine,gpenn}@cs.toronto.edu

Abstract

We consider two related problems in this paper. Given an undeciphered alphabetic writing system or mono-alphabetic cipher, determine: (1) which of its letters are vowels and which are consonants; and (2) whether the writing system is a vocalic alphabet or an abjad. We are able to show that a very simple spectral decomposition based on character co-occurrences provides nearly perfect performance with respect to answering both question types.

1 Introduction

Most of the world's writing systems are based upon *alphabets*, in which each of the basic units of speech, called *phones*, receives its own representational unit or letter. The vast majority of phones are consonants or vowels, the former being produced through a partial or full obstruction of the vocal tract, the latter, through a stable interval of resonance at several characteristic frequencies called *formants*. In the course of deciphering an alphabet, one of the first important questions to answer is which of the letters correspond to vowels, and which to consonants, a problem that has been studied as far back as Ohaver (1933). Indeed, if there is disagreement as to whether a phonetic script is an alphabet or not, a near-perfect separation of its graphemes into consonants and vowels would be very important evidence for confirming the proposition that it was.

A well-publicized, recent attempt at classifying the letters of an undeciphered alphabet as either vowels or consonants was by Kim and Snyder (2013), who used a Bayesian approach to estimating an unobserved set of parameters that cause phonetic regularities among the distributions of letters in the alphabets of known/deciphered writing systems. By contrast, the method proposed in this paper is based on a very simple spectral analysis of letter distributions within only the writing system under investigation, and it requires no training or parameter tuning. It is furthermore based on a newly confirmed empirical universal over alphabetic writing systems that is interesting in its own right, is crucial to our method's numerical stability.

Spectral analysis of vowels and consonants dates back to at least Moler and Morrison (1983), which performs very poorly. Our method can be regarded as both a simplification and improvement to Moler and Morrison (1983). On average, our method correctly classifies 97.45% of characters in any alphabetic writing system.

Another notable antecedent is Goldsmith and Xanthos (2009), who discovered essentially the same method for vowel-consonant separation in the context of spectrally analyzing phonemic transcriptions. While the premise that someone would have phonemically transcribed a text without knowing by the end which phones were vowels or consonants may seem far-fetched, Goldsmith and Xanthos (2009) draw some important conclusions for a subsequent analysis of vowel-harmonic processes that we shall not investigate further here. Goldsmith and Xanthos (2009) also cite Sukhotin (1962), whose method we evaluate below, as a precedent for their own study, possibly influenced by Guy's (1991) English gloss of Sukhotin's work, which misrepresents Sukhotin's (1962) intention as seeking to classify letters in a substitution cipher as vowels or consonants. Sukhotin's (1962) study, which was originally written in Russian, is in fact about the written form (*bukv*) of plaintext letters, not of ciphers nor of the sounds of speech. Sukhotin begins his study by posing the research question of whether, given the well-known separation of the sounds of speech into vowels and consonants, there are similar classes for letters (*podobnyh klassah k'bukvam*). The distinction be-

Proceedings of the First Workshop on Subword and Character Level Models in NLP, pages 82–91,
Copenhagen, Denmark, September 7, 2017. ©2017 Association for Computational Linguistics.

	_*h	t*e	h*_	_*a	f*t	a*_	c*t
t	1	0	0	0	0	1	0
h	0	1	0	0	0	0	0
e	0	0	1	0	0	0	0
f	0	0	0	1	0	0	0
c	0	0	0	1	0	0	0
a	0	0	0	0	1	0	1

Table 1: The binary matrix, A, for the string 'the fat cat'. Viewed as an adjacency matrix, it represents a bipartite graph.

tween written letters and phones is particularly salient in Russian, which, unlike English, has written letters that simply cannot be classified as vowels or consonants in any context or in isolation.[1]

Sukhotin (1962) made an earlier attempt at our study of writing systems, not at Goldsmith and Xanthos's (2009) study of phoneme clustering. In the present paper, we consider two applications of our method to the problem of classifying an alphabetic writing system as either an abjad (one with letters only for consonants) or a vocalic alphabet (one with letters for vowels as well).

2 A Spectral Universal over Alphabets

A *p-frame* (Stubbs and Barth, 2003) is a bit like a trigram context, except it considers one preceding and one succeeding element of context, rather than two preceding elements. The string 'the fat cat', for example, contains these, among other p-frames at the character level: '_*h', 't*e', 'h*_', '_*a', where '_' represents a space.

Given a sufficiently long corpus, C, in the alphabet, Ω, let A be the binary matrix of dimension $m \times n$, where n is the number of different letter types in Ω and m is the number of different p-frames that occur in C (see Table 1), in which $A_{ij} = 1$ iff letter i occurs in p-frame j in C.

Every m by n matrix A has a singular-value decomposition into $A = U\Sigma V^T$. Usually, we are interested in Σ, a diagonal matrix containing the *singular values* of A, but we will be more concerned here with the n by n matrix V, the columns of which, the *right singular vectors* of A, are eigenvectors of $A^T A$. V is also *orthonormal*, which

means that the inner product of any two right singular vectors, $v_i \cdot v_j$, is 0 unless $i = j$, in which case the inner product is 1 (Strang, 2005).

If the rows and columns of U, Σ and V are permuted so that the singular values of Σ appear in decreasing order, then the first two right singular vectors are the most important, in the sense that they provide the most information about A. Let x and y be these two vectors; they are columns of V, and so they are rows of V^T, as shown in Figure 1. Empirically, each x_i is proportional to both the frequency of the ith letter in C and the frequencies of the p-frame contexts in which the ith letter occurs. Again empirically, each y_i ends up being proportional to the number of contexts that the ith letter shares with other letters.

Because V is orthonormal, $\sum_i x_i y_i = 0$. Since their sum centres around zero, for some of the letters $i \in \Omega^+$, $x_i y_i$ is positive, and for other $i \in \Omega^-$, $x_i y_i$ is negative. The spectral universal we have empirically determined is that these two subsets of Ω almost perfectly separate the vowels and consonants of the writing system utilized by C. A moment's reflection will confirm that the p-frame distributions of vowels are probably very different from the p-frame distributions of consonants (Sukhotin, 1962), but the best thing about this universal is its inherent numerical stability. Table 2 shows the sums over these two sets for 15 alphabetic writing systems, expanded to 12 decimal places.

This calculation presumes a foreknowledge of what the vowels and consonants are, but if we were to order all of the letters in Ω by their value y_i, define a separator $y = b$, and then vary the parameter b so as to maximize the sum $|\sum_{i:y_i>b} x_i y_i| + |\sum_{i:y_i \le b} x_i y_i|$, $b = 0$ attains the maximum value. This is again trivial to prove in theory, but because the differences between vowel and consonant p-frames are the most important differences among all of the possible separators, empirically we may observe that $y = 0$ separates the vowels from the consonants. In other words, the actual values that the y_i attain are irrelevant; all that matters is their signs.

None of this provides any guidance as to which subset/sign contains the vowels and which, the consonants. Borrowing from the general idea behind Sukhotin's algorithm (Guy, 1991), we will assume that the most frequent letter of any alpha-

---

[1] These are the front and back "yer" that respectively mark the presence or absence of palatalization. Sukhotin (1962) knew about the special status of these letters, too; when his method classifies the "front yer" as a vowel, he expresses some satisfaction because the "front yer" did represent a vowel at an earlier stage in Russian writing.

$$A = U\Sigma V^\mathsf{T} = \begin{pmatrix} \cdot & \cdot & \cdot & \cdot & \cdot & \cdot \\ \cdot & \cdot & \cdot & \cdot & \cdot & \cdot \\ \cdot & \cdot & \cdot & \cdot & \cdot & \cdot \\ \cdot & \cdot & \cdot & \cdot & \cdot & \cdot \\ \cdot & \cdot & \cdot & \cdot & \cdot & \cdot \\ \cdot & \cdot & \cdot & \cdot & \cdot & \cdot \end{pmatrix} \begin{pmatrix} \cdot & \cdot & \cdot & \cdot & \cdot & \cdot \\ \cdot & \cdot & \cdot & \cdot & \cdot & \cdot \\ \cdot & \cdot & \cdot & \cdot & \cdot & \cdot \\ \cdot & \cdot & \cdot & \cdot & \cdot & \cdot \\ \cdot & \cdot & \cdot & \cdot & \cdot & \cdot \\ \cdot & \cdot & \cdot & \cdot & \cdot & \cdot \end{pmatrix} \begin{pmatrix} x_1 & x_2 & x_3 & x_4 & x_5 & x_6 \\ y_1 & y_2 & y_3 & y_4 & y_5 & y_6 \\ \cdot & \cdot & \cdot & \cdot & \cdot & \cdot \\ \cdot & \cdot & \cdot & \cdot & \cdot & \cdot \\ \cdot & \cdot & \cdot & \cdot & \cdot & \cdot \\ \cdot & \cdot & \cdot & \cdot & \cdot & \cdot \end{pmatrix}$$

Figure 1: Singular Value Decomposition of A.

Language	$\left|\sum x_{\text{vowels}} \cdot y_{\text{vowels}}\right|$	$\left|\sum x_{\text{consonants}} \cdot y_{\text{consonants}}\right|$
Danish	0.461778253515	0.461778253515
Dutch	0.478014338904	0.478014338904
English	0.484420669972	0.484420669972
Finnish	0.471723103373	0.471723103373
French	0.482759327181	0.482759327181
German	0.440663056154	0.440663056154
Greek	0.447065776857	0.447065776857
Hawaiian	0.432782088536	0.432782088536
Italian	0.467317672843	0.467317672843
Latin	0.4656326487	0.4656326487
Maltese	0.496082609138	0.496082609138
Portuguese	0.463359992637	0.463359992637
Russian	0.491165538014	0.491165538014
Spanish	0.478974310472	0.478974310472
Swedish	0.430570626024	0.430570626024

Table 2: Inner products of x and y (Figure 1) for 15 different writing systems, accurate to 12 places.

bet is a vowel,[2] (Vietnamese is the singular exception that we have found to this rule) and thus label the subset that contains it as the vowel container[3]. This yields Algorithm 1, which we evaluate in Table 3.[4] [5]

3 Evaluating the Vowel Identification Algorithm

Kim and Snyder (2013) report token-level accu-

racies with a macro-average of 98.85% across 503 alphabets, with a standard deviation of about 2%. Token-level accuracies are somewhat misleading, as the hyperbolic distribution of letters in all naturally occurring alphabets makes it very easy to inflate accuracies even when the class of many (rare) letters cannot be determined. Furthermore, if the classified or readable portions of corpora were at issue, then these token accuracies should have been micro-averaged, not macro-averaged, and, more importantly, they should have been smoothed by an n-gram character model to produce a more meaningful estimate.

Vowel/consonant classification is better viewed as a letter-type, not letter-instance, classification problem, in which progress is evaluated according to the percentage of letter types that are correctly classified. Semivowels or whatever ambiguous classes one wishes to define should ideally be distinguished as extra classes, or at the very least disregarded. For a level comparison with our base

---

[2] Note that we treat ò, ó, ô, and o, for example, as four distinct vowels.

[3] Out of the 26 alphabets we examine, this assumption only fails for Vietnamese, whose most frequent letter is n. This is mainly due to the large number of diacriticized vowels in Vietnamese that we treat discretely.

[4] In this and the subsequent experiments, the following writing systems were withheld as an evaluation set to prevent overfitting: Aramaic, Farsi, Hungarian, Serbian, Urdu, and Vietnamese.

[5] Each corpus was sampled from a combination of Wikipedia, Project Gutenberg and BBC World Service web pages, and consists of between 14316 and 706422 characters (median=164757). All punctuation was removed, and all letters were downcased.

Algorithm 1 Vowel and consonant classification algorithm

1: $num_{words} \leftarrow 0$
2: $num_{letters} \leftarrow length(letters)$
3: $contexts \leftarrow list\ of\ num_{letters}\ empty\ lists$
4: $frames_{keys} \leftarrow [\ ]$
5: $frames_{values} \leftarrow [\ ]$
6: $letters_{count} \leftarrow list\ of\ zeros\ of\ size\ num_{letters}$
7: $A \leftarrow [\ ]$
8: $A_{weighted} \leftarrow [\ ]$
9: **function** VOWELCONSONANTCLASSIFICATION(V, $most\_freq\_letter$)
10:     $coordinates \leftarrow zip(V[0], V[1], letters)$
11:     $cluster_1 \leftarrow triples\ where\ V[1]\ value\ > 0$
12:     $cluster_2 \leftarrow triples\ where\ V[1]\ value\ < 0$
13:     $vowels \leftarrow cluster\ that\ has\ most\_freq\_letter$
14:     $consonants \leftarrow cluster\ that\ does\ not\ have\ most\_freq\_letter$
15:     **return** $vowels, consonants$
16: **end function**
17: **function** ALGORITHM1($corpus$, max)
18:     **for all** $word \in corpus$ **do**
19:         $word \leftarrow ['\_'] + list(word) + ['\_']$
20:         $num_{words} += 1$
21:         **if** $num_{words} > max$ **then**
22:             **break**
23:         **end if**
24:         $MakePFrames(word)$ # Calculates A and $A_{weighted}$
25:     **end for**
26:     $index_{most\_freq\_letter} \leftarrow index\ of\ max(letters_{count})$
27:     $most\_freq\_letter \leftarrow letters[index_{most\_freq\_letter}]$
28:     $U, s, V \leftarrow SVD(A)$
29:     $vowels, consonants \leftarrow VowelConsonantClassification(V, most\_freq\_letter)$
30:     **return** $vowels, consonants$
31: **end function**

Language	(Moler and Morrison, 1983)				Sukhotin's Algorithm			Algorithm 1		
	NC	P	R	A	P	R	A	P	R	A
Abkhaz	4	1.00	0.67	0.94	1.00	1.00	**1.00**	1.00	1.00	**1.00**
Afrikaans	18	0.71	0.36	0.31	0.93	0.81	0.88	1	0.81	**0.91**
Czech	23	1.00	0.63	0.68	1.00	0.94	**0.98**	1.00	0.94	**0.98**
Dutch	11	1.00	1.00	**1.00**	0.83	1.00	0.96	1.00	1.00	**1.00**
Danish	26	0.67	0.67	0.56	0.88	0.93	0.91	1.00	0.93	**0.97**
English (Middle)	4	1.00	1.00	**1.00**	1	0.90	0.96	1	0.90	0.96
English (Modern)	5	1.00	1.00	**1.00**	0.71	1.00	0.92	1.00	1.00	**1.00**
English (Old)	19	0.86	0.67	0.64	1.00	1.00	**1.00**	1.00	1.00	**1.00**
Finnish	3	1.00	0.89	**0.96**	0.89	1.00	**0.96**	0.89	1.00	**0.96**
French (Modern)	29	0.43	1.00	0.60	1.00	0.79	**0.89**	1.00	0.79	**0.89**
Inuktitut	6	1.00	1.00	**1.00**	0.95	0.95	0.95	1.00	0.95	0.97
Italian	17	0.90	0.90	0.86	0.91	0.67	0.82	1.00	0.93	**0.97**
German	13	1.00	0.88	0.93	0.73	1.00	0.89	0.88	1.00	**0.96**
Greek (Ancient)	3	0.83	1.00	0.95	1.00	1.00	**1.00**	1.00	1.00	**1.00**
Greek (Modern)	3	1.00	1.00	**1.00**	1.00	1.00	**1.00**	1.00	1.00	**1.00**
Hawaiian	5	0.90	0.90	0.92	0.83	0.91	0.90	1.00	1.00	**1.00**
Hungarian	14	0.44	0.80	0.71	0.94	0.94	0.94	1.00	1.00	**1.00**
Latin	3	1.00	1.00	**1.00**	1.00	1.00	**1.00**	1.00	1.00	**1.00**
Maltese	2	1.00	1.00	**1.00**	0.83	1.00	0.96	1.00	1.00	**1.00**
Portuguese	24	0.88	1.00	0.92	1.00	0.88	**0.94**	1.00	0.88	**0.94**
Russian	5	1.00	1.00	**1.00**	1.00	1.00	**1.00**	1.00	1.00	**1.00**
Serbian	25	0.89	0.89	0.85	0.90	0.69	0.88	1.00	0.82	**0.95**
Spanish	16	0.86	0.86	0.86	0.91	1.00	0.97	1.00	1.00	**1.00**
Swedish	6	1.00	1.00	**1.00**	0.89	1.00	0.96	0.80	1.00	0.93
Tagalog	4	1.00	0.94	**0.97**	0.95	1.00	**0.97**	1.00	0.89	0.95
Vietnamese	40	0.04	0.07	0.02	0.71	0.67	0.87	0.94	1.00	**0.99**

Table 3: Algorithm 1 evaluated with type-level accuracies. Corpora were sampled from the same sources as in Table 2, but with between 25738 and 968298 characters (median = 177529). The best accuracies are highlighted. Algorithm 1 incorrectly classifies several infrequent vowels (ë,ï,œ and ù) as consonants in Modern French. P, R, and A stand for Precision, Recall, and Accuracy, respectively. NC is the number of letters not classified by Moler and Morrison's (1983) algorithm; they are not necessarily semivowels. Unclassified letters are not included in the calculation of their method's precision, recall, and accuracy, however; their results are even worse when NC letters are treated as false negatives.

lines (most are interested in vowel vs. non-vowel; Kim and Snyder (2013) experimented with distinguishing nasals as well), ambiguous letters such as English 'y' have been manually identified and discarded altogether in Table 3.

It is impossible to determine the type accuracy of Kim and Snyder's (2013) method, because they only made the raw counts of words in their corpus available[6] (not the code, nor the resulting classifications). It is also impossible to reproduce their evaluation, since they did not provide their pa-

rameter settings. In addition, their ground truth classification of graphemes into vowels and consonants was remarkably ambitious. They treated all semivowels as consonants, for example — even tokens where they act as vowels. The "front yer" palatalization marker in Russian Cyrillic was called a consonant, for example, and yet the "back yer" that blocks palatalization is called a vowel. With such arbitrary labellings of graphemes that simply should have been left out of the classification, a controlled comparison of even token accuracy is perhaps beside the point. For what it is worth, however, we could use the correct

[6]http://pages.cs.wisc.edu/~ybkim/data/ consonant_vowel_acl2013.tgz.

grapheme classifications in the 20 writing systems that constitute the overlap between the 503 that they sampled and the 26 that we did, and Algorithm 1's macro-averaged token-accuracy on these is 99.93%, whereas Sukhotin's is 96.05%.

An even greater cause for concern with this corpus is the sampling method that created it. Kim and Snyder's (2013) use of a leave-one-out protocol to evaluate their method on each of their 503 writing systems at first seems reasonable — every known writing system should be pressed into the service of analyzing an unknown one. But all of these samples are Biblical, and many of them (the English, Portuguese, Italian and Spanish samples, for example, or the French and German samples) are the same verses translated into different languages. It is not reasonable in general to expect that a sample of unknown writing would necessarily be a translation of a text from a known writing system. The overlap in character contexts between transliterated proper names and cognates makes for a very charitable transfer of knowledge between writing systems.

Across the 26 writing systems that we have evaluated, our samples are all different texts from several genres. Our method requires no training, so all of the samples can be used for evaluation, but it also cannot avail itself of transfer across writing systems. On these samples, Algorithm 1 achieves a macro-averaged type accuracy of 97.45% and a macro-averaged token accuracy of 99.39% with a standard deviation of 1.67%. Performance is very robust in the realistic context of low transfer. On the same samples, Sukhotin's algorithm has a macro-averaged type accuracy of 94.34%.

Moler and Morrison (1983)'s algorithm is less accurate than Algorithm 1. Moler and Morrison (1983) claim that their method is intended for "vowel-follows-consonant" (vfc) texts, where the proportion of vowels following consonants is greater than the proportion of vowels following vowels. Yet every writing system in our corpus is vfc, and still it performs poorly. Instead of using a binary adjacency matrix representing which letters occur within which p-frames, they calculate the number of times every possible letter pair occurs. They run SVD on the resulting matrix and use the second right and left singular vectors to plot the letters. The plot is divided into four quadrants, where letters in the fourth quadrant are clas-

sified as vowels, those in the second quadrant as consonants, and those in the first or third quadrants as "neuter," [*sic*] meaning unclassified (see NC on Table 3). Our plots, on the other hand, are split into half planes with a crisp, numerically stable separation at the x-axis between the putative vowels and putative consonants, leaving no letter unclassified unless it falls on $y = 0$, which would only occur with completely unattested letters. Given the computational power and the number of electronic multilingual sources available at the time, Moler and Morrison (1983) had no workable means of thoroughly evaluating their method.

Another important concern is stability as a function of length — many undeciphered writing systems are not well attested in terms of the number or length of their surviving samples. Our spectral method performs robustly at the 97.45% level for sparse samples down to a minimum of about 500 word types or 4000 word tokens. It is possible that below this threshold Sukhotin's algorithm would still be preferable.

Goldsmith and Xanthos (2009) only evaluate their method on one collection of written words, sampled from Finnish,[7] and they obtain the same result as we do below, with our algorithm only misclassifying the grapheme 'q'.[8] This should come as no surprise, because their method is an algebraically very close variant of ours — they compute eigenvectors on the Gram closure of our grapheme/context matrix (which they call F) instead of a singular value decomposition directly.

It may nevertheless come as a surprise that their method is so similar to ours. Their motivation consists of a lengthy discussion of graph cuts, along with a reference to Fiedler vectors, the name of the second eigenvector (the correlate to our $\bar{y}$) of a graph's Laplacian matrix, which is known to relate to the graph's algebraic connectivity. Neither Goldsmith and Xanthos (2009) nor we explicitly calculate the Laplacian matrix of a graph, and if this would-be graph happened to have more than one connected component, the Fiedler vector would not be uniquely well-defined on its Lapla-

---

[7]This is offered with the apology that Finnish is orthographically transparent, thus almost qualifying as a phonemic transcription.

[8]Goldsmith and Xanthos's (2009) explanation for this is a "problem of threshold," but our study has found that the numerical stability of the threshold is extremely accurate. Instead, the problem is the relative disconnectedness of 'q' from other graphemes owing to its sparsity, as the discussion in this paragraph will elaborate upon.

cian matrix in general.[9] Vowels and consonants rarely if ever separate into perfectly disjoint contexts; among our corpora the most disjoint is Vietnamese, in which vowels and consonants share exactly 100/645 p-frames. Out of curiosity, we evaluated our algorithm on the matrices from all 26 writing systems with their inter-CV/VC links removed. Performance degrades (macro-averaged accuracy: 89.08%) — which implies that this method is not merely computing an overall minimum graph cut — but not so badly that partitions could merely be ignoring either all of the vowels or all of the consonants. The explanation found in Goldsmith and Xanthos (2009) therefore does not account for the robustness or generality of our collective approach. Our own determination of this method, along with this universal, was entirely experimental.

A final difference to our approach is that Goldsmith and Xanthos (2009) use bigram contexts instead of p-frames, although they are aware that this choice is arbitrary. Empirically, p-frames work better than bigrams (macro-averaged type accuracy: 89.06%) as well as trigrams with two preceding elements (96.24%).

Figure 2 shows example classifications by Algorithm 1 of six different writing systems. Each letter is plotted at its (x_i, y_i) coordinate, but the classification is made using only y_i. It is worth noting that semivowels and other trouble-makers consistently fall very close to the $y = 0$ threshold. Maltese is particularly important, as it uses a vocalic alphabet with a Semitic language. Our correct handling of this case, and converse cases such as Farsi, demonstrates that we are responding to properties of alphabetic writing systems, and not of linguistic phylogeny.

4 Distinguishing Abjads from Vocalic Alphabets

Some writing systems assign syllabic or larger phonetic values to individual graphemes. Those that do not are sometimes called *alphabetic* writing systems, which is confusing because not all of them are true alphabets. There is another kind of alphabetic writing system called an *abjad*, which expresses only consonants. Arabic writing and writing systems based upon Arabic writing (whether or not the underlying language is related to the Arabic language) are the prototypical abjads; the rest (e.g., Hebrew, Aramaic) express Hatto-Semitic languages. Abjads express words in languages that have vowels, but the vowels must be inferred from context, unless, in anomalous genres, they are expressed through optional diacritics (Daniels and Bright, 1996).

We can use the spectral method presented in Section 2 to classify an alphabetic writing system as either an abjad or a true, vocalic alphabet. This is a different kind of classification problem than that of Section 3, as we are attempting here to classify the structure of entire writing systems rather than the phonetic values assigned to individual graphemes. We will consider two algorithms for distinguishing abjads from vocalic alphabets:

4.1 Algorithm 2: Divergence

This variant begins by provisionally assuming that the writing system under investigation is a vocalic alphabet, and applying Algorithm 1 to it, which involves the calculation of the aforementioned matrix, A, and the classification of every letter as a consonant or vowel. There is a related matrix W, for which W_{ij} is the number of times letter i occurs in the context of p-frame j. W is not binary. We will label the rows of W as $\hat{v}_i$ or $\hat{c}_j$ according to whether i and j are labelled as vowels or consonants by Algorithm 1. Algorithm 1 still uses A in assigning the labels, not W.

We can view each row of W as a discrete distribution over p-frame contexts. In recognition of this, Algorithm 2 calculates:

$$ N = \sum_{\hat{v}_i, \hat{v}_j} |D|(\hat{v}_i \| \hat{v}_j) - \sum_{\hat{v}_i, \hat{c}_j} |D|(\hat{v}_i \| \hat{c}_j), $$

where $D(p \| q)$ is the Kullback-Leibler divergence of p and q. We use $|D|$ to represent the absolute-value of each element-wise calculation of $\hat{v}_i \log \frac{\hat{v}_i}{\hat{v}_j \mathrm{or} \hat{c}_j}$. The distributions of putative vowels tend to be more dissimilar to one another in abjads than in true alphabets. The distributions of putative vowels are more similar to that of putative consonants in abjads than in true alphabets. Values of N are shown for 30 writing systems in Table 4.

N separates the abjads from the vocalic alphabets at about $N = -100$.

---

[9]Unless all of the connected components fortuitously had first and second eigenvalues of exactly the same magnitudes, the overall second non-zero eigenvector would not cross all of the components.

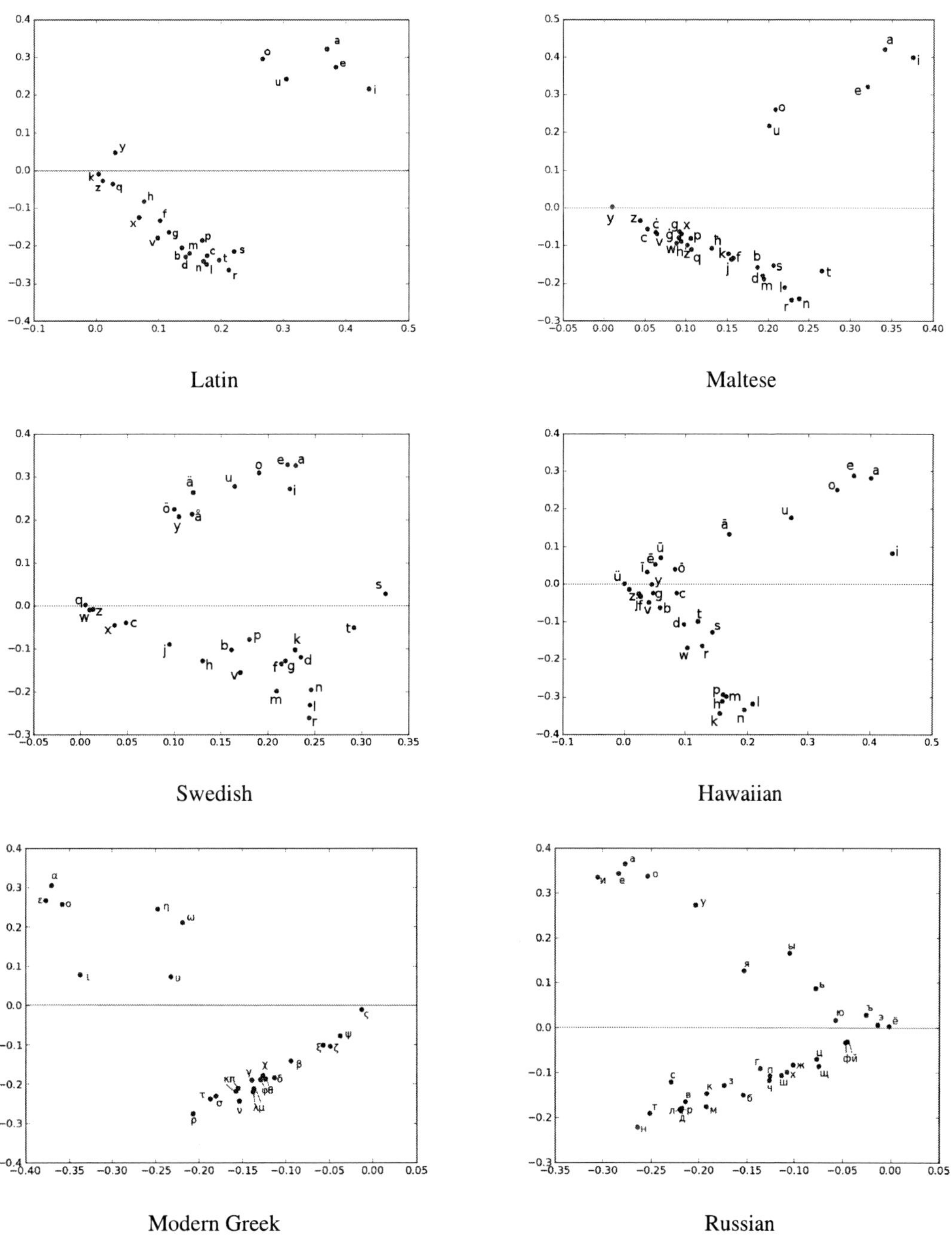

Figure 2: x and y for several writing systems.

Language	N
Hungarian	773.7
Tagalog	531.43
Inuktitut	424.12
Vietnamese	359.53
Finnish	240.26
Old English	234.52
Czech	223.96
Spanish	147.44
Russian	135.88
Swedish	121.77
Maltese	104.63
Latin	83.88
Ancient Greek	65.88
Hawaiian	57.29
Middle English	48.21
Serbian	28.07
Modern Greek	20.6
German	20.33
French	16.01
Modern English	-31.05
Portuguese	-53.19
Dutch	-57.18
Afrikaans	-73.52
Italian	-89.94
NVME	-167.63
Farsi	-185.7
Aramaic	-191.23
Hebrew	-207.32
Urdu	-220.01
Arabic	-225.36

Table 4: Values of N for Algorithm 2, calculated over corpora of roughly 5000 words each (min character tokens = 13681, max = 39936, median = 20361). NVME is the Modern English corpus with vowels removed. Abkhaz ($N = -70.94$) is not included because of its small size.

Language	V	C
Arabic	**3.75**	0.92
Hebrew	**3.63**	0.2
Urdu	**2.58**	0.22
Farsi	**2.35**	0.13
Aramaic	**1.97**	0.18
NVME	0.19	**0.69**
Abkhaz	**0.63**	0.44
Russian	**0.37**	0.29
Maltese	**0.36**	0.06
Vietnamese	0.25	**0.27**
Modern Greek	**0.14**	0.06
Dutch	**0.13**	0.04
Old English	**0.12**	0.11
Hawaiian	**0.12**	0.4
Middle English	0	**0.12**
Spanish	**0.11**	0.08
German	**0.09**	0.04
Tagalog	**0.07**	0.06
Inuktitut	**0.07**	0.05
Italian	**0.07**	0.04
Serbian	**0.07**	0.02
Portuguese	**0.05**	0.05
Afrikaans	**0.05**	0.04
Czech	**0.05**	0.01
Modern English	**0.05**	0.01
Latin	**0.04**	0.03
Finnish	**0.03**	0.03
Swedish	**0.03**	0.03
French	**0.03**	0.02
Hungarian	**0.02**	0.01

Table 5: Percentages of word tokens with no putative vowels (V) or consonants (C), as determined by Algorithm 3.

4.2 Algorithm 3: Vowelless words

For writing systems that conventionally use interword whitespace, we can alternatively apply vowel identification to the task of discriminating abjads from vocalic alphabets by examining the percentage of word tokens with no vowel graphemes.[10] This method, Algorithm 3, is implicit to Reddy and Knight's (2011) 2-state HMM analysis of part of the Voynich manuscript, in which they observed that every word was recognized as an instance of the regular language a^*b. They believed the most likely explanation is that every word was written with several consonants followed by a vowel, and that the Voynich manuscript therefore uses an abjad.

From this percentage, a decision boundary also emerges at about 1%, as shown in Table 5. NVME is not correctly classified unless one uses the greater of the percentage of words without a vowel or consonant, but this (Modern English with the Once again, putative vowels and consonants have been determined by Algorithm 1.

---

[10] In vocalic writing systems, vowelless words include typographical errors, abbreviations and, in some writing systems, words with semivowels that can occupy a syllabic mora, such as 'y' in English.

5 Conclusion and Future Work

We have shown that a very simple spectral decomposition based on character co-occurrences provides nearly perfect performance with respect to classifying both a letter as vowel or consonant and a writing system as an abjad or alphabet. Algorithm 1 does not resolve other pertinent questions, e.g., distinguishing numbers from letters, or determining which capital letters correspond to which lowercase letters. Our method of vowel/consonant classification is meant to inform existing methods of finding graphemes' corresponding sounds. An additional source for associating sound values to graphemes is comparing letter frequencies between two related languages.

Future research on associating sound values to graphemes could include extending a method similar to Algorithm 1 to other types of writing systems, such as syllabaries.

References

Peter T Daniels and William Bright. 1996. *The world's writing systems*. Oxford University Press.

J. Goldsmith and A. Xanthos. 2009. Learning phonological categories. *Language* 85(1):4–38.

Jacques BM Guy. 1991. Vowel identification: an old (but good) algorithm. *Cryptologia* 15(3):258–262.

Young-Bum Kim and Benjamin Snyder. 2013. Unsupervised Consonant-Vowel Prediction over Hundreds of Languages. In *ACL (1)*. pages 1527–1536.

Cleve Moler and Donald Morrison. 1983. Singular value analysis of cryptograms. *American Mathematical Monthly* pages 78–87.

Merle E Ohaver. 1933. *Cryptogram solving*. Etcetera Press, PO Drawer 27100, Columbus, Ohio 43227.

Sravana Reddy and Kevin Knight. 2011. What we know about the Voynich manuscript. In *Proceedings of the 5th ACL-HLT Workshop on Language Technology for Cultural Heritage, Social Sciences, and Humanities*. Association for Computational Linguistics, pages 78–86.

Gilbert Strang. 2005. *Linear Algebra and Its Applications, 4th Edition*. Brooks/Cole Publishing Company.

Michael Stubbs and Isabel Barth. 2003. Using recurrent phrases as text-type. *Functions of language* 10(1):61–104.

B.V. Sukhotin. 1962. Eksperimental'noe vydelenie klassov bukv s po- moshch'ju elektronnoj vychislitel'noj mashiny. *Problemy strukturnoj lingvistiki* 234:198–106.

Syllable-level Neural Language Model for Agglutinative Language

Seunghak Yu[*]   **Nilesh Kulkarni**[*]   **Haejun Lee**   **Jihie Kim**
Samsung Electronics Co. Ltd., South Korea
{seunghak.yu, n93.kulkarni, haejun82.lee, jihie.kim}@samsung.com

Abstract

Language models for agglutinative languages have always been hindered in past due to myriad of agglutinations possible to any given word through various affixes. We propose a method to diminish the problem of out-of-vocabulary words by introducing an embedding derived from syllables and morphemes which leverages the agglutinative property. Our model outperforms character-level embedding in perplexity by 16.87 with 9.50M parameters. Proposed method achieves state of the art performance over existing input prediction methods in terms of Key Stroke Saving and has been commercialized.

1 Introduction

Recurrent neural networks (RNNs) exhibit dynamic temporal behavior which makes them ideal architectures to model sequential data. In recent times, RNNs have shown state of the art performance on tasks of language modeling (RNN-LM), beating the statistical modeling techniques by a huge margin (Mikolov et al., 2010; Lin et al., 2015; Kim et al., 2016; Miyamoto and Cho, 2016). RNN-LMs model the probability distribution over the words in vocabulary conditioned on a given input context. The sizes of these networks are primarily dependent on their vocabulary size.

Since agglutinative languages, such as Korean, Japanese, and Turkish, have a huge number of words in the vocabulary, it is considerably hard to train word-level RNN-LM. Korean is agglutinative in its morphology; words mainly contain different morphemes to determine the meaning of the word hence increasing the vocabulary size for language model training. A given word in Korean

could have similar meaning with more than 10 variations in the suffix as shown in Table 1.

Various language modeling methods that rely on character or morpheme like segmentation of words have been developed (Ciloglu et al., 2004; Cui et al., 2014; Kim et al., 2016; Mikolov et al., 2012; Zheng et al., 2013; Ling et al., 2015). (Chen et al., 2015b) explored the idea of joint training for character and word embedding. Morpheme based segmentation has been explored in both Large Vocabulary Continuous Speech Recognition (LVCSR) tasks for Egyptian Arabic (Mousa et al., 2013) and German newspaper corpus (Cotterell and Schütze, 2015). (Sennrich et al., 2015) used subword units to perform machine translation for rare words.

Morpheme distribution has a relatively smaller frequency tail as compared to the word distribution from vocabulary, hence avoids over-fitting for tail units. However, even with morpheme segmentation the percentage of out-of-vocabulary (OOV) words is significantly high in Korean. Character embedding in Korean is unfeasible as the context of the word is not sufficiently captured by the long sequence which composes the word. We select as features syllable-level embedding which has shorter sequence length and morpheme-level embedding to capture the semantics of the word.

We deploy our model for input word prediction on mobile devices. To achieve desirable performance we are required to create a model that has as small as possible memory and CPU footprint without compromising its performance. We use differentiated softmax (Chen et al., 2015a) for the output layer. This method uses more parameters for the words that are frequent and less for the ones that occur rarely. We achieve better performance than existing approaches in terms of Key Stroke Savings (KSS) (Fowler et al., 2015) and our approach has been commercialized.

---

[*] Equal contribution

Proceedings of the First Workshop on Subword and Character Level Models in NLP, pages 92–96,
Copenhagen, Denmark, September 7, 2017. ©2017 Association for Computational Linguistics.

Word	Morpheme	English
그가	그 + 가	he
그는	그 + 는	he
그에게	그 + 에게	to him
그도	그 + 도	him(he) also
그를	그 + 를	him
그의	그 + 의	his

Table 1: Example of variation of a base word '그 (He)'. It can have more than 10 variation forms according to its postposition.

2 Proposed Method

Following sections propose a model for agglutinative language. In Section 2.1 we discuss the basic architecture of the model as detailed in Figure 1, followed by Section 2.2 that describes our embeddings. In Section 2.3 we propose an adaptation of differentiated softmax to reduce the number of model parameters and improve computation speed.

2.1 Language Model

Overall architecture of our language model consists of a) embedding layer, b) hidden layer, c) softmax layer. Embedding comprises of syllable-level and morpheme-level embedding as described in Section 2.2. We combine both embedding features and pass them through a highway network (Srivastava et al., 2015) which act as an input to the hidden layers. We use a single layer of LSTM as hidden units with architecture similar to the non-regularized LSTM model by (Zaremba et al., 2014). The hidden state of the LSTM unit is affine-transformed by the softmax function, which is a probability distribution over all the words in the output vocabulary.

2.2 Syllable & Morphological Embedding

We propose syllable-level embedding that attenuates OOV problem. (Santos and Zadrozny, 2014; Kim et al., 2016) proposed character aware neural networks using convolution filters to create character embedding for words. We use convolution neural network (CNN) based embedding method to get syllable-level embedding for words. We use 150 filters that consider uni, bi, tri and quad syllable-grams to create a feature representation for the word. This is followed by max-pooling to concatenate the features from each class of filters resulting in a syllable embedding representation

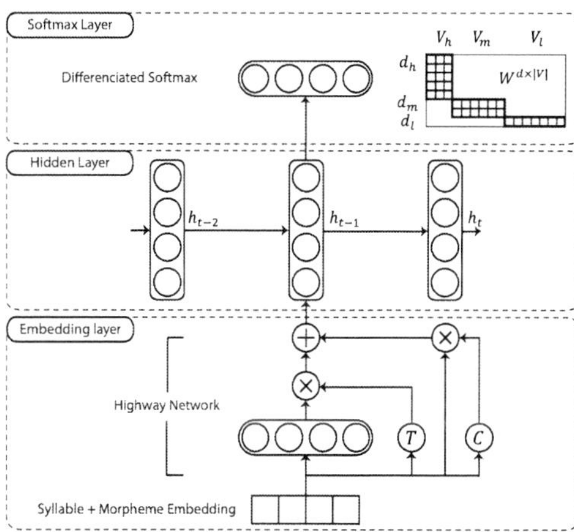

Figure 1: Overview of the proposed method. T and C are the transform gate and carry gate of the highway network respectively

for the word. Figure 2 in the left half shows an example sentence embedded using the syllable-level embedding.

Figure 3 highlights the difference between various embedding and the features they capture. The syllable embedding is used along with a morphological embedding to provide richer features for the word. The majority of words (95%) in Korean has at most three morphological units. Each word can be broken into start, middle, and end unit. We embed each morphological unit by concatenating to create a joint embedding for the word. Advantage of morphological embedding over syllable is all the sub-units have an abstract value in the language and this creates representation for words relying on the usage of these morphemes. Both morphological and syllable embeddings are concatenated and fed through a highway network (Srivastava et al., 2015) to get a refined representation for the word as shown in the embedding layer for Figure 1.

2.3 Differentiated Softmax

The output layer models a probability distribution over words in vocabulary conditioned on the given context. There is a trade-off between required memory and computational cost which determines the level of prediction. To generate a complete word, using morpheme-level predictions requires beam search which is expensive as compared to word-level predictions. Using beam search to predict the word greedily does not adhere to the com-

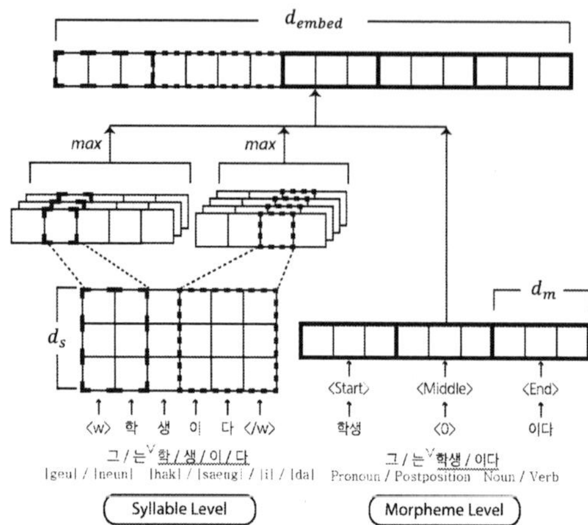

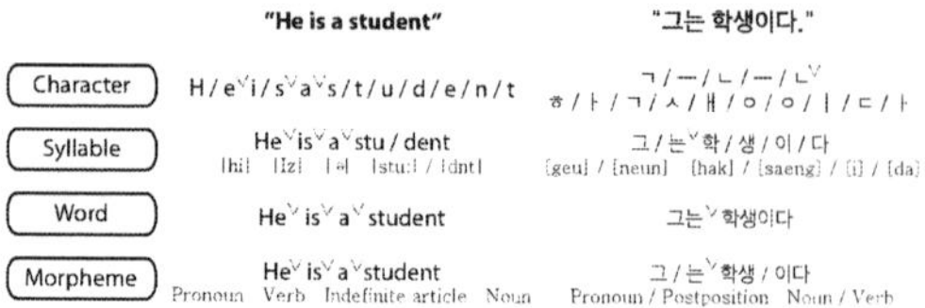

Figure 3: Comparison of various embedding levels. In case of Korean, syllable can be used as a basic unit of sequence to solve OOV with shorter sequence length compare to character level. Also, morpheme level is effective to make the size of vocabulary smaller.

Figure 2: Proposed embedding method for agglutinative languages. We take an input word as syllable and morpheme level, embed them separately and concatenate them to make an entire embedding.

putational requirements set forth for mobile devices. Thus, we have to choose word-level outputs although it requires having a vocabulary of over 0.2M words to cover 95% of the functional word forms. Computing a probability distribution function for 0.2M classes is computational intensive and overshoots the required run-time and the allocated memory to store the model parameters.

Therefore, the softmax weight matrix, $W_{softmax}$, needs to be compressed as it is contributing to huge model parameters. We initially propose to choose an appropriate rank for the $W_{softmax}$ in the following approximation problem; $W_{softmax} = W_A \times W_B$, where W_A and W_B have ranks less than r. We extend the idea of low rank matrix factorization in (Sainath et al., 2013) by further clustering words into groups and allowing a different low rank r' for each cluster. The words with high frequency are given a rank, r_1, such that $r_1 \geq r_2$ where r_2 is the low rank for the words with low frequency. The core idea being, words with higher frequency have much richer representation in higher dimensional space, whereas words with low frequency cannot utilize the higher dimensional space well.

We observe that 87% of the words appear in the tail of the distribution by the frequency of occurrence. We provide a higher rank to the top 2.5% words and much lower rank to the bottom 87%. This different treatment reduces the number of pa-

rameters and leads to better modeling.

3 Experiment Results

3.1 Setup

We apply our method to web crawled dataset consisting on news, blogs, QA. Our dataset consists of over 100M words and over 10M sentences. For morpheme-level segmentation, we use lexical analyzer and for syallable-level we just syllabify the dataset. We empirically test our model and its input vocabulary size is around 20K morphemes and 3K syllables. The embedding size for morpheme is 52 and that for syllable is 15. We use one highway layer to combine the embeddings from syllable and morpheme. Our hidden layer consists of 500 LSTM units. The differentiated softmax outputs the model's distribution over the 0.2M words in the output vocabulary with top 5K (by frequency) getting a representation dimension (low rank in $W_{softmax}$) of 152, next 20K use a representation dimension of 52 and the rest 175K get a representation dimension of 12. All the compared models have word level outputs and use differentiated softmax.

3.2 Comparison of embedding methods

We randomly select 10% of our crawled data (10M words, 1M sentences) to compare embedding methods as shown in Table 2. We test character, syllable, morpheme and word-level embeddings. The word-level embedding has the highest number of parameters but has the worst performance. As expected breaking words into their subforms improves the language model. However, our experiment reaches its peak performance when we use syllable level embeddings. To improve the performance even further we propose using syllable

Embedding	Param.	Perplexity	Vocab.
Word	15.72M	327.17	200K
Morph	6.61M	283.54	20K
Character	8.66M	235.52	40
Syl	8.71M	231.30	3K
Syl + Morph	**9.50M**	**218.65**	**23K**

Table 2: Results of different embedding methods. Param. : Total model paramerters, Vocab: Input vocabulary size, Syl : Syllable, Morph: Morpheme.

and morpheme which outperforms all the other approaches in terms of perplexity.

3.3 Performance evaluation

Proposed method shows the best performance compared to other solutions in terms of Key Stroke Savings (KSS) as shown in Table 3. KSS is a percentage of key strokes not pressed compared to a vanilla keyboard which does not have any prediction or completion capabilities. Every user typed characters using the predictions of the language model counts as key stroke saving. The dataset[1] used to evaluate KSS was manually curated to mimic user keyboard usage patterns.

The results in Table 3 for other commercialized solutions are manually evaluated due to lack of access to their language model. We use three evaluators from inspection group to cross-validate the results and remove human errors. Each evaluator performed the test independently for all the other solutions to reach a consensus. We try to minimize user personalization in predictions by creating a new user profile while evaluating KSS.

The proposed method shows 37.62% in terms of KSS and outperforms compared solutions. We have achieved more than 13% improvement over the best score among existing solutions which is 33.20% in KSS. If the user inputs a word with our solution, we require on an average 62.38% of the word prefix to recommend the intended word, while other solutions need 66.80% of the same. Figure 4 shows an example of word prediction across different solutions. In this example, the predictions from other solutions are same irrespective

---

[1]The dataset consists of 67 sentences (825 words, 7,531 characters) which are collection of formal and informal utterances from various sources. It is available at `https://github.com/meinwerk/SyllableLevelLanguageModel`

Developer	KSS(%)
Proposed	**37.62**
Swiftkey	33.20
Apple	31.90
Samsung	31.40

Table 3: Performance comparison of proposed method and other commercialized keyboard solutions by various developers.

Figure 4: Example of comparison with other commercialized solutions. Predicted words for the Context A (rain heavily) and Context B (too much rice). Other solutions make same prediction regardless of the context (only consider the last two words of context).

of the context, while the proposed method treats them differently with appropriate predictions.

4 Conclusion

We have proposed a practical method for modeling agglutinative languages, in this case Korean. We use syllable and morpheme embeddings to tackle large portion of OOV problem owing to practical limit of vocabulary size and word-level prediction with differentiated softmax to compress size of model to a form factor making it amenable to running smoothly on mobile device. Our model has 9.50M parameters and achieves better perplexity than character-level embedding by 16.87. Our proposed method outperforms the existing commercialized keyboards in terms of key stroke savings and has been commercialized. Our commercialized solution combines above model with n-gram statistics to model user behavior thus supporting personalization.

References

Welin Chen, David Grangier, and Michael Auli. 2015a. Strategies for training large vocabulary neural language models. *arXiv preprint arXiv:1512.04906* .

Xinxiong Chen, Lei Xu, Zhiyuan Liu, Maosong Sun, and Huanbo Luan. 2015b. Joint learning of character and word embeddings. In *Twenty-Fourth International Joint Conference on Artificial Intelligence*.

T Ciloglu, M Comez, and S Sahin. 2004. Language modelling for turkish as an agglutinative language. In *Signal Processing and Communications Applications Conference, 2004. Proceedings of the IEEE 12th*. IEEE, pages 461–462.

Ryan Cotterell and Hinrich Schütze. 2015. Morphological word-embeddings. In *HLT-NAACL*. pages 1287–1292.

Qing Cui, Bin Gao, Jiang Bian, Siyu Qiu, and Tie-Yan Liu. 2014. Learning effective word embedding using morphological word similarity. *arXiv preprint arXiv:1407.1687* .

Andrew Fowler, Kurt Partridge, Ciprian Chelba, Xiaojun Bi, Tom Ouyang, and Shumin Zhai. 2015. Effects of language modeling and its personalization on touchscreen typing performance. In *Proceedings of the 33rd Annual ACM Conference on Human Factors in Computing Systems*. ACM, pages 649–658.

Yoon Kim, Yacine Jernite, David Sontag, and Alexander M Rush. 2016. Character-aware neural language models. In *Thirtieth AAAI Conference on Artificial Intelligence*.

Rui Lin, Shujie Liu, Muyun Yang, Mu Li, Ming Zhou, and Sheng Li. 2015. Hierarchical recurrent neural network for document modeling. In *EMNLP*. pages 899–907.

Wang Ling, Tiago Luís, Luís Marujo, Ramón Fernandez Astudillo, Silvio Amir, Chris Dyer, Alan W Black, and Isabel Trancoso. 2015. Finding function in form: Compositional character models for open vocabulary word representation. *arXiv preprint arXiv:1508.02096* .

Tomas Mikolov, Martin Karafiát, Lukas Burget, Jan Cernockỳ, and Sanjeev Khudanpur. 2010. Recurrent neural network based language model. In *Interspeech*. volume 2, page 3.

Tomáš Mikolov, Ilya Sutskever, Anoop Deoras, Hai-Son Le, Stefan Kombrink, and Jan Cernocky. 2012. Subword language modeling with neural networks. *preprint (http://www. fit. vutbr. cz/imikolov/rnnlm/char. pdf)* .

Yasumasa Miyamoto and Kyunghyun Cho. 2016. Gated word-character recurrent language model. *arXiv preprint arXiv:1606.01700* .

Amr El-Desoky Mousa, Hong-Kwang Jeff Kuo, Lidia Mangu, and Hagen Soltau. 2013. Morpheme-based feature-rich language models using deep neural networks for lvcsr of egyptian arabic. In *Acoustics, Speech and Signal Processing (ICASSP), 2013 IEEE International Conference on*. IEEE, pages 8435–8439.

Tara N Sainath, Brian Kingsbury, Vikas Sindhwani, Ebru Arisoy, and Bhuvana Ramabhadran. 2013. Low-rank matrix factorization for deep neural network training with high-dimensional output targets. In *Acoustics, Speech and Signal Processing (ICASSP), 2013 IEEE International Conference on*. IEEE, pages 6655–6659.

Cicero D Santos and Bianca Zadrozny. 2014. Learning character-level representations for part-of-speech tagging. In *Proceedings of the 31st International Conference on Machine Learning (ICML-14)*. pages 1818–1826.

Rico Sennrich, Barry Haddow, and Alexandra Birch. 2015. Neural machine translation of rare words with subword units. *arXiv preprint arXiv:1508.07909* .

Rupesh Kumar Srivastava, Klaus Greff, and Jürgen Schmidhuber. 2015. Highway networks. *arXiv preprint arXiv:1505.00387* .

Wojciech Zaremba, Ilya Sutskever, and Oriol Vinyals. 2014. Recurrent neural network regularization. *arXiv preprint arXiv:1409.2329* .

Xiaoqing Zheng, Hanyang Chen, and Tianyu Xu. 2013. Deep learning for chinese word segmentation and pos tagging. In *EMNLP*. pages 647–657.

Character-based Bidirectional LSTM-CRF with words and characters for Japanese Named Entity Recognition

Shotaro Misawa, Motoki Taniguchi, Yasuhide Miura and Tomoko Ohkuma

Fuji Xerox Co., Ltd.

{misawa.shotaro, motoki.taniguchi, yasuhide.miura, ohkuma.tomoko}@fujixerox.co.jp

Abstract

Recently, neural models have shown superior performance over conventional models in NER tasks. These models use CNN to extract sub-word information along with RNN to predict a tag for each word. However, these models have been tested almost entirely on English texts. It remains unclear whether they perform similarly in other languages. We worked on Japanese NER using neural models and discovered two obstacles of the state-of-the-art model. First, CNN is unsuitable for extracting Japanese sub-word information. Secondly, a model predicting a tag for each word cannot extract an entity when a part of a word composes an entity. The contributions of this work are (i) verifying the effectiveness of the state-of-the-art NER model for Japanese, (ii) proposing a neural model for predicting a tag for each character using word and character information. Experimentally obtained results demonstrate that our model outperforms the state-of-the-art neural English NER model in Japanese.

1 Introduction

Named Entity Recognition (NER) is designed to extract entities such as location and product from texts. The results are used in sophisticated tasks including summarizations and recommendations. In the past several years, sequential neural models such as long-short term memory (LSTM) have been applied to NER. They have outperformed the conventional models (Huang et al., 2015). Recently, Convolutional Neural Network (CNN) was introduced into many models for extracting sub-word information from a word (Santos and Guimaraes, 2015; Ma and Hovy, 2016). The models achieved higher performance because CNN can capture capitalization, suffixes, and prefixes (Chiu and Nichols, 2015). These models predict a tag for each word assuming that words can be separated clearly by explicit word separators (e.g. blank spaces). We refer to such model as a "word-based model", even if inputs include characters.

When Japanese NER employs a recent neural model, two obstacles arise. First, extracting sub-word information by CNN is unsuitable for Japanese language. The reasons are that Japanese words tend to be shorter than English and Japanese characters have no capitalization. Secondly, the word-based model cannot extract entities when a part of a word composes an entity. Japanese language has no explicit word separators. Word boundaries occasionally become ambiguous. Therefore, the possibility exists that entity boundary does not match word boundaries. We define such phenomena as "boundary conflict". To avoid this obstacle, NER using finer-grained compose units than words are preferred in Japanese NERs (Asahara and Matsumoto, 2003; Sassano and Utsuro, 2000). We follow these approaches and expand the state-of-the-art neural NER model to predict a tag for each character: a "character-based model".

The contributions of our study are: (i) application of a state-of-the-art NER model to Japanese NER and verification of its effectiveness, and (ii) proposition of a "character-based" neural model with concatenating words and characters. Experimental results show that our model outperforms the state-of-the-art neural NER model in Japanese.

2 Related Work

Conventional Models: Conventional NER systems employ machine learning algorithms that use

Proceedings of the First Workshop on Subword and Character Level Models in NLP, pages 97–102,
Copenhagen, Denmark, September 7, 2017. ©2017 Association for Computational Linguistics.

inputs which are hand-crafted features such as POS tags. Support Vector Machine (Isozaki and Kazawa, 2002), maximum entropy models (Bender et al., 2003), Hidden Markov Models (Zhou and Su, 2002) and CRF (Klinger, 2011; Chen et al., 2006; Marcinczuk, 2015) were applied.

Word-based Neural Models: A neural model was applied to sequence labeling tasks also in NER (Collobert et al., 2011). Modified models using Bi-directional LSTM (BLSTM) or Stacked LSTM were proposed (Huang et al., 2015; Lample et al., 2016). Recently, new approaches introducing CNN or LSTM for extracting sub-word information from character inputs have been found to outperform other models (Lample et al., 2016). Rei et al. (2016) proposed the model using an attention mechanism whose inputs are words and characters. Above all, BLSTM-CNNs-CRF (Ma and Hovy, 2016) achieved state-of-the-art performance on the standard English corpus: CoNLL2003 (Tjong Kim Sang and De Meulder, 2003).

Character-based Neural Models: Kuru et al. (2016) proposed a character-based neural model. This model, which inputs only characters, exhibits good performance on the condition that no external knowledge is used. This model predicts a tag for each character and forces that predicted tags in a word are the same. Therefore, it is unsuitable for languages in which boundary conflicts occur.

Japanese NER: For Japanese NER, many models using conventional algorithms have been proposed (Iwakura, 2011; Sasano and Kurohashi, 2008). Most such models are character-based models to deal with boundary conflicts.

Tomori et al. (2016) applied a neural model to Japanese NER. This study uses non-sequential neural networks with inputs that are hand-crafted features. This model uses no recent advanced approaches for NER, such as word embedding or CNN to extract sub-word information. Therefore, the effectiveness of recent neural models for Japanese NER has not been evaluated.

3 Japanese NER and Characteristics

One common definition of entity categories for Japanese NER is Sekine's extended named entity hierarchy (Sekine et al., 2002). This definition includes 30 entity categories. This study used the corpus annotated in Mainichi newspaper articles (Hashimoto et al., 2008).

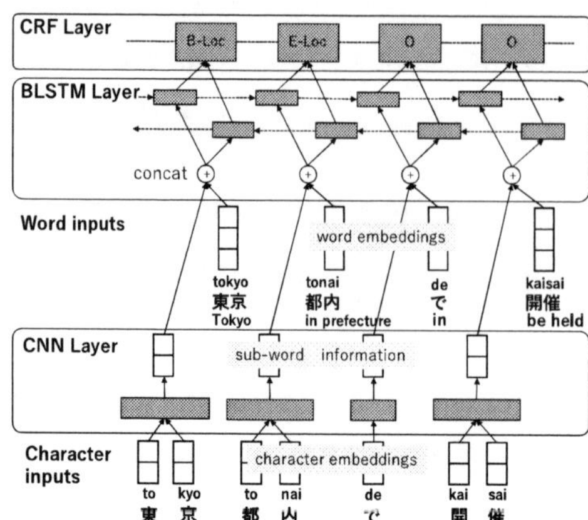

Figure 1: Structure of BLSTM-CNNs-CRF. The superscripts on Japanese show pronunciations. The subscripts on Japanese words are translations.

Japanese language is written without blank spaces. Therefore, word segmentations that are made using morphological analysis are needed to use word information. However, some word segmentations cause boundary conflicts. As an example, one can consider the extraction of the correct entity "*Tokyoto*" (Tokyo prefecture) from "*Tokyotonai*" (in Tokyo prefecture).

Tokyo/*tonai* (Tokyo / in pref.): word boundary

Tokyoto/*nai* (Tokyo pref. / in): entity boundary

These slashes show word and entity boundaries. The entity boundary does not match the word boundary. Therefore, the entity candidates by word-based models are "*Tokyo*" and "*Tokyotonai*." It is impossible to extract the entity "*Tokyoto*".

Word lengths of Japanese language tend to be shorter than those of English. The average word length in entities in CoNLL 2003 (Reuters news service) is 6.43 characters. That in the Mainichi newspaper corpus is 1.95. Therefore, it is difficult to extract sub-word information in Japanese in a manner that is suitable for English.

4 NER Models

4.1 Word-based neural model

In this study, we specifically examine BLSTM-CNNs-CRF (Ma and Hovy, 2016) because it achieves state-of-the-art performance in the CoNLL 2003 corpus. Figure 1 presents the architecture of this model. This word-based model combines CNN, BLSTM, and CRF layers. We describe each layer of this model as the following.

CNN Layer: This layer is aimed at extracting sub-word information. The inputs are character embeddings of a word. This layer consists of convolution and pooling layers. The convolution layer produces a matrix for a word with consideration of the sub-word. The pooling layer compresses the matrix for each dimension of character embedding.

BLSTM Layer: BLSTM (Graves and Schmidhuber, 2005) is an approach to treat sequential data. The output of CNN and word embedding are concatenated as an input of BLSTM.

CRF Layer: This layer was designed to select the best tag sequence from all possible tag sequences with consideration of outputs from BLSTM and correlations between adjacent tags. This layer introduces a transition score for each transition pattern between adjacent tags. The objective function is calculated using the sum of the outputs from BLSTM and the transition scores for a sequence.

4.2 Character-based neural model

To resolve the obstacles when applying a recent neural model, we propose character-based BLSTM-CRF model (Char-BLSTM-CRF). This model, which consists of BLSTM and CRF layers, predicts a tag for every character independently. Figure 2 presents the model structure.

This model gives an input for each character to predict a tag for a character independently. Additionally, we introduce word information with character information as inputs of this model. Character information is a character embedding and word information is the embedding of the word containing the character. That is, the same word embedding will be used as inputs of characters constructing a word. This enables us to utilize pre-training of word embeddings with the effectiveness shown in English (Ma and Hovy, 2016).

We assume that it is difficult for the CNN layer to extract the Japanese sub-word information. Moreover, we assume that sufficient information can be extracted from a simple character input. Consequently, the model uses no CNN layer.

5 Experiments

5.1 Experiment Conditions

We evaluate our models using the Mainichi newspaper corpus. We specifically examine the four categories of the highest frequency: *Product, Location, Organization, Time*. Table 1 presents

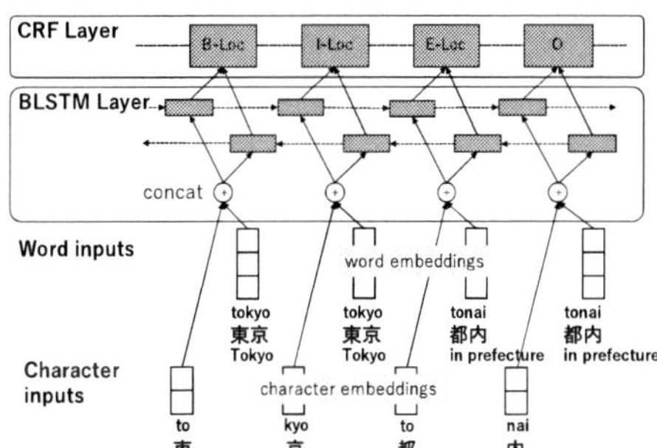

Figure 2: Structure of Char-BLSTM-CRF.

	Train	Dev.	Test
Articles	5,424	678	682
Sentences	62,373	8,032	7,689
Words	1,591,781	200,843	197,649
Product (NE)	39,734	5,087	5,120
Location (NE)	24,981	3,238	3,251
Organization (NE)	19,119	2,535	2,690
Time (NE)	17,252	2,216	2,148

Table 1: Statistics of the corpus.

statistics related to this corpus. We prepared pre-trained word embeddings using skip-gram model (Mikolov et al., 2013). Seven years (1995–1996 and 1998–2002) of Mainichi newspaper articles which include almost 500 million words are used for pre-training. We conduct parameter tuning using the development dataset. We choose the unit number of LSTM as 300, the size of word embedding as 500, that of character embedding as 50, the maximum epoch as 20, and the batch size as 60. We use Adam (Kingma and Ba, 2014), with the learning rate of 0.001 for optimization. We use MeCab (Kudo, 2005) for word segmentation. Other conditions are the same as those reported for an earlier study (Ma and Hovy, 2016).

5.2 Results

Table 2 presents F1 scores of models. We compare BLSTM-CNNs-CRF, Char-BLSTM-CRF, and character-based conventional CRF. To verify the effectiveness of the CNN layer and the CRF layer in BLSTM-CNNs-CRF, we use additional word-based models of two types with a component changed from BLSTM-CNNs-CRF. BLSTM-CRF is a model with eliminated the CNN layer and character inputs. BLSTM-CNNs is a model with the CRF layer replaced by a softmax layer. To evaluate the performance improvement of character inputs, word inputs and pre-training, we prepared additional three configurations of Char-BLSTM-CRF: without word, without character, without pre-training.

99

	BLSTM -CRF	BLSTM -CNNs	BLSTM -CNNs -CRF	CRF	Char-BLSTM -CRF w/o word	Char-BLSTM -CRF w/o char	Char-BLSTM -CRF w/o pretraining	Char- BLSTM -CRF
input	word	word+character			character	word	word+character	
output	word				character			
Product	†83.89	80.83	83.82	80.72	78.12	84.28	80.13	**84.46**
Location	†88.57	87.52	88.46	87.54	86.77	91.30	87.63	**91.47**
Organization	85.87	82.07	†**85.99**	79.62	77.72	85.26	80.79	85.56
Time	†94.39	92.50	93.51	93.00	93.35	94.03	93.55	**94.44**
Average	†87.16	84.59	86.98	84.25	82.81	87.80	84.33	**88.06**

Table 2: F1 score of each models. Average is a weighted average. † expresses the best result in the word-based models for each entity category. Bold means the best result in all models for each entity category. "output" means the unit of prediction; "input" shows information used as inputs.

Entity Category	*Pro.*	*Loc.*	*Org.*	*Time*
Word Length in Entity	1.99	2.07	2.51	1.20

Table 3: Averaged word length in entity.

	Pro.	*Loc.*	*Org.*	*Time*
Total Conflicts	66	75	23	7
Extracted Entities	25	68	8	3

Table 4: Number of entities with boundary conflicts and that of entities extracted by Char-BLSTM-CRF.

Word-based Neural Models: Among word-based models, BLSTM-CNNs-CRF is the best model for *Organization*. Also, BLSTM-CRF is the best model for *Product*, *Location*, and *Time*. We confirm that cutting-edge neural models are suitable for Japanese language because each model outperforms CRF.

When comparing BLSTM-CNNs and BLSTM-CNNs-CRF, the CRF layer contributes to improvement by 2.39 pt. When comparing BLSTM-CRF and BLSTM-CNNs-CRF, the CNN layer is worse by 0.18 pt. Here, the CNN layer and the CRF layer improve by 2.36 pt and 1.75 pt in English (Ma and Hovy, 2016). Therefore, the CRF layer performs similarly but the CNN layer performs differently. The CNN layer enhances the model flexibility. Nevertheless, this layer can scarcely extract information from characters because Japanese words are shorter than English, according to Section 3.

Table 3 shows the averaged word length after splitting an entity into words for each entity category. Words composing *Time* entities is the shortest. Therefore, information is scarce, especially in *Time*. In contrast, the words composing *Organization* is long. Therefore, CNN can extract information from characters in a word in *Organization*. This is the reason why BLSTM-CNNs-CRF performs better than BLSTM-CRF in *Organization*.

Character-based Neural Models: The results of averaged F1 scores show that Char-BLSTM-CRF is more suitable for Japanese than word-based models. When comparing four configurations of Char-BLSTM-CRF, pre-training is critically important for performance. Character input also con-tributes to the performance improvement in Char-BLSTM-CRF, although the input degrades the performance in a word-based model.

Total Conflicts in the table 4 is the total number of entities with boundary conflicts in the test data. Extracted Entities in the table is the number of entities that Char-BLSTM-CRF extracts among the entities with boundary conflicts. Results show that the model extracts entities with boundary conflicts which cannot be extracted by word-based models. The number of entities with boundary conflicts extracted by Char-BLSTM-CRF is the largest in *Location*. When comparing the performance of Char-BLSTM-CRF and BLSTM-CRF for each entity category, the largest performance improvement of 2.90 pt is achieved in *Location*. By extracting 68 entities with boundary conflicts in *Location*, Char-BLSTM-CRF achieves about 2 pt improvement out of total 2.90 pt. It can be said that almost all improvements of Char-BLSTM-CRF are from extracting these entities.

In contrast, Char-BLSTM-CRF is inappropriate for *Organization*. The averaged word length of entities that are not extracted accurately by BLSTM-CNNs-CRF is 4.07; that by Char-BLSTM-CRF is 4.87. It can be said that Char-BLSTM-CRF is un-suitable for extracting long words. We infer that the inputs of LSTM become redundant and that LSTM does not work efficiently. Especially, the averaged word length of *Organization* is long according to Table 3. For that reason, the character-based model is inappropriate in *Organization*.

6 Conclusions

As described in this paper, we verified the effectiveness of the state-of-the-art neural NER model for Japanese. The experimentally obtained results show that the model outperforms conventional CRF in Japanese. Results show that the CNN layer works improperly for Japanese because words of the Japanese language are short.

We proposed a character-based neural model incorporating words and characters: Char-BLSTM-CRF. This model outperforms a state-of-the-art neural NER model in Japanese, especially for the entity category consisting of short words. Our future work will examine reduction of redundancy in character-based model by preparing and combining different LSTMs for word and character inputs. Also to examine the effects of pre-training of characters in Char-BLSTM-CRF is our future work.

References

Masayuki Asahara and Yuji Matsumoto. 2003. Japanese named entity extraction with redundant morphological analysis. In *Proceedings of the 7th Conference of the North American Chapter of the Association for Computational Linguistics on Human Language Technology-Volume 1*, pages 8–15.

Oliver Bender, Franz Josef Och, and Hermann Ney. 2003. Maximum entropy models for named entity recognition. In *Proceedings of the 7th Conference on North American Chapter of the Association for Computational Linguistics on Human Language Technology-Volume4*, pages 148–151.

Wenliang Chen, Yujie Zhang, and Hitoshi Isahara. 2006. Chinese named entity recognition with conditional random fields. In *Proceedings of the 5th Special Interest Group of Chinese Language Processing Workshop*, pages 118–121.

Jason PC Chiu and Eric Nichols. 2015. Named entity recognition with bidirectional lstm-cnns. *arXiv preprint arXiv:1511.08308.*

Ronan Collobert, Jason Weston, Léon Bottou, Michael Karlen, Koray Kavukcuoglu, and Pavel Kuksa. 2011. Natural language processing (almost) from scratch. *Journal of Machine Learning Research*, 12(Aug):2493–2537.

Alex Graves and Jürgen Schmidhuber. 2005. Framewise phoneme classification with bidirectional lstm and other neural network architectures. *Neural Networks*, 18(5):602–610.

Taiichi Hashimoto, Takashi Inui, and Koji Murakami. 2008. Constructing extended named entity annotated corpora (in japanese). *The Special Interest Group Technical Reports of the Information Processing Society of Japan*, 113:113–120.

Zhiheng Huang, Wei Xu, and Kai Yu. 2015. Bidirectional lstm-crf models for sequence tagging. *arXiv preprint arXiv:1508.01991.*

Hideki Isozaki and Hideto Kazawa. 2002. Efficient support vector classifiers for named entity recognition. In *Proceedings of the 19th international conference on Computational linguistics-Volume 1*, pages 1–7.

Tomoya Iwakura. 2011. A named entity recognition method using rules acquired from unlabeled data. In *Proceedings of the 8th International Conference on Recent Advances in Natural Language Processing*, pages 170–177.

Diederik Kingma and Jimmy Ba. 2014. Adam: A method for stochastic optimization. *arXiv preprint arXiv:1412.6980.*

Roman Klinger. 2011. Automatically selected skip edges in conditional random fields for named entity recognition. In *Proceedings of the 8th International Conference on Recent Advances in Natural Language Processing*, pages 580–585.

Taku Kudo. 2005. Mecab: Yet another part-of-speech and morphological analyzer. *http://taku910.github.io/mecab/.*

Onur Kuru, Arkan Ozan Can, and Deniz Yuret. 2016. Charner: Character-level named entity recognition. In *Proceedings of the 26th International Conference on Computational Linguistics*, pages 911–921.

Guillaume Lample, Miguel Ballesteros, Sandeep Subramanian, Kazuya Kawakami, and Chris Dyer. 2016. Neural architectures for named entity recognition. *arXiv preprint arXiv:1603.01360.*

Xuezhe Ma and Eduard Hovy. 2016. End-to-end sequence labeling via bi-directional lstm-cnns-crf. *arXiv preprint arXiv:1603.01354.*

Michal Marcinczuk. 2015. Automatic construction of complex features in conditional random fields for named entities recognition. In *Proceedings of the 10th International Conference on Recent Advances in Natural Language Processing*, pages 413–419.

Tomas Mikolov, Kai Chen, Greg Corrado, and Jeffrey Dean. 2013. Efficient estimation of word representations in vector space. *arXiv preprint arXiv:1301.3781.*

Marek Rei, Gamal Crichton, and Sampo Pyysalo. 2016. Attending to characters in neural sequence labeling models. In *Proceedings of the 26th International Conference on Computational Linguistics*, pages 309–318.

Cicero Nogueira dos Santos and Victor Guimaraes. 2015. Boosting named entity recognition with neural character embeddings. *arXiv preprint arXiv:1505.05008.*

Ryohei Sasano and Sadao Kurohashi. 2008. Japanese named entity recognition using structural natural language processing. In *Proceedings of the 3rd International Joint Conference on Natural Language Processing*, pages 607–612.

Manabu Sassano and Takehito Utsuro. 2000. Named entity chunking techniques in supervised learning for japanese named entity recognition. In *Proceedings of the 18th conference on Computational linguistics-Volume 2*, pages 705–711.

Satoshi Sekine, Kiyoshi Sudo, and Chikashi Nobata. 2002. Extended named entity hierarchy. In *Proceedings of 3rd International Conference on Language Resources and Evaluation*, pages 1818–1824.

Erik F Tjong Kim Sang and Fien De Meulder. 2003. Introduction to the conll-2003 shared task: Language-independent named entity recognition. In *Proceedings of the 7th conference on North American Chapter of the Association for Computational Linguistics on Human Language Technology-Volume 4*, pages 142–147.

Suzushi Tomori, Takashi Ninomiya, and Shinsuke Mori. 2016. Domain specific named entity recognition referring to the real world by deep neural networks. In *proceedings of the 54th Annual Meeting of the Association for Computational Linguistics*, pages 236–242.

GuoDong Zhou and Jian Su. 2002. Named entity recognition using an hmm-based chunk tagger. In *proceedings of the 40th Annual Meeting on Association for Computational Linguistics*, pages 473–480.

Word Representation Models for Morphologically Rich Languages in Neural Machine Translation

Ekaterina Vylomova and **Trevor Cohn** and **Xuanli He**
The University of Melbourne
Melbourne, VIC, Australia
evylomova@gmail.com trevor.cohn@unimelb.edu.au
xuanlih@student.unimelb.edu.au

Gholamreza Haffari
Monash University
Clayton, VIC, Australia
gholamreza.haffari@monash.edu

Abstract

Out-of-vocabulary words present a great challenge for Machine Translation. Recently various character-level compositional models were proposed to address this issue. In current research we incorporate two most popular neural architectures, namely LSTM and CNN, into hard- and soft-attentional models of translation for character-level representation of the source. We propose semantic and morphological intrinsic evaluation of encoder-level representations. Our analysis of the learned representations reveals that character-based LSTM seems to be better at capturing morphological aspects compared to character-based CNN. We also show that a hard-attentional model provides better character-level representations compared to standard 'soft' attention.

1 Introduction

Models of end-to-end machine translation based on neural networks can produce excellent translations, rivalling or surpassing traditional statistical machine translation systems (Kalchbrenner and Blunsom, 2013; Sutskever et al., 2014; Bahdanau et al., 2015). A central challenge in neural MT is handling rare and uncommon words. Conventional neural MT models use a fixed modest-size vocabulary, such that the identity of rare words are lost, which makes their translation exceedingly difficult. Accordingly, sentences containing rare words tend to be translated much more poorly than those containing only common words (Sutskever et al., 2014; Bahdanau et al., 2015). The rare word problem is exacerbated when translating from morphologically rich languages, where the several morphological variants of words result in a huge vocabulary with a heavy tail. For example in Russian, there are at least 70 word forms for dog, encoding case, gender, age, number, sentiment and other semantic connotations. Many of them share a common lemma, and contain regular morphological affixation; consequently much of the information required for translation is present, but not in an accessible form for models of neural MT.

In many cases the OOV problem is addressed by incorporating character-level word representations largely belonging to one of two classes, namely convolutional neural networks (CNNs) and recurrent neural networks based on long-short term memory (LSTM) units (Hochreiter and Schmidhuber, 1997). But there was no investigation of what each of the models captures and how well they can model morphology in particular. In this paper, we fill this gap by evaluating of encoder-level representations of OOV words. To get the representations, we incorporate LSTM and CNN word representation models into two types of attentional machine translation models. Our evaluation includes both intrinsic and extrinsic metrics, where we compare these approaches based on their translation performance as well as their ability to recover synonyms for the rare words. Intrinsic analysis shows that there is only minor differences in end translation performance, although detailed analysis shows that character-based LSTM is overally best at capturing morphological regularities.

103

Proceedings of the First Workshop on Subword and Character Level Models in NLP, pages 103–108,
Copenhagen, Denmark, September 7, 2017. ©2017 Association for Computational Linguistics.

2 Related Work

Most neural models for NLP rely on words as their basic units, and consequently face the problem of how to handle tokens in the test set that are out-of-vocabulary (OOV). Often these words are assigned a special UNK token, which comes at the expense of modelling accuracy. One solution to OOV problem is modelling sub-word units, using a model of a word from its composite morphemes. Luong et al. (2013) proposed a recursive combination of morphs using affine transformation, however this is unable to differentiate between the compositional and non-compositional cases. Botha and Blunsom (2014) tackle this problem by forming word representations from adding a sum of each word's morpheme embeddings to its word embedding. Morpheme based methods rely on good morphological analysers, however these are only available for a limited set of languages. Unsupervised analysers (Creutz and Lagus, 2007) are prone to segmentation errors, particularly on fusional or polysynthetic languages. In these settings, character-level word representations may be more appropriate.

Several authors have proposed convolutional neural networks over character sequences, as part of models of part of speech tagging (Santos and Zadrozny, 2014), named entity recognition (Ma and Hovy, 2016; Chiu and Nichols, 2015), language (Kim et al., 2015) and machine translation (Costa-jussà and Fonollosa, 2016; Belinkov et al., 2017). The latter one presents an in-depth analysis of representations learned by neural MT models. Another strand of research has looked at recurrent architectures, using long-short term memory units (Ling et al., 2015; Ballesteros et al., 2015) which can capture long orthographic patterns in the character sequence, as well as non-compositionality. (Lample et al., 2016) shows that incorporating biLSTM character-level word representations improves accuracy in named entity recognition task.

All of the aforementioned models were shown to either perform similar or even outperform standard word-embedding approaches. With a few notable exceptions (Vania and Lopez, 2017; Heigold et al., 2017), there was no systematic investigation of the various modelling architectures. In our work we address the question of what linguistic lexical aspects are best encoded in each type of architecture, and their efficacy as part of a machine translation model when translating from morpho-

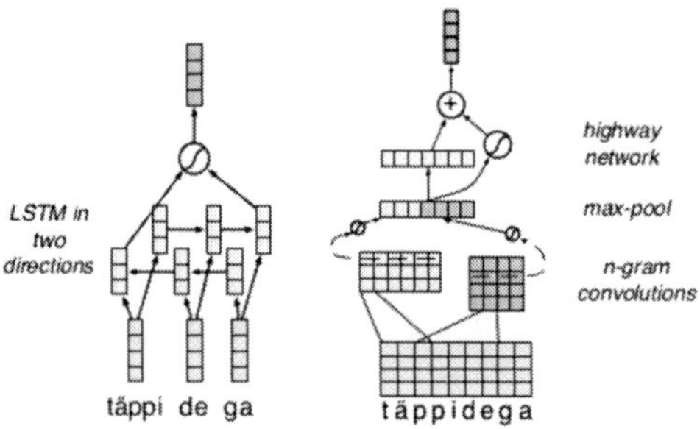

Figure 1: Model architecture for the several approaches to learning word representations, showing from left: BiLSTM over characters and the character convolution.

logically rich languages.

3 Models

Now we turn to the problem of learning word representations. We consider character level encoding methods which we compare to the baseline word embedding approach. We test two types of character representations: LSTM recurrent neural networks (RNN) and convolutional neural network (CNN).

For each type of character encoder we learn two word representations: one estimated from the characters and the word embedding.[1] Then we run max pooling over both embeddings to obtain the word representation, $\mathbf{r}_w = \boldsymbol{m}_w \oslash \boldsymbol{e}_w$, where $\boldsymbol{m}_w$ is the embedding of word w and $\boldsymbol{e}_w$ is the sub-word encoding. The max pooling operation $\oslash$ captures non-compositionality in the semantic meaning of a word relative to its sub-parts. We assume that the model would favour unit-based embeddings for rare words and word-based for more common ones.

Each word is expressed with its constituent units as follows. Let $\mathcal{U}$ be the vocabulary of sub-word units, i.e., characters, E_u be the dimensionality of unit embeddings, and $M \in \mathbf{R}^{E_u \times |\mathcal{U}|}$ be the matrix of unit embeddings. Suppose that a word w from the source dictionary is made up of a sequence of units $\mathcal{U}_w := [u_1, \ldots, u_{|w|}]$, where $|w|$ stands for the number of constituent units in the word. The resulting word representations are then fed to both attentional models as the source word embeddings.

---

[1] We only include word embeddings for common words; rare words share a UNK embedding.

3.1 Bidirectional LSTM Encoder

The encoding of the word is formulated using a pair of LSTMs (denoted *biLSTM*) one operating left-to-right over the input sequence and another operating right-to-left, $h_j^{\rightarrow} = \text{LSTM}(h_{j-1}^{\rightarrow}, m_{u_j})$ and $h_j^{\leftarrow} = \text{LSTM}(h_{j+1}^{\leftarrow}, m_{u_j})$ where $h_j^{\rightarrow}$ and $h_j^{\leftarrow}$ are the LSTM hidden states.[2] These are fed into perceptron with a single hidden layer and a tanh activation function to form the word representation, $e_w = \text{MLP}\left(h_{|\mathcal{U}_w|}^{\rightarrow}, h_1^{\leftarrow}\right)$.

3.2 Convolutional Encoder

Another word encoder we consider is a convolutional neural network, inspired by a similar approach in language modelling (Kim et al., 2016). Let $U_w \in \mathbb{R}^{E_u \times |\mathcal{U}|_w}$ denote the unit-level representation of w, where the jth column corresponds to the unit embedding of u_j. The idea of unit-level CNN is to apply a *kernel* $\mathbf{Q}_l \in \mathbb{R}^{E_u \times k_l}$ with the width k_l to U_w to obtain a feature map $\mathbf{f_l} \in \mathbb{R}^{|\mathcal{U}|_w - k_l + 1}$. More formally, for the jth element of the feature map the convolutional representation is

$$\mathbf{f_l}(j) = \tanh(\langle U_{w,j}, \mathbf{Q}_l \rangle + b)$$

where $U_{w,j} \in \mathbb{R}^{E_u \times k_l}$ is a slice from U_w which spans the representations of the jth unit and its preceding $k_l - 1$ units, and

$$\langle A, B \rangle = \sum_{i,j} A_{ij} B_{ij} = \text{Tr}\left(AB^T\right)$$

denotes the Frobenius inner product. For example, suppose that the input has size $[4 \times 9]$, and a kernel has size $[4 \times 3]$ with a sliding step being 1. Then, we obtain a $[1 \times 7]$ feature map. This process implements a character n-gram, where n is equal to the width of the filter. The word representation is then derived by max pooling the feature maps of the kernels:

$$\forall l: \quad \mathbf{r}_w(l) = \max_j \mathbf{f_l}(j)$$

In order to capture interactions between the character n-grams obtained by the filters, a *highway network* (Srivastava et al., 2015) is applied after the max pooling layer,

$$e_w = t \odot \text{MLP}(r_w) + (1 - t) \odot r_w,$$

where $t = \text{MLP}_\sigma(r_w)$ is a sigmoid gating function which modulates between a tanh MLP transformation of the input (left component) and preserving the input as is (right component).

Language	Ru-En	Et-En
Phrase-based Baseline	15.02	24.40
AM BILSTM$_{\text{char}}$	16.01	26.34
OSM BILSTM$_{\text{char}}$	15.81	26.14
AM CNN$_{\text{char}}$	15.90	26.14
OSM CNN$_{\text{char}}$	15.94	25.97
AM BILSTM$_{\text{word}}$	15.93	26.33
OSM BILSTM$_{\text{word}}$	15.70	26.03

Table 2: BLEU scores for re-ranking the test sets.

4 Experiments

Datasets. We use parallel bilingual data from Europarl for Estonian-English (Koehn, 2005), and web-crawled parallel data for Russian-English (Antonova and Misyurev, 2011). For preprocessing, we tokenize, lower-case, and filter out sentences longer than 30 words. We apply a frequency threshold of 5, replacing low-frequency words with a special UNK token. Table 1 presents the corpus statistics.

4.1 Extrinsic Evaluation: MT

We apply the character level models in the encoder of the neural attentional (Bahdanau et al., 2015) (AM, soft-attentional) and neural operation sequence (Vylomova et al., 2016) (OSM, hard-attentional) models, replacing the source word embedding component with a BiLSTM or CNN over characters. To evaluate translations, we re-ranked moses[3] 100-best output translations using the attentional models. The re-ranker includes standard features from moses plus an extra feature(s) for each of the models. For the AM we supply the log probability of the candidate translation, and for the OSM we add two extra features corresponding to the generated alignment and the translation probabilities. The weights of the re-ranker are then trained using MERT (Och, 2003) with 100 restarts to optimise BLEU.

Table 2 presents BLEU score results. As seen, re-ranking based on neural models' scores outperforms the phrase-based baseline. However, the translation quality of the neural models are not significantly different. We assume that this is due to re-ranking of moses translations rather than decoding. Also note that here we do not address the problem of OOV on the decoding side.

4.2 Intrinsic Evaluation

We now take a closer look at the embeddings learned by the models, based on how well they

---

[2] The memory cells are computed as part of the recurrence, suppressed here for clarity.

[3] `https://github.com/moses-smt`.

Set	Train		Development		Test		
	tokens	types	tokens	types	tokens	types	OOV rate
Ru-En	1,639K-1,809K	145K-65K	150K-168K	35K-18K	150K-167K	35K-18K	45%
Et-En	1,411K-1,857K	90K-25K	141K-188K	21K-9K	142K-189K	21K-8K	45%

Table 1: Corpus statistics for parallel data between Russian/Estonian and English. The OOV rate are the fraction of word types in the source language that are in the test set but are below the frequency cut-off or unseen in training.

capture the *semantic* and *morphological* information in the nearest neighbour words. Learning representations for low frequency words is harder than that for high-frequency words, since low frequency words cannot capitalise as reliably on their contexts. Therefore, we split the test lexicon into 6 parts according to their frequency in the training set. Since we set out word frequency threshold to 5 for the training set, all words appearing in the lowest frequency band [0,4] are OOVs for the test set. For each word of the test set, we take its top-20 nearest neighbours from the whole training lexicon using cosine similarity.

Semantic Evaluation. We investigate how well the nearest neighbours are interchangable with a query word in the translation process. So we formalise the notion of semantics of the source words based on their translations in the target language. We use *pivoting* to define the probability of a candidate word e' to be the synonym of the query word e, $p(e'|e) = \sum_f p(f|e)p(e'|f)$, where f is a target language word, and the translation probabilities inside the summation are estimated using a word-based translation model trained on the entire initial bilingual corpora. We then take the top-5 most probable words as the gold synonyms for each query word of the test set.[4]

We measure the quality of predicted nearest neighbours using the multi-label accuracy[5], $\frac{1}{|S|} \sum_{w \in S} \mathbf{1}_{[G(w) \cap N(w) \neq \varnothing]}$ where $G(w)$ and $N(w)$ are the sets of gold standard synonyms and nearest neighbors for w respectively; the function $\mathbf{1}_{[C]}$ is one if the condition C is true, and zero otherwise. In other words, it is the fraction of words in S whose nearest neighbours and gold standard synonyms have non-empty overlap.

Table 3 presents the semantic evaluation results. As seen, for the *vanilla* (soft) attentional model word- and character-level representations perform

---

[4]We remove query words whose frequency is less than a threshold in the initial bilingual corpora, since pivoting may not result in high quality synonyms for such words.

[5]We evaluated using mean reciprocal rank (MRR) measure as well, and obtained results consistent with the multi-label accuracy (omitted due to space constraints).

Model Freq.	0-4	5-9	10-14	15-19	20-50	50+
Russian						
AM BILSTM$_{word}$	-	0.32	0.52	0.65	**0.81**	**0.95**
OSM BILSTM$_{word}$	-	0.36	0.49	0.61	0.76	0.91
AM BILSTM$_{char}$	0.21	0.33	0.49	0.58	0.71	0.85
OSM BILSTM$_{char}$	0.16	0.34	0.48	0.59	0.71	0.85
AM CNN$_{char}$	0.13	0.23	0.38	0.47	0.61	0.84
OSM CNN$_{char}$	**0.43**	**0.71**	**0.77**	**0.77**	**0.81**	0.81
Estonian						
AM BILSTM$_{word}$	-	0.39	0.53	0.63	0.72	0.88
OSM BILSTM$_{word}$	-	0.48	0.62	0.70	**0.79**	**0.90**
AM BILSTM$_{char}$	0.12	0.30	0.37	0.45	0.52	0.70
OSM BILSTM$_{char}$	0.13	0.39	0.48	0.55	0.63	0.78
AM CNN$_{char}$	0.12	0.25	0.33	0.42	0.52	0.75
OSM CNN$_{char}$	**0.48**	**0.70**	**0.75**	**0.76**	0.78	0.78

Table 3: Semantic evaluation of nearest neighbours using multi-label accuracy on words in different frequency bands.

quite similar. In case of the *hard* attentional model we OSM CNN$_{char}$ outperforms other representations by a large margin.

Morphological Evaluation. We now turn to evaluating the morphological component. We only focus on Russian since it has a notoriously hard morphology. We run another morphological analyser, *mystem* (Segalovich, 2003), to generate *linguistically tagged* morphological analyses for a word, e.g. POS tags, case, person, plurality, etc. We represent each morphological analysis with a bit vector, where each 1 bit indicates the presence of a specific grammatical feature. Each word is then assigned a set of bit vectors corresponding to the set of its morphological analyses. As the *morphology similarity* between two words, we take the minimum of Hamming similarity[6] between the corresponding two sets of bit vectors. Table 4(a) shows the average morphology similarity between the words and their nearest neighbours across the frequency bands. Likewise, we represent the words based on their lemma features; Table 4(b) shows the average lemma similarity.

Table 5 lists top five nearest neighbours for OOV words produced by the OSM models. BiLSTMs better capture morphological similarities expressed in suffixes and prefixes. We assume this

---

[6]The Hamming similarity is the number of bits having the same value in two given bit vectors.

Ras+po+*lag*+a+ušč+ej

Disposing (inpraes,dat,sg,partcp,plen,f,ipf,intr)

OSM CNN$_{char}$	OSM BILSTM$_{char}$
ras+po+lag+a+ušč+iy	ras+slab+l+ja+ušč+ej
disposing (inpraes,nom,sg,partcp,plen,m,ipf,inan,intr)	*relaxing (inpraes,dat,sg,partcp,plen,f,ipf)*
ras+po+lag+a+ušč+im	so+pro+voj+d+a+ušč+ej
disposing (inpraes,ins,sg,partcp,plen,m,ipf,intrn)	*accompanying (inpraes,dat,sg,partcp,plen,f,ipf,tran)*
ras+po+lag+a+ušč+ie	ras+slab+l+ja+ušč+uju
disposing (inpraes,nom,pl,partcp,plen,ipf,intr)	*relaxing (inpraes,acc,sg,partcp,plen,f,ipf)*
ras+po+lag+a+ušč+ih	ras+po+lag+a+ušč+iy
disposing (inpraes,gen,pl,partcp,plen,ipf,intr)	*disposing (inpraes,nom,sg,partcp,plen,m,ipf,inan,intr)*
ras+po+lag+a+ušč+i+e+sja	pro+dvig+a+ušč+ej
disposing (inpraes,nom,pl,partcp,plen,ipf,act)	*promoting (inpraes,dat,sg,partcp,plen,f,ipf,act)*

S+*konfigur*+ir+ova+í

Configure (v,pf,tran,inf)

OSM CNN$_{char}$	OSM BILSTM$_{char}$
s+konfigur+ir+ui+te	konfigur+ir+ova+í
configure (v,pf,tran,pl,imper,2p)	*configure (v,ipf,tran,inf)*
s+konfigur+ova+li	s+korrekt+ir+ova+í
configured (v,pf,tran,praet,pl,indic)	*adjust (v,pf,tran,inf)*
s+konfigur+ova+n	s+*koordin*+ir+ova+í
configured (v,pf,tran,praet,sg,partcp,brev,m,pass)	*coordinate (v,pf,tran,inf)*
s+konstru+ir+ova+í	s+fokus+ir+ova+í
construct (v,pf,tran,inf)	*focus (v,pf,tran,in)*
s+kompil+ir+ova+í	s+kompil+ir+ova+í
compile (v,pf,tran,inf)	*compile (v,pf,tran,inf)*

Table 5: Analysis of the five most similar Russian words (initial word is OOV), under the OSM CNN$_{char}$ and OSM BILSTM$_{char}$ word encodings based on cosine similarity. The diacritic ´ indicates softness. **POS tags**: *s*-noun, *a*-adjective, *v*-verb; **Gender**: *m*-masculine, *f*-feminine, *n*-neuter; **Number**: *sg*-singular, *pl*-plural; **Case**: *nom*-nominative, *gen*-genitive, *dat*-dative, *acc*-accusative, *ins*-instrumental, *abl*-prepositional, *loc*-locative; **Tense**: *praes*-present, *inpraes*-continuous, *praet*-past, *pf*-perfect, *ipf*-imperfect; *indic*-indicative; **Transitivity**: *trans*-transitive, *intr*-intransitive; **Adjective form**: *br*-brevity, *plen*-full form, *poss*-possessive; **Comparative**: *supr*-superlative, *comp*-comparative; **Noun person**: *1p*-first, *2p*-second, *3p*-third;

Model \ Freq.	0-4	5-9	10-14	15-19	20-50	50+
AM BILSTM$_{word}$	-	0.70	0.73	075	0.78	0.82
OSM BILSTM$_{word}$	-	0.74	0.77	0.78	0.81	0.84
AM BILSTM$_{char}$	0.90	0.82	0.83	0.83	0.84	0.82
OSM BILSTM$_{char}$	**0.91**	**0.84**	**0.85**	**0.85**	**0.86**	**0.86**
AM CNN$_{char}$	0.82	0.76	0.77	0.78	0.79	0.81
OSM CNN$_{char}$	0.79	0.80	0.79	0.79	0.79	0.79

(a)

Model \ Freq.	0-4	5-9	10-14	15-19	20-50	50+
AM BILSTM$_{word}$	-	0.02	0.04	0.07	0.11	0.18
OSM BILSTM$_{word}$	-	0.03	0.05	0.06	0.09	0.15
AM BILSTM$_{char}$	0.08	0.06	0.10	0.11	0.12	0.21
OSM BILSTM$_{char}$	0.05	0.05	0.08	0.10	0.13	0.18
AM CNN$_{char}$	0.04	0.02	0.05	0.06	0.1	0.15
OSM CNN$_{char}$	**0.20**	**0.37**	**0.41**	**0.42**	**0.44**	**0.41**

(b)

Table 4: Morphology analysis for nearest neighbours based on (a) Grammar tag features, and (b) Lemma features, evaluated on Russian.

is due to the fact that they are naturally biased towards most recent inputs. CNNs, on the other hand, are more invariant of character positions and provide whole-word similarity.

5 Conclusion

We studied two types of attentional models augmented by CNN and LSTM encodings. Our experiments demonstrate that representation of out-of-vocabulary words with their sub-word units on the source side did not lead to a significant improvement in overall quality of machine translation; however LSTMs applied to character sequences are more capable at learning morphological patterns. Moreover, a hard attention mechanism leads to better capturing of semantic and morphological regularities.

References

Alexandra Antonova and Alexey Misyurev. 2011. Building a web-based parallel corpus and filtering out machine-translated text. In *Proceedings of the 4th Workshop on Building and Using Comparable Corpora: Comparable Corpora and the Web*. Association for Computational Linguistics, pages 136–144.

Dzmitry Bahdanau, Kyunghyun Cho, and Yoshua Bengio. 2015. Neural machine translation by jointly learning to align and translate. In *Proceedings of the International Conference on Learning Representations (ICLR)*. San Diego, CA.

Miguel Ballesteros, Chris Dyer, and Noah A Smith. 2015. Improved transition-based parsing by modeling characters instead of words with lstms. *arXiv preprint arXiv:1508.00657* .

Yonatan Belinkov, Nadir Durrani, Fahim Dalvi, Hassan Sajjad, and James Glass. 2017. What do neural machine translation models learn about morphology? *arXiv preprint arXiv:1704.03471* .

Jan A Botha and Phil Blunsom. 2014. Compositional morphology for word representations and language modelling. *arXiv preprint arXiv:1405.4273* .

Jason PC Chiu and Eric Nichols. 2015. Named entity recognition with bidirectional lstm-cnns. *arXiv preprint arXiv:1511.08308* .

Marta Costa-jussà and Jose Fonollosa. 2016. Character-based neural machine translation. *arXiv preprint arXiv:1603.00810* .

Mathias Creutz and Krista Lagus. 2007. Unsupervised models for morpheme segmentation and morphology learning. *ACM Transactions on Speech and Language Processing (TSLP)* 4(1):3.

Georg Heigold, G ünter Neumann, and Josef van Genabith. 2017. An extensive empirical evaluation of character-based morphological tagging for 14 languages. In *Proceedings of the 15th Conference of the European Chapter of the Association for Computational Linguistics*. volume 1, pages 505–513.

Sepp Hochreiter and Jürgen Schmidhuber. 1997. Long short-term memory. *Neural computation* 9(8):1735–1780.

Nal Kalchbrenner and Phil Blunsom. 2013. Recurrent continuous translation models. In *EMNLP*. pages 1700–1709.

Yoon Kim, Yacine Jernite, David Sontag, and Alexander Rush. 2016. Character-aware neural language models. In *Proceedings of the Thirtieth AAAI Conference on Artificial Intelligence (AAAI-16)*.

Yoon Kim, Yacine Jernite, David Sontag, and Alexander M Rush. 2015. Character-aware neural language models. *arXiv preprint arXiv:1508.06615* .

Philipp Koehn. 2005. Europarl: A parallel corpus for statistical machine translation. In *MT summit*. volume 5, pages 79–86.

Guillaume Lample, Miguel Ballesteros, Sandeep Subramanian, Kazuya Kawakami, and Chris Dyer. 2016. Neural architectures for named entity recognition. *arXiv preprint arXiv:1603.01360* .

Wang Ling, Tiago Luís, Luís Marujo, Ramón Fernandez Astudillo, Silvio Amir, Chris Dyer, Alan W Black, and Isabel Trancoso. 2015. Finding function in form: Compositional character models for open vocabulary word representation. *arXiv preprint arXiv:1508.02096* .

Thang Luong, Richard Socher, and Christopher D Manning. 2013. Better word representations with recursive neural networks for morphology. In *CoNLL*. Citeseer, pages 104–113.

Xuezhe Ma and Eduard Hovy. 2016. End-to-end sequence labeling via bi-directional lstm-cnns-crf. *arXiv preprint arXiv:1603.01354* .

Franz Josef Och. 2003. Minimum error rate training in statistical machine translation. In *Proceedings of the 41st Annual Meeting on Association for Computational Linguistics-Volume 1*. Association for Computational Linguistics, pages 160–167.

Cicero D. Santos and Bianca Zadrozny. 2014. Learning character-level representations for part-of-speech tagging. In *Proceedings of the 31st International Conference on Machine Learning (ICML-14)*. pages 1818–1826.

Ilya Segalovich. 2003. A fast morphological algorithm with unknown word guessing induced by a dictionary for a web search engine. In *MLMTA*. Citeseer, pages 273–280.

Rupesh K Srivastava, Klaus Greff, and Jürgen Schmidhuber. 2015. Training very deep networks. In *Advances in Neural Information Processing Systems*. pages 2368–2376.

Ilya Sutskever, Oriol Vinyals, and Quoc VV Le. 2014. Sequence to sequence learning with neural networks. In *Neural Information Processing Systems (NIPS)*. Montréal, pages 3104–3112.

Clara Vania and Adam Lopez. 2017. From characters to words to in between: Do we capture morphology? *arXiv preprint arXiv:1704.08352* .

Ekaterina Vylomova, Trevor Cohn, Xuanli He, and Gholamreza Haffari. 2016. Word representation models for morphologically rich languages in neural machine translation. *arXiv preprint arXiv:1606.04217* .

Spell-Checking based on Syllabification and Character-level Graphs for a Peruvian Agglutinative Language

Carlo Alva
Facultad de Ciencias e Ingeniería
Pontificia Universidad Católica del Perú
`carlo.alva@pucp.pe`

Arturo Oncevay-Marcos
Departamento de Ingeniería, GRPIAA
Pontificia Universidad Católica del Perú
`arturo.oncevay@pucp.edu.pe`

Abstract

There are several native languages in Peru which are mostly agglutinative. These languages are transmitted from generation to generation mainly in oral form, causing different forms of writing across different communities. For this reason, there are recent efforts to standardize the spelling in the written texts, and it would be beneficial to support these tasks with an automatic tool such as a spell-checker. In this way, this spelling corrector is being developed based on two steps: an automatic rule-based syllabification method and a character-level graph to detect the degree of error in a misspelled word. The experiments were realized on Shipibo-konibo, a highly agglutinative and Amazonian language, and the results obtained have been promising in a dataset built for the purpose.

1 Introduction

In Peru, there are several native languages through the diverse native communities in the Amazonian region, such as Asháninka, Kakataibo, Shipibo-konibo, among others (Rivera, 2001). These languages, in spite of being very different from each other (47 languages in 21 linguistic families), share some features related to their morphology and the context in which they are used.

Regarding the morphology of the Amazonian languages, they are highly agglutinative, where suffixes predominates over prefixes. This characteristic distances them a lot from Spanish, the main official language in the country, and even the structural order is also different.

On the other side, these languages are used and transmitted mainly in an oral way, such as story-telling, poetry and in everyday life in the native communities. This causes differences in the way of writing between communities, and even among people in the same community (Aikman, 1999). For this reason, the texts that were written in these languages did not have an orthographic standard to guide them.

Thus, it is a must to support the educational process of this languages for this communities, and from the computational side, the main way to help them would be through the development of automatic tools or functions that process the specific language, in order to assist tasks related to generate written material such as educational books.

In that way, this project aims to develop a spell-checker focused on Shipibo-konibo, an amazonian language that is one of the most studied by linguists (Valenzuela, 2003) and also there are efforts from the computer science field to develop a basic toolkit for it (Pereira et al., 2017).

As this kind of language possess a rich morphology, the spelling corrector would focus on process sub words parts, such as syllables and characters, developing data structures and functions that could help in the process of identifying a misspelled word and suggesting potential corrected alternatives.

This study is organize as follows: In the next section, there will be described some studies related to the implementation of spelling correctors focusing on low-resource languages or language-independent models. Then, the sub word approach for the resources used (data structures and functions) will be detailed. After that, Section 4 describes the proposed spelling corrector, while Section 5 presents the experimentation and results obtained. Finally, the conclusions and future work are discussed in Section 6.

Proceedings of the First Workshop on Subword and Character Level Models in NLP, pages 109–116,
Copenhagen, Denmark, September 7, 2017. ©2017 Association for Computational Linguistics.

2   Related work

The related works focus on studies regarding the development of spell-checkers in a low-resource scenario or with a language independent approach.

Firstly, Barari and QasemiZadeh presented a tool called "CloniZER Spell Checker Adaptive". It consists of an adaptive method that uses internal error pattern recognition based on a ternary search tree. Thanks to this approach, the spell-checker was independent of the language because it was not based on specific rules from a specific language or corpus (this could be replaced). An interesting part in this approach resides is the support of the tree with variable weighted edges. The weights modifications are made through the interaction with a user, since the method learns from a mean of error patterns and thus the suggestion of solutions keeps improving.

Another source found is Abdullah and Rahman, who performed a generic spelling correction engine for South Asian languages, which uses circular lists where words are grouped by phonetic similarity and with an algorithm adapted from the Recursive Simulation (Lee, 1997) is constructed the possibly correct word that has similar to the misspelled word. However an interesting help they used was an additional dictionary of words, where they kept the misspelled words that the users wrote. This method is favorable for languages that have similarity with other phonetically, such as the group of languages of the Pano family in which the shipibo-konibo is.

Aduriz et al., who presented a corrector based on morphologies, in which a morphological analysis is used to perform morphological decompositions at two levels for spelling errors and for typographical errors uses a recognition of morphemes in the generation of correct words. This approach is interesting since they additionally use a lexicon that they are improving and a set of rules that help to map the lexical level and the surface level due to the morphological transformation (phonological representation of the morphemes).

Finally, Wasala et al. presented a proofreader for an African language. In this it was used a statistical model based on n-grams, this approach is based on assigning probabilities to a sequence of words where the sequence is determined by n-gram. An example of a 2-gram or bigram is: "try this". The chosen approach offers relative ease of construction and avoids the problem of hav-

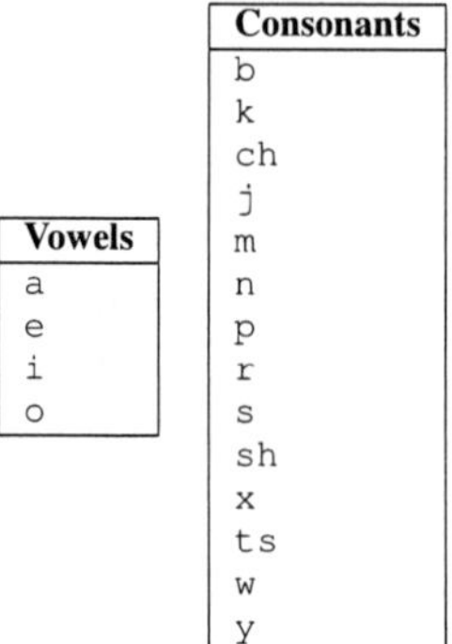

Table 1:   Vowels and consonants in shipibo-konibo.

ing few linguistic resources. The algorithm that is proposed for the orthographic correction uses 4 modules. These are: pre-processing, generation of permutations, selection of best suggestions, and post-processing. The interesting thing about this algorithm is that after preprocessing it performs a word search with similar sounds or phonemes, thus generating possible solutions, which are then improved based on the statistics of n-grams applying from unigramas to trigrams.

3   Subword Resources

As a first step, it is necessary to specify what type of resources, such as data structures, were used for the development of the spell checker.

3.1   Character-level Graph

The first structure that is needed is a graph as is shown in Figure 1. The nodes represent the characters that are used in the Shipibo-konibo (SHP) vocabulary, while the vertexes are the (weighted) relationships between each pair of them (this information is extracted from a corpus). Specifically, the alphabet of SHP contains 4 vowels and 15 consonants, as it can be seen in Table1. It is important to note that all the nodes will not be used in the whole process, due to the proposed n-gram based approach.

3.2   Syllable-level Graph

Another structure, needed to improve the possible algorithm solution, is a syllable-level graph. The nodes are the syllables that could be formed in the SHP grammar, and the vertexes represent the potential proximity relationship between 2 syllables (that is extracted from a corpus also). The number

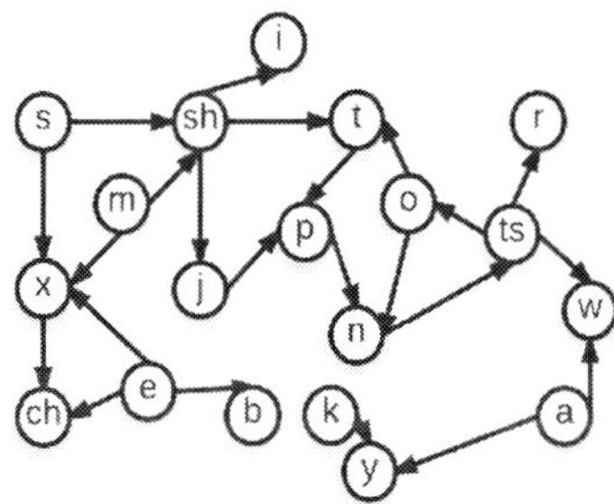

Figure 1: Character-level Graph Structure

Attack	Core	Coda
	Vowel	
Consonant	Vowel	
	Vowel	Consonant
Consonant	Vowel	Consonant

Table 2: Syllabic pattern

of grammatically correct syllables in SHP is 576, and with these syllables, all the word entries of a SHP dictionary could be generated.

3.2.1 Syllabification function

There are 4 syllabic patterns in the SHP language, and these are represented in Table 2. There are 3 positions named Attack, Core and Coda.

The syllabification function helps in the improvement of the solutions selection of the correction algorithm. It has been developed based on the existing rules in the Shipibo konibo grammar, and it helped the process because it allowed to separate each word of the dictionary in syllables to create the syllables graph. In addition, the use of the syllabification functions is a filter that is used to identify whether a word is well written or not.

3.3 Dictionary for previous corrections

As another needed resource, there is an own built dictionary structure that saves the previous misspelled word that has already been corrected, in order to avoid the same error correction again. The key is the misspelled word, and this is associated with a list of words corrected previously as is shown in Figure 2.

4 Proposed Spelling Corrector

First, the text is tokenized. After that, there is a verification process for each word to know if the term have been corrected before, or belongs to the

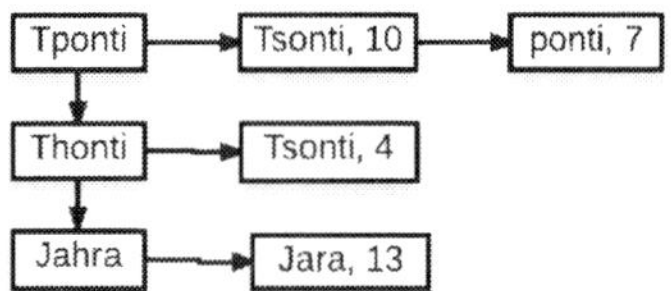

Figure 2: Sample of a misspelled-corrected dictionary

Spanish language, or exceeds a modified language model. In those cases the suggestion is sent directly as it can be appreciated in Figure 3. In other case, the word goes to the correction process, in which a graph is traversed in order to be able to identify possible correct words. Also, a filter is used where the word must be syllabified and finally a score is applied while traversing a graph of syllables and other score with the edit-distance. The results are ranked by score and assigned as suggestions to each corrected word.

4.1 Spell-checking algorithm

4.1.1 Identifying a misspelled word

First, the text is tokenized, and the numbers and punctuation are removed. The position of these filtered characters are saved, in order to replace them after the correction process is complete. Besides, the text is transformed to lowercase letters and the accent marks are removed.

As there is a dictionary structure that stores previous corrections, a search of the misspelled word is performed.

If the terms are not found in the previous dictionary structure, it is necessary to identify if they belong to the Spanish language using a corpus(Davies, 2002), a feature shared with other native languages in Perú.

Words that are not found in this Spanish corpus, are evaluated by the syllable language model. This model sum-up the weights assigned by each syllable found in the word, if this value can't surpass an empirical calculated threshold, is marked as a misspelled word an it will be the input for the next stage.

4.1.2 Correcting a misspelled word

For this stage, both graphs of letter and syllables described in the previous section are loaded. Each word that has to be corrected is evaluated. In this way, the number of vowels in the word allows to approximate number of syllables that can be iden-

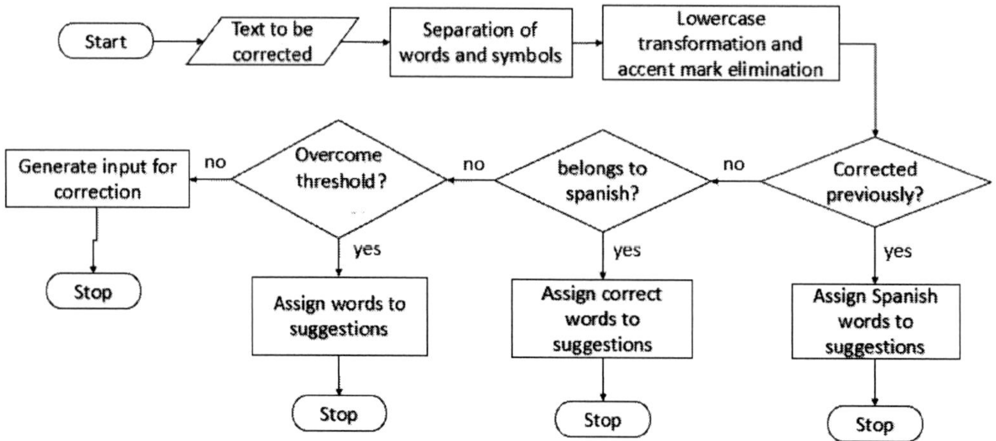

Figure 3: Identifying a misspelled word

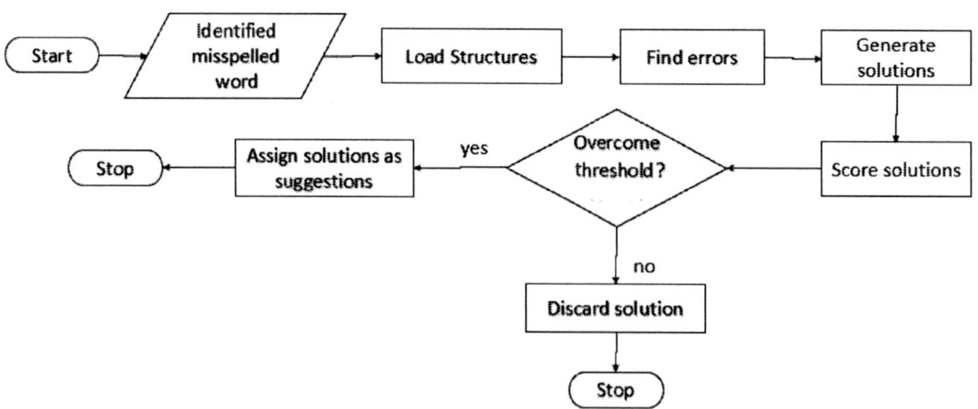

Figure 4: Correcting a misspelled word

112

tified. Since the absence or increasing of a vowel may be an error, it is considered a little higher range of syllables that can form the word: [number of syllables - 1; number of syllables + 1]. This helps in the generation of the possible correct solutions of each word.

The next step is the solution search. This is done by recursively traversing the misspelled word letter by letter. In this way, each possible syllable combination is contrasted versus the rule-based syllabification model and the range of syllables considered. Also, each solution receive a value calculated by the sum of the repetition of each own letter in the dictionary and the value of the unions in the graph. While traversing the misspelled word by finding a mistake, different paths are generated, the first one is from deleting the wrong letter, the next is when making a change of letter with the previous one, and the other paths are generated by changing the wrong letter with related letters in the graph. In this way, when creating several paths are generating different solutions.

Once the search for correct solutions is completed, they are evaluated through a modified language model. For that purpose the second graph containing syllables and the repetitions of the connections between syllables are used. In order to start the process, each possible solution is separated into syllables and the sum of the connections of these syllables is calculated using the graph. Additionally, the edit distance with Damerau-Levenshtein is calculated. At the end of calculating the two values, a 90% multiplication was performed on Damerau-Levenshtein and 10% on the sum of syllabic relationships, these values of 90% and 10% were chosen after testing to identify which optimized results. Finalized the calculations to each word, there are chosen the three possible correct words with the best values to be returned as solution.

4.2 Suggestions component

The suggestions component has been defined so that the user can make corrections to the solution that the application provides, allowing to improve the results since it will not have a totally accurate correction and adding new elements to the corrected list structure. It starts when the user selects the corrected word, activating a menu with the additional suggested words that were obtained when performing the correction. Then, the user selects the option that seems more precise and it is changed in the corrected text. Once this change is made, an additional change is made to the internal structures, where the correct word is added to the corrected list structure and the values are updated in the internal graph that is handled for the correction algorithm.

5   Experimentation and Results

An experiment will be carried out to establish the effectiveness of the spelling checker using metrics (van Huyssteen et al., 2004) to evaluate this type of projects.

5.1   Dataset

To construct the dataset there was more than one source. The first is a dictionary of shipibo-konibo and Spanish which through a preprocessing has been updated to the new rules of writing and consists of 5486 words. The second source is separated texts by domain (educational, legal and religious) that was translated from Spanish to Shipibo-Konibo. The educational domain consists of 2097 sentences consisting of 16789 words, the legal domain consists of 957 sentences consisting of 16794 words and the religious domain consists of 13482 sentences consisting of 212921 words. This is the initial dataset that helps to construct the graphs that are needed in the correction algorithm.

The dataset is available at a website project.[1]

5.2   Design of the experiment

To perform the experiment, where the effectiveness of the algorithm will be tested, it has been decided to use different sentences extracted from the shipibo-konibo dictionary (Lauriout et al., 1993). These sentences correspond to the examples of each dictionary entry. As the dictionary is not with the new official changes, proceeded to perform a pre-processing to update all the words in the example sentences.

After cleaning, 2 types of tests will be generated. The first test is to randomly add a character to some words in the sentence. On the other hand, the second test adds, deletes or changes characters of some words at random in the sentence.

Three columns are created in a table: in the first column the original sentence which is already cleaned, in the second column the sentence with the first type of error and in the last column the

Sentence	Sentence for test type 1
nokon wái óroa pekaora ea náshiai	nyokon wái aóroa poekaora eda náshiai
eara nénoa iki	eara nénopa iki
rámara títa ka cónko iki	rámara títaa ka cónko ikii

Table 3: Example of sentences for the test 1

Sentence	Sentence for test type 2
nokon wái óroa pekaora ea náshiai	nokon wáji óra dpekaora a náshiai
eara nénoa iki	eaora néoa oiki
rámara títa ka cónko iki	rámara títa k cónko iki

Table 4: Example of sentences for the test 2

Data	Value
True positive	7099
True negative	6276
False positive	14200
False negative	128
Correction in the first position of the suggestion	13340
Correction in some position of the suggestions	7959
No correct suggestion	6404
No suggestion	533

Table 5: Experiment type 1 data

Data	Value
True positive	3504
True negative	9769
False positive	14242
False negative	111
Correction in the first position of the suggestion	12695
Correction in some position of the suggestions	5051
No correct suggestion	9980
No suggestion	510

Table 6: Experiment type 2 data

sentence with more than 1 type of error. The file with the generated tables is used as input to perform the experiment.

5.3 Results

Correction of the 2 types of test was done with 5121 sentences. In order to identify the correct functioning, the Recall, Precision, measure of suggestions and general performance metrics were proposed for the evaluation of spell checkers (van Huyssteen et al., 2004). When counting the number of words in sentences, the result was 55786 words, these included correct words and misspelled words which will allow a better evaluation of the metrics. To calculate the recall and precision of the results:

- True positives (Tp): Misspelled word that are well corrected.

- True negatives (Tn): Misspelled word that are poorly corrected.

- False positives (Fp): Correct word that are well corrected.

- False negatives (Fn): Correct word that are poorly corrected.

To calculate the measure of suggestions a score is used depending on the suggestion of correction that will be applied to all corrections. Upon completion, a sum of all the scores obtained from the corrections will be made and divided by the number of positive ones to find the value of the suggestion measure. The scores used are:

- Correction in the first position of the suggestions: 1 point

- Correction in some position of the suggestions: 0.5 points

- No correct suggestion: -0.5 points

- No suggestion: 0 points

With the values in Tables 5 and 6, it was possible to calculate the recall and precision metrics with the formulas 1 and 2:

$$recall = \frac{Tp}{Tp + Fp} \qquad (1)$$

$$precision = \frac{Tp}{Tp + Tn} \qquad (2)$$

Finally, to find the value of overall performance of the corrector, the following formula 3 is used:

$$overall = \frac{Tp + Fp}{Tp + Tn + Fp + Fn} \qquad (3)$$

With the results obtained in Table 7 and Table 8, the values of the Recall and precision metrics are low, however this is because the spell-checker has yet to be improved to better identify the errors.

Data	Value
Recall	0.33
Precision	0.53
Suggested Measure	14117.5 points
Overall Performance	0.76

Table 7: Resulting metric type 1

Data	Value
Recall	0.19
Precision	0.26
Suggested Measure	10230.5 points
Overall Performance	0.64

Table 8: Resulting metric type 2

Top	Type of errors 1	Type of errors 2
1	13400	12695
3	722	376
5	665	337
7	6572	4338

Table 9: Number of words in top suggestions by type of errors

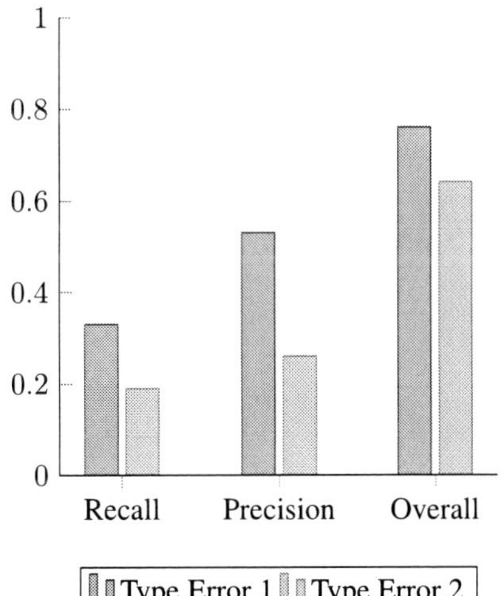

Figure 5: Metrics by type of error

we use four elements: the first position, the top-3, the top-5 and the top-7. These results can be seen in Table 9. In most cases, the corrected suggestions are in the first positions and low values in the next positions in both types of errors.

6 Conclusions and Future Work

In this study, it was proposed a hybrid approach for the development of a spell-checker for Shipibo-konibo. This method was supported with the implementation of linguistic rules (in the syllabification process) and the information obtained from different text corpus for the language. One of the difficult tasks was the use of recursion at the following of different paths when finding an error in the words (since it could be possible to change the character, add or remove it). That is why it was used a cutoff depth that help not to create long paths.

Finally the results were obtained, however they were not very promising because the approach followed is not enough to obtain a precise correction. However, as a future work, a context analysis will be integrated, using embedded words with a character-level model to identify terms that should not be corrected, because they may be well written but are not suitable in the context of a sentence.

Acknowledgments

For this study, the authors acknowledge the support of the "Consejo Nacional de Ciencia, Tecnología e Innovación Tecnológica" (CONCYTEC Perú) under the contract 225-2015-FONDECYT.

What would improve its effectiveness is to be able to better detect words that do not need to be really corrected, because as can be appreciate, many of the words that are corrected are words that did not need it. An approach to face this problem is to take advantage of the available corpus to perform a search of the word and identify in the corpus if it already exists. This would avoid unnecessary correction, but would mean an increase in the time due to a search for each word that although in short texts would not be much difference, in longer texts it would be noticed.

Despite the low numbers in recall and precision as can see in Figure 5, the spell-checker get a good result at the general level because it is considered within the correct result that both misspelled and well written words, when corrected, offer a correct result. In addition, it can be seen that more than half the time a good correction proposal has been found and 25% of the time these corrections are in the first position as a suggestion in the two types of tests performed.

There was another experiment where it can be found the ranking of the suggestions, for this case

References

ABA Abdullah and Ashfaq Rahman. 2003. A generic spell checker engine for south asian languages. In *Conference on Software Engineering and Applications (SEA 2003)*. pages 3–5.

Itziar Aduriz, MIRIAM Urkia, INAKI Alegria, XABIER Artola, NEREA Ezeiza, and KEPA Sarasola. 1997. A spelling corrector for basque based on morphology. *Literary and Linguistic Computing* 12(1):31–38.

Sheila Aikman. 1999. *Intercultural education and literacy: An ethnographic study of indigenous knowledge and learning in the Peruvian Amazon*, volume 7. John Benjamins Publishing.

Loghman Barari and Behrang QasemiZadeh. 2005. CloniZER spell checker adaptive language independent spell checker. In *AIML 2005 Conference CICC, Cairo, Egypt*. pages 19–21.

M Davies. 2002. Corpus del español: 100 million words, 1200s-1900s. *Available online at* http://www.corpusdelespanol.org.

Erwin Lauriout, Dwight Day, and James Loriot. 1993. Diccionario shipibo-castellano .

Lung-fei Lee. 1997. A smooth likelihood simulator for dynamic disequilibrium models. *Journal of econometrics* 78(2):257–294.

Jose Pereira, Rodolfo Mercado, Andres Melgar, Marco Sobrevilla-Cabezudo, and Arturo Oncevay-Marcos. 2017. Ship-lemmatagger: building an NLP toolkit for a peruvian native language. In *Text, Speech, and Dialogue: 20th International Conference, TSD 2017*. Springer (In-press).

Andrés Chirinos Rivera. 2001. *Atlas lingüístico del Perú*, volume 6. Centro Bartolomé de Las Casas.

Pilar Valenzuela. 2003. *Transitivity in shipibo-konibo grammar*. Ph.D. thesis, University of Oregon.

Gerhard B van Huyssteen, ER Eiselen, and MJ Puttkammer. 2004. Re-evaluating evaluation metrics for spelling checker evaluations. In *Proceedings of First Workshop on International Proofing Tools and Language Technologies*. pages 91–99.

Ruwan Asanka Wasala, Ruwan Weerasinghe, Randil Pushpananda, Chamila Liyanage, and Eranga Jayalatharachchi. 2011. An open-source data driven spell checker for sinhala. *ICTer* 3(1).

What do we need to know about an unknown word when parsing German

Bich-Ngoc Do[*] and **Ines Rehbein**[♣] and **Anette Frank**[*]
Leibniz ScienceCampus
Universität Heidelberg[*] / Institut für Deutsche Sprache Mannheim[♣]
Germany
`{do|rehbein|frank}@cl.uni-heidelberg.de`

Abstract

We propose a new type of subword embedding designed to provide more information about unknown compounds, a major source for OOV words in German. We present an extrinsic evaluation where we use the *compound* embeddings as input to a neural dependency parser and compare the results to the ones obtained with other types of embeddings. Our evaluation shows that adding compound embeddings yields a significant improvement of 2% LAS over using word embeddings when no POS information is available. When adding POS embeddings to the input, however, the effect levels out. This suggests that it is not the missing information about the semantics of the unknown words that causes problems for parsing German, but the lack of morphological information for unknown words. To augment our evaluation, we also test the new embeddings in a language modelling task that requires both syntactic and semantic information.

1 Introduction

Parsing morphologically rich languages (MRLs) is a challenging task. One of the main problems is the high proportion of unknown words in the data, due to the high number of different inflected forms. In some languages, this problem is made even worse by *compounding*, a highly productive word formation process. Thus, handling unknown words is crucial for parsing MRLs and especially for German where compounding is a frequent phenomenon.

While word embeddings are a promising way to learn a general representation that captures syntactic and semantic properties of a word, they have

not fully solved the sparse data problem. Recent studies are exploring representations at the subword level that can provide information even for rare and unseen words. Well-known examples are character and character-ngram-based embeddings (Sperr et al., 2013; dos Santos and Zadrozny, 2014; Ling et al., 2015; Vania and Lopez, 2017), morphological embeddings (Luong et al., 2013; Botha and Blunsom, 2014; Cotterell and Schütze, 2015; Cao and Rei, 2016), or byte embeddings (Plank et al., 2016; Gillick et al., 2016).

Ballesteros et al. (2015) were the first to integrate character-based embeddings into a syntactic parser and compared the effect for different languages with different levels of morphological richness. They showed that replacing word embeddings with character-based embeddings can be useful, especially for parsing agglutinative languages. Since then, character-based embeddings have become an ingredient in many parsing systems.

Other work has addressed the compounding problem on the level of word embeddings. Dima et al. have tried to model compound compositionality for English (Dima and Hinrichs, 2015) and German (Dima, 2015). However, experiments were on the semantic level, and the compounds were restricted to two components only. To the best of our knowledge, nobody has tried compound embeddings to tackle the unknown word problem in statistical parsing.

2 The problem with compounds

Compounds are words that include more than one stem. In some languages (e.g. English), the individual components are separated by spaces, while in other languages, such as German, they are merged into a new word form. Compounding is highly productive and thus, in languages like German, a major source of new, unseen words. Take,

Proceedings of the First Workshop on Subword and Character Level Models in NLP, pages 117–123,
Copenhagen, Denmark, September 7, 2017. ©2017 Association for Computational Linguistics.

Threshold	en	de
1	13.17	37.18
2	19.48	48.78
3	24.39	55.59
4	28.36	60.51
5	31.90	64.12

Table 1: The percentage of unknown words in the *test* data set with respect to different levels of cut-off threshold in the *training* data. Threshold of 1 means no words in the training data are discarded.

for example, the German compound *Verbraucher-schutzgesetz* (consumer protection law). While all three parts are reasonably frequent and thus have a good chance of being included in a sufficiently large data set, the *merged* compound itself, most probably, is not.

This poses a problem for most statistical parsers. In our work, we focus on recent neural dependency parsers which, instead of using hand-crafted feature templates, directly learn the features from the training data (Chen and Manning, 2014; Zhang et al., 2017). These parsers usually introduce an UNKNOWN token for out-of-vocabulary words. A well-known technique for computing the embeddings of the UNKNOWN token is to discard infrequent words below a certain *threshold* and also treat them as *unknown*.

To illustrate the differential effect of this practice for languages that write compounds with word-internal spaces versus languages that use run-together compounds, let us take a look at the English Penn Treebank (PTB) (Marcus et al., 1993) and the German data set from the SPMRL 2014 shared task (Seddah et al., 2014), and compare the ratio of sparse or unknown words in the test sets for both treebanks with regard to different frequency thresholds. Table 1 shows that the ratio of words to be declared *unknown* is more than twice as high in the German data, due to a high amount of unknown common nouns. At a cutoff threshold of 5, the most frequent POS for unknown words in the German data are common nouns (47.4%) and proper nouns (17.3%). In the English data, however, proper names are the most frequent source for UNKNOWNs (35.4%) and common nouns only amount to 24.1%. One of the main reasons for this difference between the two Germanic languages is the high productivity of German compounds. We thus hypothesize that the high ratio of compounds will have a major impact on parsing German, which we address with our new *compound* embeddings.

3 Character vs Compound Embeddings

In a neural parsing system, each word is represented by a vector stored in a lookup table. One way to reduce the negative effect of unknown words in the vocabulary and also, if only indirectly, provide a treatment for compound words, is to replace the word lookup table by **character-based embeddings** (Ling et al., 2015). In this approach, each word is treated as a sequence of characters and the representation for each word is constructed from the representations for its characters, using a bi-directional long short-term memory network (LSTM) (Hochreiter and Schmidhuber, 1997). Given word w as a sequence of characters $(c_1, c_2, ..., c_m)$ and e_c as the vector representation of character c, we can compute the representation e_w^{char} of word w as follows:

$$s_t^F = \text{LSTM}_F(e_{c_t}, s_{t-1}^F) \tag{1}$$

$$s_t^B = \text{LSTM}_B(e_{c_t}, s_{t+1}^B) \tag{2}$$

$$e_w^{\text{char}} = D^F s_m^F + D^B s_0^B + b \tag{3}$$

where s_t^F and s_t^B are the hidden states of the forward and backward LSTMs at time t; D^F, D^B and b are the weight and bias vectors.

We now outline our compositional model for **compound embeddings**. We assume that most compounds have a transparent meaning that can be inferred from the meaning of its components and hypothesize that providing the parser with subword embeddings that combine the representations of the individual components will help the model to handle unseen compounds. To that end, we first split each compound into lexemes and then combine the sequence of lexemes as we did for the character-based embeddings, using a bi-directional LSTM.

For compound splitting, we use the IMS splitter (Weller and Heid, 2012) which adopts a frequency-based approach with additional linguistic features. The input information for the splitter (frequencies, POS and lemmas) was extracted from SdeWac (Faaß and Eckart, 2013), a cleaned-up version of the *deWac* corpus (Baroni et al., 2009) with automatic POS tags and lemmas.

4 Experiments

4.1 Parsing Model

Our parsing model is an extension of the *head-selection* parser of Zhang et al. (2017) (figure 1). Given the sentence $S = (w_0, w_1, ..., w_N)$ and x_i as the *input representation* of word w_i, the model

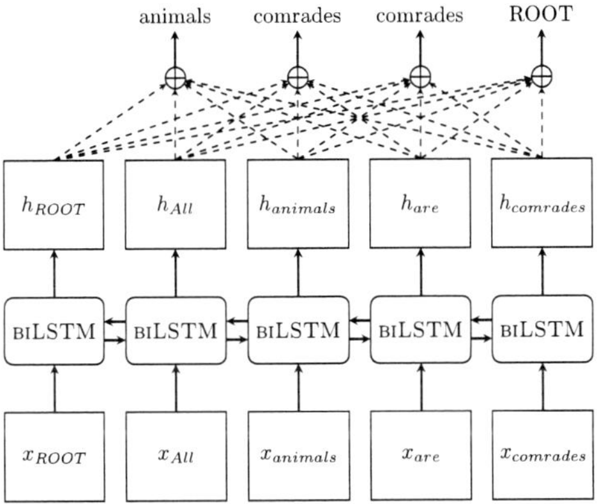

Figure 1: The parsing as head selection model

uses a bi-directional LSTM to learn a *feature vector* for each word in S:

$$h_i^F = \text{LSTM}_F(x_i, h_{i-1}^F) \qquad (4)$$
$$h_i^B = \text{LSTM}_B(x_i, h_{i+1}^B) \qquad (5)$$
$$h_i = [h_i^F; h_i^B] \qquad (6)$$

The feature vector h_i of word w_i is the concatenation of the hidden states from the forward and backward passes of the bi-direction LSTM. An artificial root node w_0 token is appended at the beginning of each sentence.

Unlabeled parsing is modeled as choosing the most probable head for each word in a sentence. In sentence $S = (w_0, w_1, ..., w_N)$, the probability of word w_j being the head of w_i is calculated as:

$$P_{\text{head}}(w_j \mid w_i, S) = \frac{\exp(g(a_j, a_i))}{\sum_{k=0}^{N} \exp(g(a_k, a_i))} \qquad (7)$$

where g is a neural network that predicts a score for the feature vectors h_i and h_j as follows:

$$g(a_j, a_i) = v_a^\top \cdot \tanh(U_a \cdot a_j + W_a \cdot a_i) \qquad (8)$$

Finally, an additional neural network is used to assign the grammatical function label to each edge in the unlabeled tree. The input to that network is the concatenation of the input representations and the learned feature vectors of head j and dependent i:

$$[x_i; x_j; h_i; h_j] \qquad (9)$$

Note that in our implementation we use a single hidden-layer rectifier network instead of the two-layer rectifier network in Zhang et al. (2017), since we achieve better results with only one hidden layer.

Module	Hyperparameter	Value
Word emb.	size	300
POS emb.	size	40
Character-based emb.	character embedding size	50
	hidden size	100
Compound emb.	lexeme embedding size	50
	hidden size	100
BiLSTM	hidden size	300
Regularization	L2	1e-3
	input dropout rate	0.05
	dropout rate	0.5
	max-norm	5.0
Optimization	optimizer	Adam
	learning rate	0.001
	1st momentum	0.9
	2st momentum	0.999
	no. epochs	15
Others	word cutoff threshold	5

Table 2: Hyperparameters used in all experiments

4.2 Input representations

To assess the effect of different compound handling techniques on parsing performance, we systematically vary the input information for the parser, as described below:

Word Embeddings (+word) Each word w in the lexicon is represented as a vector e_w in the lookup table. We do not use any pre-trained embeddings; all embeddings are initialized randomly.

POS Embeddings (+pos) If word w has POS tag p, we add an embedding e_p for tag p to the input information.

Character-Based Embeddings (+char) In addition to the word embeddings e_w from the lookup table, we also use the character-based embeddings e_w^{char} of word w (equation 3).

Compound Embeddings (+comp) The compound embedding e_w^{comp} of word w is calculated based on the lexeme embeddings (see section 3).

When combining different types of information in the input, we use the *concatenation* of each embedding type.

4.3 Training

We train our own implementation of the parser, following Zhang et al. (2017). For optimization, we used Adam (Kingma and Ba, 2015) with default parameters. All models were trained in 15 epochs and the training process was regularized using common techniques like L2 regularization, max-norm and dropout (Srivastava et al., 2014). We chose all hyperparameters for our

		Input	**UAS**	**LAS**
+pos	**b1**	`+word,pos`	90.50	88.06
	b2	`head:+word,pos`	90.46	88.13
		`+comp,pos`	90.23	87.93
		`+comp,word,pos`	90.39	88.10
		`+char,pos`	90.53	88.49
		`+word,char,pos`	**90.69**	**88.56**
-pos	**b1**	`+word`	86.27	83.08
	b2	`head:+word`	87.00	83.97
		`+word,comp`	88.29	85.42
		`+word,char`	**90.42**	**88.20**

Table 3: Results for different input combinations

experiments manually, following suggestions by Zhang et al. (2017) (see table 2).

We report parsing performance (UAS and LAS) *with punctuation* on the German data set from the SPMRL 2014 shared task. The training set contains 40,472 sentences and the development and test sets both include 5,000 sentences.

The compound splitting (section 3) affected about one third of the lexemes in the lexicon, all of them nouns. Of all the unknown words in the test set (64.12% at a cutoff threshold of 5, see table 1), 24.92% now consist of known lexemes, 73.79% have only one unknown lexeme, and only 1.29% have more than one unknown component.

We compare our results against two baselines, (b1) using the original words for parsing and (b2) a greedy baseline *head*, where we discard all compound components except the rightmost one, since in most cases, the rightmost lexeme is the head of the compound. Baseline (b2) reduces the number of unknown words in the data by 10%.

4.4 Results

Table 3 (+pos) shows results for different combinations of input information. The `+word,pos` setting (baseline b1) is the one implemented in the original parser. The results show that our special treatment of compounds does not have the desired effect. In both settings, using only the head words (b2) and using compound embeddings, we see only minor changes in parsing accuracy and when replacing word with compound embeddings, results actually decrease. This strongly suggests that the parsing model is often able to make the right decision without actually knowing the word.

Adding the character embeddings improves the LAS by 0.5%, but does not have a significant effect on the UAS. Since German is a richly inflected, semi-free word order language, this suggests that the character-based embeddings have learned *morphological* information from the sur-

Label	Freq.	`-char`		`+char`	
		P	R	P	R
SB	6,638	**90.7**	91.2	90.6	**92.2**
OA	3,184	82.3	85.7	**83.3**	**87.5**
DA	568	73.2	55.3	**78.9**	**63.9**
AG	2,241	91.3	91.5	**94.2**	**93.9**
OG	21	**100.0**	4.8	N/A	0.0
PD	1,045	82.5	74.3	**84.8**	**80.8**

Table 4: Precision (P) and recall (R) for core grammatical functions with/without character-based embeddings. SB: subj, OA: accusative obj, DA: dative obj, AG: genitive attribute, OG: genitive obj, PD: predicate.

face of the words that helps assign the correct grammatical function for each head-dependent pair. Table 4 confirms this by showing the improvements we get for the core arguments when adding character-based embeddings.

The effect of POS tags In the next set of experiments, we exclude the POS tag information to isolate the effect of the different techniques for handling compounds. Table 3 (-pos) shows that without POS information, we now see a significant effect. The greedy baseline that keeps only the head word for each compound increases UAS and LAS by 0.7% and 0.9% respectively, and our compound embeddings now improve both scores by more than 2%. Using character-based embeddings in combination with word embeddings, however, yields comparable results to the `+word,pos` system. We take that as evidence that the character-based embeddings implicitly learn morphological information that is complementary to the information included in the word embeddings. Our results are in line with previous results from the literature, claiming that character-based embeddings are able to capture morphological information (Ling et al., 2015; Cao and Rei, 2016; Kim et al., 2016).

Our results also corroborate findings by Köhn (2016) who evaluates different types of *word* embeddings in a syntax-based classification task, reporting that the embeddings yielded improvements *only* when no POS information was given.

4.5 Language Modeling

To validate our results in a different setting, we also test the compound embeddings in a language modeling task. Language models (LM) are an important ingredient in many NLP applications, e.g. in speech recognition and machine translation, and they require both syntactic and semantic information.

Model	Word	Compound	Char
Perplexity	36.954	35.987	**32.273**

Table 5: Perplexity for different language models on German texts from Wikipedia.

In our experiment, we use the framework[1] and setup described in Vania and Lopez (2017) to build a language model for German texts. The framework includes implementations for word and subword-based (morpheme, character or character n-gram) embeddings and uses either bidirectional LSTMs or addition as the combination function of subwords.

The German data sets are from the preprocessed Wikipedia data (Al-Rfou et al., 2013). Hyperlinks have been removed and the input texts have been lower-cased before learning the word- and compound-based embeddings. For the character-based embeddings, the upper-cased letters have been preserved. We split the data into training, development and test sets, with approximately 1.2M, 150K and 150K tokens, respectively. For training and evaluation we closely follow Vania and Lopez (2017).

We report results for three language models. The *word* model and the *character* model (using a bidirectional LSTM as composition function)[2] are already implemented in the framework. For the *compound* embeddings, we first split the compounds in the data sets as described in section 3 and then combine them, again using a bidirectional LSTM as composition function.

The results are shown in table 5. Using compound-based embeddings yields better perplexity in comparison to the vanilla word model, but the compound model is still far behind the character-based embeddings which obtain the lowest perplexity. The results for the language model thus confirm the trend observed in the parsing experiments.

5 Discussion

In both tasks, parsing and language modelling, the character-based embeddings clearly outperformed the compound-based embeddings. This suggests that the character-based embeddings are able to pick up structural information that is important for both tasks.

For parsing, the results for the compound-based embeddings were even below the ones for the word embeddings when including POS information in the input. This implies that the information needed for *parsing* unknown words is not so much information about the semantics of a word but, crucially, morphological information. This was confirmed by the improved results for using character-based embeddings instead of the compound-based ones, where we were able to make up for the decrease in LAS that resulted from removing POS information from the input.

Our results are important, as they show that unknown words are not per se a problem for parsing, as long as we are able to learn something about their morphological properties.

6 Conclusions and future work

In the paper, we introduced a new type of subword embedding, the *compound* embedding. The new embeddings are designed to provide more information about unknown compounds which constitute a major part of OOV words in German.

We evaluated the embeddings in dependency parsing and showed that although the compound-based embeddings outperformed word embeddings when *no* POS information was available, the character-based model showed a performance superior to the one for word and compound embeddings. For language modelling, where not only syntactic but also semantic information is important, the results follow the same trend.

This leaves us with two avenues for future work. To provide an improved handling of OOV words for parsing, we need to optimise subword embeddings to represent morphological information for unknown words. In addition, we would like to test the compound embeddings in a purely *semantic* task where we can explore their full potential.

Acknowledgments

This research has been conducted within the Leibniz Science Campus "Empirical Linguistics and Computational Modeling", funded by the Leibniz Association under grant no. SAS-2015-IDS-LWC and by the Ministry of Science, Research, and Art (MWK) of the state of Baden-Württemberg.

---

[1] https://github.com/claravania/subword-lstm-lm

[2] These are the same character-based embeddings that we used in the parsing experiment (sections 4.3, 4.4).

References

Rami Al-Rfou, Bryan Perozzi, and Steven Skiena. 2013. Polyglot: Distributed word representations for multilingual NLP. In *Proceedings of the Seventeenth Conference on Computational Natural Language Learning*. Association for Computational Linguistics, Sofia, Bulgaria, pages 183–192.

Miguel Ballesteros, Chris Dyer, and Noah A. Smith. 2015. Improved transition-based parsing by modeling characters instead of words with LSTMs. In *Proceedings of the 2015 Conference on Empirical Methods in Natural Language Processing*. Association for Computational Linguistics, Lisbon, Portugal, pages 349–359.

Marco Baroni, Silvia Bernardini, Adriano Ferraresi, and Eros Zanchetta. 2009. The WaCky wide web: A collection of very large linguistically processed web-crawled corpora. *Language Resources and Evaluation* 43(3):209–226.

Jan A. Botha and Phil Blunsom. 2014. Compositional morphology for word representations and language modelling. In *Proceedings of the 31st International Conference on Machine Learning*. Beijing, China, ICML 2014.

Kris Cao and Marek Rei. 2016. A joint model for word embedding and word morphology. In *Proceedings of the 1st Workshop on Representation Learning for NLP*. Berlin, Germany, RepL4NLP-2016.

Danqi Chen and Christopher D. Manning. 2014. A fast and accurate dependency parser using neural networks. In *Proceedings of the 2014 Conference on Empirical Methods in Natural Language Processing (EMNLP)*. Association for Computational Linguistics, Doha, Qatar, pages 740–750.

Ryan Cotterell and Hinrich Schütze. 2015. Morphological word-embeddings. In *The 2015 Conference of the North American Chapter of the Association for Computational Linguistics: Human Language Technologies, Denver, Colorado, USA, May 31 - June 5, 2015*. NAACL HLT 2015, pages 1287–1292.

Corina Dima. 2015. Reverse-engineering language: A study on the semantic compositionality of German compounds. In *Proceedings of the 2015 Conference on Empirical Methods in Natural Language Processing*. Association for Computational Linguistics, Lisbon, Portugal, pages 1637–1642.

Corina Dima and Erhard Hinrichs. 2015. Automatic noun compound interpretation using deep neural networks and word embeddings. In *Proceedings of the 11th International Conference on Computational Semantics*. Association for Computational Linguistics, London, UK, pages 173–183.

Cícero Nogueira dos Santos and Bianca Zadrozny. 2014. Learning character-level representations for part-of-speech tagging. In *Proceedings of the 31th International Conference on Machine Learning, ICML 2014, Beijing, China, 21-26 June 2014*. pages 1818–1826.

Gertrud Faaß and Kerstin Eckart. 2013. SdeWaC - A corpus of parsable sentences from the web. In *Language Processing and Knowledge in the Web: 25th International Conference, GSCL 2013, Darmstadt, Germany, September 25-27, 2013. Proceedings*. Springer, Berlin, Heidelberg, pages 61–68.

Dan Gillick, Cliff Brunk, Oriol Vinyals, and Amarnag Subramanya. 2016. Multilingual language processing from bytes. In *The 2016 Conference of the North American Chapter of the Association for Computational Linguistics: Human Language Technologies*. San Diego California, USA, NAACL HLT 2016, pages 1296–1306.

Sepp Hochreiter and Jürgen Schmidhuber. 1997. Long short-term memory. *Neural Computing* 9(8):1735–1780.

Yoon Kim, Yacine Jernite, David Sontag, and Alexander M. Rush. 2016. Character-aware neural language models. In *Proceedings of the Thirtieth AAAI Conference on Artificial Intelligence*. AAAI Press, AAAI'16, pages 2741–2749.

Diederik Kingma and Jimmy Ba. 2015. Adam: A method for stochastic optimization. In *The International Conference on Learning Representations*. San Diego.

Arne Köhn. 2016. Evaluating embeddings using syntax-based classification tasks as a proxy for parser performance. In *Proceedings of the 1st Workshop on Evaluating Vector Space Representations for NLP*. Berlin, Germany, pages 67–71.

Wang Ling, Tiago Luís, Luís Marujo, Ramón Fernandez Astudillo, Silvio Amir, Chris Dyer, Alan W Black, and Isabel Trancoso. 2015. Finding function in form: Compositional character models for open vocabulary word representation. In *Proceedings of the 2015 Conference on Empirical Methods in Natural Language Processing*. Association for Computational Linguistics, Lisbon, Portugal, pages 1520–1530.

Thang Luong, Richard Socher, and Christopher D. Manning. 2013. Better word representations with recursive neural networks for morphology. In *Proceedings of the Seventeenth Conference on Computational Natural Language Learning*. Sofia, Bulgaria, CoNLL 2013, pages 104–113.

Mitchell P. Marcus, Mary Ann Marcinkiewicz, and Beatrice Santorini. 1993. Building a large annotated corpus of English: the Penn treebank. *Computational Linguistics* 19(2):313–330.

Barbara Plank, Anders Søgaard, and Yoav Goldberg. 2016. Multilingual part-of-speech tagging with bidirectional long short-term memory models and auxiliary loss. In *Proceedings of the 54th Annual*

Meeting of the Association for Computational Linguistics. Berlin, Germany, ACL 2016.

Djamé Seddah, Sandra Kübler, and Reut Tsarfaty. 2014. Introducing the SPMRL 2014 shared task on parsing morphologically-rich languages. In *Proceedings of the First Joint Workshop on Statistical Parsing of Morphologically Rich Languages and Syntactic Analysis of Non-Canonical Languages*. Dublin City University, Dublin, Ireland, pages 103–109.

Henning Sperr, Jan Niehues, and Alex Waibel. 2013. Letter n-gram-based input encoding for continuous space language models. In *Proceedings of the Workshop on Continuous Vector Space Models and their Compositionality*. Sofia, Bulgaria, pages 30–39.

Nitish Srivastava, Geoffrey Hinton, Alex Krizhevsky, Ilya Sutskever, and Ruslan Salakhutdinov. 2014. Dropout: A simple way to prevent neural networks from overfitting. *Journal of Machine Learning Research* 15:1929–1958.

Clara Vania and Adam Lopez. 2017. From characters to words to in between: Do we capture morphology? In *Proceedings of the 55th Annual Meeting of the Association for Computational Linguistics*. Association for Computational Linguistics.

Marion Weller and Ulrich Heid. 2012. Analyzing and aligning German compound nouns. In *Proceedings of the Eight International Conference on Language Resources and Evaluation (LREC'12)*. European Language Resources Association (ELRA), Istanbul, Turkey.

Xingxing Zhang, Jianpeng Cheng, and Mirella Lapata. 2017. Dependency parsing as head selection. In *Proceedings of the 15th Conference of the European Chapter of the Association for Computational Linguistics: Volume 1, Long Papers*. Association for Computational Linguistics, Valencia, Spain, pages 665–676.

A General-Purpose Tagger with Convolutional Neural Networks

Xiang Yu and **Agnieszka Falenska** and **Ngoc Thang Vu**
Institut für Maschinelle Sprachverarbeitung
Universität Stuttgart
{xiangyu,falensaa,thangvu}@ims.uni-stuttgart.de

Abstract

We present a general-purpose tagger based on convolutional neural networks (CNN), used for both composing word vectors and encoding context information. The CNN tagger is robust across different tagging tasks: without task-specific tuning of hyper-parameters, it achieves state-of-the-art results in part-of-speech tagging, morphological tagging and supertagging. The CNN tagger is also robust against the out-of-vocabulary problem; it performs well on artificially unnormalized texts.

1   Introduction

Recently, character composition models have shown great success in many NLP tasks, mainly because of their robustness in dealing with out-of-vocabulary (OOV) words by capturing sub-word informations. Among the character composition models, bidirectional long short-term memory (LSTM) models and convolutional neural networks (CNN) are widely applied in many tasks, e.g. part-of-speech (POS) tagging (dos Santos and Zadrozny, 2014; Plank et al., 2016), named entity recognition (dos Santos and Guimarães, 2015), language modeling (Ling et al., 2015; Kim et al., 2016), machine translation (Costa-jussà and Fonollosa, 2016) and dependency parsing (Ballesteros et al., 2015; Yu and Vu, 2017).

In this paper, we present a state-of-the-art general-purpose tagger that uses CNNs both to compose word representations from characters and to encode context information for tagging.[1] We show that the CNN model is more capable than

the LSTM model for both functions, and more stable for unseen or unnormalized words, which is the main benefit of character composition models.

Yu and Vu (2017) compared the performance of CNN and LSTM as character composition model for dependency parsing, and concluded that CNN performs better than LSTM. In this paper, we show that this is also the case for POS tagging. Furthermore, we extend the scope to morphological tagging and supertagging, in which the tag set is much larger or long-distance dependencies between words are more important.

In these three tagging tasks, we compare our tagger with the bilstm-aux tagger (Plank et al., 2016) and the CRF-based morphological tagger MarMot (Müller et al., 2013) as baselines. The CNN tagger shows robust performance across the three tasks, and achieves the highest average accuracies in all tasks. It considerably outperforms the LSTM tagger in morphological tagging and both baselines in supertagging.

To test the robustness of the taggers against the OOV problem, we also conduct experiments on unnormalized text by artificially corrupting words in the normal dev sets. With the increasing degree of unnormalization, the performance of the CNN tagger degrades much slower than the other two, which suggests that the CNN tagger is more robust against unnormalized text.

Therefore we conclude that our CNN tagger is a robust state-of-the-art general-purpose tagger that can effectively compose word representation from characters and encode context information.

2   Model

Our proposed CNN tagger has two main components: the character composition model and the context encoding model. Both components are essentially very similar CNN models, capturing dif-

---

[1]The tagger is available at http://www.ims.uni-stuttgart.de/institut/mitarbeiter/xiangyu/index.en.html

Proceedings of the First Workshop on Subword and Character Level Models in NLP, pages 124–129,
Copenhagen, Denmark, September 7, 2017. ©2017 Association for Computational Linguistics.

ferent levels of information: the first CNN captures morphological information from character n-grams, the second one captures contextual information from word n-grams. Figure 1 shows a diagram of both models of the tagger.

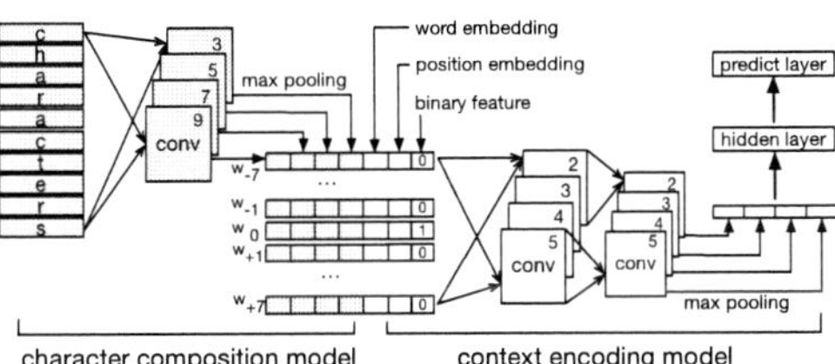

Figure 1: Diagram of the CNN tagger.

2.1 Character Composition Model

The character composition model is similar to Yu and Vu (2017), where several convolution filters are used to capture character n-grams of different sizes. The outputs of each convolution filter are fed through a max pooling layer, and the pooling outputs are concatenated to represent the word.

2.2 Context Encoding Model

The context encoding model captures the context information of the target word by scanning through the word representations of its context window. The word representation could be only word embeddings ($\vec{w}$), only composed vectors ($\vec{c}$), or the concatenation of both ($\vec{w} + \vec{c}$).

A context window consists of N words to both sides of the target word and the target word itself. To indicate the target word, we concatenate a binary feature to each of the word representations with 1 indicating the target and 0 otherwise, similar to Vu et al. (2016). Additional to the binary feature, we also concatenate a position embedding to encode the relative position of each context word, similar to Gehring et al. (2017).

2.3 Hyper-parameters

For the character composition model, we take a fixed input size of 32 characters for each word, with padding on both sides or cutting from the middle if needed. We apply four convolution filters with sizes of 3, 5, 7, and 9. Each filter has an output channel of 25 dimensions, thus the composed vector is 100-dimensional. We apply Gaussian noise with standard deviation of 0.1 on the composed vector during training.

For the context encoding model, we take a context window of 15 (7 words to both sides of the target word) as input and predict the tag of the target word. We also apply four convolution filters with sizes of 2, 3, 4 and 5, each filter is stacked by another filter with the same size, and the output has 128 dimensions, thus the context representation is 512-dimensional. We apply one 512-dimensional hidden layer with ReLU non-linearity before the prediction layer. We apply dropout with probability of 0.1 after the hidden layer during training.

The model is trained with averaged stochastic gradient descent with a learning rate of 0.1, momentum of 0.9 and mini-batch size of 100. We apply L2 regularization with a rate of 10^{-5} on all the parameters of the network except the embeddings.

3 Experiments

3.1 Data

We use treebanks from version 1.2 of Universal Dependencies[2] (UD), and in the case of several treebanks for one language, we only use the canonical one. There are in total 22 treebanks, as in Plank et al. (2016).[3] Each treebank splits into train, dev, and test sets, we use the dev sets for early stop training.

In order to compare to more previous works on POS tagging, we additionally experiment POS tagging on the more established Penn Treebank Wall Street Journal (WSJ) data set (Marcus et al., 1993). We use the standard splitting, where sections 0-18 are used for training, 19-21 for tuning, and 22-24 for testing (Collins, 2002).

3.2 Tasks

We evaluate the taggers on three tagging tasks: POS tagging (**POS**), morphological tagging (**MORPH**) and supertagging (**SUPER**).

For POS tagging we use Universal POS tags, which are an extension of Petrov et al. (2012). The universal tag set tries to capture the "universal" properties of words and facilitate cross-lingual learning. Therefore the tag set is very coarse and leaves out most of the language-specific properties to morphological features.

Morphological tags encode the language-specific morphological features of the words, e.g., number, gender, case. They are represented in the

---

[2] http://universaldependencies.org

[3] We use all training data for Czech, while Plank et al. (2016) only use a subset.

UD treebanks as one string which contains several key-value pairs of morphological features.[4]

Supertags (Joshi and Bangalore, 1994) are tags that encode more syntactic information than standard POS tags, e.g. the head direction or the subcategorization frame. We use dependency-based supertags (Foth et al., 2006) which are extracted from the dependency treebanks. Adding such tags into feature models of statistical dependency parsers significantly improves their performance (Ouchi et al., 2014; Faleńska et al., 2015). Supertags can be designed with different levels of granularity. We use the standard Model 1 from Ouchi et al. (2014), where each tag consists of head direction, dependency label and dependent directions. The SUPER task is more difficult than POS and MORPH because it generally requires taking long-distance dependencies between words into consideration.

These three tagging tasks differ strongly in tag set sizes. Generally, the POS set sizes for all the languages are no more than 17 and SUPER set sizes are around 200. When treating morphological features as a string (i.e. not splitting into key-value pairs), the sizes of the MORPH tag sets range from about 100 up to 2000.

3.3 Setups

As baselines to our models, we take the two state-of-the-art taggers MarMot[5] (denoted as **CRF**) and bilstm-aux[6] (denoted as **LSTM**). We train the taggers with the recommended hyper-parameters from the documentations.

To ensure a fair comparison (especially between LSTM and CNN), we generally treat the three tasks equally, and do not apply task-specific tuning on them, i.e., using the same features and same model hyper-parameters in each single task. Also, we do not use any pre-trained word embeddings.

For the LSTM tagger, we use the recommended hyper-parameters from the documentation[7] including 64-dimensional word embeddings ($\vec{w}$) and 100-dimensional composed vectors ($\vec{c}$). We train the $\vec{w}$, $\vec{c}$ and $\vec{w}+\vec{c}$ models as in Plank et al. (2016).

---

[4]German, French and Indonesian do not have MORPH tags in UD-1.2, thus not evaluated in this task.

[5]http://cistern.cis.lmu.de/marmot/

[6]https://github.com/bplank/bilstm-aux

[7]We use the most recent version of the tagger and stacking 3 layers of LSTM as recommended. The average accuracy for POS in our evaluation is slightly lower than reported in the paper, presumably due to different versions of the tagger, but it does not influence the conclusion.

We train the CNN taggers with the same dimensionalities for word representations.

For the CRF tagger, we predict POS and MORPH jointly as in the standard setting, which performs much better than with separate predictions, as shown in Müller et al. (2013). Also, the CRF tagger splits the morphological tags into key-value pairs, whereas the two neural-based taggers treat the whole string as a tag.[8] We predict SUPER as a separate task.

3.4 Results

The test results for the three tasks are shown in Table 1 in three groups. The first group of seven columns are the results for POS, where both LSTM and CNN have three variations of input features: word only ($\vec{w}$), character only ($\vec{c}$) and both ($\vec{w}+\vec{c}$). For MORPH and SUPER, we only use the $\vec{w}+\vec{c}$ setting for both LSTM and CNN.

On macro-average, three taggers perform close in the POS task, with the CNN tagger being slightly better. In the MORPH task, CNN is again slightly ahead of CRF, while LSTM is about 2 points behind. In the SUPER task, CNN outperforms both taggers by a large margin: 2 points higher than LSTM and 8 points higher than CRF.

While considering the input features of the LSTM and CNN taggers, both taggers perform close with $\vec{w}$ as input, which suggests that the two taggers are comparable in encoding context for POS. However, with only $\vec{c}$, CNN performs much better than LSTM (95.54 vs. 92.61), and close to $\vec{w}+\vec{c}$ (96.18). Also, $\vec{c}$ consistently outperforms $\vec{w}$ for all languages with CNN. This suggests that the CNN model alone is capable of learning most of the information that the word-level model can learn, while the LSTM model is not.

The more interesting cases are MORPH and SUPER, where CNN performs much higher than LSTM. One potential explanation for the considerably large difference is that the LSTM tagger may be more sensitive to hyper-parameters and requires task specific tuning. We use the same setting which is tuned for the POS task, thus it underperforms in the other tasks. Another factor could be the large tag sets in MORPH tagging task, which are larger than POS in orders of magnitudes, especially for *cs*, *eu*, *fi*, *hr*, *pl*, and *sl*, all of which have more than 500 distinct tags, and the LSTM

---

[8]Since we use the CRF tagger as a non-neural baseline, we prefer to use the settings which maximize its performances rather than rigorously equal but suboptimal settings.

| | **POS** | | | | | | | **MORPH** | | | **SUPER** | | |
	CRF	LSTM $\vec{w}$	LSTM $\vec{c}$	LSTM $\vec{w}+\vec{c}$	CNN $\vec{w}$	CNN $\vec{c}$	CNN $\vec{w}+\vec{c}$	CRF	LSTM $\vec{w}+\vec{c}$	CNN $\vec{w}+\vec{c}$	CRF	LSTM $\vec{w}+\vec{c}$	CNN $\vec{w}+\vec{c}$
ar	98.83	95.05	98.35	98.88	95.30	98.89	**99.00**	98.11	97.91	**98.45**	79.67	83.70	**85.51**
bg	98.11	94.96	96.94	98.07	95.25	97.79	**98.20**	**95.12**	92.28	94.85	78.91	85.91	**87.64**
cs	98.74	96.12	92.98	98.40	96.36	98.35	**98.79**	93.81	90.21	**94.45**	76.33	81.43	**87.46**
da	95.96	91.74	94.29	**96.06**	92.08	95.24	95.92	**95.50**	94.15	95.14	73.83	81.00	**81.82**
de	**92.77**	89.91	88.97	92.57	90.21	92.44	92.73	-	-	-	70.56	77.58	**79.69**
en	94.49	91.58	88.99	94.17	92.64	93.76	**94.76**	95.69	95.45	**95.88**	75.57	83.27	**85.87**
es	95.28	93.27	91.41	94.62	93.95	95.36	**95.65**	96.14	95.26	**96.34**	78.07	83.80	**86.27**
eu	94.79	88.70	89.80	93.99	89.69	94.31	**94.94**	**89.60**	84.32	89.06	70.44	77.88	**80.43**
fa	96.82	95.67	94.73	96.95	95.97	96.12	**97.12**	**96.56**	96.37	96.50	76.76	83.21	**83.25**
fi	**95.79**	87.78	84.41	94.16	88.24	94.33	95.31	**94.33**	87.33	93.82	70.69	76.65	**82.63**
fr	95.98	94.34	91.82	95.85	94.56	95.68	**96.27**	-	-	-	78.36	84.01	**85.44**
he	95.48	93.81	92.96	95.62	93.81	94.68	**96.04**	92.92	91.27	**93.29**	76.73	82.56	**85.44**
hi	96.36	95.66	91.12	96.23	96.04	95.77	**96.69**	90.93	90.78	**92.11**	85.54	89.62	**90.08**
hr	**95.56**	88.10	94.47	94.69	88.92	94.76	95.05	87.25	84.56	**87.73**	71.42	77.77	**79.27**
id	**93.51**	90.40	90.76	92.97	91.15	92.32	93.44	-	-	-	75.37	80.55	**81.63**
it	**97.74**	96.04	94.64	97.55	96.54	97.08	97.62	**97.63**	97.13	97.47	84.02	89.10	**90.89**
nl	91.03	85.09	86.52	92.23	83.74	92.05	**93.11**	92.32	91.26	**93.12**	67.04	77.71	**79.68**
no	97.61	94.39	93.32	97.49	94.60	97.05	**97.65**	96.03	94.85	95.74	79.99	86.45	**89.41**
pl	**96.92**	89.53	95.05	96.30	90.48	96.41	96.83	**87.74**	82.34	87.13	76.09	80.00	**83.45**
pt	**97.78**	94.20	94.95	97.53	94.41	97.22	97.46	94.99	94.75	**95.76**	78.68	86.02	**87.42**
sl	96.60	90.43	96.35	**97.42**	91.02	96.89	97.16	90.41	86.47	**91.94**	76.35	85.67	**86.45**
sv	96.23	93.04	94.48	96.20	93.27	95.38	**96.28**	**95.65**	94.08	95.30	73.81	81.04	**83.34**
avg	96.02	92.26	92.61	95.82	92.65	95.54	**96.18**	93.72	91.62	**93.90**	76.10	82.50	**84.69**

Table 1: Tagging accuracies of the three taggers in the three tasks on the test sets of UD 1.2, the highest accuracy for each task on each language is marked in boldface.

tagger performs poorly on these languages. In the SUPER task, where the information from long-distance context is more important, CNN performs much better than both CRF and LSTM. CRF simply has a much smaller context window, thus the poor performance. The LSTM model theoretically can model long-distance contexts, but the information may gradually fade away during the recurrence, whereas the CNN model treat all words equally as long as they are in the context window.

On the more established WSJ data set, Table 2 shows the tagging performances of the CNN model along with some previous works as reference. Generally, the differences among the taggers are very small, we could not conclude any one being considerably better on this data set. This result is expected since English is not a morphologically rich language and WSJ is large data set and has a relatively low OOV rate. Note that the Convnet tagger by dos Santos and Zadrozny (2014) used pre-trained word embeddings while our CNN tagger does not.

3.5 Unnormalized Text

It is a common scenario to use a model trained with news data to process text from social media, which could include intentional or unintentional

WSJ	Accuracy
CRF (Müller et al., 2013)	97.30
Convnet (dos Santos and Zadrozny, 2014)	97.32
bi-LSTM (Ling et al., 2015)	97.36
bi-LSTM (Plank et al., 2016)	97.22
CNN (this work)	97.30

Table 2: Tagging accuracy on the WSJ test set.

misspellings. Unfortunately, we do not have social media data for all the languages. However, we design an experiment to simulate unnormalized text, by systematically editing the words in the dev sets with one of the four operations: insertion, deletion, substitution, and swap. For example, if we modify a word *abcdef* at position 2 (0-based), the modified words would be *abxcdef*, *abdef*, *abxdef*, and *abdcef*, where x is a random character from the alphabet of the language.

For each operation, we create a group of modified dev sets, where all words longer than two characters are edited by the operation with a probability of 0.25, 0.5, 0.75, or 1. For each language, we use the models trained on the normal training sets and predict POS for the modified dev sets. The average accuracies are shown in Figure 2.

Generally, all models suffer from the increasing degrees of unnormalization, but CNN always degrades the least and slowest. In the extreme case where almost all words are unnormalized, CNN performs 4 to 8 points higher than LSTM and 4 to 12 points higher than CRF. This suggests that the CNN is more robust to misspelt words.

While looking into the specific cases of misspelling, CNN is less sensitive to substitution, while insertion and deletion have stronger effect, and swap degrades its performance the most. In the case of substitution, the distortion to the character n-gram patterns are smaller than varying the lengths, i.e. insertion and deletion, thus has smaller negative impact. However, in the case of swap, the effect is similar to substituting two characters instead of one, thus larger degradation. LSTM and CRF on the other hand, are affected the most by substitution.

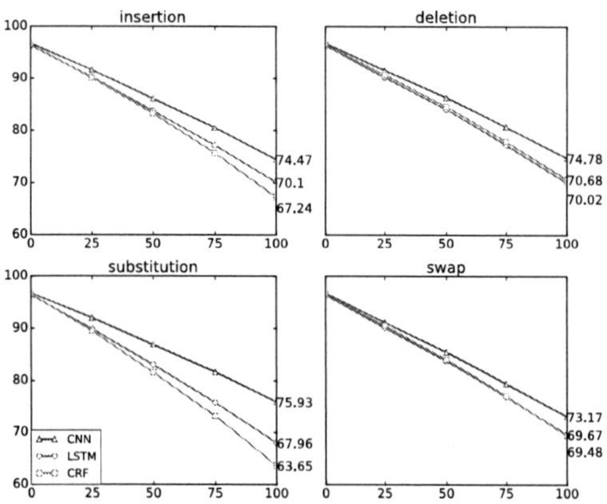

Figure 2: POS tagging accuracies on the dev sets with the four modifications of different degrees.

4 Conclusion

In this paper, we propose a general-purpose tagger that uses two CNNs for both character composition and context encoding. On the universal dependency treebanks (v1.2), the tagger achieves state-of-the-art or comparable results for POS tagging and morphological tagging, and to the best of our knowledge, it performs by far the best for supertagging. The tagger works well across different tagging tasks without tuning the hyper-parameters, and it is also robust against unnormalized text.

Our tagger uses a greedy window-based approach, which mainly aims at showing the effectiveness of CNN in composing word representations and encoding contexts. However, a globally normalized decoding method, e.g. beam-search or sentence-level inference as in Collobert et al. (2011), could potentially further improve the tagger's performance, which is left for future work.

Acknowledgments

This work was supported by the German Research Foundation (DFG) in project D8 of SFB 732. We also thank our colleagues in the IMS and the anonymous reviewers for the suggestions.

References

Miguel Ballesteros, Chris Dyer, and A. Noah Smith. 2015. Improved transition-based parsing by modeling characters instead of words with lstms. In *Proceedings of the 2015 Conference on Empirical Methods in Natural Language Processing*. Association for Computational Linguistics, pages 349–359. https://doi.org/10.18653/v1/D15-1041.

Michael Collins. 2002. Discriminative training methods for hidden markov models: Theory and experiments with perceptron algorithms. In *Proceedings of the ACL-02 conference on Empirical methods in natural language processing-Volume 10*. Association for Computational Linguistics, pages 1–8.

Ronan Collobert, Jason Weston, Léon Bottou, Michael Karlen, Koray Kavukcuoglu, and Pavel Kuksa. 2011. Natural language processing (almost) from scratch. *Journal of Machine Learning Research* 12(Aug):2493–2537.

R. Marta Costa-jussà and R. José A. Fonollosa. 2016. Character-based neural machine translation. In *Proceedings of the 54th Annual Meeting of the Association for Computational Linguistics (Volume 2: Short Papers)*. Association for Computational Linguistics, pages 357–361. https://doi.org/10.18653/v1/P16-2058.

Cicero dos Santos and Victor Guimarães. 2015. Boosting named entity recognition with neural character embeddings. In *Proceedings of the Fifth Named Entity Workshop*. Association for Computational Linguistics, pages 25–33. https://doi.org/10.18653/v1/W15-3904.

Cicero dos Santos and Bianca Zadrozny. 2014. Learning character-level representations for part-of-speech tagging. In *Proceedings of the 31st International Conference on Machine Learning (ICML-14)*. pages 1818–1826.

Agnieszka Faleńska, Anders Björkelund, Özlem Çetinoğlu, and Wolfgang Seeker. 2015. Stacking or supertagging for dependency parsing – what's the difference? In *Proceedings of the 14th International Conference on Parsing Technologies*. Association for Computational Linguistics, Bilbao, Spain, pages 118–129. http://www.aclweb.org/anthology/W15-2215.

Kilian A. Foth, Tomas By, and Wolfgang Menzel. 2006. Guiding a constraint dependency parser with supertags. In *ACL 2006, 21st International Conference on Computational Linguistics and 44th Annual Meeting of the Association for Computational Linguistics, Proceedings of the Conference, Sydney, Australia, 17-21 July 2006*. http://aclweb.org/anthology/P06-1037.

Jonas Gehring, Michael Auli, David Grangier, Denis Yarats, and Yann N Dauphin. 2017. Convolutional sequence to sequence learning. *arXiv preprint arXiv:1705.03122* .

Aravind K. Joshi and Srinivas Bangalore. 1994. Disambiguation of Super Parts of Speech (or Supertags): Almost Parsing. In *Proceedings of the 15th Conference on Computational Linguistics - Volume 1*. Association for Computational Linguistics, Stroudsburg, PA, USA, COLING '94, pages 154–160. https://doi.org/10.3115/991886.991912.

Yoon Kim, Yacine Jernite, David Sontag, and Alexander M. Rush. 2016. Character-aware neural language models. In *Proceedings of the Thirtieth AAAI Conference on Artificial Intelligence, February 12-17, 2016, Phoenix, Arizona, USA.*. AAAI Press, pages 2741–2749.

Wang Ling, Chris Dyer, W. Alan Black, Isabel Trancoso, Ramon Fermandez, Silvio Amir, Luis Marujo, and Tiago Luis. 2015. Finding function in form: Compositional character models for open vocabulary word representation. In *Proceedings of the 2015 Conference on Empirical Methods in Natural Language Processing*. Association for Computational Linguistics, pages 1520–1530. https://doi.org/10.18653/v1/D15-1176.

Mitchell P. Marcus, Mary Ann Marcinkiewicz, and Beatrice Santorini. 1993. Building a large annotated corpus of english: The penn treebank. *Computational Linguistics* pages 313–330. http://dl.acm.org/citation.cfm?id=972470.972475.

Thomas Müller, Helmut Schmid, and Hinrich Schütze. 2013. Efficient Higher-Order CRFs for Morphological Tagging. In *In Proceedings of EMNLP*.

Hiroki Ouchi, Kevin Duh, and Yuji Matsumoto. 2014. Improving Dependency Parsers with Supertags. In *Proceedings of the 14th Conference of the European Chapter of the Association for Computational Linguistics, Volume 2: Short Papers*. Association for Computational Linguistics, Gothenburg, Sweden, pages 154–158. http://www.aclweb.org/anthology/E14-4030.

Slav Petrov, Dipanjan Das, and Ryan McDonald. 2012. A universal part-of-speech tagset. In *Proceedings of the Eight International Conference on Language Resources and Evaluation (LREC'12)*. European Language Resources Association (ELRA), Istanbul, Turkey.

Barbara Plank, Anders Søgaard, and Yoav Goldberg. 2016. Multilingual part-of-speech tagging with bidirectional long short-term memory models and auxiliary loss. In *Proceedings of the 54th Annual Meeting of the Association for Computational Linguistics (Volume 2: Short Papers)*. Association for Computational Linguistics, pages 412–418. https://doi.org/10.18653/v1/P16-2067.

Ngoc Thang Vu, Heike Adel, Pankaj Gupta, and Hinrich Schütze. 2016. Combining recurrent and convolutional neural networks for relation classification. In *Proceedings of the 2016 Conference of the North American Chapter of the Association for Computational Linguistics: Human Language Technologies*. Association for Computational Linguistics, pages 534–539. https://doi.org/10.18653/v1/N16-1065.

Xiang Yu and Ngoc Thang Vu. 2017. Character composition model with convolutional neural networks for dependency parsing on morphologically rich languages. In *Proceedings of the 55th Annual Meeting of the Association for Computational Linguistics (Volume 2: Short Papers)*. Association for Computational Linguistics, Vancouver, Canada.

Reconstruction of Word Embeddings from Sub-Word Parameters

Karl Stratos
Toyota Technological Institute at Chicago
`stratos@ttic.edu`

Abstract

Pre-trained word embeddings improve the performance of a neural model at the cost of increasing the model size. We propose to benefit from this resource without paying the cost by operating strictly at the sub-lexical level. Our approach is quite simple: before task-specific training, we first optimize sub-word parameters to reconstruct pre-trained word embeddings using various distance measures. We report interesting results on a variety of tasks: word similarity, word analogy, and part-of-speech tagging.

1 Introduction

Word embeddings trained from a large quantity of unlabled text are often important for a neural model to reach state-of-the-art performance. They are shown to improve the accuracy of part-of-speech (POS) tagging from 97.13 to 97.55 (Ma and Hovy, 2016), the F1 score of named-entity recognition (NER) from 83.63 to 90.94 (Lample et al., 2016), and the UAS of dependency parsing from 93.1 to 93.9 (Kiperwasser and Goldberg, 2016). On the other hand, the benefit comes at the cost of a bigger model which now stores these embeddings as additional parameters.

In this study, we propose to benefit from this resource without paying the cost by operating strictly at the sub-lexical level. Specifically, we optimize the character-level parameters of the model to reconstruct the word embeddings prior to task-specific training. We frame the problem as distance minimization and consider various metrics suitable for different applications, for example Manhattan distance and negative cosine similarity.

While our approach is simple, the underlying learning problem is a challenging one; the sub-word parameters must reproduce the topology of word embeddings which are not always morphologically coherent (e.g., the meaning of `fox` does not follow any common morphological pattern). Nonetheless, we observe that the model can still learn useful patterns. We evaluate our approach on a variety of tasks: word similarity, word analogy, and POS tagging. We report certain, albeit small, improvement on these tasks, which indicates that the word topology transformation based on pre-training can be beneficial.

2 Related Work

Faruqui et al. (2015) "retrofit" embeddings against semantic lexicons such as PPDB or WordNet. Cotterell et al. (2016) leverage existing morphological lexicons to incorporate sub-word components. The aim and scope of our work are clearly different: we are interested in training a strictly sub-lexical model that only operates over characters (which has the benefit of smaller model size) and yet somehow exploit pre-trained word embeddings in the process.

Our work is also related to *knowledge distillation* which refers to training a smaller "student" network to perform better by learning from a larger "teacher" network. We adopt this terminology and refer to pre-trained word embeddings as the teacher and sub-lexical embeddings as the student. This problem has mostly been considered for classification and framed as matching the probabilities of the student to the probabilities of the teacher (Ba and Caruana, 2014; Li et al., 2014; Kim and Rush, 2016). In contrast, we work directly with representations in Euclidean space.

Proceedings of the First Workshop on Subword and Character Level Models in NLP, pages 130–135,
Copenhagen, Denmark, September 7, 2017. ©2017 Association for Computational Linguistics.

3 Reconstruction Method

Let $\mathcal{W}$ denote the set of word types. For each word $w \in \mathcal{W}$, we assume a pre-trained word embedding $x^w \in \mathbb{R}^d$ and a representation $h^w \in \mathbb{R}^d$ computed by sub-word model parameters Θ; we defer how to define h^w until later. The reconstruction error with respect to a distance function $D : \mathbb{R}^d \times \mathbb{R}^d \to \mathbb{R}$ is given by

$$L_D(\Theta) = \sum_{w \in \mathcal{W}} D(x^w, h^w) \qquad (1)$$

where x^w is constant and h^w is a function of Θ. Since we use gradient descent to optimize (1), we can define $D(u, v)$ to be any continuous function measuring the discrepency between u and v, for example,

$$D_1(u, v) := \sum_{i=1}^{d} |u_i - v_i| \qquad \text{(Manhattan)}$$

$$D_{\sqrt{2}}(u, v) := \sqrt{\sum_{i=1}^{d} |u_i - v_i|^2} \qquad \text{(Euclidean)}$$

$$D_2(u, v) := \sum_{i=1}^{d} |u_i - v_i|^2 \qquad \text{(squared error)}$$

$$D_\infty(u, v) := \max_{i=1}^{d} |u_i - v_i| \qquad (l_\infty \text{ distance})$$

$$D_{\cos}(u, v) := \frac{-u^\top v}{||u||_2 \, ||v||_2} \qquad \text{(negative cosine)}$$

Unlike other common losses used in the neural network literature such as negative log likelihood or the hinge loss, L_D has a direct geometric interpretation illustrated in Figure 1. We first optimize (1) over sub-word model parameters Θ for a set number of epochs, and then proceed to optimize a task-specific loss $L(\Theta, \Theta')$ where Θ' denotes all other model parameters.

3.1 Analysis of a Linear Model

In general, h^w can be a complicated function of Θ. But we can gain some insight by analyzing the simple case of a linear model, which corresponds to the top layer of a neural network. More specifically, we assume the form

$$h_i^w = \theta_i^\top z^w \qquad \forall i = 1 \ldots d$$

where $z^w \in \mathbb{R}^{d'}$ is fixed and $\Theta = \{\theta_1 \ldots \theta_d\} \subset \mathbb{R}^{d'}$ is the only parameter to be optimized.

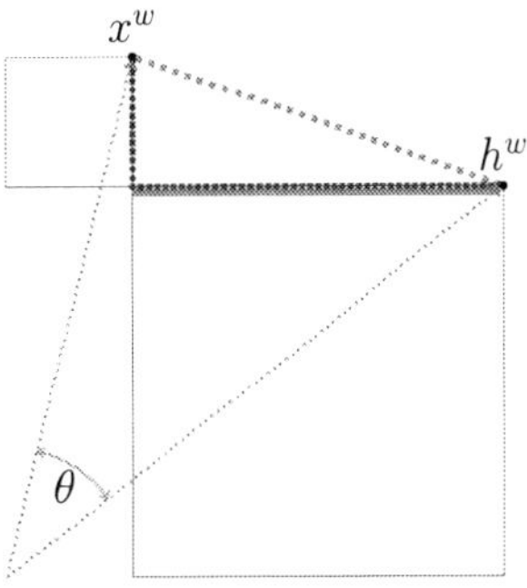

Figure 1: Geometric losses corresponding to different distance metrics: Manhattan distance (blue), Euclidean distance (green), squared error (yellow), l_∞ distance (red), and negative cosine similarity $(-\cos \theta)$.

Manhattan distance The error $L_{D_1}(\Theta)$ is now

$$L_{D_1}(\Theta) = \sum_{w \in \mathcal{W}} \sum_{i=1}^{d} \left| x_i^w - \theta_i^\top z^w \right| = \sum_{i=1}^{d} \text{LAD}_i(\theta_i)$$

where $\text{LAD}_i(\theta) := \sum_{w \in \mathcal{W}} \left| x_i^w - \theta_i^\top z^w \right|$ is least absolute deviations (LAD). It is well-known that the LAD criterion is robust to outliers. To see this, if $z^w = (1/d')\mathbf{1}$ for all $w \in \mathcal{W}$, then a minimizer of $\text{LAD}_i(\theta)$ is given analytically by

$$\theta_i^* = \text{median} \{x_i^w : w \in \mathcal{W}\}$$

where the median resists extreme values (e.g., the median of both $\{1, 2, 3\}$ and $\{1, 2, 999\}$ is 2). Thus using Manhattan distance can be useful when teacher word embeddings are noisy or there are occasional exceptions in morphological patterns that are best ignored.

Squared error The error $L_{D_2}(\Theta)$ is now

$$L_{D_2}(\Theta) = \sum_{w \in \mathcal{W}} \sum_{i=1}^{d} \left| x_i^w - \theta_i^\top z^w \right|^2 = \sum_{i=1}^{d} \text{OLS}_i(\theta_i)$$

where $\text{OLS}_i(\theta) := \sum_{w \in \mathcal{W}} \left| x_i^w - \theta^\top z^w \right|^2$ is ordinary least squares (OLS). Thus if the matrix $Z \in \mathbb{R}^{|\mathcal{W}| \times d'}$ with z^w as rows has rank d', the unique solution is given by $\theta_i^* = (Z^\top Z)^{-1} Z^\top x_i^w$. Let $\bar{h}_i^w = (\theta_i^*)^\top z^w$ denote the optimal sub-word embedding value. It is well-known that the change in $\bar{h}_i^w$ caused by removing x_i^w from the dataset is proportional to the residual $x_i^w - \bar{h}_i^w$ (Davidson et al.,

1993). In other words, squared error is sensitive to outliers and may not be as suitable as Manhattan distance for fitting noisy or incoherent word embeddings.

Other distance metrics Euclidean distance is geometrically intuitive but less mathematically convenient than squared error, thus we choose not to focus on it. l_∞ distance penalizes the dimension with maximum absolute difference and can be useful if calculating one coordinate at a time is convenient. Finally, negative cosine similarity penalizes the angle between embeddings. This is suitable when we only care about directions and not magnitude, for instance in word similarity where we measure cosine similarities between word embeddings.

There are distance metrics not discussed here that may be appropriate in certain situations. For instance, the KL divergence is a natural (assymetric) measure if word embeddings are distributions (e.g., over context words). More generally, we can consider the wide class of metrics in the Bregman divergence (Banerjee et al., 2005).

4   Sub-Word Architecture

We now describe how we define word embedding $h^w \in \mathbb{R}^d$ from sub-word parameters. We use a character-based embedding scheme closely following Lample et al. (2016). We use an LSTM simply as a mapping $\phi : \mathbb{R}^d \times \mathbb{R}^{d'} \to \mathbb{R}^{d'}$ that takes an input vector x and a state vector h to output a new state vector $h' = \phi(x, h)$. See Hochreiter and Schmidhuber (1997) for a detailed description.

4.1   Character Model

Let $\mathcal{C}$ denote the set of character types. The model parameters Θ associated with this layer are

- $e^c \in \mathbb{R}^{d_c}$ for each $c \in \mathcal{C}$

- Character LSTMs $\phi_f^{\mathcal{C}}, \phi_b^{\mathcal{C}} : \mathbb{R}^{d_c} \times \mathbb{R}^{d_c} \to \mathbb{R}^{d_c}$

- $W^f, W^b \in \mathbb{R}^{d \times d_c}$, $b^{\mathcal{C}} \in \mathbb{R}^d$

Let $w(j) \in \mathcal{C}$ denote the character of $w \in \mathcal{W}$ at position j. The model computes $h^w \in \mathbb{R}^d$ as

$$f_j^{\mathcal{C}} = \phi_f^{\mathcal{C}}\left(e^{w(j)}, f_{j-1}^{\mathcal{C}}\right) \qquad \forall j = 1 \ldots |w|$$

$$b_j^{\mathcal{C}} = \phi_b^{\mathcal{C}}\left(e^{w(j)}, b_{j+1}^{\mathcal{C}}\right) \qquad \forall j = |w| \ldots 1$$

$$z^w = W^f f_{|w|}^{\mathcal{C}} + W^b b_1^{\mathcal{C}} + b^{\mathcal{C}}$$

$$h_i^w = \max\left\{0, z_i^w\right\} \quad \forall i = 1 \ldots d \qquad (2)$$

We also experiment with a highway network (Srivastava et al., 2015) which has been shown to be beneficial for image recognition (He et al., 2015) and language modeling (Kim et al., 2016). In this case, Θ includes additional parameters $W^{\text{highway}} \in \mathbb{R}^{d \times d}$ and $b^{\text{highway}} \in \mathbb{R}^d$. A new character-level embedding $\tilde{h}^w$ is computed as

$$t = \sigma\left(W^{\text{highway}} h^w + b^{\text{highway}}\right)$$

$$\tilde{h}^w = t \odot h^w + (\mathbf{1} - t) \odot z^w \qquad (3)$$

where $\sigma(\cdot) \in [0, 1]$ denotes an element-wise sigmoid function and $\odot$ the element-wise multiplication. This allows the network to skip nonlinearity by making t_i close to 0. We find that the additional highway network is beneficial in certain cases. We will use either (2) or (3) in our experiments depending on the task.

5   Experiments

Implementation We implement our models using the DyNet library. We use the Adam optimizer (Kingma and Ba, 2014) and apply dropout at all LSTM layers (Hinton et al., 2012). For POS tagging and parsing, we perform a 5×5 grid search over learning rates $0.0001 \ldots 0.0005$ and dropout rates $0.1 \ldots 0.5$ and choose the configuration that gives the best performance on the dev set. We use the highway network (3) for word analogy and parsing and (2) for others. Note that the character embedding dimension d_c must match the dimension of the pre-trained word embeddings.

Teacher Word Embeddings We use 100-dimensional word embeddings identical to those used by Dyer et al. (2015) which are computed with a variant of the skip n-gram model (Ling et al., 2015). These embeddings have been shown to be effective in various tasks (Dyer et al., 2015; Lample et al., 2016).

5.1   Word Similarity and Analogy

Data For word similarity, we use three public datasets WordSim-353, MEN, and Stanford Rare Word. Each contains 353, 3000, and 2034 word pairs annotated with similarity scores. The evaluation is conducted by computing the cosine of the angle θ between each word pair (w_1, w_2) under the model (2):

$$\cos(\theta) = \frac{\left(h^{w_1}\right)^\top h^{w_2}}{||h^{w_1}||_2 \, ||h^{w_2}||_2} \qquad (4)$$

	number of reconstruction epochs				
metric	0	10	20	30	50
D_1	0.03	0.09	0.11	0.12	0.13
D_2	0.03	0.12	0.12	0.14	**0.15**
D_∞	0.03	0.12	0.10	0.09	0.10
$D_{\cos}$	0.03	**0.13**	**0.15**	**0.15**	**0.15**

Table 1: Effect of reconstruction on word similarity: the teacher word embeddings obtain score 0.50.

Embedding	Syntactic	Semantic
random	**65.21**	1.13
D_1	26.32	2.20
D_2	27.56	**2.47**
D_∞	45.68	1.74
$D_{\cos}$	23.77	2.22
teacher	57.42	59.58

Table 2: Effect of reconstruction on word analogy (10 reconstruction epochs).

and computing the Spearman's correlation coefficient with the human scores. We report the average correlation across these datasets. For word analogy, we use the 8000 syntactic analogy questions from the dataset of Mikolov et al. (2013b) and 8869 semantic analogy questions from the dataset of Mikolov et al. (2013a). We use the multiplicative technique of Levy and Goldberg (2014) for answering analogy questions.

Result Table 1 shows word similarity scores for different numbers of reconstruction training epochs. The teacher word embeddings obtain 0.5. The sub-word model improves performance from the initial score of 0.03 up to 0.16. In particular, the negative cosine distance metric which directly optimizes the relevant quantity (4) is consistently best performing.

Table 2 shows the accuracy on the syntactic and semantic analogy datasets. An interesting finding in our experiment is that for syntactic analogy, **a randomly initialized character-based model outperforms the pre-trained embeddings** and thus reconstruction only decreases the performance. We suspect that this is because much of the syntactic regularities is already captured by the architecture. Many questions involves only simplistic transformation, for instance adding r in wise : wiser $\sim$ free : x. The model correctly answers such questions simply by following its architecture, though it is unable to answer less regular questions (e.g., see : saw $\sim$ keep : x).

Semantic analogy questions have no such morphological regularities (e.g., Athens : Greece $\sim$ Havana : x) and are challenging to sub-lexical models. Nonetheless, the model is able to make a minor improvement in accuracy.

5.2 POS Tagging

We perform POS tagging on the Penn WSJ treebank with 45 tags using a BiLSTM model de-

model	accuracy	lookup
FULL	97.20	43211
FULL+EMB	97.32	252365
CHAR	96.93	80
CHAR(D_1)	**97.17**	93
CHAR(D_2)	97.08	93
CHAR(D_∞)	97.06	93
CHAR$(D_{\cos})$	97.08	93

Table 3: POS tagging accuracy with different definitions of v^w (see the main text). The final column shows the number of lookup parameters.

scribed in Lample et al. (2016). Given a vector sequence $(v^{w_1} \dots v^{w_n})$ corresponding to a sentence $(w_1 \dots w_n) \in \mathcal{W}^n$, the BiLSTM model produces feature vectors $(h_1 \dots h_n)$. We adhere to the simplest approach of making a local prediction at each position i by a feedforward network on h_i,

$$p(t_i|h_i) \propto \exp\left(W^2 f(W^1 h_i + b^1) + b^2\right)$$

where $f_i(v) = \max\{0, v_i\}$ and W^1, W^2, b^1, b^2 are additional parameters. The model is trained by optimizing log likelihood. We consider the following choices of v^w:

- FULL: $v^w = e^w \oplus h^w$ uses both word-level lookup parameter e^w and character-level embedding h^w (2).

- FULL+EMB: Same as FULL but the lookup parameters e^w are initialized with pre-trained word embeddings.

- CHAR: $v^w = h^w$ uses characters only.

- CHAR(D): Same as CHAR but optimized for 10 epochs to reconstruct pre-trained word embeddings with distance metric D.

Table 3 shows the accuracy of these models. We see that pre-trained word embeddings boost the

`beautiful`	wonderful	prettiest	gorgeous	smartest	jolly	famous	sensual
	baleful	bagful	basketful	bountiful	boastful	bashful	behavioural
	bountiful	peaceful	disdainful	perpetual	primaeval	successul	purposeful
`amazing`	incredible	wonderful	remarkable	terrific	marvellous	astonishing	unbelievable
	awaking	arming	aging	awakening	angling	agonizing	among
	arousing	amusing	awarding	applauding	allaying	awaking	assaying
`Springfield`	Glendale	Kennesaw	Gainesville	Lynchburg	Youngstown	Kutztown	Harrisburg
	Spanish-ruled	Serbian-held	Serbian-led	Spangled	Serbian-controlled	Schofield	Sharif-led
	Stubblefield	Smithfield	Stansfield	Butterfield	Littlefield	Bitterfeld	Sinfield

Table 4: Nearest neighbor examples: for each word, the three rows respectively show its nearest neighbors using pre-trained word embeddings, student embeddings at random initialization (3), and student embeddings optimized for 10 epochs using D_1.

performance of FULL from 97.20 to 97.32. When we use the strictly character-based model CHAR without reconstruction, the performance drops to 96.93. But with reconstruction, the model recovers some of the lost accuracy. In particular, reconstructing with the Manhattan distance metric gives the largeset improvement and yields 97.17.

5.3 Analysis of Student Embeddings

Table 4 shows examples of nearest neighbors. For each example, the first row corresponds to the teacher, the second to the student (3) at random initialization, and the third to the student optimized for 10 epochs using D_1. The student embeddings at random initialization are already capable of capturing morphological regularities such as `-ful` and `-ing`. With reconstruction, there is a subtle change in the topology. For instance, the nearest neighbors of `beautiful` change from `baleful` and `bagful` to `bountiful` and `peaceful`. For `Springfield`, nearest neighbors change from unrelated words such as `Spanish-ruled` to fellow nouns such as `Stubblefield`.

6 Conclusion

We have presented a simple method for a sublexical model to leverage pre-trained word embeddings. We have shown that by recontructing the embeddings before task-specific training, the model can improve over random initialization on a variety of tasks. The reconstruction task is a challenging learning problem; while our model learns useful patterns, it is far from perfect. An important future direction is to improve reconstruction with other choices of architecture.

References

Jimmy Ba and Rich Caruana. 2014. Do deep nets really need to be deep? In *Advances in neural information processing systems*. pages 2654–2662.

Dzmitry Bahdanau, Kyunghyun Cho, and Yoshua Bengio. 2014. Neural machine translation by jointly learning to align and translate. *arXiv preprint arXiv:1409.0473* .

Arindam Banerjee, Srujana Merugu, Inderjit S Dhillon, and Joydeep Ghosh. 2005. Clustering with bregman divergences. *Journal of machine learning research* 6(Oct):1705–1749.

Lyle Campbell and Mauricio J Mixco. 2007. *A glossary of historical linguistics*. Edinburgh University Press.

Jason PC Chiu and Eric Nichols. 2015. Named entity recognition with bidirectional lstm-cnns. *arXiv preprint arXiv:1511.08308* .

Ryan Cotterell, Hinrich Schütze, and Jason Eisner. 2016. Morphological smoothing and extrapolation of word embeddings. In *Proceedings of the 54th Annual Meeting of the Association for Computational Linguistics*. volume 1, pages 1651–1660.

Russell Davidson, James G MacKinnon, et al. 1993. Estimation and inference in econometrics .

Chris Dyer, Miguel Ballesteros, Wang Ling, Austin Matthews, and Noah A Smith. 2015. Transition-based dependency parsing with stack long short-term memory. *arXiv preprint arXiv:1505.08075* .

Manaal Faruqui, Jesse Dodge, Sujay K. Jauhar, Chris Dyer, Eduard Hovy, and Noah A. Smith. 2015. Retrofitting word vectors to semantic lexicons. In *Proceedings of NAACL*.

Alex Graves. 2012. Neural networks. In *Supervised Sequence Labelling with Recurrent Neural Networks*, Springer, pages 15–35.

Kaiming He, Xiangyu Zhang, Shaoqing Ren, and Jian Sun. 2015. Deep residual learning for image recognition. *arXiv preprint arXiv:1512.03385* .

Geoffrey E Hinton, Nitish Srivastava, Alex Krizhevsky, Ilya Sutskever, and Ruslan R Salakhutdinov. 2012. Improving neural networks by preventing co-adaptation of feature detectors. *arXiv preprint arXiv:1207.0580* .

Sepp Hochreiter and Jürgen Schmidhuber. 1997. Long short-term memory. *Neural computation* 9(8):1735–1780.

Yoon Kim, Yacine Jernite, David Sontag, and Alexander M Rush. 2016. Character-aware neural language models. In *Thirtieth AAAI Conference on Artificial Intelligence*.

Yoon Kim and Alexander M Rush. 2016. Sequence-level knowledge distillation. *arXiv preprint arXiv:1606.07947* .

Diederik Kingma and Jimmy Ba. 2014. Adam: A method for stochastic optimization. *arXiv preprint arXiv:1412.6980* .

Eliyahu Kiperwasser and Yoav Goldberg. 2016. Simple and accurate dependency parsing using bidirectional lstm feature representations. *Transactions of the Association for Computational Linguistics* 4:313–327.

Guillaume Lample, Miguel Ballesteros, Sandeep Subramanian, Kazuya Kawakami, and Chris Dyer. 2016. Neural architectures for named entity recognition. *arXiv preprint arXiv:1603.01360* .

Geunbae Lee, Jong-Hyeok Lee, and Kyunghee Kim. 1994. Phonemie-level, speech and natural, language integration for agglutinative languages. *GGGGGGGG 0* .

Omer Levy and Yoav Goldberg. 2014. Linguistic regularities in sparse and explicit word representations. In *Proceedings of the Computational Natural Language Learning*. page 171.

Jinyu Li, Rui Zhao, Jui-Ting Huang, and Yifan Gong. 2014. Learning small-size dnn with output-distribution-based criteria. In *INTERSPEECH*. pages 1910–1914.

Wang Ling, Lin Chu-Cheng, Yulia Tsvetkov, and Silvio Amir. 2015. Not all contexts are created equal: Better word representations with variable attention .

Xuezhe Ma and Eduard Hovy. 2016. End-to-end sequence labeling via bi-directional lstm-cnns-crf. *arXiv preprint arXiv:1603.01354* .

Ryan T McDonald, Joakim Nivre, Yvonne Quirmbach-Brundage, Yoav Goldberg, Dipanjan Das, Kuzman Ganchev, Keith B Hall, Slav Petrov, Hao Zhang, Oscar Täckström, et al. 2013. Universal dependency annotation for multilingual parsing. In *ACL (2)*. pages 92–97.

Tomas Mikolov, Kai Chen, Greg Corrado, and Jeffrey Dean. 2013a. Efficient estimation of word representations in vector space. *arXiv preprint arXiv:1301.3781* .

Tomas Mikolov, Wen-tau Yih, and Geoffrey Zweig. 2013b. Linguistic regularities in continuous space word representations. In *HLT-NAACL*. volume 13, pages 746–751.

Sakriani Sakti, Andrew Finch, Ryosuke Isotani, Hisashi Kawai, and Satoshi Nakamura. 2010. Korean pronunciation variation modeling with probabilistic bayesian networks. In *Universal Communication Symposium (IUCS), 2010 4th International*. IEEE, pages 52–57.

Mike Schuster and Kuldip K Paliwal. 1997. Bidirectional recurrent neural networks. *IEEE Transactions on Signal Processing* 45(11):2673–2681.

Jae Jung Song. 2006. *The Korean language: Structure, use and context*. Routledge.

Rupesh Kumar Srivastava, Klaus Greff, and Jürgen Schmidhuber. 2015. Highway networks. *arXiv preprint arXiv:1505.00387* .

Karl Stratos, Michael Collins, and Daniel Hsu. 2015. Model-based word embeddings from decompositions of count matrices. In *Proceedings of the 53rd Annual Meeting of the Association for Computational Linguistics and the 7th International Joint Conference on Natural Language Processing (Volume 1: Long Papers)*. Association for Computational Linguistics, Beijing, China, pages 1282–1291.

Inflection Generation for Spanish Verbs using Supervised Learning

Cristina Barros
Department of Software
and Computing Systems
University of Alicante
Apdo. de Correos 99
E-03080, Alicante, Spain
cbarros@dlsi.ua.es

Dimitra Gkatzia
School of Computing
Edinburgh Napier University
Edinburgh, EH10 5DT, UK
d.gkatzia@napier.ac.uk

Elena Lloret
Department of Software
and Computing Systems
University of Alicante
Apdo. de Correos 99
E-03080, Alicante, Spain
elloret@dlsi.ua.es

Abstract

We present a novel supervised approach to inflection generation for verbs in Spanish. Our system takes as input the verb's lemma form and the desired features such as person, number, tense, and is able to predict the appropriate grammatical conjugation. Even though our approach learns from fewer examples comparing to previous work, it is able to deal with all the Spanish moods (indicative, subjunctive and imperative) in contrast to previous work which only focuses on indicative and subjunctive moods. We show that in an intrinsic evaluation, our system achieves 99% accuracy, outperforming (although not significantly) two competitive state-of-art systems. The successful results obtained clearly indicate that our approach could be integrated into wider approaches related to text generation in Spanish.

1 Introduction

Existing Natural Language Generation (NLG) approaches are usually applied to non morphological rich languages, such as English, where the morphological inflection of the word during the generation process can be addressed using simple handwritten rules or existing libraries such as SimpleNLG (Gatt and Reiter, 2009). In contrast, when it comes to morphological rich languages, such as Spanish, the use of rules can lead to incorrect inflection of a word, thus generating ungrammatical or meaningless texts. Our ultimate goal is to implement a morphological inflection approach for Spanish sentences within an NLG system based on the use of lexicons. However, lexicons lack some verbs' information, specifically, regarding grammatical moods (i.e., the grammatical features of verbs used for denoting modality - statement of facts, desires, commands, etc.). To create lexicons for all the verb inflections and moods would be a very time-consuming and costly task, so in this context the use of machine learning approaches can benefit the inflection of unseen verb forms. Based on this, the research challenge we tackle is defined as follows: given a Spanish verb in its base form (i.e., its lemma), we want to automatically generate all the inflections for that verb. This is very useful for tasks involving natural language generation (e.g., text generation, machine translation), since the generated texts would sound more natural and grammatically correct.

Our contributions to the field are as follows: we present a novel and efficient method for tackling the challenge of inflection generation for Spanish verbs using an ensemble of algorithms; we provide a high-quality dataset which includes inflection rules of Spanish verbs for all the grammatical moods (i.e. indicative, subjunctive and imperative, being this last one do not tackled by the current approaches); our models are trained with fewer resources than the state-of-art methods; and finally, our method outperforms the state-of-the-art methods achieving a 2% higher accuracy.

The rest of the paper is shaped as follows: In the next section (Section 2) we refer to the related work on inflection generation. In Section 3, we describe the overall methodology and the dataset used to train our model. In Section 4, we present a comparison to the state-of-art inflection generation approaches and in Section 5, we discuss the results. Finally, in Section 6, directions for future work are discussed.

2 Related Work

Morphological inflection has been addressed from different perspectives within the area of Compu-

Proceedings of the First Workshop on Subword and Character Level Models in NLP, pages 136–141,
Copenhagen, Denmark, September 7, 2017. ©2017 Association for Computational Linguistics.

tational Linguistics, commonly for morphological rich languages, such as German, Spanish, Finnish or Arabic, as well as less morphological rich languages such as English.

Previous work has used supervised or semi-supervised learning (Durrett and DeNero, 2013; Ahlberg et al., 2014; Nicolai et al., 2015; Faruqui et al., 2016) to learn from large datasets of morphological rules on word forms in order to apply them to inflect the desired words. Other approaches have relied on linguistic information, such as morphemes and phonology (Cotterell et al., 2016); morphosyntactic disambiguation rules (Suárez et al., 2005); and, graphical models (Dreyer and Eisner, 2009).

Recently, the morphological inflection has been also addressed at SIGMORPHON 2016 Shared Task (Cotterell et al., 2016) where, given a lemma with its part-of-speech, a target inflected form had to be generated (task 1). This task was addressed through several approaches, including align and transduce (Alegria and Etxeberria, 2016; Nicolai et al., 2016; Liu and Mao, 2016); recurrent neural networks (Kann and Schütze, 2016; Aharoni et al., 2016; Östling, 2016); and, linguistic-inspired heuristics approaches (Taji et al., 2016; Sorokin, 2016). Overall, recurrent neural networks approaches performed better, being (Kann and Schütze, 2016) the best performing system in the shared task, obtaining around 98%.

Furthermore, the work described here differs from existing statistical surface realisation methods which use phrase-based learning (e.g., (Konstas and Lapata, 2012)) since they do not usually include morphological inflection. In this respect, our work is more similar to (Dušek and Jurčíček, 2013), where the inflected word forms are learnt through multi-class logistic regression by predicting edit scripts. The aforementioned data-driven methods achieve high accuracy in predicting the appropriate inflection by learning from huge datasets. For example, Durret and DeNero (2013) use 11400 amount of data (i.e. the total number of instances or rules used to predict the inflections of a verb). In contrast, we use almost half to train our system (4556 instances), and we achieve comparable or better results for Spanish. Finally, the work presented here relies on ensembles of classifiers which has been proved successful for content selection in data-to-text systems (Gkatzia et al., 2014).

3 Methodology

In order to perform the inflection task, we first created a dataset to be used for training machine learning algorithms to inflect verbs in Spanish. As part of this submission we will make our dataset freely available[1]. Then, we trained a model capable of predicting the appropriate inflection of a verb automatically, given a verb base form. Next, each of the stages of the proposed approach are described in more detail.

3.1 Dataset Creation

For the purposes of this research, we created a parallel dataset of Spanish base forms and their corresponding inflected form. The Spanish verbs can be divided into regular and irregular verbs, where all the regular verbs share the same inflection patterns whereas, the irregular ones do not and can completely vary from one verb to another, as it is shown in Figure 1.

Regular		Irregular	
Base form	Inf. Form	Base form	Inf. Form
partir	parta	ir	vaya
añadir =	añada	decir ≠	diga
compartir	comparta	argüir	arguya

Figure 1: Differences between regular and irregular verbs in Spanish, for the first singular person of the present tense and in the subjunctive mood.

Therefore, we constructed a dataset, containing the necessary examples of inflection for all the tenses in the Spanish language, by consulting the *Real Academia Española*[2] and the *Enciclopedia Libre Universal en Español*[3]. We further considered that a verb can be divided in three parts: (1) *ending*, (2) *ending stem*, and (3) *penSyl*. An example is shown in Figure 2. This information will be later used as features within the dataset. In Spanish, the verbs can be classified depending on their *ending*, specifically, the verbs ended by "-ar", "-er" and "-ir" belong to the first, second an third conjugation, respectively. Moreover, for the feature *penSyl*, the previous syllable of the ending, formed by the whole syllable, or its dominant vowel is extracted. Finally, the *ending stem* is the closest consonant to the ending.

---

[1]Our dataset for the Spanish verbs inflection is available here: https://github.com/cbarrosua/infDataset

[2]http://www.rae.es/diccionario-panhispanico-de-dudas/apendices/modelos-de-conjugacion-verbal

[3]http://enciclopedia.us.es/index.php/Categoría:Verbos

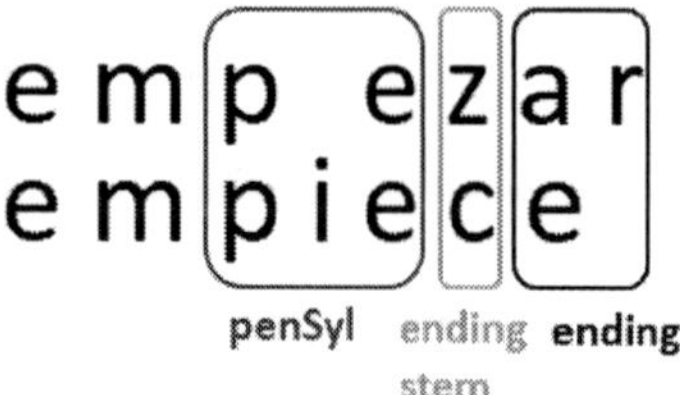

Figure 2: Division of the Spanish verb *to begin* and its inflection for the first singular person of the present tense and in the subjunctive mood.

Besides the previous features obtained from the verb, other features, such as *suff1*, *suff2* or *stemC1* were included because in Spanish some verbs have several variations of an inflection for the same tense, person and number. Therefore, our dataset is finally composed of the following features: (1) *ending*, (2) *ending stem*, (3) *penSyl*, (4) *person*, (5) *number*, (6) *tense*, (7) *mood*, (8) *suff1*, (9) *suff2*, (10) *stemC1*, (11) *stemC2*, (12) *stemC3*. In particular, *suff1* and *suff2* are the inflection predicted for the suffix of the verb form; and *stemC1*, *stemC2* and *stemC3*, refer to the inflection predicted for the penSyl of the verb form. An example of an entry of the dataset is shown in Table 1. Overall, there are 4556 possible inflections. An example of a verb and several of its inflections is shown in Table 2.

3.2 Obtaining the Model and Reconstructing the Verb

As mentioned earlier, our learning task is formed as follows: given a set of 7 features, select the inflection which is most appropriate for the verb. The set of 7 features are as follows: (1) *ending*, (2) *ending stem*, (3) *penSyl*, (4) *person*, (5) *number*, (6) *tense*, (7) *mood*. Using these features, we trained a group of individual models for each of the features described in Section 3.1, which represents a potential inflection value. We used the WEKA (Frank et al., 2016) implementation of the Random Forest algorithm to train the models for the *stemC3* and *stemC2* features, and the Random Tree algorithm to train the models for the *suff1*, *suff2* and *stemC1* features.

Once the models were trained, we predicted all the possible inflections given a verb in its base form, i.e., all the tenses for each mood in Spanish. For accomplishing this task, we first analysed the base form to extract the necessary fea-

tures for the inflection. In this manner, the base form was divided into syllables, taking the penultimate one to obtain the *penSyl* feature. Since all verbs in Spanish always end with "-ar", "-er" and "-ir", as described in the previous section, we split the last syllable into the *ending* and *ending stem* features. Then, for each model we predicted its potential inflection using these extracted features combined with the ones related to the verb tense, i.e., the number, person, etc. Finally, the predicted inflections were employed to replace the features previously identified in the base form, leading to the reconstruction of the base form into the desired inflection, as it can be seen in Figure 3.

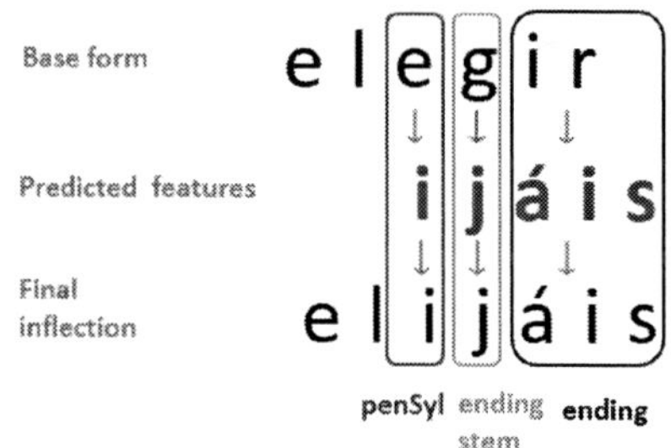

Figure 3: Reconstruction of the verb *elegir* (to choose) with the features predicted by the models.

4 Experiments

We compared our system (RandFT) with two very competitive baselines described below by measuring the accuracy of their output for Spanish verb inflections. The baselines are as follows:

- **Durret13**: This system automatically extracts the orthographic transformation rules of the morphology from labeled examples, and then learns which of those transformations to apply in different contexts by using a semi-Markov conditional random field (CRF) model.

- **Ahlberg14**: This system uses a semi-supervised approach to generalise inflection paradigms from inflection tables by using a finite-state construction.

We reproduced the experiments presented in Durrett and DeNero (2013) and in Ahlberg et al. (2014). In order to compare our system with both baselines, we employed the test set of examples (200 different verbs) which was made available

verb pattern	ending	endingstem	penSyl	person	number	tense	mood	suff1	suff2	stemC1	stemC2	stemC3
amar	ar	ANY	ANY	1	0	1	1	ara	ase	ANY	ANY	ANY
	ar	ANY	ANY	2	0	1	1	aras	ases	ANY	ANY	ANY
	ar	ANY	ANY	3	0	1	1	ara	ase	ANY	ANY	ANY
yacer	er	ANY	yac	1	0	0	0	o	ANY	yazc	yazg	yag
	er	ANY	yac	2	0	0	0	es	ANY	yac	ANY	ANY
	er	ANY	yac	3	0	0	0	e	ANY	yac	ANY	ANY

Table 1: Example of the 1st, 2nd and 3rd singular person of the subjunctive past tense of "amar" (*to love*); and the 1st, 2nd and 3rd singular person of present tense in indicative mood of "yacer" (*to lie*). We assigned the term *ANY* to indicate that the value of a feature does not need to change during the inflection with respect to its value in the base form.

Verb: regar (*to water*)	
Features	**Inflection**
ar, g, e, 1P, Sing, Pres., Ind	riego
ar, g, e, 2P, Sing, Pres., Sub	riegues
ar, g, e, 2P, Plural, Cond., Ind	regaríais
ar, g, e, 3P, Sing, Past I., Sub	regara, regase

Table 2: Example of some possible inflections for the verb "regar" (*to water*) (Pres. = present; Cond. = conditional; Past I. = imperfect past; Ind = Indicative; Sub = subjunctive).

Approach	Correctly predicted verb tables	Correctly predicted verb forms
RandFT	99%	99.98%
Durret13	97%	99.76%
Ahlberg14	96%	99.52%

Table 3: Accuracy of predicting inflection of verb tables and individual verb forms given only the base form, evaluated with an unseen test set of 200 verbs. For the imperative mood, our system achieves 100% accuracy, however the baselines do not predict the imperative form.

by Durrett and DeNero (2013), since this test set included verbs with both uncommon and regular forms. This test set does not included any entry that appeared in the training data. For the experiments, we generated all the verb inflections for the 200 base forms. Furthermore, the aforementioned baselines do not predict all the grammatical moods that exist in the Spanish language (both baselines are only able to predict the indicative and subjunctive mood, but not the imperative one, which is not easy, especially for irregular forms). Therefore, we used an additional test-set to evaluate this grammatical mood. We created the additional test-set by employing information from the Freeling's lexicon for the imperative forms of these 200 verbs (Padró and Stanilovsky, 2012).

5 Results and Discussion

The results obtained, together with the results of Durrett and DeNero (2013) and Ahlberg et al. (2014), are shown in Table 3, where we compared the inflection of the same verb tenses as Durret and Ahlberg using the test set described in the previous section. Our group of classifiers (RandFT), trained with our generalised dataset for Spanish, obtained a higher overall accuracy (but not significantly) regarding the state-of-the-art baselines systems.

In addition, our model can correctly perform the inflection of the imperative mood, which was not included in the baseline systems. This grammatical mood, which forms commands or requests, contains unique imperative forms among the irregular Spanish verbs, as shown in Table 4. For this experiment, our system achieves 100% accuracy when evaluated on the additional test set. Furthermore, our model contributes to the improvement of naturalness and expressivity of NLG (Barros et al., 2017).

Base form–*Inflected form*
contar–*cuenta*; **errar**–*yerra*; **haber**–*he*; **hacer**–*haz*; **oler**–*huele*; **ir**–*ve*; **oír**–*oye*; **decir**–*di*

Table 4: Variability of inflection in the imperative mood for the 2nd person singular of the present.

Error Analysis: Although our system obtains almost 100% accuracy, it fails on the inflection of the participles of extremely rare irregular verbs (e.g., **verb**: ejabrir → **generated**: ejabrido → **correct**: ejabierto). These errors could be corrected by adding specific rules for these cases.

6 Conclusion and Future Work

This paper presented a robust light-weight supervised approach to obtain the inflected forms of any Spanish verb for any of its moods (indicative, subjunctive and imperative). This approach uses an ensemble of supervised learning algorithms to learn how the verbs are composed in order to obtain the inflection of a verb given its base form. Our method obtained accuracy close to 100%, outperforming existing state-of-the-art approaches. In addition, our method is able to further predict the inflection of the imperative mood, which was not tackled by previous work. In future, we plan to test our inflection approach for other languages, as well as other types of words (not only verbs). Furthermore, we also plan to compare this approach with the ones obtaining the best results (i.e. the ones employing recurrent neural networks) in the reinflection task of the SIGMORPHON 2016 Shared Task. Our short-term goal would be to integrate it within a surface realisation method, which will allow us to inflect whole sentences in different ways and tenses, thus improving the generation capabilities of current NLG systems.

Acknowledgments

This research work has been partially funded by the Generalitat Valenciana through the projects "DIIM2.0: Desarrollo de técnicas Inteligentes e Interactivas de Minería y generación de información sobre la web 2.0" (PROMETEOII/2014/001); and partially funded by the Spanish Government through projects TIN2015-65100-R, TIN2015-65136-C2-2-R, as well as by the project "Análisis de Sentimientos Aplicado a la Prevención del Suicidio en las Redes Sociales (ASAP)" funded by Ayudas Fundación BBVA a equipos de investigación científica.

References

Roee Aharoni, Yoav Goldberg, and Yonatan Belinkov. 2016. Improving sequence to sequence learning for morphological inflection generation: The biu-mit systems for the sigmorphon 2016 shared task for morphological reinflection. In *Proceedings of the 14th Annual SIGMORPHON Workshop on Computational Research in Phonetics, Phonology, and Morphology*. Association for Computational Linguistics, pages 41–48.

Malin Ahlberg, Markus Forsberg, and Mans Hulden. 2014. Semi-supervised learning of morphological paradigms and lexicons. In *Proceedings of the 14th Conference of the European Chapter of the Association for Computational Linguistics*. pages 569–578.

Iñaki Alegria and Izaskun Etxeberria. 2016. Ehu at the sigmorphon 2016 shared task. a simple proposal: Grapheme-to-phoneme for inflection. In *Proceedings of the 14th Annual SIGMORPHON Workshop on Computational Research in Phonetics, Phonology, and Morphology*. Association for Computational Linguistics, pages 27–30.

Cristina Barros, Dimitra Gkatzia, and Elena Lloret. 2017. Improving the naturalness and expressivity of language generation for spanish. In *Proceedings of the 10th International Conference on Natural Language Generation (INLG)*.

Ryan Cotterell, Christo Kirov, John Sylak-Glassman, David Yarowsky, Jason Eisner, and Mans Hulden. 2016. The sigmorphon 2016 shared task—morphological reinflection. In *Proceedings of the 2016 Meeting of SIGMORPHON*. Association for Computational Linguistics.

Markus Dreyer and Jason Eisner. 2009. Graphical models over multiple strings. In *Proceedings of the 2009 Conference on Empirical Methods in Natural Language Processing: Volume 1 - Volume 1*. Association for Computational Linguistics, pages 101–110.

Greg Durrett and John DeNero. 2013. Supervised learning of complete morphological paradigms. In *Proceedings of the North American Chapter of the Association for Computational Linguistics*. pages 1185–1195.

Ondřej Dušek and Filip Jurčíček. 2013. Robust multilingual statistical morphological generation models. In *51st Annual Meeting of the Association for Computational Linguistics: Proceedings of the Student Research Workshop*. Association of Computational Linguistics, pages 158–164.

Manaal Faruqui, Yulia Tsvetkov, Graham Neubig, and Chris Dyer. 2016. Morphological inflection generation using character sequence to sequence learning. In *NAACL HLT 2016, The 2016 Conference of the North American Chapter of the Association for Computational Linguistics: Human Language Technologies*. pages 634–643.

Eibe Frank, Mark A. Hall, and Ian H. Witten. 2016. *The WEKA Workbench. Online Appendix for "Data Mining: Practical Machine Learning Tools and Techniques"*. Morgan Kaufmann, 4 edition.

Albert Gatt and Ehud Reiter. 2009. Simplenlg: A realisation engine for practical applications. In *Proceedings of the 12th European Workshop on Natural Language Generation (ENLG)*.

Dimitra Gkatzia, Helen Hastie, and Oliver Lemon. 2014. Comparing multi-label classification with reinforcement learning for summarisation of time-series data. In *52nd Annual Meeting of the Association for Computational Linguistics (ACL)*.

Katharina Kann and Hinrich Schütze. 2016. Med: The lmu system for the sigmorphon 2016 shared task on morphological reinflection. In *Proceedings of the 14th SIGMORPHON Workshop on Computational Research in Phonetics, Phonology, and Morphology*. Association for Computational Linguistics, pages 62–70.

Ioannis Konstas and Mirella Lapata. 2012. Concept-to-text generation via discriminative reranking. In *Proceedings of the 50th Annual Meeting of the Association for Computational Linguistics*. pages 369–378.

Ling Liu and Lingshuang Jack Mao. 2016. Morphological reinflection with conditional random fields and unsupervised features. In *Proceedings of the 14th Annual SIGMORPHON Workshop on Computational Research in Phonetics, Phonology, and Morphology*. Association for Computational Linguistics, pages 36–40.

Garrett Nicolai, Colin Cherry, and Grzegorz Kondrak. 2015. Inflection generation as discriminative string transduction. In *NAACL HLT 2015, The 2015 Conference of the North American Chapter of the Association for Computational Linguistics: Human Language Technologies*. pages 922–931.

Garrett Nicolai, Bradley Hauer, Adam St. Arnaud, and Grzegorz Kondrak. 2016. Morphological reinflection via discriminative string transduction. In *Proceedings of the 14th Annual SIGMORPHON Workshop on Computational Research in Phonetics, Phonology, and Morphology*. Association for Computational Linguistics, pages 31–35.

Robert Östling. 2016. Morphological reinflection with convolutional neural networks. In *Proceedings of the 14th SIGMORPHON Workshop on Computational Research in Phonetics, Phonology, and Morphology*. Association for Computational Linguistics, pages 23–26.

Lluís Padró and Evgeny Stanilovsky. 2012. Freeling 3.0: Towards wider multilinguality. In *Proceedings of the Eight International Conference on Language Resources and Evaluation*.

Alexey Sorokin. 2016. Using longest common subsequence and character models to predict word forms. In *Proceedings of the 14th SIGMORPHON Workshop on Computational Research in Phonetics, Phonology, and Morphology*. Association for Computational Linguistics, pages 54–61.

Octavio Santana Suárez, José Rafael Pérez Aguiar, Luis Javier Losada García, and Francisco Javier Carreras Riudavets. 2005. Spanish morphosyntactic disambiguator. In *Proceedings of the Association for Computers and the Humanities and the Association for Literary and Linguistic Computing*. pages 201–204.

Dima Taji, Ramy Eskander, Nizar Habash, and Owen Rambow. 2016. The columbia university - new york university abu dhabi sigmorphon 2016 morphological reinflection shared task submission. In *Proceedings of the 14th SIGMORPHON Workshop on Computational Research in Phonetics, Phonology, and Morphology*. Association for Computational Linguistics, pages 71–75.

Neural Paraphrase Identification of Questions
with Noisy Pretraining

Gaurav Singh Tomar **Thyago Duque** **Oscar Täckström**
Jakob Uszkoreit **Dipanjan Das**
Google Inc.
{gtomar, duque, oscart, uszkoreit, dipanjand}@google.com

Abstract

We present a solution to the problem of paraphrase identification of questions. We focus on a recent dataset of question pairs annotated with binary paraphrase labels and show that a variant of the decomposable attention model (Parikh et al., 2016) results in accurate performance on this task, while being far simpler than many competing neural architectures. Furthermore, when the model is pretrained on a noisy dataset of automatically collected question paraphrases, it obtains the best reported performance on the dataset.

1 Introduction

Question paraphrase identification is a widely useful NLP application. For example, in question-and-answer (QA) forums ubiquitous on the Web, there are vast numbers of duplicate questions. Identifying these duplicates and consolidating their answers increases the efficiency of such QA forums. Moreover, identifying questions with the same semantic content could help Web-scale question answering systems that are increasingly concentrating on retrieving focused answers to users' queries.

Here, we focus on a recent dataset published by the QA website Quora.com containing over 400K annotated question pairs containing binary paraphrase labels.[1] We believe that this dataset presents a great opportunity to the NLP research community and practitioners due to its scale and quality; it can result in systems that accurately identify duplicate questions, thus increasing the quality of many QA forums. We examine a simple model family, the *decomposable attention model* of Parikh et al. (2016), that has shown promise in modeling natural

language inference and has inspired recent work on similar tasks (Chen et al., 2016; Kim et al., 2017).

We present two contributions. First, to mitigate data sparsity, we modify the input representation of the decomposable attention model to use sums of character n-gram embeddings instead of word embeddings. We show that this model trained on the Quora dataset produces comparable or better results with respect to several complex neural architectures, all using pretrained word embeddings. Second, to significantly improve our model performance, we pretrain *all* our model parameters on the noisy, automatically collected question-paraphrase corpus Paralex (Fader et al., 2013), followed by fine-tuning the parameters on the Quora dataset. This two-stage training procedure achieves the best result on the Quora dataset to date, and is also significantly better than learning *only* the character n-gram embeddings during the pretraining stage.

2 Related Work

Paraphrase identification is a well-studied task in NLP (Das and Smith, 2009; Chang et al., 2010; He et al., 2015; Wang et al., 2016, *inter alia*). Here, we focus on an instance, that of finding questions with identical meaning. Lei et al. (2016) consider a related task leveraging the AskUbuntu corpus (dos Santos et al., 2015), but it contains two orders of magnitude less annotations, thus limiting the quality of any model. Most relevant to this work is that of Wang et al. (2017), who present the best results on the Quora dataset prior to this work. The *bilateral multi-perspective matching* model (BiMPM) of Wang et al. uses a character-based LSTM (Hochreiter and Schmidhuber, 1997) at its input representation layer, a layer of bi-LSTMs for computing context information, four different types of multi-perspective matching layers, an additional bi-LSTM aggregation layer, followed by a

---

[1] See https://data.quora.com/First-Quora-Dataset-Release-Question-Pairs.

Proceedings of the First Workshop on Subword and Character Level Models in NLP, pages 142–147,
Copenhagen, Denmark, September 7, 2017. ©2017 Association for Computational Linguistics.

two-layer feedforward network for prediction. In contrast, the decomposable attention model uses four simple feedforward networks to (self-)attend, compare and predict, leading to a more efficient architecture. BiMPM falls short of our best performing model pretrained on noisy paraphrase data and uses more parameters than our best model.

Character-level modeling of text is a popular approach. While conceptually simple, character n-gram embeddings are a highly competitive representation (Huang et al., 2013; Wieting et al., 2016; Bojanowski et al., 2016). More complex representations built directly from individual characters have also been proposed (Sennrich et al., 2016; Luong and Manning, 2016; Kim et al., 2016; Chung et al., 2016; Ling et al., 2015). These representations are robust to out-of-vocabulary items, often producing improved results. Our pretraining procedure is reminiscent of several recent papers (Wieting et al., 2016, *inter alia*) who aim for general purpose character n-gram embeddings. In contrast, we pretrain all model parameters on automatic but in-domain paraphrase data. We employ the same neural architecture as our end task, similar to prior work on multi-task learning (Søgaard and Goldberg, 2016, *inter alia*), but use a simpler learning setup.

3 Approach

Our starting point is the decomposable attention model (Parikh et al., 2016, DECATT henceforth), which despite its simplicity and efficiency has been shown to work remarkably well for the related task of natural language inference (Bowman et al., 2015). We extend this model with character n-gram embeddings and noisy pretraining for the task of question paraphrase identification.

3.1 Problem Formulation

Let $\mathbf{a} = (a_1, \ldots, a_{\ell_a})$ and $\mathbf{b} = (b_1, \ldots, b_{\ell_b})$ be two input texts consisting of ℓ_a and ℓ_b tokens, respectively. We assume that each $a_i, b_j \in \mathbb{R}^d$ is encoded in a vector of dimension d. A context window of size c is subsequently applied, such that the input to the model $(\bar{\mathbf{a}}, \bar{\mathbf{b}})$ consists of partly overlapping phrases $\bar{a}_i = [a_{i-c}, \ldots, a_i, \ldots, a_{i+c}], \bar{b}_j = [b_{j-c}, \ldots, b_j, \ldots, b_{j+c}] \in \mathbb{R}^{2c+1 \times d}$. The model is estimated using training data in the form of labeled pairs $\{\mathbf{a}^{(n)}, \mathbf{b}^{(n)}, \mathbf{y}^{(n)}\}_{n=1}^{N}$, where $\mathbf{y}^{(n)} \in \{0, 1\}$ is a binary label indicating whether $\mathbf{a}$ is a paraphrase of $\mathbf{b}$ or not. Our goal is to predict the correct label $\mathbf{y}$ given a pair of previously unseen texts $(\mathbf{a}, \mathbf{b})$.

3.2 The Decomposable Attention Model

The DECATT model divides the prediction into three steps: *Attend*, *Compare* and *Aggregate*. Due to lack of space, we only provide a brief outline below and refer to Parikh et al. (2016) for further details on each of these steps.

Attend. First, the elements of $\bar{\mathbf{a}}$ and $\bar{\mathbf{b}}$ are aligned using a variant of neural attention (Bahdanau et al., 2015) to decompose the problem into the comparison of aligned phrases.

$$e_{ij} := F(\bar{a}_i)^{\top} F(\bar{b}_j) \,. \tag{1}$$

The function F is a feedforward network. The aligned phrases are computed as follows:

$$\beta_i := \sum_{j=1}^{\ell_b} \frac{\exp(e_{ij})}{\sum_{k=1}^{\ell_b} \exp(e_{ik})} \bar{b}_j \,,$$

$$\alpha_j := \sum_{i=1}^{\ell_a} \frac{\exp(e_{ij})}{\sum_{k=1}^{\ell_a} \exp(e_{kj})} \bar{a}_i \,. \tag{2}$$

Here β_i is the subphrase in $\bar{\mathbf{b}}$ that is (softly) aligned to $\bar{a}_i$ and vice versa for α_j. Optionally, the inputs $\bar{\mathbf{a}}$ and $\bar{\mathbf{b}}$ to (1) can be replaced by input representations passed through a "self-attention" step to capture longer context. In this optional step, we modify the input representations using "self-attention" to encode compositional relationships between words within each sentence, as proposed by (Cheng et al., 2016). Similar to (1), we define

$$f_{ij} := F_{self}(\bar{a}_i)^{\top} F'_{self}(\bar{a}_j) \,. \tag{3}$$

The function F_{self} and F'_{self} are feedforward networks. The self-aligned phrases are then computed as follows:

$$a'_i := \sum_{j=1}^{\ell_a} \frac{\exp(f_{ij} + d_{i-j})}{\sum_{k=1}^{\ell_a} \exp(f_{ik} + d_{i-k})} a_j \,. \tag{4}$$

where d_{i-j} is a learned distance-sensitive bias term. Subsequent steps then use modified input representations defined as $\bar{a}_i := [a_i, a'_i]$ and $\bar{b}_i := [b_i, b'_i]$.

Compare. Second, we separately compare the aligned phrases $\{(\bar{a}_i, \beta_i)\}_{i=1}^{\ell_a}$ and $\{(\bar{b}_j, \alpha_j)\}_{j=1}^{\ell_b}$ using a feedforward network G:

$$v_{1,i} := G([\bar{a}_i, \beta_i]) \quad \forall i \in \langle 1, \ldots, \ell_a \rangle \,,$$

$$v_{2,j} := G([\bar{b}_j, \alpha_j]) \quad \forall j \in \langle 1, \ldots, \ell_b \rangle \,. \tag{5}$$

where the brackets $[\cdot, \cdot]$ denote concatenation.

Aggregate. Finally, the sets $\{\mathbf{v}_{1,i}\}_{i=1}^{\ell_a}$ and $\{\mathbf{v}_{2,j}\}_{j=1}^{\ell_b}$ are aggregated by summation. The sum of two sets is concatenated and passed through another feedforward network followed by a linear layer, to predict the label $\hat{y}$.

3.3 Character n-Gram Word Encodings

Parikh et al. assume that each token $a_i, b_j \in \mathbb{R}^d$ is directly embedded in a vector of dimension d; in practice, they used pretrained word embeddings. Inspired by prior work mentioned in Section 2, we use an alternative approach and instead represent each token as a sum of its embedded character n-grams. This allows for more effective parameter sharing at a small additional computational cost. As observed in Section 4, this leads to better results compared to word embeddings.

3.4 Noisy Pretraining

While character n-gram encodings help in effective parameter sharing, data sparsity remains an issue. Pretraining embeddings with a task-agnostic objective on large-scale corpora (Pennington et al., 2014) is a common remedy to this problem. However, such pretraining is limited in the following ways. First, it only applies to the input representation, leaving subsequent parts of the model to random initialization. Second, there may be a domain mismatch unless embeddings are pretrained on the same domain as the end task (e.g., questions). Finally, since the objective used for pretraining differs from that of the end task (e.g., paraphrase identification), the embeddings may be suboptimal.

As an alternative to task-agnostic pretraining of embeddings on a very large corpus, we propose to pretrain all parameters of the model on a modest-sized corpus of automatically gathered, and therefore noisy examples, drawn from a similar domain.[2] As observed in Section 4, such noisy pretraining of the full model results in more accurate performance compared to using pretrained embeddings, as well as compared to only pretraining embeddings on the noisy in-domain corpus.[3]

---

[2]Paralex is gathered from WikiAnswers, a QA forum.

[3]The Quora data is similar to the Paralex corpus and we exploit this by pretraining our entire model on the latter. It can be argued that not all sentence pair modeling tasks may benefit similarly from the Paralex corpus and a detailed empirical study is warranted to investigate that; in this work, we restrict our scope to only the question paraphrase identification task, a very useful NLP application by itself.

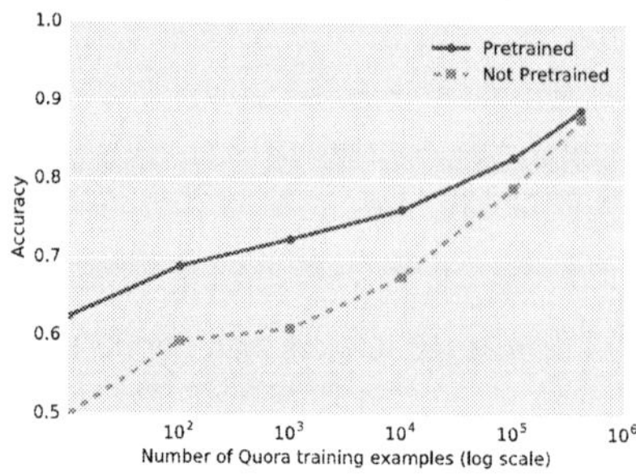

Figure 1: Learning curves for the Quora development set with and without pretraining on Paralex.

4 Experiments

4.1 Implementation Details

Datasets We evaluate our models on the Quora question paraphrase dataset which contains over 400,000 question pairs with binary labels. We use the same data and split as Wang et al. (2017), with 10,000 question pairs each for development and test, who also provide preprocessed and tokenized question pairs.[4] We duplicated the training set, which has approximately 36% positive and 64% negative pairs, by adding question pairs in reverse order (since our model is not symmetric). When pretraining the full model parameters, we use the Paralex corpus (Fader et al., 2013), which consists of 36 million noisy paraphrase pairs including duplicate reversed paraphrases. We created 64 million artificial negative paraphrase pairs (reflecting the class balance of the Quora training set) by combining the following three types of negatives in equal proportions: (1) random unrelated questions, (2) random questions that share a single word, and (3) random questions that share all but one word.[5]

Hyperparameters We tuned the following hyperparameters by grid search on the development set (settings for our best model are in parenthesis): embedding dimension (300), shape of all feedforward networks (two layers with 400 and 200 width), character n-gram sizes (5), context size (1), learning rate (0.1 for both pretraining and tuning), batch size (256 for pretraining and 64 for tuning), dropout ratio (0.1 for tuning) and prediction threshold (positive paraphrase for a score ≥ 0.3). We examined whether self-attention helps or not for all model variants, and found that it does for our best model. Note that we tried multiple orders of character n-

---

[4]This split is available at https://zhiguowang.github.io.

[5]More complex sampling procedures are possible, for example, by using pretrained word embeddings.

ID	Question 1	Question 2	DECATT$_{glove}$	DECATT$_{char}$	pt-DECATT$_{char}$	Gold
A	How shall I start my preparation for IIT-JEE in class 10?	Should I start preparing for the IIT JEE in class 10 only?	N	Y	Y	Y
B	What is fama french three factor model?	What is Fama-French three factor model?	N	Y	Y	Y
C	How does PayPal work in India?	Does PayPal work in India? What features of PayPal are available in India?	Y	Y	N	N
D	What are the similarities between British English and American English?	What are the similarities between American English and British English?	N	N	Y	Y
E	How is buying land on the moon a good investment? Why do people buy land on the moon?	At $20 an acre, isn't buying moon plots a solid investment?	N	N	N	Y
F	What can wrestlers do to prevent cauliflower ears?	Why do wrestlers have deformed ears?	N	N	N	Y

Table 1: Example wins and losses from the DECATT$_{glove}$, DECATT$_{char}$ and the pt-DECATT$_{char}$ models.

Method	Dev Acc	Test Acc
Siamese-CNN	-	79.60
Multi-Perspective CNN	-	81.38
Siamese-LSTM	-	82.58
Multi-Perspective-LSTM	-	83.21
L.D.C	-	85.55
BiMPM	88.69	88.17
FFNN$_{word}$	85.07	84.35
FFNN$_{char}$	86.01	85.06
DECATT$_{word}$	86.04	85.27
DECATT$_{glove}$	87.42	86.52
DECATT$_{char}$	87.78	86.84
DECATT$_{paralex-char}$	87.80	87.77
pt-DECATT$_{word}$	88.44	87.54
pt-DECATT$_{char}$	**88.89**	**88.40**

Table 2: Results on the Quora development and test sets in terms of accuracy. The first six rows are taken from (Wang et al., 2017).

grams with n $\in \{3, 4, 5\}$ both individually and separately but 5-grams alone worked better than these alternatives.

Baselines We implemented several baseline models. In our first two baselines, each question is represented by concatenating the sum of its unigram word embeddings and the sum of its trigram vectors, where each trigram vector is a concatenation of 3 adjacent word embeddings. The two question representations are then concatenated and fed to a feedforward network of shape [800, 400, 200]. We call these FFNN$_{word}$ and FFNN$_{char}$; in the latter, word embeddings are just sums of character n-gram embeddings. Second, we compare purely supervised variants of decomposable attention model, namely a word-based model with-

out any pretrained embeddings (DECATT$_{word}$), a word-based model with GloVe (Pennington et al., 2014) embeddings (DECATT$_{glove}$), a character n-gram model (DECATT$_{char}$) without pretrained embeddings and DECATT$_{paralex-char}$ whose character n-gram embeddings are pretrained with Paralex while all other parameters are learned from scratch on Quora. Finally we present a baseline where a word-based model is pretrained completely on Paralex (pt-DECATT$_{word}$) and our best model which is a character n-gram model pretrained completely on Paralex (pt-DECATT$_{char}$). Note that in case of character n-gram based models, for tokens shorter than n characters, we backoff and emit the token itself. Also, boundary markers were added at the beginning and end of each word.

4.2 Results

Other than our baselines, we compare with Wang et al. (2017) in Table 2. We observe that the simple FFNN baselines work better than more complex Siamese and Multi-Perspective CNN or LSTM models, more so if character n-gram based embeddings are used. Our basic decomposable attention model DECATT$_{word}$ without pre-trained embeddings is better than most of the models, all of which used GloVe embeddings. An interesting observation is that DECATT$_{char}$ model without any pretrained embeddings outperforms DECATT$_{glove}$ that uses task-agnostic GloVe embeddings. Furthermore, when character n-gram embeddings are pre-trained in a task-specific manner in DECATT$_{paralex-char}$ model, we observe a significant boost in performance. [6]

The final two rows of the table show results achieved by pt-DECATT$_{word}$ and pt-DECATT$_{char}$.

---

[6]Note that Paralex is orders of magnitude smaller than the corpus used to pretrain GloVe.

We note that the former falls short of the DE-CATT$_{\text{paralex}-\text{char}}$, which shows that character n-gram representations are powerful. Finally, we note that our best performing model is pt-DECATT$_{\text{char}}$, which leverages the full power of character embeddings and pretraining the model on Paralex.

Noisy pretraining gives more significant gains in case of smaller human annotated data as can be seen in Figure 1 where non-pretrained DECATT$_{\text{char}}$ and pretrained pt-DECATT$_{\text{char}}$ are compared on a logarithmic scale of number of Quora examples. It also gives an important insight into trade off between having more but costly human annotated data versus cheap but noisy pretraining. Table 1 shows some example predictions from the DE-CATT$_{\text{glove}}$, DECATT$_{\text{char}}$ and the pt-DECATT$_{\text{char}}$ models. The GloVe-trained model often makes mistakes related to spelling and tokenization artifacts. We observed that hyperparameter tuning resulted in settings where non-pretrained models did not use self-attention while the pretrained character based model did, thus learning better long term context at its input layer; this is reflected in example D which shows an alternation that our best model captures. Finally, E and F show pairs that present complex paraphrases that none of our models capture.

5   Conclusion and Future Work

We presented a focused contribution on question paraphrase identification, on the recently published Quora corpus. First, we showed that replacing the word embeddings of the decomposable attention model of Parikh et al. (2016) with character n-gram embeddings results in significantly better accuracy on this task. Second, we showed that pretraining the full model on automatically labeled noisy, but task-specific data results in further improvements. Our methods perform better than several complex neural architectures and achieve state of the art. While conceptually simple, we believe that these are two important insights that may be more widely applicable within the field of natural language understanding. We leave investigation of this claim to future work that may involve evaluation on related tasks such as recognizing textual entailment.

References

Dzmitry Bahdanau, Kyunghyun Cho, and Yoshua Bengio. 2015. Neural machine translation by jointly learning to align and translate. In *Proceedings of ICLR*.

Piotr Bojanowski, Edouard Grave, Armand Joulin, and Tomas Mikolov. 2016. Enriching word vectors with subword information. *arXiv* 1607.04606.

Samuel R. Bowman, Gabor Angeli, Christopher Potts, and Christopher D. Manning. 2015. A large annotated corpus for learning natural language inference. In *Proceedings of EMNLP*.

Ming-Wei Chang, Dan Goldwasser, Dan Roth, and Vivek Srikumar. 2010. Discriminative learning over constrained latent representations. In *Proceedings of HLT-NAACL*.

Qian Chen, Xiaodan Zhu, Zhen-Hua Ling, Si Wei, and Hui Jiang. 2016. Enhancing and combining sequential and tree LSTM for natural language inference. *arXiv 1609.06038* .

Jianpeng Cheng, Li Dong, and Mirella Lapata. 2016. Long short-term memory-networks for machine reading. In *Proceedings of the 2016 Conference on Empirical Methods in Natural Language Processing*. Association for Computational Linguistics, Austin, Texas, pages 551–561. https://aclweb.org/anthology/D16-1053.

Junyoung Chung, Kyunghyun Cho, and Yoshua Bengio. 2016. A character-level decoder without explicit segmentation for neural machine translation. In *Proceedings of ACL*.

Dipanjan Das and Noah A. Smith. 2009. Paraphrase identification as probabilistic quasi-synchronous recognition. In *Proceedings of ACL-IJCNLP*.

Cicero dos Santos, Luciano Barbosa, Dasha Bogdanova, and Bianca Zadrozny. 2015. Learning hybrid representations to retrieve semantically equivalent questions. In *Proceedings of ACL*.

Anthony Fader, Luke Zettlemoyer, and Oren Etzioni. 2013. Paraphrase-driven learning for open question answering. In *Proceedings of ACL*.

Hua He, Kevin Gimpel, and Jimmy Lin. 2015. Multi-perspective sentence similarity modeling with convolutional neural networks. In *Proceedings of EMNLP*.

Sepp Hochreiter and Jürgen Schmidhuber. 1997. Long short-term memory. *Neural Computation* 9(8):1735–1780.

Po-Sen Huang, Xiaodong He, Jianfeng Gao, Li Deng, Alex Acero, and Larry Heck. 2013. Learning deep structured semantic models for web search using clickthrough data. In *Proceedings of CIKM*.

Yoon Kim, Carl Denton, Loung Hoang, and Alexander M. Rush. 2017. Neural machine translation by jointly learning to align and translate. In *Proceedings of ICLR*.

Yoon Kim, Yacine Jernite, David Sontag, and Alexander M. Rush. 2016. Character-aware neural language models. In *Proceedings of AAAI*.

Tao Lei, Hrishikesh Joshi, Regina Barzilay, Tommi Jaakkola, Kateryna Tymoshenko, Alessandro Moschitti, and Lluís Màrquez. 2016. Semi-supervised question retrieval with gated convolutions. In *Proceedings of NAACL*.

Wang Ling, Chris Dyer, Alan W Black, Isabel Trancoso, Ramon Fermandez, Silvio Amir, Luis Marujo, and Tiago Luis. 2015. Finding function in form: Compositional character models for open vocabulary word representation. In *Proceedings of EMNLP*.

Minh-Thang Luong and Christopher D. Manning. 2016. Achieving open vocabulary neural machine translation with hybrid word-character models. In *Proceedings of ACL*.

Ankur Parikh, Oscar Täckström, Dipanjan Das, and Jakob Uszkoreit. 2016. A decomposable attention model for natural language inference. In *Proceedings of EMNLP*.

Jeffrey Pennington, Richard Socher, and Christopher D. Manning. 2014. GloVe: Global vectors for word representation. In *Proceedings of EMNLP*.

Rico Sennrich, Barry Haddow, and Alexandra Birch. 2016. Neural machine translation of rare words with subword units. In *Proceedings of ACL*.

Anders Søgaard and Yoav Goldberg. 2016. Deep multi-task learning with low level tasks supervised at lower layers. In *Proceedings of ACL*.

Zhiguo Wang, Wael Hamza, and Radu Florian. 2017. Bilateral multi-perspective matching for natural language sentences. In *Proceedings of IJCAI*.

Zhiguo Wang, Haitao Mi, and Abraham Ittycheriah. 2016. Sentence similarity learning by lexical decomposition and composition. In *Proceedings of COLING*.

John Wieting, Mohit Bansal, Kevin Gimpel, and Karen Livescu. 2016. Charagram: Embedding words and sentences via character n-grams. In *Proceedings of EMNLP*.

Sub-character Neural Language Modelling in Japanese

Viet Nguyen   Julian Brooke   Timothy Baldwin
School of Computing and Information Systems
The University of Melbourne

vn@student.unimelb.edu.au, jabrooke@unimelb.edu.au, tb@ldwin.net

Abstract

In East Asian languages such as Japanese and Chinese, the semantics of a character are (somewhat) reflected in its sub-character elements. This paper examines the effect of using sub-characters for language modeling in Japanese. This is achieved by decomposing characters according to a range of character decomposition datasets, and training a neural language model over variously decomposed character representations. Our results indicate that language modelling can be improved through the inclusion of sub-characters, though this result depends on a good choice of decomposition dataset and the appropriate granularity of decomposition.

1 Introduction

The Japanese language makes use of Chinese-derived ideographs ("kanji") which contain sub-character elements ("bushu") that to varying degrees reflect the semantics of the character. For example, the character 鯨 (*kujira* "whale") consists of two sub-characters: 魚 (*sakana* "fish") and 京 (*kyou* "capital city"). Similarly, the character 鮃 (*hirame* "flounder") consists of the sub-characters 魚 (*sakana* "fish") and 平 (*hira* "something broad and flat"). Here, the sub-character 魚 (*sakana* "fish") is a semantically significant element which appears in characters relating to marine life. Current Japanese language models do not capture sub-character information, and hence lack the ability to capture such generalisations.

A key limitation of word-based language modelling is the tendency to produce poor esti-mations for rare or OOV (out-of-vocabulary) words, and character-based language models have been shown to solve some of the sparsity problem in English by modeling how words are constructed (Graves, 2013). We take inspiration from this work, but observe for Japanese that since the kanji portion of the Japanese writing system contains thousands rather than dozens of characters, a character-based language model will still be susceptible to sparsity. Given that a large number of Japanese characters can be decomposed into sub-characters, we examine the question of whether sub-character language models can achieve similar gains in language model quality to character language models in English.

In this paper we train sub-character language models for Japanese based on decom-positions available in several existing kanji datasets. Our results suggest that decompos-ing characters is of value, but that the results are sensitive to the nature and granularity of the decomposition.

2 Kanji Datasets

In order to investigate the usefulness of sub-character decomposition for language models, we need some way of deriving these bushu from kanji. Here, we consider four kanji datasets that provide decompositions for kanji char-acters: GLYPHWIKI, IDS, KANJIVG, and KRADFILE. An example kanji decomposi-tion under the four datasets is provided in Fig-ure 1.

2.1 GlyphWiki

GLYPHWIKI[1] is a community-driven wiki that stores information about kanji characters

---

[1] http://glyphwiki.org

Proceedings of the First Workshop on Subword and Character Level Models in NLP, pages 148–153,
Copenhagen, Denmark, September 7, 2017. ©2017 Association for Computational Linguistics.

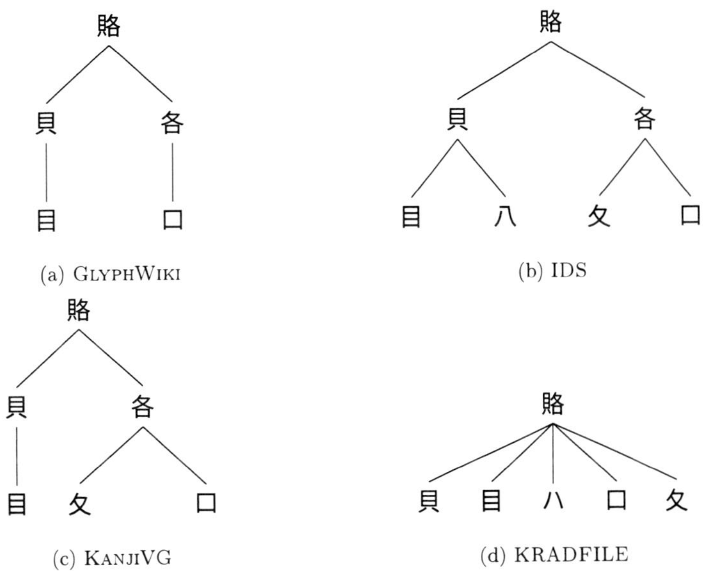

(a) GLYPHWIKI   (b) IDS

(c) KANJIVG   (d) KRADFILE

Figure 1: A visualisation of a full decomposition of the character 賂 (*mainai* "bribe") according to the four kanji datasets.

such as their decompositions into bushu, and their usage as bushu in other kanji. Decomposition information in GLYPHWIKI is collected by user contribution.

2.2 IDS

IDS[2] is based on an open source project which uses character processing methods to create descriptions of character components (Morioka and Wittern, 2002). The decompositions in IDS are generated automatically, using character topic maps to draw associations between kanji and their constituent elements.

In Figure 1b we see that IDS provides a more detailed breakdown than GLYPHWIKI, including two bushu that are not found in GLYPHWIKI. At the first level of decomposition, though, they are identical.

2.3 KanjiVG

KANJIVG[3] is a collection of images that provides information about kanji and their decompositions. Decomposition information for KANJIVG is derived from the analysis of strokes used to write kanji characters (Apel and Quint, 2004). Although KANJIVG does allow for the decomposition of characters down

to the stroke level, we exclude all strokes in this research as we do not consider strokes to reflect semantic meaning.

Note in Figure 1c that the decomposition is different to IDS, because KANJIVG specifies that the bottom elements of the bushu character 貝 (*kai* "shell") are strokes rather than bushu, meaning they are excluded from decomposition.

2.4 KRADFILE

KRADFILE[4] represents a flat decomposition of kanji into their constituent bushu. One key aspect of KRADFILE that differs from the other datasets is the use of a relatively limited set of bushu. Additionally, unlike the other datasets, KRADFILE does not list bushu in an order consistent with their appearance in the kanji. Furthermore, KRADFILE provides a single exhaustive decomposition for all kanji characters and their bushu. Because of this, we consider KRADFILE to have only a single, indivisible layer of decomposition.

2.5 Dataset Comparison

Table 1 shows descriptive statistics for the four datasets and their decompositions.

---

[2] https://github.com/cjkvi/cjkvi-ids
[3] http://kanjivg.tagaini.net/

[4] http://users.monash.edu/~jwb/kradinf.html

149

	GlyphWiki	IDS	KanjiVG	KRADFILE
Characters	18761	20970	6744	12156
Unique bushu	2834	3104	1327	254
Average bushu per kanji	1.9	2.1	2.2	4.5
Average branching factor	1.5	2.1	1.9	4.5
Average depth	2.7	3.1	2.9	1.0

Table 1: Statistics for the four kanji datasets

The *Characters* row of the table describes the total number of characters in each dataset that have a decomposition. KanjiVG contains a much smaller number of kanji than the other two datasets, although note that in modern Japanese, kanji is generally restricted to 2,136 *jouyou* kanji (Bond and Baldwin, 2016). All four datasets have full coverage over our corpus.

Unique bushu describes the number of characters that have been used as bushu. In general, if a kanji character is found in the decomposition of another kanji character, then it is counted as a bushu. While most of the datasets use thousands of bushu, KRADFILE is notable in that it uses a much smaller bushu set. With respect to *Average bushu per kanji*, there is strong similarity between Glyph-Wiki, IDS and KanjiVG, but KRADFILE produces almost double the number of bushu because the decompositions are exhaustive.

Average branching factor describes the average number of bushu found through exhaustively decomposing over every kanji and its bushu (an example of exhaustive decomposition — which we call "deep decomposition" — can be seen in Figure 2). Because KRADFILE provides a single layer of decomposition that is complete and indivisible, we cannot decompose each bushu any further. Therefore, KRADFILE has an average depth of 1.

3   Experimental Setup

For our experiments, we use version 1.5 of the NAIST text corpus (Iida et al., 2007), a collection of Japanese newspaper articles which is widely used in Japanese NLP research (Imamura et al., 2009; Sasano and Kurohashi, 2011). The corpus consists of roughly 1.7 million character tokens, of which roughly 42% are kanji. To build and test our models we use 5-fold cross-validation.

Our language models are standard neural network models, implemented in Tensorflow; they consist of a embedding layer, with embeddings for each character (including kanji, bushu, and other elements of the Japanese writing systems) which are learned during training, a standard unidirectional LSTM (Sundermeyer et al., 2012), and a layer which maps the output of the LSTM to a vector representing the probability of the next character; the hidden (embedding) size of the LSTM for our experiments is 128. We train the language model by minimizing the cross-entropy between the output probabilities and the one-hot vector corresponding to the correct answer, using the Adam optimizer with a batch size of 128 and a learning rate of 0.002.

In addition to the four kanji datasets, we consider two kinds of decomposition: shallow and deep. Shallow decomposition refers to using only the first layer of decomposition of a kanji character, whereas deep expansion refers to an exhaustive decomposition of the kanji and all of its bushu. We use these two methods to explore whether semantic information is reflected in deeper levels of decomposition. In general, we aim to compare the performance of a language model based on the way kanji are decomposed and the depth of their decompositions.

Figure 2 includes examples of both shallow and deep decompositions, for kanji including 賂 (*mainai* "bribe") from Figure 1b. Decomposition is done in a left-to-right in-order traversal.

It is possible for multiple kanji to share the same bushu. For example, according to KanjiVG, the characters 由 (*yoshi* "cause/reason"), 甲 (*kou* "carapace/shell"), and 申 (*saru* "monkey") are decomposed into 田 (*ta*

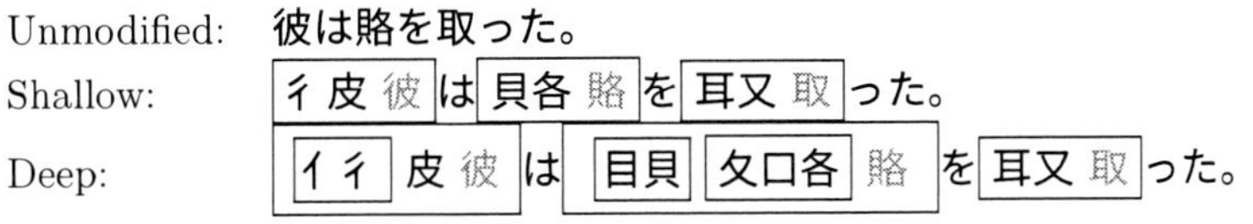

Figure 2: Examples of shallow and deep decomposition using KANJIVG, with original characters highlighted in red. Boxes denote characters that have been decomposed.

k	BASELINE	GLYPHWIKI		IDS		KANJIVG		KRADFILE
		SHALLOW	DEEP	SHALLOW	DEEP	SHALLOW	DEEP	
1	77.76	34.31	40.68	37.11	47.75	40.04	47.04	160.94
2	38.17	33.34	37.52	33.75	48.54	35.91	45.20	89.17
3	59.41	39.72	49.02	44.73	63.69	45.95	57.79	99.79
4	70.40	50.70	61.68	50.79	62.00	50.79	64.68	125.67
5	60.05	50.83	52.65	52.12	68.58	53.03	71.00	155.00
Average	61.16	41.78	48.31	43.70	58.11	44.74	57.14	126.11

Table 2: Language model perplexity based on the different decompositions

"rice field") and 丨 (*tatebou* "vertical line"). Because of this, using just the decomposition of a character can actually lead to a loss of information. Thus, we postpend all decomposition sequences with the original kanji character to preserve the mapping of bushu to its original kanji.

We evaluate based on perplexity, normalizing the product of the probability of the (sub-)characters in our test set by the character length of the corpus (lower perplexity is better). Because decomposing characters affects the superficial length of the corpus, however, we note that in the cases of decomposition we are normalizing using the original (undecomposed) corpus length in all cases, and not the decomposed token length. This reflects the fact that by adding decompositions of a character we are not really adding new text to the corpus. Both regular and decomposed language models in fact predict exactly the original contents of the corpus, but for the decomposed models the uncertainty associated with each kanji is distributed among the predictions of its bushu (and the postpended kanji), and can be retrieved simply by multiplying all the individual probabilities together.

4 Results

Table 2 shows the perplexity for each of the sub-character language models, for the two possible decomposition depths, as compared to a baseline where no decomposition occurs. We report perplexity for each fold of our 5-fold cross-validation, as well as the average.

First, we note that while most of the sub-character language models showed some improvement over the undecomposed baseline, KRADFILE performed substantially worse, with a mean perplexity score almost twice as high as that of the baseline. One potential problem with KRADFILE is that it provides only deep, exhaustive decompostions. Other limitations of using KRADFILE for language modelling are the lack of order in how bushu are arranged, and the fact that the bushu are limited to a specific set of characters. We can conclude that it is not a useful dataset for this purpose.

The best-performing dataset was GLYPH-WIKI, with shallow decomposition. Not only was this configuration markedly better than the baseline on average, it also beat every other option on every fold of our cross-validation. The results for KANJIVG and IDS were similar, but slightly worse. Interestingly, based on the statistics in Table 1, GLYPH-WIKI is the most conservative of the datasets in terms of the average number of decomposed bushu. We also found that the best results all involved shallow decomposition, which may reflect the fact that the most semantically-salient bushu tend to appear at the first level of composition; this result was also consistent across folds for IDS and KANJIVG. Taken together, these results indicate that some decomposition is useful for building Japanese language models, but too much decomposition is not advisable.

5   Related Work

Working at the character level has proven useful in language modelling in English, as well as related applications such as building word representations (Graves, 2013; Ling et al., 2015). With regards to ideographic languages, there is work in information retrieval that has considered the appropriate representation for indexing; the focus has typically been word versus character (Kwok, 1997; Baldwin, 2009), but Fujii and Croft (1993) considered (though ultimately rejected) sub-character based indexing. In terms of investigations of the usefulness of sub-character representations for neural network models in ideographic languages, relevant work includes recent papers that use sub-character information to assist in the training of character embeddings for Chinese (Sun et al., 2014; Li et al., 2015; Yin et al., 2016) or build sub-character embeddings directly (Shi et al., 2015), demonstrating that sub-character information is useful for representing semantics in Chinese. However, our work differs not only in language and task, but also in our use of decomposition, since the work done in Chinese has primarily focused on a single semantically relevant sub-character (known as the radical), despite the fact that other sub-characters do provide additional semantic information in some characters.

6   Conclusion and Future Work

In this paper we have explored the idea of decomposing Japanese kanji to improve language modeling using neural network models. Our results indicate that it is possible to improve the predictive power of a language model using decomposition, as measured by perplexity, but the effectiveness of this does depend on the properties of the kanji database: whereas GLYPHWIKI is a useful resource for our purpose, KRADFILE is clearly not.

With respect to future work, we have thus far explored only a subset of the options with regards to the decomposition and ordering of sub-characters, and we would also like to consider more sophisticated models which integrate the structure of the kanji instead of flattening it, and applying our sub-character modeling to other sequential tasks such as part-of-speech tagging. Given the correspondence between kanji and Chinese characters, a comparison of the two languages with regards to the usefulness of decomposition would be worth exploring. We are also interested in performing an intrinsic evaluation of the character- and bushu-level embeddings learned through language modelling, e.g. relative to character-level similarity datasets such as that of Yencken and Baldwin (2006).

References

Ulrich Apel and Julien Quint. 2004. Building a graphetic dictionary for Japanese kanji: character look up based on brush strokes or stroke groups, and the display of kanji as path data. In *Proceedings of the Workshop on Enhancing and Using Electronic Dictionaries*. Geneva, Switzerland, pages 36–39.

Timothy Baldwin. 2009. The hare and the tortoise: speed and accuracy in translation retrieval. *Machine Translation* 23(4):195–240.

Francis Bond and Timothy Baldwin. 2016. Introduction to Japanese computational linguistics. In Francis Bond, Timothy Baldwin, Kentaro Inui, Shun Ishizaki, Hiroshi Nakagawa, and Akira Shimazu, editors, *Readings in Japanese Natural Language Processing*, CSLI Publications, Stanford, USA, pages 1–28.

Hideo Fujii and W. Bruce Croft. 1993. A comparison of indexing techniques for Japanese text retrieval. In *Proceedings of the 16th Annual International ACM SIGIR Conference on Research and Development in Information Retrieval*. Pittsburgh, USA, pages 237–246.

Alex Graves. 2013. Generating sequences with recurrent neural networks. *CoRR* abs/1308.0850.

Ryu Iida, Mamoru Komachi, Kentaro Inui, and Yuji Matsumoto. 2007. Annotating a Japanese text corpus with predicate-argument and coreference relations. In *Proceedings of the Linguistic Annotation Workshop*. Prague, Czech Republic, pages 132–139.

Kenji Imamura, Kuniko Saito, and Tomoko Izumi. 2009. Discriminative approach to predicate-argument structure analysis with zero-anaphora resolution. In *Proceedings of the ACL-IJCNLP 2009 Conference Short Papers*. Singapore, pages 85–88.

Kui-Lam Kwok. 1997. Comparing representations in Chinese information retrieval. In *Proceedings of the 20th Annual International ACM SIGIR Conference on Research and Development in Information Retrieval*. Philadelphia, USA, pages 34–41.

Yanran Li, Wenjie Li, Fei Sun, and Sujian Li. 2015. Component-enhanced Chinese character embeddings. In *Proceedings of the 2015 Conference on Empirical Methods in Natural Language Processing*. Lisbon, Portugal, pages 829–834.

Wang Ling, Chris Dyer, Alan W Black, Isabel Trancoso, Ramon Fermandez, Silvio Amir, Luis Marujo, and Tiago Luis. 2015. Finding function in form: Compositional character models for open vocabulary word representation. In *Proceedings of the 2015 Conference on Empirical Methods in Natural Language Processing*. Lisbon, Portugal, pages 1520–1530.

Tomohiko Morioka and Christian Wittern. 2002. *Moji Dētabēsu ni Motoduku Moji Object Gijutsu no Kōchiku*. In *Proceedings of IPSJ 2002*. (in Japanese).

Ryohei Sasano and Sadao Kurohashi. 2011. A discriminative approach to Japanese zero anaphora resolution with large-scale lexicalized case frames. In *Proceedings of the 5th International Joint Conference on Natural Language Processing (IJCNLP 2011)*. Chiang Mai, Thailand, pages 758–766.

Xinlei Shi, Junjie Zhai, Xudong Yang, Zehua Xie, and Chao Liu. 2015. Radical embedding: Delving deeper to Chinese radicals. In *Proceedings of the 53rd Annual Meeting of the Association for Computational Linguistics and the 7th International Joint Conference on Natural Language Processing*. Beijing, China, pages 594–598.

Yaming Sun, Lei Lin, Nan Yang, Zhenzhou Ji, and Xiaolong Wang. 2014. Radical-enhanced Chinese character embedding. In *Proceedings of the 21st International Conference on Neural Information Processing (ICONIP 2014)*. Kuching, Malaysia, pages 279–286.

Martin Sundermeyer, Ralf Schlüter, and Hermann Ney. 2012. LSTM neural networks for language modeling. In *Proceedings of the 13th Annual Conference of the International Speech Communication Association (Interspeech 2012)*. Portland, USA, pages 194–197.

Lars Yencken and Timothy Baldwin. 2006. Modelling the orthographic neighbourhood for Japanese kanji. In *Proceedings of the 21st International Conference on the Computer Processing of Oriental Languages (ICCPOL 2006)*. Singapore, pages 321–332.

Rongchao Yin, Quan Wang, Rui Li, Peng Li, and Bin Wang. 2016. Multi-granularity Chinese word embedding. In *Proceedings of the 2016 Conference on Empirical Methods in Natural Language Processing*. Austin, USA, pages 981–986.

Byte-based Neural Machine Translation

Marta R. Costa-jussà, Carlos Escolano and **José A. R. Fonollosa**
TALP Research Center, Universitat Politècnica de Catalunya, Barcelona
marta.ruiz@upc.edu, carlos.escolano@tsc.upc.edu, jose.fonollosa@upc.edu

Abstract

This paper presents experiments comparing character-based and byte-based neural machine translation systems. The main motivation of the byte-based neural machine translation system is to build multilingual neural machine translation systems that can share the same vocabulary. We compare the performance of both systems in several language pairs and we see that the performance in test is similar for most language pairs while the training time is slightly reduced in the case of byte-based neural machine translation.

1 Introduction

Multilingual neural machine translation is raising interest in the community because it re-opens the possibility of an interlingual architecture. the main advantage of the current setting is that interlingua is not manually designed but it seems that it can be automatically extracted (Johnson et al., 2016). In addition, this multilingual environment seems to allow to build translation systems among language pairs that do not have parallel corpus available (Johnson et al., 2016), what is called "zero-shot translation".

These two motivations (interlingua and zero-shot translation) are strong enough to motivate the entire commmunity to experiment towards multilingual architectures. Recently, there have appeared works in multilingual word representations (Schwenk et al., 2017; España-Bonet et al., 2017)

Most multilingual works are at the level of words. As multilingual character research we can find (Lee et al., 2016) which goes from many-to-one languages in translation and achieves improvements for several language pairs. Previous work on character-based neural machine transla-

tion includes (Ling et al., 2015; Costa-jussà and Fonollosa, 2016), among others.

We want to explore multilingual character-based neural machine translation with a diversity of languages, including languages as Chinese. In case of using languages with different alphabets, the character dictionary can not be shared or it has to be considerably augmented. In order to keep the dictionary to the order of hundreds, we want to explore how byte-based neural machine translation behaves. In this paper, we propose to use the fully-character neural machine translation architecture (Lee et al., 2016) but using bytes instead of characters. We compare the performance of character against byte-based neural machine translation among similar languages (Catalan/Spanish and Portuguese/Brazilian) and relatively far languages (in terms of alphabet) (German/Finnish/Turkish-English).

As far as we are concerned, we are not aware of any research work in neural machine translation that has experimented with bytes. Related work can be found int the area of natural language processing. Gillick et al. (2016) propose an neural network that reads text as bytes and use this model in tasks of Part-of-Speech and Named Entity Recognition. The recent investigation of Irie et al (2017) describes the use of a byte-level convolutional layer (instead of character-level) in the neural language model (Irie et al., 2017), which is applied to low resource speech recognition.

2 Character-based Neural Machine Translation

Our system uses the architecture from (Lee et al., 2016) where a character-level neural MT model that maps the source character sequence to the target character sequence. The main difference in the encoder architecture of the standard neural

154

Proceedings of the First Workshop on Subword and Character Level Models in NLP, pages 154–158,
Copenhagen, Denmark, September 7, 2017. ©2017 Association for Computational Linguistics.

MT model from (Bahdanau et al., 2015) is that instead of using word embeddings, the system uses character embeddings based on previous works like (Kim et al., 2015; Costa-jussà and Fonollosa, 2016). The architecture uses character embeddings include convolution layers, max pooling and highway network layers. The character embeddings from the decoder are the input of the bidirectional recurrent neural network. The main difference in the decoder architecture is that the single-layer feedforward network computes the attention score of next target character (instead of word) to be generated with every source segment representation. And afterwards, a two-layer character-level decoder takes the source context vector from the attention mechanism and predicts each target character.

3 Byte-based Neural Machine Translation

The byte-based Neural Machine Translation changes the character representation of words to the byte representation. Each sentence is represented as the concatenation of bytes that form its characters in *utf-8* encoding. No explicit vocabulay is used but we can consider the byte representation as a vocabulary of 256 positions in which every possible byte can be represented. This modifications provides the following improvements over the previously seen architecture.

- Both languages share the same representation. If a word is identical in the source and in the target language they share the same representation when converted into sequences to be fed in the network. This is an advantage over the character-based representation, which dictionary is language-dependent.

- This representation uses a limited set of tokens of size 256 independently of the language. Therefore, the system is not affected by the size of character vocabulary. Note that there are languages that have a very rich explicit morphological representation or that have a wide range of characters (e.g. Chinese). However, the byte-based decoding also produces a sequence of correct bytes in a similar way that character level translation works compared to word-based systems.

- All words are theoretically representable by the system even if they have not been previ-

uosly seen in the training. This is due to the fact that every single character of word can be seen as a concatenation of bytes and the full range of possible bytes is covered by the system.

4 Experimental Framework

In this section we detail experimental corpora, architecture and parameters that we used.

4.1 Data and Preprocessing

For Catalan-Spanish, We use a large corpus extracted from ten years of the paper edition of a bilingual Catalan newspaper, El Periódico (Costa-jussà et al., 2014). The Spanish-Catalan corpus is partially available via ELDA (Evaluations and Language Resources Dis-tribution Agency) in catalog number ELRA-W0053. Development and test sets are extracted from the same corpus.

For Portuguese-Brazilian, we used the OPUS corpus (Tiedemann, 2012) which is a growing collection of translated texts from the web. In particular, for Portuguese-Brazilian the source corpus are from Ubuntu and GNOME. We extracted the parallel text from translation memories (TMX format) and from the complete text, we extracted a collection of development and test set.

Finally, we used WMT 2017 [1] corpus data for German, Finish and Turkish to English. For the three language pairs, we used all data parallel data provided in the evaluation. For German-English, we used: *europarl v.7, news commentary v.12, common crawl* and *rapid corpus of EU press releases*. For Finnish-English, we used *europarl v.8, wiki headlines* and *rapid corpus of EU press releases*. For Turkish-English, we used *setimes2*. The German and Finish test set is the news 2015 evaluation set, for Turkish the test set is the news 2016 evaluation set.

Preprocessing consisted in cleaning empty sentences, limiting sentences up to 50 words, tokenization and truecasing for each language using tools from Moses (Koehn et al., 2007). Table 1 shows details about the corpus statistics after pre-processing.

4.2 Parameters

Both character and byte-based systems share the same parameters. Further research may explore different parameters for the byte-based system,

---

[1] http://www.statmt.org/wmt17/translation-task.html

LP	L	Set	S	W	V
EsCa	Es	Train	6478618	165170227	736873
		Dev	2244	55478	12237
		Test	2244	55988	12218
	Ca	Train	6478618	178954335	713445
		Dev	2244	60130	11734
		Test	2244	60693	11691
PtBr	Pt	Train	4280310	33954616	362592
		Dev	2000	16122	4155
		Test	2000	16012	4141
	Br	Train	4280310	33600508	320972
		Dev	2000	15963	3939
		Test	2000	15663	3964
DeEn	De	Train	9659106	2 03634165	1721113
		Dev	2999	62362	12674
		Test	2169	44085	9895
	En	Train	9659106	210205446	954387
		Dev	2999	64503	9506
		Test	2169	46830	7871
FiEn	Fi	Train	2468673	3 7755811	863898
		Dev	3000	47779	16236
		Test	2870	43069	15748
	En	Train	2468673	52262051	240625
		Dev	3000	63519	9059
		Test	2870	60149	8961
TuEn	Tu	Train	200290	42 48508	158276
		Dev	1001	16954	6463
		Test	3000	54128	15898
	En	Train	299290	4713025	73906
		Dev	1001	22136	4318
		Test	3000	66394	9503

Table 1: Corpus Statistics. Number of sentences (S),words (W), vocabulary (V).

Language	Bytes
Spanish	1.026
Catalan	1.040
German	1.015
Finnish	1.044
Turkish	1.087
English	1.000
Portuguese	1.027
Brazilian Portuguese	1.028
Chinese	2.108

Table 2: Mean bytes for character for all the languages tested, Chinese added for comparison.

since we are adopting for the byte-based systems the character-based parameters from previous research (Lee et al., 2016).

For the embedding of the source sentence, we use set of convolutional layers which number kernels are (200-200-250-250-300-300-300-300) and their lengths are (1-2-3-4-5-6-7-8) respectively. Additionally 4 highway layers are employed. And a bidirectional LSTM layer of 512 units for encoding. The maximum souce sentence's length is 450 during training and 500 for decoding both during training and sampling.

4.3 Byte differences among language pairs

Characters may be represented by a single or several bytes. English and its close languages usually have a correspondance of character and byte (a character is represented by a single byte). Therefore, these languages are not really affected by this representation, mainly because the ASCII encoding makes possible to represent all possible characters in a single byte which results in a similar length representation in both baseline and proposed system.

However, in other languages (e.g. Turkish, Finnish...) which contain stressed characters (among other modifications), a single character in *utf-8* may be a concatenation of several bytes. For these cases, the performance of the byte-based system differs from the character-based system.

Table 2 shows the mean number of bytes for character changes for different languages. As the languages are more similiar to English the difference between bytes and characters changes. For all the languages tested in our experiments using all latin alphabet the differences are small and resultant sentence length is similar to its character counterpart.

On the other hand for languages that use a different alphabet such as Chinese we can observe how for each character more than two bytes have to be correctly generated.

5 Results

This section compares the performance of the byte-based neural machine translation system with the character-based in terms of translation quality and training time. In order to compare training times all systems have been trained in the same machine using an *NVIDIA TITAN X* with 12GB of RAM.

Table 3 shows BLEU results and number for close languages Catalan-Spanish and Portuguese-Brazilian in both directions. Comparison between character and byte-based models shows that by using a byte-base system comparable results to the ones obtained using a character-based system. In our experiments, we have observed that the byte-based system tends to converge at least a couple of hundred iterations earlier than the character-based system.

Table 4 shows BLEU results for distant languages German, Finish and Turkish into English. Comparison between character and byte-based models shows how even in distance languages similar or even equal results can be obtained us-

Language	System	BLEU
esca	char	87.12
	byte	86.91
caes	char	82.43
	byte	81.27
ptbr	char	48.54
	byte	48.28
brpt	char	46.41
	byte	47.20

Table 3: Close languages. BLEU results.

Language	System	BLEU
tren	char	5.87
	byte	4.75
deen	char	28.63
	byte	25.29
fien	char	14.75
	byte	14.75

Table 4: Distant languages. BLEU results.

ing the byte-based system. For the case of Turkish and English (and training for an equal number of iterations), results are lower than the ones obtained by the char-based system but given the reduced size of the corpus variance in the results can be caused by other factors. For Finnish-English, we achieved the same results with several hundred training iterations less. In the case of the German-English pair, results show that the char-based approach provides quite better results than the proposed byte-based system but also it is worth mentioning that when using bytes, the results converged several hundred training iterations before than when using the baseline system.

6 Conclusions

This paper shows an experimental comparison between char-based neural machine translation and byte-based neural machine translation. Variability has been found in the results for different language pairs ranging for -3.3 to $+0.8$ BLEU points. Also the main advantage of the proposed system compared to the baseline system is that it tends to require less training iterations which translates in a reduction of training time that can vary from several days to even two weeks.

Further work includes the experimentation of multilingual neural machine translation using byte-based system. In addition, we want to include in our experimentation languages with complete different alphabets such as Chinese and we will investigate if byte-based neural machine translation system proposes malformed characters. In future research, we will test different parameters such as changing the number of convolutional filters.

Acknowledgements

This work is supported by the Spanish Ministerio de Economía y Competitividad and Fondo Europeo de Desarrollo Regional, through contract TEC2015-69266-P (MINECO/FEDER, UE) and the postdoctoral senior grant *Ramón y Cajal*.

References

Dzmitry Bahdanau, Kyunghyun Cho, and Yoshua Bengio. 2015. Neural machine translation by jointly learning to align and translate. volume abs/1409.0473. http://arxiv.org/abs/1409.0473.

Marta R. Costa-jussà and José A. R. Fonollosa. 2016. Character-based neural machine translation. In *Proceedings of the 54th Annual Meeting of the Association for Computational Linguistics (Volume 2: Short Papers)*. Association for Computational Linguistics, Berlin, Germany, pages 357–361. http://anthology.aclweb.org/P16-2058.

Marta R. Costa-jussà, March Poch, José A.R. Fonollosa, Mireia Farrús, and José B. Mariño. 2014. A large Spanish-Catalna parallel corpus release for Machine Translation. *Computing and Informatics Journal* 33.

Cristina España-Bonet, Ádám Csaba Varga, Alberto Barrón-Cedeño, and Josef van Genabith. 2017. An empirical analysis of nmt-derived interlingual embeddings and their use in parallel sentence identification. *CoRR* abs/1704.05415. http://arxiv.org/abs/1704.05415.

Dan Gillick, Cliff Brunk, Oriol Vinyals, and Amarnag Subramanya. 2016. Multilingual language processing from bytes. In *Proceedings of the 2016 Conference of the North American Chapter of the Association for Computational Linguistics: Human Language Technologies*. San Diego, California, pages 1296–1306.

Kazuki Irie, Pavel Golik, Ralf Schlter, and Hermann Ney. 2017. Investigations on byte-level convolutional neural networks for language modeling in low resource speech recognition page 5.

Melvin Johnson, Mike Schuster, Quoc V. Le, Maxim Krikun, Yonghui Wu, Zhifeng Chen, Nikhil Thorat, Fernanda B. Viégas, Martin Wattenberg, Greg Corrado, Macduff Hughes, and Jeffrey Dean. 2016. Google's multilingual neural machine translation system: Enabling zero-shot translation. *CoRR* abs/1611.04558. http://arxiv.org/abs/1611.04558.

Yoon Kim, Yacine Jernite, David Sontag, and Alexander M. Rush. 2015. Character-aware neural language models. *CoRR* abs/1508.06615. http://arxiv.org/abs/1508.06615.

Philipp Koehn, Hieu Hoang, Alexandra Birch, Chris Callison-Burch, Marcello Federico, Nicola Bertoldi, Brooke Cowan, Wade Shen, Christine Moran, Richard Zens, Chris Dyer, Ondřej Bojar, Alexandra Constantin, and Evan Herbst. 2007. Moses: Open source toolkit for statistical machine translation. In *Proceedings of the 45th Annual Meeting of the ACL on Interactive Poster and Demonstration Sessions*. Association for Computational Linguistics, Stroudsburg, PA, USA, ACL '07, pages 177–180. http://dl.acm.org/citation.cfm?id=1557769.1557821.

Jason Lee, Kyunghyun Cho, and Thomas Hofmann. 2016. Fully character-level neural machine translation without explicit segmentation. *CoRR* abs/1610.03017. http://arxiv.org/abs/1610.03017.

Wang Ling, Isabel Trancoso, Chris Dyer, and Alan W. Black. 2015. Character-based neural machine translation. *CoRR* abs/1511.04586.

Holger Schwenk, Ke Tran, Orhan Firat, and Matthijs Douze. 2017. Learning joint multilingual sentence representations with neural machine translation. *CoRR* abs/1704.04154. http://arxiv.org/abs/1704.04154.

Jörg Tiedemann. 2012. Parallel data, tools and interfaces in opus. In *Proceedings of the Eighth International Conference on Language Resources and Evaluation (LREC-2012)*. European Language Resources Association (ELRA), Istanbul, Turkey, pages 2214–2218.

Improving Opinion-Target Extraction with Character-Level Word Embeddings

Soufian Jebbara and **Philipp Cimiano**
Semantic Computing Group, Bielefeld University
{sjebbara, cimiano}@cit-ec.uni-bielefeld.de

Abstract

Fine-grained sentiment analysis received increasing attention in recent years. Extracting opinion target expressions (OTE) in reviews is often an important step in fine-grained, aspect-based sentiment analysis. Retrieving this information from user-generated text, however, can be difficult. Customer reviews, for instance, are prone to contain misspelled words and are difficult to process due to their domain-specific language. In this work, we investigate whether character-level models can improve the performance for the identification of opinion target expressions. We integrate information about the character structure of a word into a sequence labeling system using character-level word embeddings and show their positive impact on the systems performance. Specifically, we obtain an increase by 3.3 points F_1-score with respect to our baseline model. In further experiments, we reveal encoded character patterns of the learned embeddings and give a nuanced view of the performance differences of both models.

1 Introduction

In recent years, there has been an increased interest in developing sentiment analysis models that predict sentiment at a more fine-grained level than at the level of a complete document. A key task within fine-grained sentiment analysis consists in identifying so called opinion target expressions (OTE). These are the objects of a sentiment expression. Consider the following example:

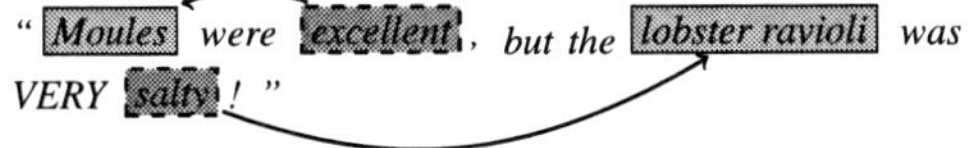

where blue boxes mark opinion targets, (dashed) red boxes the opinion terms and arrows the respective relations. In this example, there are two sentiment statements, one positive and one negative. The positive one is indicated by the word *excellent* and is expressed towards the *Moules*. The second, negative sentiment, is indicated by the word *salty* and is expressed towards the *lobster ravioli*.

In this work, we consider the task of identifying such opinion target expressions in reviews as a sequence labeling problem. A particular challenge involved in OTE identification stems from the fact that online reviews can be of low quality and contain misspelled words, novel word creations, rare words etc. We thus hypothesize that including character-embeddings might be beneficial in the context of OTE extraction, allowing a model to be robust to spelling errors as well as generalize to unseen words. A further challenge is that an OTE can span multiple tokens.

In this work, we thus investigate whether a character-based approach is capable of using the additional low-level information to improve upon a standard word-based baseline. We hypothesize that character-level word embeddings capture relevant information for opinion target expression extraction that regular (skip-gram) word embeddings lack. We propose a neural network model that learns and utilizes character-level word embeddings to extract opinion target expressions and examine its characteristics. Our experimental analysis shows that with an increase of 3.3 points F_1-score, the character information is indeed valuable for the task. Further experiments reveal encoded character patterns of the learned embeddings and give a nuanced view of the performance differences of both models.

The rest of the paper is structured as follows: Section 2 discusses related work from two domains: fine-grained sentiment analysis and

Proceedings of the First Workshop on Subword and Character Level Models in NLP, pages 159–167,
Copenhagen, Denmark, September 7, 2017. ©2017 Association for Computational Linguistics.

character-level neural text processing. In Section 3, we describe our approach to address opinion target extraction and present the recurrent neural network models that we use to measure the impact of character information on the task. We carry out our evaluation and analysis in Section 4 and examine the learned character-level word embeddings in more detail. Finally, Section 5 summarizes our findings and presents directions for future work.

2   Related Work

Our work brings together the domains of fine-grained sentiment analysis on the one side and character-level neural text processing on the other side. In this section we give a brief overview of both domains and point out parallels to previous work.

Fine-Grained Sentiment Analysis   San Vicente et al. (2015) present a system that addresses opinion target extraction as a sequence labeling problem based on a perceptron algorithm with local features.

Toh and Wang (2014) propose a Conditional Random Field (CRF) as a sequence labeling model that includes a variety of features such as Part-of-Speech (POS) tags and dependencies, word clusters and WordNet taxonomies.

Jakob and Gurevych (2010) follow a very similar approach that addresses opinion target extraction as a sequence labeling problem using CRFs. Their approach includes features derived from words, POS tags and dependency paths, and performs well in a single and cross-domain setting.

Klinger and Cimiano (2013a,b) model the task of joint aspect and opinion term extraction using probabilistic graphical models and rely on Markov Chain Monte Carlo methods for inference. They demonstrate the impact of a joint architecture on the task with a strong impact on the extraction of aspect terms, but less so for the extraction of opinion terms.

Character-Level Neural Network Models
Character-level neural network models are gaining interest in many research areas such as language modeling (Kim et al., 2016), spelling correction (Sakaguchi et al., 2017), text classification (Zhang et al., 2015) and more. Most similar works from the area of character-level word representations can be found in (dos Santos and Zadrozny, 2014; dos Santos et al., 2015;

Ma and Hovy, 2016). In these works, word and character level representations are successfully learned and combined to improve Part-of-Speech (POS) tagging and Named Entity Recognition (NER).

dos Santos and Zadrozny (2014) and dos Santos et al. (2015) apply a convolutional neural network (CNN) to the raw character sequence that detects character patterns and represents them as a fixed-sized embedding vector. The concatenated sequence of word and character-level embeddings is then used to predict POS or NER tags for each word.

Ma and Hovy (2016) use a similar CNN-based word structure model. However, the subsequent processing of the embedded word sequence is carried out using a bidirectional Long Short-Term Memory network (LSTM).

An example of character-level text classification not requiring any tokenization is given by Zhang et al. (2015). In their work, the authors perform text classification using character-level CNNs on very large datasets and obtain comparable results to traditional models based on words. Their findings suggest that the standard tokenization of text is indeed something to be reconsidered.

3   Model

In this work, we approach the task of extracting opinion target expressions by phrasing it as a sequence labeling problem. Doing so allows us to extract an arbitrary number of multi-word expressions in a given text. We use the **IOB** scheme (Tjong Kim Sang and Veenstra, 1999) to represent OTEs as a sequence of tags. According to this scheme, each word in our text receives one of 3 tags, namely **I**, **O** or **B** that indicate if the word is at the **B**eginning[1], **I**nside or **O**utside of an expression:

The	wine	list	is	also	really	nice	.
O	**I**	**I**	O	O	O	O	O

The task is thus reduced to mapping a sequence of words to a sequence of tags. We model the sequence labeling task using recurrent neural networks (RNN). RNNs allow us to easily integrate character-level knowledge into the model in the form of character-level word embeddings. To

---

[1] Note that the **B** token is only used to indicate the boundary of two consecutive phrases.

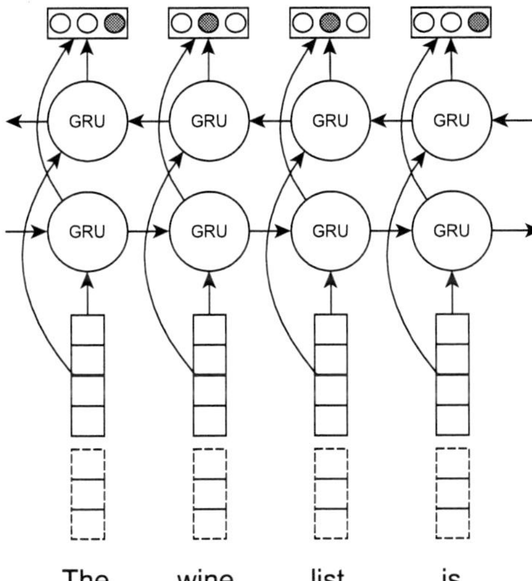

Figure 1: Illustration of the RNN sequence labeling model. The dashed boxes represent the character-level word embeddings that are only present in the character-enhanced model.

quantify the impact of these embeddings, we compare it to a baseline model that only uses word level embeddings.

3.1 Baseline Model

The proposed baseline model is a recurrent neural network that receives a word sequence $\mathbf{w} = \{\mathbf{w}_1, \ldots, \mathbf{w}_n\}$ as input features and predicts an output sequence of IOB tags $\mathbf{t} = \{\mathbf{t}_1, \ldots, \mathbf{t}_n\}$. Figure 1 illustrates the baseline neural network.

Formally, the word sequence is passed to a word embedding layer that maps each word $\mathbf{w}_i$ to its d^{wrd}-dimensional embedding vector $\mathbf{x}_i^{wrd}$ by means of an embedding matrix $\mathbf{W}^{wrd} \in \mathbb{R}^{d^{wrd} \times |V^{wrd}|}$:

$$\mathbf{x}_i^{wrd} = \mathbf{W}^{wrd} \mathbf{e}^{\mathbf{w}_i}$$

where V^{wrd} is the vocabulary of the word embeddings and $\mathbf{e}^{\mathbf{w}_i}$ is a one-hot vector of size $|V^{wrd}|$ representing the word $\mathbf{w}_i$.

The sequence of word embedding vectors is passed to a bidirectional layer (Schuster and Paliwal, 1997) of Gated Recurrent Units (GRU, Cho et al. (2014)). The GRU uses a combination of update and reset gates to improve its ability to learn long range information comparable to Long Short-Term Memory cells (Chung et al., 2014). The computation of a single GRU layer at timestep[2] i is as follows:

$$\mathbf{z}_i = \sigma(\mathbf{W}^z \mathbf{x}_i + \mathbf{U}^z \mathbf{h}_{i-1} + \mathbf{b}^z)$$
$$\mathbf{r}_i = \sigma(\mathbf{W}^r \mathbf{x}_i + \mathbf{U}^r \mathbf{h}_{i-1} + \mathbf{b}^r)$$
$$\mathbf{h}_i = (1 - \mathbf{z}_i) \odot \mathbf{h}_{i-1} + \mathbf{z}_i \odot \mathbf{g}_i$$
$$\mathbf{g}_i = f(\mathbf{W}^h \mathbf{x}_i + \mathbf{U}^h (\mathbf{r}_i \odot \mathbf{h}_{i-1}) + \mathbf{b}^h)$$

where $\mathbf{x}_i$ is an element of a generic input sequence and $\mathbf{g}_i$ the computed output. $\mathbf{z}_i$ is the update gate and $\mathbf{r}_i$ the forget gate, σ is the sigmoid activation function and f is a non-linearity for which we chose the ELU (Clevert et al., 2016) activation function.

The bidirectional GRU is a variant of the GRU that processes the input sequence in forward and backward direction. The hidden states of the forward pass and the backward pass are concatenated to produce a single hidden state sequence:

$$\mathbf{g} = \{[\overrightarrow{\mathbf{g}}_1 : \overleftarrow{\mathbf{g}}_1], \ldots, [\overrightarrow{\mathbf{g}}_n : \overleftarrow{\mathbf{g}}_n]\}$$

where $\overrightarrow{\mathbf{g}}_i$ and $\overleftarrow{\mathbf{g}}_i$ are the hidden states for the forward and backward GRU layer, respectively. We choose the dimensionality of the parameters of the word-level GRU layers such that $\overrightarrow{\mathbf{g}}_i, \overleftarrow{\mathbf{g}}_i \in \mathbb{R}^{r^{wrd}/2}$, where r^{wrd} is a hyperparameter of the model.

The bidirectional connections allow the model to include words appearing before and after each timestep into the computation of the hidden states. The resulting sequence of hidden states $\mathbf{g}$ presumably incorporates the necessary context for each word in its corresponding hidden state. In a last step, each hidden state $\mathbf{g}_i$ is projected to a probability distribution $\mathbf{q}_i$ over all possible output tags, namely $\mathbf{I}$, $\mathbf{O}$ and $\mathbf{B}$, using a standard feedforward layer with a softmax activation function:

$$\mathbf{q}_i = softmax(\mathbf{W}^{tag} \mathbf{g}_i + \mathbf{b}^{tag})$$

with $\mathbf{W}^{tag} \in \mathbb{R}^{d^{tag} \times r^{wrd}}$ and $\mathbf{b}^{tag} \in \mathbb{R}^{d^{tag}}$. For each word, we choose the tag with the highest probability as the predicted IOB tag. The predicted tag sequence can be decoded into a set of opinion term expressions using the IOB scheme in reverse.

The trainable parameters of this model are $\mathbf{W}^{wrd}$, $\mathbf{W}^{tag}$, $\mathbf{b}^{tag}$, and the parameters of the GRU $\mathbf{W}^h$, $\mathbf{U}^h$, $\mathbf{b}^h$, $\mathbf{W}^z$, $\mathbf{U}^z$, $\mathbf{b}^z$, $\mathbf{W}^r$, $\mathbf{U}^r$, $\mathbf{b}^r$ (for both directions).

---

[2] Each word in the input sequence is considered a timestep.

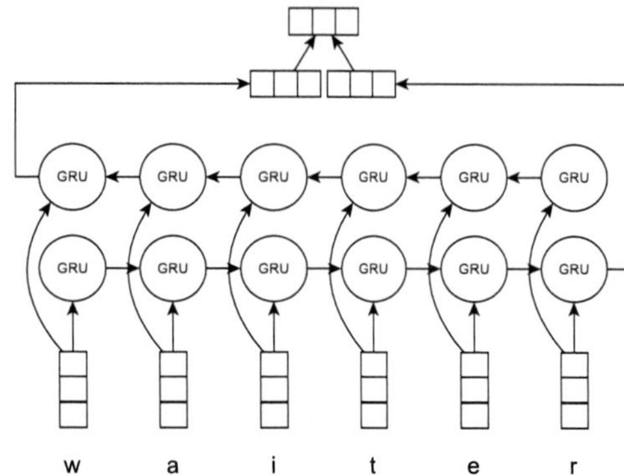

Figure 2: Illustration of the RNN character-level word embedding model. The output of this sub network is later concatenated with the regular word embeddings.

3.2 Character-Enhanced Model

We propose a variation of the baseline model from Section 3.1 that incorporates character-level information in the process of opinion target extraction. Our goal is to confirm the hypothesis that character information poses a valuable source of information for this task. Following previous work in this direction, we incorporate the character information in the form of character-level word embeddings. Figure 2 illustrates the character-level word model. Given the character sequence $\mathbf{c} = \{c_1, \ldots, c_n\}$ of a word w, we first transform each character c_i to its corresponding d^{chr}-dimensional character embedding $\mathbf{x}_i^{chr}$ using a character embedding matrix $\mathbf{W}^{chr} \in \mathbb{R}^{d^{chr} \times |V^{chr}|}$:

$$\mathbf{x}_i^{chr} = \mathbf{W}^{chr} \mathbf{e}^{c_i}.$$

Analogously to the procedure for word embeddings, V^{chr} is the character vocabulary and $\mathbf{e}^{c_i}$ is a one-hot vector of size $|V^{chr}|$ representing the character c_i. As before, the sequence of character embeddings is passed through a bidirectional GRU layer that produces two sequences of hidden states, $\overrightarrow{\mathbf{g}}$ and $\overleftarrow{\mathbf{g}}$. We choose the dimensionality of the parameters such that $\overrightarrow{\mathbf{g}}_i, \overleftarrow{\mathbf{g}}_i \in \mathbb{R}^{d^{chr}}$.

To represent the sequence of characters as a fixed-sized vector, we concatenate the final hidden states[3] of both sequences and obtain a single representation $\mathbf{g} = [\overrightarrow{\mathbf{g}_n} : \overleftarrow{\mathbf{g}_1}]$ for the character sequence. Lastly, the concatenated hidden state $\mathbf{g}$ is

transformed to the final character-level word embedding using a linear feedforward layer:

$$\mathbf{x}^{cw} = \mathbf{W}^{cw}\mathbf{g} + \mathbf{b}^{cw}$$

with $\mathbf{W}^{cw} \in \mathbb{R}^{d^{chr} \times 2 \cdot d^{chr}}$ and $\mathbf{b}^{cw} \in \mathbb{R}^{d^{chr}}$.

To incorporate the word model in the overall neural network model, we pass the corresponding character sequence of each word in $\mathbf{w} = \{\mathbf{w}_1, \ldots, \mathbf{w}_n\}$ through the character model to obtain $\mathbf{x}^{cw} = \{\mathbf{x}_1^{cw}, \ldots, \mathbf{x}^{cw}\}$. The resulting character-level embeddings are then concatenated with the word level embeddings:

$$\widetilde{\mathbf{x}} = \{[\mathbf{x}_1^w : \mathbf{x}_1^{cw}], \ldots, [\mathbf{x}_n^w : \mathbf{x}_n^{cw}]\}$$

The augmented sequence $\widetilde{\mathbf{x}}$ replaces $\mathbf{x}$ in the baseline model and is passed through the remaining layers of the network. Since $\widetilde{\mathbf{x}}$ contains word and character-level information, the subsequent RNN and projection layers can make use of the additional information to improve the extraction of opinion target expressions.

The trainable parameters of this model are $\mathbf{W}^w, \mathbf{W}^c, \mathbf{W}^{cw}, \mathbf{b}^{cw}, \mathbf{W}^{tag}, \mathbf{b}^{tag}$, and the parameters of the GRU $\mathbf{W}^h, \mathbf{U}^h, \mathbf{b}^h, \mathbf{W}^z, \mathbf{U}^z, \mathbf{b}^z, \mathbf{W}^r, \mathbf{U}^r, \mathbf{b}^r$ for the word and character-level RNN (and for both directions).

3.3 Network Training

The optimization of the model parameters is done by minimizing the classification error for each word in the sequence using the cross-entropy loss. The optimization is carried out using a mini-batch size of 5 with the stochastic optimization technique *Adam* (Kingma and Ba, 2015). We clip the norm of the gradients to 5 and regularize our network quite rigorously using L2 regularization of 10^{-5} on $\mathbf{W}^{tag}$ and $\mathbf{W}^{cw}$, as well as Dropout (Srivastava et al., 2014) in various positions in our network. Specifically, we apply Dropout with a drop probability of 0.5 to the character and word embeddings, the output of the character-level GRUs, as well as the input and hidden sequence of the word-level GRUs as proposed in (Gal and Ghahramani, 2016). Initial experiments suggested that this strong regularization is necessary due to the moderate size of the training dataset. The networks are implemented using the machine learning framework *Keras* (Chollet, 2015).

The word embedding matrix $\mathbf{W}^{wrd}$ is initialized with a pretrained matrix of skip-gram embeddings trained on a corpus of amazon reviews

---

[3]Note that the final hidden state of the backwards directed GRU is the hidden state that corresponds to the first character in the sequence.

Dataset	#Sent.	#OTEs	#Chars per OTE
Train	2000	1880	2 -80
Test	676	650	3-50

Table 1: Relevant statistics of the SemEval 2016 dataset (Task 5, restaurant domain).

Model	$|V^{wrd}|$	r^{wrd}	d^{chr}	$\varnothing\ F_1$
`word-only`	50000	60	–	0.6713
`char+word`	50000	100	100	**0.6936**

Table 2: Results of a search for hyperparameters. The column $\varnothing\ F_1$ gives the best mean F_1-score for the best performing training epoch across cross-validation models.

(McAuley et al., 2015). Earlier work showed that using a domain specific corpus in the pretraining stage significantly improves performance for similar tasks (Jebbara and Cimiano, 2016).

4 Experiments and Evaluation

In this section, we evaluate the impact of using character-level word embeddings on the task of extracting opinion target expressions from user-generated reviews. For this, we compare the character-enhanced model from Section 3.2 to the baseline RNN of Section 3.1. We start by describing the used dataset in Section 4.1. To select a fitting set of hyperparameters for each model, we perform a 5-fold cross validation on the training portion of our dataset. Using the best hyperparameters, we evaluate both models on the test portion of the data and investigate the models' properties with respect to the induced character information in Sections 4.3 and 4.4. Evaluation is carried out in terms of F_1-score of expected opinion target expressions and retrieved opinion term expressions using exact matches[4]. The research code is publicly available at `https://github.com/sjebbara/clwe-ote`.

4.1 Dataset

In our experiments, we use the data for the SemEval aspect-based sentiment analysis challenge of the year 2016 (Task 5, (Pontiki et al., 2016)). The used dataset consists of review sentences from the restaurant domain with annotations for opinion target expressions. Table 1 gives a summary of the dataset.

4.2 Hyperparameter Selection

We set the dimensionality d^{wrd} of the pretrained word embeddings to 100 and perform a grid search on a subset of the hyperparameters to find a suitable solution to be used in the final system configuration. We evaluate each candidate set of hyperparameters using a 5-fold cross validation on the

training data. The search is performed for each model (`word-only` and `char+word`). We experiment with:

- the size of the word vocabulary[5] $|V^{wrd}| \in \{10000, 20000, 50000\}$ (with respect to the most frequent words),

- the size of the sentence level RNN hidden layer $r^{wrd} \in \{60, 100, 200\}$,

- and the size of the character-level RNN and the corresponding character-level word embedding vector $d^{chr} \in \{20, 50, 100\}$.

Table 2 shows the best hyperparameters for each model. As expected, the search indicates that it is always better to increase the size of the word vocabulary V^{wrd}. The best model using both word and character-level information performs on average about 2.2 points F_1-score better than the best model that only uses word-level information. For the following evaluations, we instantiate and train our models according to these hyperparameters.

4.3 Results on Test

For the evaluation on the test set, we use the previously found hyperparameters and instantiate our models. We train both models on 80% of the training set and use the remaining 20% as a validation set for early stopping (Caruana et al., 2001). The `word-only` model reaches its best performance at epoch 35 and the `char+word` model peaks at epoch 73.

The performances of both models are given in Table 3. The results confirm our hypothesis and the findings from the cross validation that the character-level word embeddings offer a substantial improvement (3.3 points F_1-score) over the `word-only` baseline model.

---

[4]We use the provided evaluation code from the organizers of the SemEval 2016 challenge.

[5]The size of the word vocabulary is the main factor in terms of (GPU) memory usage.

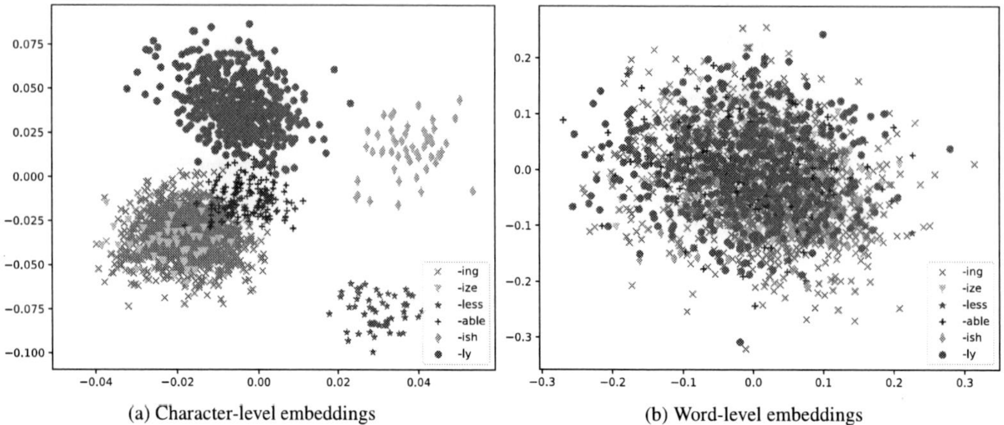

(a) Character-level embeddings   (b) Word-level embeddings

Figure 3: Visualization of suffix information of the two employed types of embeddings.

Model	F_1-score
word-only	0.6260
char+word	**0.6586**

Table 3: Results on the test set for best performing hyperparameters. The previous findings of the usefulness of character-level word embeddings are confirmed by the results of the test set.

4.4 Analysis

In this Section, we investigate what the character-level word embeddings encode and if there are specific cases in which the character-enhanced model performs better than the baseline.

Visualization Our initial experiments in visualizing the learned model suggested that the character-level word embeddings encode morphological features of a word. To confirm this assumption, we visualize the learned embeddings using suffix information. We extract a subset of the 2000 most frequently occurring words from reviews that end on one of the following suffixes: -ing, -ly, -able, -ish, -less, -ize. We project the character-level word embeddings of the words to a 2 dimensional space using T-SNE (van der Maaten and Hinton, 2008) and plot them as a scatter plot. By highlighting each word according to its suffix, we see that the character-level embeddings are grouped according to their suffixes (see Figure 3a). Performing the same procedure with the regular skip-gram word embeddings results in no clear separation between the 6 suffix groups (see Figure 3b).

Previous work in the direction of aspect-based sentiment analysis shows a positive impact of POS tag features for the extraction of opinion phrases and opinion target expressions (Toh and Wang, 2014; Jebbara and Cimiano, 2016). It stands to reason if the character-level word embeddings act in a similar way. The morphological information of character-level word embeddings (as shown in Figure 3a) might help to disambiguate word occurrences with respect to their linguistic function in the sentence, similar to the positive effect of POS tags for this task. We leave the verification of this hypothesis for future work.

Out-of-Vocabulary Errors Next, we are interested in seeing if the improvement in F_1-score can be backtraced to Out-of-Vocabulary (OOV) word errors. For this, we compute the F_1-score on 3 different subsets of sentences for the word-only model and the char+word model:

- no OOV: This subset only contains sentences for which all words are part of the known vocabulary.

- OOV sent.: This subset contains sentences that contain an unknown word at some position in the sentence.

- OOV op.: The subset of sentences that contain at least one opinion target expression with an unknown word.

Figure 4a shows F_1-scores for different subsets. Surprisingly, we can see that the F_1-scores rise and fall similarly for both models regardless of

164

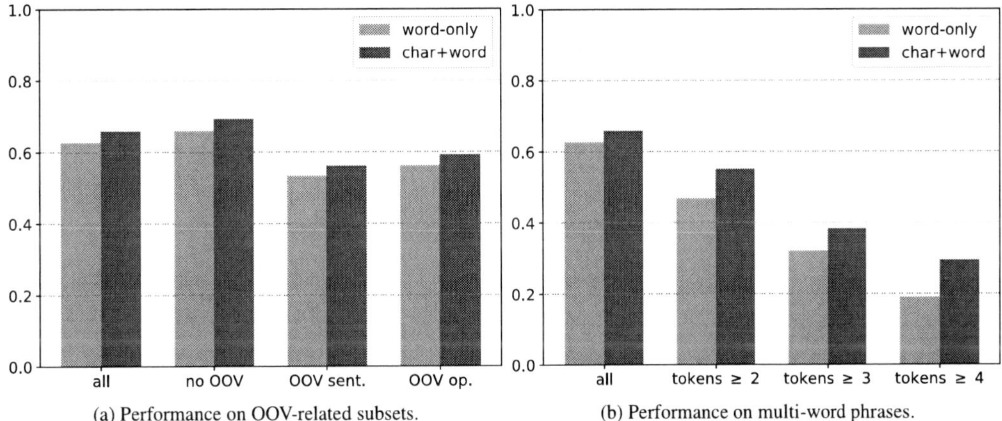

(a) Performance on OOV-related subsets.   (b) Performance on multi-word phrases.

Figure 4: Illustration of performance differences for different subsets of sentences.

Word	atmosphere	restaurant	service
Nearest Neighbors	*atomosphere* ambience *atmoshpere*	*restaraunt* eatery *restuarant*	customer *serivce* costumer

Table 4: Three commonly used words in restaurant reviews and their 3 nearest neighbors in the embedding space. Often, misspelled versions (*italic*) of the original word are among its closest neighbors.

the evaluated subset. This suggests, that the positive influence of the character information does not particularly help in those cases where the text contains previously unseen words (e.g. misspelled words). We assume that the positive impact on these cases is mitigated since the domain specific skip-gram word embeddings already contain various writing errors that frequently occur in customer reviews. This can be seen in Table 4, which shows the nearest neighbors of exemplary words in the skip-gram embedding space. We see that common writing mistakes are often already captured by the word embeddings.

Multi-Word Expressions Another possible cause for the performance difference of both models might be related to the length of opinion target expressions[6]. This hypothesis is motivated by the idea that e.g. variations in spelling with respect to hyphenation (e.g. *bartenders* vs. *bar tenders* or *wait staff* vs. *wait-staff*) could have less of an influence on the character-based model than on the word-based model. To test this idea, we consider subsets of sentences that contain at least one OTE that is a multi-word expression of

---

[6]In terms of words.

more than or equal to k words. The performance differences for $k \in \{2, 3, 4\}$ are visualized in Figure 4b.

The first thing to notice is that both models are strongly affected by the length of the OTEs. Longer expressions seem to be harder to extract in general. However, we can observe that the character model is influenced by the length of an OTE to a lesser degree. While the difference in F_1-score for all sentences between the word-only model and char+word model is about 3.3, the differences for OTEs composed of more than or equal to 2, 3, and 4 words are 8.4, 6.1 and 10.4, respectively.

5 Conclusion

There is a growing interest in character and subword-level models for natural language processing in recent years. Tokenization is a crucial step for many applications, yet neglects the information that can be gained from the character structure of a word itself.

In this work, we were able to show that character-level information assists in the task of opinion target extraction, an important step in aspect-based sentiment analysis. We compared a model using only word-level features to a more sophisticated model that also includes character-level word embeddings. We showed that the more complex character model consistently outperforms the baseline model with a substantial margin of 3.3 points F_1-score. A visualization of the learned embeddings revealed encoded morphological regularities that we could not find in our skip-gram word embeddings. Through experiments on different subsets of the data, we linked the positive influence of the character-level word embeddings to the difficulty of extracting multi-word expressions. We did not observe a performance difference for Out-of-Vocabulary cases.

However, it is not entirely clear how exactly the additional character information contributes to the task of extracting opinion target expression. In general, we suspect that the morphological information of character-level word embeddings helps to disambiguate word occurrences similarly to the positive effect of POS tags for OTE extraction. A confirmation of this hypothesis remains for future work.

Another interesting direction for future work is the pretraining of parts of the network to enrich the character-based word representation. We believe that character-level language models pose an interesting candidate for this.

The positive results of this work and the remaining research questions suggest a need to focus further research effort in the direction of character-level neural network models in order to improve token-based approaches or even replace the need for tokenization altogether.

Acknowledgments

This research was supported by the Cluster of Excellence Cognitive Interaction Technology 'CITEC' (EXC 277) at Bielefeld University, which is funded by the German Research Foundation (DFG).

References

Rich Caruana, Steve Lawrence, and C. Lee Giles. 2001. Overfitting in neural nets: Backpropagation, conjugate gradient, and early stopping. In T. K. Leen, T. G. Dietterich, and V. Tresp, editors, *Advances in Neural Information Processing Systems 13*, MIT Press, pages 402–408.

Kyunghyun Cho, Bart Van Merriënboer, Çalar Gülçehre, Dzmitry Bahdanau, Fethi Bougares, Holger Schwenk, and Yoshua Bengio. 2014. Learning phrase representations using rnn encoder–decoder for statistical machine translation. In *Proceedings of the 2014 Conference on Empirical Methods in Natural Language Processing (EMNLP)*. Association for Computational Linguistics, Doha, Qatar, pages 1724–1734.

Francois Chollet. 2015. Keras -theano-based deep learning library. https://github.com/fchollet/keras.

Junyoung Chung, Çaglar Gülçehre, Kyunghyun Cho, and Yoshua Bengio. 2014. Empirical evaluation of gated recurrent neural networks on sequence modeling. In *NIPS Deep Learning Workshop*.

Djork-Arné Clevert, Thomas Unterthiner, and Sepp Hochreiter. 2016. Fast and accurate deep network learning by exponential linear units (ELUs). In *Proceedings of the International Conference on Learning Representations (ICLR)*.

Cicero dos Santos, Victor Guimaraes, RJ Niterói, and Rio de Janeiro. 2015. Boosting named entity recognition with neural character embeddings. In *Proceedings of NEWS 2015 The Fifth Named Entities Workshop*. page 25.

Cicero dos Santos and Bianca Zadrozny. 2014. Learning character-level representations for part-of-speech tagging. In *Proceedings of the 31st International Conference on Machine Learning*. pages 1818–1826.

Yarin Gal and Zoubin Ghahramani. 2016. A theoretically grounded application of dropout in recurrent neural networks. In *Advances in Neural Information Processing Systems 29 (NIPS)*.

Niklas Jakob and Iryna Gurevych. 2010. Extracting opinion targets in a single-and cross-domain setting with conditional random fields. In *Proceedings of the Conference on Empirical Methods in Natural Language Processing*. pages 1035–1045.

Soufian Jebbara and Philipp Cimiano. 2016. Aspect-Based Relational Sentiment Analysis Using a Stacked Neural Network Architecture. In *ECAI 2016 - 22nd European Conference on Artificial Intelligence, 29 August-2 September 2016, The Hague, The Netherlands - Including Prestigious Applications of Artificial Intelligence (PAIS 2016)*. pages 1123—-1131. https://doi.org/10.3233/978-1-61499-672-9-1123.

Yoon Kim, Yacine Jernite, David Sontag, and Alexander M. Rush. 2016. Character-aware neural language models. In *Proceedings of the Thirtieth AAAI Conference on Artificial Intelligence, February 12-17, 2016, Phoenix, Arizona, USA.*. pages 2741–2749.

Diederik Kingma and Jimmy Ba. 2015. Adam: A Method for Stochastic Optimization. In *Proceedings of the International Conference on Learning Representations*.

Roman Klinger and Philipp Cimiano. 2013a. Bidirectional inter-dependencies of subjective expressions and targets and their value for a joint model. In *Proceedings of the 51st Annual Meeting of the Association for Computational Linguistics (ACL), Volume 2: Short Papers*. pages 848–854.

Roman Klinger and Philipp Cimiano. 2013b. Joint and pipeline probabilistic models for fine-grained sentiment analysis: Extracting aspects, subjective phrases and their relations. In *Proceedings of the 13th IEEE International Conference on Data Mining Workshops (ICDM)*. pages 937–944. https://doi.org/10.1109/ICDMW.2013.13.

Xuezhe Ma and Eduard Hovy. 2016. End-to-end sequence labeling via bi-directional lstm-cnns-crf. In *Proceedings of the 54th Annual Meeting of the Association for Computational Linguistics (ACL 2016)*. Association for Computational Linguistics, volume 1.

Julian McAuley, Rahul Pandey, and Jure Leskovec. 2015. Inferring networks of substitutable and complementary products. In *Proceedings of the 21th ACM SIGKDD International Conference on Knowledge Discovery and Data Mining (KDD '15)*. ACM, New York, NY, USA, pages 785–794. https://doi.org/10.1145/2783258.2783381.

Maria Pontiki, Dimitris Galanis, Haris Papageorgiou, Ion Androutsopoulos, Suresh Manandhar, Mohammad Al-Smadi, Mahmoud Al-Ayyoub, Yanyan Zhao, Bing Qin, Orphée De Clercq, Véronique Hoste, Marianna Apidianaki, Xavier Tannier, Natalia V. Loukachevitch, Evgeniy Kotelnikov, Núria Bel, Salud María Jiménez Zafra, and Gülsen Eryigit. 2016. Semeval-2016 task 5: Aspect based sentiment analysis. In *Proceedings of the 10th International Workshop on Semantic Evaluation, SemEval@NAACL-HLT 2016, San Diego, CA, USA, June 16-17, 2016*. pages 19–30. http://aclweb.org/anthology/S/S16/S16-1002.pdf.

Keisuke Sakaguchi, Kevin Duh, Matt Post, and Benjamin Van Durme. 2017. Robsut wrod reocginiton via semi-character recurrent neural network. In *Proceedings of the Thirty-First AAAI Conference on Artificial Intelligence, February 4-9, 2017, San Francisco, California, USA.*. pages 3281–3287.

Iñaki San Vicente, Xabier Saralegi, and Rodrigo Agerri. 2015. Elixa: A modular and flexible ABSA platform. In *Proceedings of the 9th International Workshop on Semantic Evaluation*. Association for Computational Linguistics, Denver, Colorado, pages 748–752.

M. Schuster and K. K Paliwal. 1997. Bidirectional recurrent neural networks. *IEEE Transactions on Signal Processing* 45(11):2673–2681. https://doi.org/10.1109/78.650093.

Nitish Srivastava, Geoffrey Hinton, Alex Krizhevsky, Ilya Sutskever, and Ruslan Salakhutdinov. 2014. Dropout: A simple way to prevent neural networks from overfitting. *Journal of Machine Learning Research* 15:1929–1958. http://jmlr.org/papers/v15/srivastava14a.html.

Erik F. Tjong Kim Sang and Jorn Veenstra. 1999. Representing text chunks. In *Proceedings of European Chapter of the ACL (EACL)*. Bergen, Norway, pages 173–179.

Zhiqiang Toh and Wenting Wang. 2014. DLIREC: Aspect Term Extraction and Term Polarity Classification System. In *Proceedings of the 8th International Workshop on Semantic Evaluation*. pages 235–240.

Laurens van der Maaten and Geoffrey E. Hinton. 2008. Visualizing high-dimensional data using t-sne. *Journal of Machine Learning Research* 9:2579–2605.

Xiang Zhang, Junbo Zhao, and Yann LeCun. 2015. Character-level convolutional networks for text classification. In *Advances in neural information processing systems*. pages 649–657.

Author Index

Association for Computational Linguistics
209 N. Eighth Street
Stroudsburg, Pennsylvania 18360

ISBN 978-1-5108-4748-4